"Most histories of tourism take the perspective of the tourist, and so the settler's-eye view provided by Andrew Watson is unique."

– RICHARD W. JUDD,
author of *The Untilled Garden: Natural History and the Origins of American Conservation, 1730–1850*

"Andrew Watson has produced a timely, readable study with new insights into the evolving interrelationships and interdependencies of the different groups of people who have, either seasonally or permanently, tried to make Muskoka their home."

– RICHARD TATLEY, Muskoka historian

The Nature | History | Society series is devoted to the publication of high-quality scholarship in environmental history and allied fields. Its broad compass is signalled by its title: *nature* because it takes the natural world seriously; *history* because it aims to foster work that has temporal depth; and *society* because its essential concern is with the interface between nature and society, broadly conceived. The series is avowedly interdisciplinary and is open to the work of anthropologists, ecologists, historians, geographers, literary scholars, political scientists, sociologists, and others whose interests resonate with its mandate. It offers a timely outlet for lively, innovative, and well-written work on the interaction of people and nature through time in North America.

General Editor: Graeme Wynn, University of British Columbia

A list of titles in the series appears at the end of the book.

Making Muskoka

Tourism, Rural Identity, and Sustainability, 1870–1920

ANDREW WATSON

FOREWORD BY GRAEME WYNN

UBC Press • Vancouver • Toronto

© UBC Press 2022

All rights reserved. No part of this publication may be reproduced, stored in a retrieval system, or transmitted, in any form or by any means, without prior written permission of the publisher, or, in Canada, in the case of photocopying or other reprographic copying, a licence from Access Copyright, www.accesscopyright.ca.

31 30 29 28 27 26 25 24 23 22   5 4 3 2 1

Printed in Canada on FSC-certified ancient-forest-free paper (100% post-consumer recycled) that is processed chlorine- and acid-free.

Library and Archives Canada Cataloguing in Publication

Title: Making Muskoka: tourism, rural identity, and sustainability, 1870-1920 / Andrew Watson; foreword by Graeme Wynn.
Names: Watson, Andrew (Andrew K.), author.
Series: Nature, history, society.
Description: Series statement: Nature, history, society | Includes bibliographical references and index.
Identifiers:
Canadiana (print) 20220261997 | Canadiana (ebook) 20220262101 |
ISBN 9780774867832 (hardcover) | ISBN 9780774867849 (paperback) |
ISBN 9780774867856 (PDF) | ISBN 9780774867863 (EPUB)
Subjects: LCSH: Tourism — Ontario — Muskoka (District municipality) — History — 19th century. | LCSH: Tourism — Ontario — Muskoka (District municipality) — History — 20th century. | LCSH: Rural development — Ontario — Muskoka (District municipality) — History — 19th century. | LCSH: Rural development — Ontario — Muskoka (District municipality) — History — 20th century. | LCSH: Sustainable development — Ontario — Muskoka (District municipality) — History — 19th century. | LCSH: Sustainable development — Ontario — Muskoka (District municipality) — History — 20th century. | LCSH: Muskoka (Ont.: District municipality) — History — 19th century. | LCSH: Muskoka (Ont.: District municipality) — History — 20th century.
Classification: LCC G155.C3 W38 2022 | DDC 338.4/791097131609034 — dc23

Canadä

UBC Press gratefully acknowledges the financial support for our publishing program of the Government of Canada (through the Canada Book Fund), the Canada Council for the Arts, and the British Columbia Arts Council.

This book has been published with the help of a grant from the Canadian Federation for the Humanities and Social Sciences, through the Awards to Scholarly Publications Program, using funds provided by the Social Sciences and Humanities Research Council of Canada.

UBC Press
The University of British Columbia
2029 West Mall
Vancouver, BC V6T 1Z2
www.ubcpress.ca

Dedicated to Maurice Jr. Labelle

PLAY THE PERSON, NOT THE CARDS

Contents

List of Illustrations / viii

Foreword: Edge Effects / x
Graeme Wynn

Acknowledgments / xxiv

Introduction / 3

1 Rural Identity and Resettlement of the Canadian Shield, 1860–80 / 19

2 Indigenous Identity, Settler Colonialism, and Tourism, 1850–1920 / 48

3 Rural Identity and Tourism, 1870–1900 / 77

4 The Promise of Wood-Resource Harvesting, 1870–1920 / 104

5 Fossil Fuels, Consumer Culture, and the Tourism Economy, 1900–20 / 133

Conclusion / 164

Appendix: A Note on Sources / 175

Notes / 178

Bibliography / 214

Index / 231

Illustrations

0.1 Granite outcroppings, 1908 / 5

0.2 Muskoka River watershed / 6

0.3 Muskoka River watershed 11,000 years ago / 16

1.1 Muskoka Colonization Road, c. 1873 / 21

1.2 Early artistic impression of Lake Joseph, c. 1880 / 25

1.3 Steamer *Nipissing,* c. 1879 / 26

1.4 Isolated farm in Stephenson Township, 1875 / 30

1.5 Captain Harston's second home on Buck Lake, c. 1900 / 33

1.6 Cleared land at Buck Lake, c. 1900 / 34

1.7 Patents obtained by township, 1875–79 / 36

1.8 Abandoned locations by township, 1875–79 / 37

2.1 First Nations men, 1844 / 57

2.2 First Nations reserves in Muskoka area, c. 1900 / 59

2.3 Rama, 1844 / 60

2.4 First Nations camp, 1904 / 73

2.5 Indigenous women bringing berries to market, c. 1880 / 73

3.1 Muskoka Club, 1866 / 81

3.2 Cottages on the lower lakes, 1899 / 83

3.3 Ferndale House, c. 1890 / 85

3.4 Solid Comfort Camp, 1900 / 86

Illustrations

3.5 Cottage on Lake Rosseau, c. 1908 / 90

3.6 Cottage on Lake Joseph, 1895 / 90

3.7 Maclennan cottage, Wegamind Island, 1907 / 92

3.8 Canoes and the *Muskoka*, c. 1881 / 96

3.9 Overlooking the town of Rosseau, c. 1890 / 98

3.10 Supply boat *Constance*, c. 1900 / 98

3.11 Interior of the *Constance*, c. 1900 / 99

3.12 Crowds and supply boat *Mink*, c. 1910 / 101

3.13 Interior of the *Mink*, date unknown / 102

4.1 Tugboat towing a log boom, c. 1900 / 108

4.2 Feet of white pine sawlogs, Ontario, 1874–1920 / 109

4.3 Logs on the South Muskoka River, 1918 / 112

4.4 Kaufman sawmill, c. 1908 / 118

4.5 Settlers who sold logs to Snider, 1902–7 / 120

4.6 Muskoka Leather Company tannery, 1910 / 122

4.7 A group at Lake Rosseau, c. 1908 / 125

4.8 Muskoka Leather Company tanbark sources, 1886–1906 / 127

4.9 Anglo-Canadian Leather tannery, Bracebridge, 1896 / 129

4.10 Anglo-Canadian Leather tannery, Huntsville, 1911 / 130

4.11 Anglo-Canadian Leather tannery, Huntsville, 1921 / 130

5.1 The lower lakes, c. 1913 / 140

5.2 Advertisement for Scarcliff, 1918 / 141

5.3 Summit House, c. 1907 / 142

5.4 Advertisement for Ernescliffe, 1918 / 143

5.5 Eaton's *Campers' Supplies* supplement, 1900 / 145

5.6 Eaton's *Summer Holiday Needs* catalogue, 1903 / 147

5.7 Steamboat *Sagamo*, 1908 / 152

5.8 Small crowd watching a regatta, 1907 / 153

5.9 Steamboat *Muskoka*, date unknown / 154

5.10 Men shovelling coal on the *Sagamo*, date unknown / 154

5.11 Disappearing Propeller Boat advertisement, 1918 / 159

5.12 A crush of boats at a regatta, 1909 / 161

FOREWORD

Edge Effects

Graeme Wynn

An edge, we might say, is the line where an object or area begins or ends. So we think of the edge of a table, or a cliff edge. Simple. But a moment's reflection brings other edges to mind: the sharpened side of a blade; the advantage derived from practice; the threshold of disaster; being nervous (on edge); to nudge (off the road); to win narrowly (edge out the competition); and so on. Edges, it seems, can be narrow or wide, real or imagined, material or metaphorical.

This is a book about various edges – geological, ecological, cultural, economic, sociological, and political – and their effects. Its focus – on the Muskoka Lakes region of Ontario in the half century after 1870 – is relatively tight, but it speaks more broadly to important questions about the nature of Canadian development, the encounter between Indigenous peoples and newcomers to their territory, and the larger implications of settler colonialism across the globe. As an environmental historian, Andrew Watson also pays attention to the aspirations, struggles, and everyday lives of those who came to Muskoka during these years, to the ways in which they shaped the landscape, to the factors that impinged on the sustainability of their endeavours, and to the intractability of the environment that they sought to turn to their purposes. The result is a thought-provoking perspective on a storied, well-studied, widely known, and much-mythologized swathe of Canada.

In emphasizing the many edges (and the discussions of their effects) encountered in these pages, I draw inspiration from both the pioneering American ecologist Frederic Edward Clements and the wildlife manager

Foreword

and environmental philosopher Aldo Leopold.[1] Clements, a student of plant succession who developed the idea that plant assemblages progressed through a dynamic, orderly series of stages to produce identifiable climax communities, had to bound plant communities in order to name them, but he detected more-or-less gradual transitions (rather than sharp edges) between most communities.[2] These he called "ecotones," literally places where ecologies were in tension.[3] Whether wide or narrow, they are marked by a shift in dominance among species. Recognizing the greater diversity of plant species in ecotones, Leopold posited in 1933 that certain types of birds and game would be more abundant along these transitional edges, where they might benefit either from access to different types of environment, or the array of species and habitats available, or both.[4] In this view, edges are "good" because their effect is to enhance the number and variety of living things in (today we would say "the biodiversity of") an area.

Interviewed after the publication of *Edge Effects,* her eighth book of poetry, Jan Conn (who is also a biologist) reflected on the ways in which her creative writing often superimposed "one horizon upon another."[5] She was intrigued, she noted, by thresholds – places that enabled movement between, or into and out of, different realms. In her view, such edges offered "fascinating places to linger as one is neither here nor there. Yet." They were also revealing places in which to observe people and characters seeking entry or exit. They "might be trying to leave the past (another country, or realm) behind, and focus on the present," but they could never ignore the past, which "stretches out in front like a series of lakes during a thunderstorm," and must "be navigated and explored ... to reach the present." Accustomed to shifting realms in her biological research (from an individual to a population to a species to a community), Conn is less interested in "the middle (of anything)" than the edges of everything, where excitement happens; metaphorical kaleidoscopes are as valuable as actual microscopes and telescopes in our efforts to know the world. More recently, the historian Shannon Stunden Bower also adapted ecological understandings of ecotones and edge effects to suggest that scholars who straddle two or more scholarly fields – or studies that do the same – offer some of the richest, most innovative work in Canadian environmental history.[6] These invigorating reflections – suggesting that "edges" are places where fragments-in-flux coalesce into new forms, and that cross-disciplinary inquiry can be particularly productive of new insights – are worth bearing in mind in measuring the value of Andrew Watson's *Making Muskoka: Tourism, Rural Identity, and Sustainability, 1870–1920.*

Muskoka lies on the southern margin of the Canadian Shield – and that is the first edge of consequence to the story recounted in these pages. About 160 kilometres and barely a two-hour drive north of Toronto along Highway 400 on a good day, gently rolling farmland gives way to a more spartan landscape of exposed gneiss and granite bedrock, lakes, and forest. At approximately 45 degrees north latitude, this geological boundary marks the symbolic southern edge of northern Ontario. Sharp as this distinction might seem to motorists moving along the highway, it turns, on closer inspection, into a series of blurry lines. Ancient bedrock subject, over many thousands of years, to the erosive forces of ice, wind, and water defines the Shield, but landscapes are complex and dynamic entities. As the great Laurentian ice sheet advanced, it scoured surfaces and carved hollows; as the ice retreated, meltwater deposited accumulated sediment (clay, sand, and gravel) differentially, filling troughs and basins. With the weight of ice removed, the surface of the earth began to rebound, unevenly, altering drainage patterns. At the local scale, this produced an intricate, interdigitated mix of physical features.

Over the ensuing millennia, flora and fauna colonized these various habitats, further enhancing their diversity. Lichen attached to the bedrock; juniper and corydalis found root in its cracks; and as mineral soils accumulated, eastern white pines and red pines took root. Alder, aspen, and white birch also found their niches. Spaghnum, ferns, and cotton grass invaded ponds. With time and the development of better soils, white oak and other species more common to the south appeared here and there, making this edge a zone of vegetational transition or ecotone. Today, promotional literature for Six Mile Lake Provincial Park, located immediately south of the Muskoka watershed and right on the blurry boundary of the Shield, notes that the kilometre-long Living Edge Trail "crosses such a variety of landscapes and habitats that it seems much longer."[7]

In the middle years of the nineteenth century, this fuzzy edge was both snare and delusion. As the press of immigrant numbers increased and the relatively bountiful ecumene south of the Shield filled with farms, a strong expansionist impulse led settlers and government officials to look north for opportunities. Logging interests had already begun to exploit the pine forests of the Shield fringe. Boosters stressed the land's potential for farming, and the colonial government surveyed almost five million acres for settlement as they established a loose network of rudimentary east-west and south-north roads to promote colonization.[8] Hopes for agricultural development were high. But efforts to encourage settlement of the so-called Ottawa-Huron Tract rested, in part, on a misreading of the landscape, one that found promise in relatively thin acidic soils; underplayed the extent of swamps and bogs, barrens, and bare rocks; and ignored the climatic challenge of cooler shorter growing seasons. Either blind to the realities with which they were dealing, or intent on establishing a different version of it, enthusiasts combined naïveté, and perhaps still somewhat inchoate ambition, to conjure what historian John Walsh characterizes as "landscapes of longing" or "dreamscapes" envisaging what the Shield fringe *might* become. In 1856, a leading government official informed immigrants and others in search of land that the southern edge of the Shield was "capable of sustaining a population of some eight millions of people."[9] Fifteen years later, the government agent for settlement along the Muskoka Road had apparently written "not less than 83 Editorials and Letters in defence of the country."[10]

By most immediate and material measures, the attempt to turn this generally agriculturally marginal terrain into productive farms fell short of the boosters' hopes. Land grants along the Colonization Roads were free, but the 100 acres (40 hectares) came with conditions: to secure title, settlers were required, within four years, to build a house, reside in it, and to cultivate at least twelve acres (5 hectares). Hundreds, even thousands, of aspiring farmers moved north, to pour their energies into the earth. Some were fortunate, resilient, and made a go of things for several years; others sank quickly into despair and moved on. Township by township and road transect by road transect, surveys revealed patches of "[r]ich, sandy soils" alongside "inferior land" that was "[h]illy and broken," full of "large boulders and rocks."[11] Because (in historian Derek Murray's fine phrase) "topography defied the logic of the grid," free grant lots varied greatly in potential, and because few settlers were able to inspect the land before selecting their properties, grantees pinned their hopes on a gamble. One microscale effect of the variability and hard-to-read qualities of this edge was that fate became a substantial arbitrator of individual fortunes.

Overall, settlement was slow to take root. In 1860, there were barely 1,100 families along all of the Colonization Roads in the Ottawa-Huron Tract. Two years later, only thirty-eight newcomers took up grants along the Muskoka Road (along the route of today's Highway 11 through Bracebridge), raising the total number of settlers along its length to 287. Such numbers were hardly redolent of roaring success, and those distressed by unrequited dreams of an agricultural empire found the fanfare of official enthusiasm for colonization heartless. One contemporary critic described the Ottawa-Huron Tract as "one of the most inaccessible and poorest regions in America." In this bleak assessment, grants may have been free, but "the land was not worth the having."[12] This verdict also likely rested, in part, on a misreading of the poor circumstances and modest aspirations of many settlers for whom a piece of land and the prospect of survival may have been sufficient. For all that, Arthur Lower, probably the first professional historian to write about efforts to settle the Shield fringe, was undoubtedly correct in observing that "every additional log cabin built seems to have been a precious acquisition."[13]

Lower was well aware of the agricultural limitations of the Shield. He also understood the agrarian ambitions of the mid-nineteenth century, when "the settler sat enthroned," and (with his broader vision of Canada progressing from colony to nation never far from mind), he portrayed this biogeographical edge as a "barrier," a rampart that individual settlers might attack but from which they would, ere long, be forced back. Beyond, the forested fastness was interrupted by only a few patches of good land, and "the national estate," which extended in the 1850s only to the borders of Rupert's Land, "stood revealed as a rather sorry affair."[14] This perception was troubling, because it seemed to contemporaries that without successful settlement of the Ottawa-Huron Tract, "Canada would remain a mere frontier strip bordering the margin of the St. Lawrence and the Great Lakes."[15]

In this reading, the edge of the Shield provoked an early reckoning with the harsh realities of northern circumstances. It was the proximate and most obvious marker of the niggardly, reluctant, and bounded territory that was Canada's lot – a view that has in some degree underpinned influential interpretations of the country's development ever since.[16] By comparison with the United States, where the history of settlement is often presented as a story of "extension and abundance," of the steady successful march of people across a continent, the trajectory of Canadian development has often seemed difficult, intermittent, and coloured by "discontinuity, paradox and limitations."[17] The seemingly inexorable expansion of the United States – a "gigantic geographic growth" predicated on the geopolitical process of imperialism, defined as territorial encroachment – stands as counterpoint to the hard-won and tenuous extension of the Canadian archipelago from coast to coast (to coast).[18] Such interpretations signal, in some degree, the limitations of the Canadian ecumene; they, too, are edge effects, reflections, at the macro scale, on the implications of the Laurentian barrier (and others) in the shaping of the Canadian imagination.

A quarter century ago, the historian John Walsh found further interpretive salience in the collapse of agrarian dreams on the granitic limits of the Shield. Influenced by recent scholarship on governmentality, he read efforts to survey and settle the Ottawa-Huron Tract as a continuation of trends discernible in the 1840s and as a pivotal moment in Canadian state formation. Emphasizing the financial and administrative resources that the government of Canada West invested in this colonization project, the bureaucratic network that managed and implemented it and the unusually detailed (for the time) monitoring, record-keeping, and judgment of set-tlers and their activities, Walsh makes the plausible argument that all of this was not simply an effort to extend agricultural settlement; it was also, and importantly, an attempt to "assert the state's authority to govern, and thus to order, both society and political economy."[19] Although the admin-istrative ambitions of the state far exceeded its capacity to realize them, this early experiment in the extension of a liberal order laid the strategic and practical foundations of nation building in the North West after 1870.[20]

Reverberations from the mid-nineteenth century encounter with the Shield edge also encouraged contemporary Canadians to think differently about their emerging country. In the years after Confederation, the terri-tory that was once regarded as a place of opportunity for emigrants-soon-to-become-farmers was reconfigured in the minds and speeches of many influential Canadians as a harsh and lonely northern realm – but not one without benefits. "May not our snow and frost give us what is of more value than gold and silver," asked Robert Grant Haliburton, rhetorically, before asserting that it would, by promoting the development of "a healthy, hardy, virtuous dominant race."[21]

Even as efforts at agricultural colonization faltered, nationalist senti-ment, economic interests, a developing taste for therapeutic holidays, and the tangled strands of enthusiasm for wilderness, northern-ness, adventure, and escape led central Canadians to recalibrate the merits of the Shield fringe – and generated new cultural and economic edge effects. If farmers struggled to tame this wild region, it might better be turned to purposes other than agriculture. Lumbermen, who had long called for "a fair line of demarcation" between settlement and forest land (not least because settlers' fires often burned beyond their lot lines) urged the maintenance of Crown title (and the lease of timber rights) in place of efforts to extend a fee-simple agrarian empire across the north country.[22] Others were attracted by the many tree-fringed lakes of this wild, rugged land. As railroad companies and entrepreneurial locals saw opportunities, pamphlets and newspaper stories emphasized the grandeur of Muskoka and the health benefits of spending summers there. By century's end, the edge of the Shield was being compared to the Scottish Highlands, and described as "a paradise

xvi   Foreword

of lakes, rocks[,] hills, and woodland, a perfect place to hunt and fish, renew one's health, and step back in time to a simpler way of life."[23] To accommodate a growing stream of visitors, hotels and cottages sprang up on islands and lake shores of the Muskoka watershed and elsewhere.

As Ontario and Quebec urbanized, the elixir-like properties of northern climes appeared in new forms. While observers documented the extent and consequences of poverty, poor housing, and inadequate sanitation among those who lived in the crowded industrial quarters of the country's major cities, even affluent urbanites were warned against the debilitating dangers of "brain-fag" and the ills that might flow from experiencing "that uneasy, cooped in office feeling." Initially at least, public concerns about the health of Canadians were substantially imported disquiets, reflecting the circumstances and anxieties of Britain and the largest cities of the eastern United States.[24] But they found their mark. Amid growing anxiety about over-work and "overcivilization," neurasthenia (otherwise described as an "impoverishment of nervous force") vexed doctors and patients alike. "The papers," observed one commentator in the *Canadian Magazine* in 1908, "are filled with advertisements of tonics and nerve pills," and magazines, she alleged, ran articles with titles such as "Worry: the Disease of the Age."[25] In Muskoka, one could slough off the "dust and folly" of the city by taking "A Rest Cure in a Canoe."[26]

At much the same time, Tom Thomson and others who became famous in the 1920s as "The Group of Seven" began to paint along the southern edge of the Shield, from Georgian Bay to Algonquin Park. Seeking to develop a distinctly Canadian style of art, they used vivid colours and bold brush strokes to portray a particular version of the landscape. Aiming to capture on canvas their reactions to the settings in which they painted, and to illustrate how these places differed from Europe and Britain in "air, mood and spirit," they created striking images which, they implied, jettisoned "all preconceived ideas and rule-of-thumb reactions."[27] In truth, members of the Group were influenced by contemporary Scandinavian artists whose works (viewed by Lawren Harris and J.E.H. MacDonald in Buffalo in 1913) offered "bold, vigorous, and uncompromising [images] embodying direct experience of the great north." Almost two decades later, MacDonald's commentary on the work of Edvard Munch – that "he aims to paint the soul of things, the inner feeling rather than the outward form" – might as well have been applied to the work of the Group.[28] Works such as "The Red Maple" (A.Y. Jackson, 1914), "The West Wind" (Tom Thomson, 1916–17); "The Jack Pine" (Thomson, 1916–17); "A September Gale, Georgian Bay" (Arthur Lismer, 1921); "The Solemn Land" (J.E.H.

Foreword

MacDonald, 1921); and "Afternoon Sun, Lake Superior" (Lawren Harris, 1924) all, typically devoid of any trace of human activity, depicted the grandeur and solitude of the "untouched" north country in ways that resonated with both the wilderness ethos and a rising sense of Canadian nationalism after the First World War.[29]

The general outlines of this story – into which this book settles – are of course well established. But Watson brings novel perspectives to bear on important parts of the commonly accepted narrative. He does so as someone who knows and loves the Muskoka landscape, and whose understanding is inflected by this as well as by the ideas and concerns of recent scholarship. Working at this interface, he seeks to raise fresh questions about important, previously underplayed, aspects of the story of Muskoka's development. To this end, Watson pays attention to the everyday lives (and the intersections among them) of Indigenous people and the settlers, tourists, or folks with an eye to the main chance who came to Muskoka in the half century after 1870. By engaging, more assiduously than most scholars who have written of this time and place, with the challenges, aspirations, prospects, and experiences of those on the ground (or the lakes) of Muskoka, he is able to add further edges to our understanding of the place, and to probe both the local and the larger effects of these developments.

The most basic of Watson's interpretive edges is the multifaceted one between settler and tourist, capital and labour, pleasure and toil. At once cultural, economic, and sociological, its effects cascade through the pages of this book. Different though the yin and yang of each of these dyads may seem, they were (and are) inextricably linked one to the other. Their entanglements shaped the development of Muskoka and are integral to the fuller understanding of this place provided by *Making Muskoka*. Distilled to its essence, Watson's argument runs approximately thus: settlers came to Muskoka as the Ottawa-Huron Tract was opened up. Like others elsewhere, they encountered poor soils and generally unpropitious conditions for agriculture and (as also happened elsewhere) some were able to get by well enough for the time being by selling produce and labour to nearby lumbering camps. But Muskoka differed from settlement frontiers elsewhere in North America because rich people/tourists/pleasure seekers arrived there at much the same time as those who came to settle and toil. Quickly, the two groups developed a sustaining, symbiotic relationship: settlers found work serving the rich, who also provided a market for the surplus produce of settler farms and tourists enhanced the leisure and pleasure they sought by contracting the services of local residents to erect and maintain buildings; replenish ice houses; cut firewood; and supply eggs, milk, and vegetables in season. This was particularly important and beneficial to settlers on better land near the lakes, with their easy access to tourist hotels and cottages. Great though the gulf between them might have been, these settlers and many tourists became interdependent. For settlers on more remote lots, back from the water, options were more limited. Lumbering provided off-farm revenues for some, but as the frontier of exploitation moved northward in the final years of the century, the time and cost of hauling hay and produce to camps increased, and those who worked in the woods were necessarily away from home for longer periods. Some farmers were able to fall back on local logging and garnered enough from their labours to supplement other income and maintain their homesteads. In almost all cases, these pages reveal, settlers who came to Muskoka to farm depended more or less heavily on other activities to survive. Occupational pluralism or the co-integration of activity in different economic sectors became a way of scraping together a living on the edge of the Shield.

A second important side of Watson's analysis focuses on the Indigenous presence on the Shield fringe and the effects of the growing newcomer presence among it. This contact zone is revealed to be a somewhat ragged, multifarious edge. Neither group was homogeneous, the experiences and aspirations of encounter differed among individuals belonging to the two groups, and though much was fluid in late-nineteenth-century Muskoka, the burdens of change lay more heavily on the lives of first peoples than on those who came into this territory to farm or to recuperate. As Watson indicates, the Anishinaabeg lived across the southern edge of the Shield and ranged across it for generations to fish, hunt, trap, and trade before those of European descent came into the territory. Initial contacts with French map-makers and missionaries were mostly fleeting. Anishinaabeg leaders signed treaties with British officials at the turn of the nineteenth century, and some of them were involved in the defence of York in the War of 1812. They were not averse to change. Three bands joined the short-lived settlement at Coldwater established by the government of Upper Canada to encourage farming among Indigenous people, and later took up reserves farther north. Never numerous – their number approximately tripled during the period covered in this book, to three thousand or so – the Anishinaabeg adapted to the effects of Euro-Canadian development, taking employment in and around local sawmills, and hunting and trapping across the extensive areas beyond the settlement fringe, even as regulations sought to limit their access to traditional fishing places.

Expanding tourism brought new challenges and new opportunities for Indigenous people in the region. Those who came north in hopes that hunting and fishing would restore their innate but waning vigour favoured restrictions, in the guise of conservation laws, on Indigenous capture of the prey they sought. But sportsmen from afar also appreciated the benefits of finely tuned local knowledge. Indigenous men were hired as guides and to do the hard work involved in canoeing and camping. Tourists and sportsmen also created a market for Indigenous craftwork, from moccasins and snowshoes to baskets and birchbark canoes. Considerable quantities of such goods were manufactured by women and other family members for sale each summer – sales that were often encouraged when vendors dressed in traditional clothing to present themselves as "authentic Indians." In Watson's telling, these developments enabled the integration of Indigenous skills into the Euro-Canadian economy, sustained the intergenerational transfer of Indigenous knowledge, and marked the resilience of the Indigenous inhabitants of the area who repurposed their traditional knowledge to sustain their identities.

Discussions of identity and sustainability are threaded through the pages of *Making Muskoka,* from first to last, and frame its central arguments. Here identity is a malleable concept, but one anchored in engagement with the material world even as it reflected the discourse that people used. Watson sees the (rural) identities of the Anishinaabeg, the tourists, and the settlers of Muskoka forged through their encounters with the physical realities of the Canadian Shield. For the Anishinaabeg, this meant the development of a migratory existence that traversed the boundary of the Shield as they moved, seasonally, between southern fishing locations and northern hunting grounds. Tourists likewise spent only part of the year in Muskoka, but they were there to play, not work. Their identities turned on two pivots, the more northerly of which was a tangle of contradictions: it embraced the idea of "wilderness" as it chipped away at its existence; it disrupted and forced change on Indigenous lifeways even as it relied on the skills of reified "authentic Indians" whose ways of being were inexorably changed and challenged by the tourists' presence; and it urged "conservation" of fish and game, yet saw few reasons not to dump toxic chemicals on the forest when the hemlock looper began to defoliate trees and "spoil" the appearance of the visitors' "beautiful playground" late in the 1920s.[30] Most settlers identified themselves as farmers to census takers, but environmental limitations drove almost all of them into dependence on a variety of activities; people lived on their farms, but agricultural activity was often integrated with work of various kinds that took place elsewhere. Occupational pluralism was not uncommon in nineteenth- and twentieth-century North America, but Muskoka stood apart from other places because settlement and tourism developed almost simultaneously. Settlers "reshaped ideas of improvement," which were commonplace at the time, "into a negotiation between the limited agricultural potential of the Shield and the aesthetic expectations of visitors" (p. 12).

This is to say that the presence of "rich folks" was integral to the persistence of settlers on "poor soils."[31] But having identified that, Watson asks how sustainable this symbiosis (and others that emerged in Muskoka through these years) proved to be. Answers differ. Some arrangements lasted longer than others. Much depended on personal circumstances: age, family size, tolerance of hardship, aspirations and expectations; all factored into the equation. For the historian posing this question, responses also depend on when and where one looks. Circumstances might sustain certain activities or lifeways of a particular group even as they undercut the viability of a different group in other ways. Tourism sustained settlers close to Muskoka's lakes more robustly than it did backwoods settlers during the 1880s and 1890s. Although many settlers depended on work in logging camps to supplement the yield of their farms in the 1870s and 1880s, smaller-scale local wood extraction contributed more effectively than logging camps to their economic viability after the turn of the century. The Anishinaabeg, on the other hand, used and adapted their environmental knowledge and traditional skills to sustain themselves at a time when colonization was undermining Indigenous ways of life elsewhere. Ultimately, however, the point is that "nothing is forever." Sustainability, defined in these pages as "the *potential* for a society, or a particular feature of a society, to reproduce patterns of economic exchange, social relationships, and environmental conditions," is a relative concept intended to help understand change over time (p. 12).

This point, and the interpretive edge of this book, is sharpened by the discussion in Chapter 5 of the modifications that marked land and life in Muskoka after 1900. Here Watson emphasizes the remaking of symbiotic arrangements forged in the last decades of the previous century by the shift to fossil fuels and the rise of consumer society.[32] Like most such transitions, this shift was more gradual than precipitous: fuelwood continued to burn in cottage fireplaces; hotel kitchens used locally produced eggs, dairy, and vegetables (indeed many such establishments ran their own farms or gardens); and local "handymen" long put their skills to work building docks and repairing the ravages of time and winter on all manner of structures. Settlers also cut and sold cordwood to fuel the

Foreword

several supply boats that traversed the lakes, but costs, convenience, and efficiency increasingly favoured the use of coal imported from Pennsylvania to heat the boilers of these steamers.

Technological change provides an important backbeat to the story unfolded in these pages. Railroads underpinned early tourism developments in Muskoka. Steamboats on the lakes opened new parts of the watershed to resort hotels and cottages. Their operations were facilitated by the excavation of shallow channels and the construction of locks to manage water levels. Early in the twentieth century, gasoline-powered motorboats offered cottagers greater freedom of mobility. They eventually undermined the viability of basic supply boat services, although some vessels continued to ply the waters carrying passengers and mail, and *Peerless II* delivered oil and gasoline to resorts and marinas around the lakes until the last decade of the twentieth century. Even the fundamental instrument that brought the allure, and possibilities, of modern consumer culture into the hinterland – the Eaton's catalogue – was made more effective by improvements in printing technology. A text-only publication when it began in 1884, it added illustrations three years later, colour pages in 1915, and photographs four years after that. After 1900, the catalogue offered increasingly effective competition to local retailers, pitching prompt (and for larger orders, cost-free) delivery of a wide range of goods, from linens and furniture, to fresh produce and canned meat from urban slaughterhouses. All of this connected Muskoka to the world in new ways. The protection afforded small-scale local producers by their relative geographical isolation broke down as industrial scale production and mass marketing brought competition from afar to their doorsteps.

One harbinger of a new era was the arrival, in 1909, of a chaffeur-driven automobile at The Summit House near Port Cockburn ("the most comfortable hotel on the Muskoka Lakes"). Driven from Ohio, it necessarily made the last leg of its journey (from Gravenhurst) in the cargo hold of a supply boat, but the hotel owner saw the future, and an opportunity, in this novelty. He lost little time in turning one of the many photographs of the vehicle in front of his property into a postcard with the tagline "U Auto Come to Summit House."[33] Little more than a decade later, extensions to the road network, a growing number of automobiles, and the production of electricity from gasoline generators extended the processes of modernization and withdrawal from dependence on local labour in local nature.[34] By the late 1920s, some resort operators were concerned that the region's reputation as a summer haven on the edge of "civilization" was being diluted. Less constrained by supply-boat schedules, many visitors opted for shorter stays in the region's hotels; such transient tourism changed the social dynamics of the resort experience. Remote establishments lost business to new tourist camps and cabin courts accessible by road, and private cottages proliferated. Increasing numbers of tourists relied on goods and energy from outside Muskoka. For some, these developments and their continuation signalled that vacationing on the Shield fringe "was less about getting *back* to nature than it was about domesticating, colonizing, and conquering nature."[35]

In the end, *Making Muskoka* is a story of change – of change in landscapes, technologies, attitudes, and aspirations; of the ways in which people thought of themselves, their relations with the land, and with each other; and about the viability of those arrangements. Even the briefest review of recent writing about Muskoka, and more broadly about "Ontario cottage country," reveals that all of these things have continued to change into the twenty-first century.[36] Yet the long view also reveals continuities. This is a complicated and contested history. As in most situations, past and present, busy, buzzing reality has to be simplified or purified to be understood. But groupings to this end are rarely watertight or homogeneous; categories leak and incorporate contradictions. At one level, the distinction with which this book begins – Fanny Potts's identification of two classes of people, butterflies and bees, in Muskoka – is a marvellously helpful characterization. At another, it serves to deflect our attention away from the dynamic, fluid, and endlessly adaptive realities of lives lived, and the fact that the lines between such classifications are blurry, their edges far from impermeable.

Over time, some settlers became fully invested in the tourist economy as hotel and resort proprietors. True, they worked rather than played, but the nature of their work and their associations with the wealthy patrons of their establishments were of a different order from those of settlers who continued to scrape together an existence from a range of tasks on and off their poor soils. Less poetically than Potts, we might think of her two categories as outsiders and insiders. Again, however, categories shift. For those early adventurers who camped in Muskoka in 1860 and founded the Muskoka Club, settlers and lumberers were clearly "outsiders" bent on destroying the landscape that back-to-nature enthusiasts treasured. Settlers who became hotelkeepers might have become "insiders" insofar as they promoted the back-to-nature ethos. Those who built pretentious resort hotels and emphasized their fashionability (rather than opportunities for recreation in nature) would fall among the "outsiders." These sorts of divisions resurfaced in later years, when affluent newcomers built ever

Foreword

more grandiose "cottages" on the lakes, giving rise to characterizations of "Millionaires Row" (on Lake Muskoka), and in the twenty-first century "Billionaires Row" (on Lake Joseph), and disparaging dismissals from "old-timer insiders" that these were people who "didn't know how to cottage."[37]

Amid this swirl of conflicting perceptions and changing meanings, this book serves to remind us of the ways in which rural communities in the past have responded variously to the economic and personal challenges, the technological shifts, the cross-currents of political and sociological development, and the diverse environments that they have encountered. In doing so, it reveals both the resilience and ingenuity of those who preceded us. Here in Muskoka (perhaps an edge or threshold par excellence), as in so many other times and places, some found resolve in their efforts to domesticate the earth; others found strength in their embrace of more congruent human relations with the natural world; yet others, buffeted by circumstances, did what they could to come through the tumult of their times. Few were invariably clear about their motivations or entirely constant in their convictions. And all the while the nature they sought to beat back, to admire, to exploit, or to ignore worked its own agency across the local scene. Pause the story of Muskoka at any two points a decade or two apart between 1870 and 2020, and the later freeze-frame would bear only passing resemblance to the one that came before. People have lived on, visited, and used the southern edge of the Canadian Shield for hundreds of years. The ways in which they thought about themselves in this place varied and changed, and although humans sustained themselves here for generations, the ways in which they did so differed through time, across space, and in reflection of diverse shifting influences. To know this is to better understand the trials and tribulations of those who preceded us and to be reminded, as we ourselves "beat on, boats against the current, borne back ceaselessly into the past," that whatever future we seek, it will not be realized without strong commitment, serious endeavour, a sense of where we have come from, and a great deal of fortitude.[38]

Acknowledgments

My soul resides on an island in Muskoka. But I am a settler. I am not indigenous to Muskoka. Like most of the people in the story that follows, I visit Muskoka for only part of every year. But my identity, who I think I am, and how I see the world, have been shaped by the place my family and I call "the cottage." I started visiting it when I was very young. My parents brought my brother and sister and me to the cottage for two months every summer. And my father came every summer with his parents and siblings when he was young. The cottage was built in 1886 on land purchased from the Crown in 1873. The people who had it built, and each generation of settler families who spent their summers there since, including my own, have dispossessed the Anishinaabeg people who called (and continue to call) this part of the world home. This book cannot undo that injustice, but it can acknowledge that my own past, and my ongoing relationship with a place that means everything to me, is part of a larger history of colonialism, dispossession, and violence that shaped, and continues to shape, the lives of Indigenous peoples in Canada.

The financial costs associated with the research for this book were offset with very generous funding and support from the Social Sciences and Humanities Research Council, the Ontario Graduate Scholarship Program, the Graduate Program in History, and the Faculty of Graduate Studies at York University, as well as the Department of History, the Historical GIS Lab, and the College of Arts and Science at the University of Saskatchewan.

I received a great deal of help and encouragement from many people at the libraries and archives I visited for my research. The staff at both the

Acknowledgments

Archives of Ontario and Library and Archives Canada were very helpful. At the University of Waterloo, staff aided me in finding the records of the Muskoka Lakes Association. In Huntsville, staff at Muskoka Heritage Place and the Huntsville Public Library were very helpful in allowing me to explore their archives and special collections. In Gravenhurst, Marion and Cyril Fry very kindly assisted me in locating material in the archives of the Gravenhurst Public Library; and Mary Storey allowed me generous access to the archives of the Muskoka Steamship and Historical Society. Similarly, in Port Carling, Doug Smith gave me access to the archives of the Muskoka Lakes Museum. Conversations with local historians Richard Tatley and Ken Veitch helped steer me in the right direction.

I was very lucky to have the support and critical feedback from members of the Network in Canadian History and Environment's New Scholars Group, the Toronto Environmental History Network reading group, and the Saskatoon Environmental History Writing Group, who read several chapters at various stages. Many of their suggestions and comments got me thinking about the project in important new ways. A very special thanks goes to my writing group, Ben Bryce and Brittany Luby, who gave me deadlines; read almost all my chapters; and provided wonderful, detailed, and insightful feedback. I was also very fortunate to benefit from the generous insights of Erika Dyck, who read the entire book and talked with me about it so many times in so many ways.

I presented research from this project at meetings of the Canadian Historical Association, the Canadian Environmental Studies Association, the American Society for Environmental History, the York Indigenous Peoples Speakers Series, and the Quelques Arpents de Neige workshop.

I was lucky to benefit from the wonderful work of Justin Fisher, Abby Vadeboncoeur, and Eric Leinberger, who helped me create the Historical Geographic Information Systems maps in this book. Rilla Friesen and Deborah Kerr provided careful copy edits, and Megan Brand consistently and patiently guided me through the production stages.

I received very thoughtful and constructive comments from two reviewers that helped me make this book much better. I am also thankful for the time and effort Graeme Wynn put into helping me improve it, long after I thought I was done. From our very first conversation, my editor at UBC Press, James MacNevin, provided careful, thoughtful, encouraging, and calming guidance through the publication process. I'm so grateful for our many conversations and all the time he took to help me understand the process and maintain the confidence to see it through. Any remaining errors are my own.

Acknowledgments

We don't talk about mental health as much as we should, especially in academia. I was sometimes crippled by self-doubt and feelings that I was not good enough to get this book finished. This is not anyone's fault; there is no place for blame and shame. But it took me a long time, and caused me and my loved ones a lot of pain, while trying to figure out healthier ways of dealing with the pressures of this kind of work. It's easy to be hard on yourself, and on the people who love you most, when you are struggling. It's harder to do the work to take care of and respect yourself, to be vulnerable with people who care about you, and to both learn to respect yourself and trust them when they try to take care of you. Talking with RossAnn Edwards made that work easier.

I have the best of friends, and I'm fortunate to work with so many amazing colleagues. For all their understanding and support, I'm so grateful to Jennifer Bonnell, Lesley Bunbury, James Caven, Jim Clifford, Colin Coates, Geoff Cunfer, Colin Duncan, Susan Gray, Richard Hoffmann, Sean Kheraj, Katie Labelle, Brian MacDowall, Josh MacFadyen, Ian Milligan, Ian Mosby, Tom Peace, Carolyn Podruchny, Dan Rück, Ruth Sandwell, Graham Strickert, Anastasia Tataryn, and Colin Whitfield. When I needed him most, Moe Labelle kept checking in and showing up in ways that I will never be able to repay, and it is to him, and what he taught me, that I dedicate this book.

The most important thank yous go to my family. Thank you, Daria, for teaching me to see everything in new ways. Thank you, Angus, for teaching me it's ok to know what you want. Thank you, Milo, for teaching me to respect my feelings. Thank you, Amelia, for teaching me about determination. Thank you, Felix, for teaching me about integrity. Thank you, Carmen, for teaching me that everything has value. Thank you, Ivan, for teaching me to listen properly. Thank you, Gillian, for teaching me to be vulnerable. Thank you, Neil, for teaching me to pay attention to the details. Thank you, Erika, for teaching me about trust and empathy and for inspiring me to do the hard work of getting healthy. Thank you, Kerry, for teaching me to be patient and forgiving. Thank you, Keith, for teaching me to keep learning. I am who I am because of your love and what I've learned from each of you.

Making Muskoka

Introduction

In 1904, settler Fanny Potts observed that "for the past few years the population of Muskoka has been gradually dividing itself into two classes – tourists and settlers, otherwise capital and labor, pleasure and toil, butterflies and bees, whichever you like to call them."[1] By the time she wrote these words, Muskoka had become a tourism mecca, attracting affluent visitors from cities to the south who sought recreation, leisure, and recuperation at a lakeside wilderness retreat. Since then, the popular imagination of Muskoka, located roughly 150 kilometres north of Lake Ontario at the southern edge of the Canadian Shield, has been dominated by fashionable resort hotels and opulent summer cottages on the rugged shores of a lake. Indeed, most perceptions of Muskoka, including historical ones, do not extend any further than the view one would have standing next to the shore looking out at the lake, or sitting on the water looking back at the shore. The version of Muskoka that most people know privileges the tourist's experience and rarely moves inland beyond a narrow ribbon of land next to the lakeshore. It captures only part of Muskoka's history and obscures the experiences of the people who made tourism possible.

This book explores the role tourism played in the colonization of the southern edge of the Canadian Shield in Ontario during the late nineteenth and early twentieth centuries, and considers how the communities that lived in this region became more or less sustainable over time. I argue that during the first generation of resettlement between the 1870s and the 1890s, tourism provided many settlers in Muskoka with a more sustainable basis for constructing and reproducing their rural identity

4   Introduction

than commercial agriculture or large-scale wood-resource harvesting, and that the rise of consumer culture and fossil fuels after 1900 eroded their control over tourism and resulted in less sustainable arrangements than had existed during the 1880s and 1890s. Furthermore, in the context of the dispossession and devastation wrought by settler colonialism, tourism also provided important opportunities for members of Anishinaabeg and Haudenosaunee First Nations to protect their Indigenous identities at a time when the provincial and federal governments restricted social, cultural, political, and economic life on- and off-reserve. I pay attention to the region's environmental limitations and occupational pluralism to show that rural people constructed identities, which combined elements of both a temporary, seasonal presence and a permanent, sedentary occupation on the Canadian Shield.

To better understand the people who supported tourism in Muskoka, this book introduces the concepts of rural identity and sustainability to help explain how settlers negotiated inherited colonial ideas about liberalism, improvement, and private property with the material realities and economic opportunities in a place that was unsuited to agriculture and sedentary life. I conceptualize rural identity as a means of investigating the emergent properties of a way of life, rather than as an entirely deliberate social or political category. I also accept that people in the past may not have been fully conscious of how the material world shaped their identity. I challenge the notion that identity is strictly a social construction and demonstrate how it was shaped, in part, by the material realities of the environment in which people lived and by their interactions with that environment through economic activity. Rural identity is a malleable concept that can help to account for how and why people adjusted when they encountered new environments, engaged in new occupations, and responded to new social relationships. During the late nineteenth century, rural ways of life throughout North America displayed many similarities, and the concept of rural identity therefore provides a useful framework to reveal what made Muskoka distinct. Given their desire to extend an agrarian society into an environment unsuited to sedentary occupation, an important aim of this book is to assess how sustainable the rural identities were that people in Muskoka constructed and reproduced between 1870 and 1920. Sustainability provides a helpful framework because it allows for a comparison of economic, social, and environmental dimensions of rural identity across space and over time.

When the government opened Muskoka for Euro-Canadian settlement during the late nineteenth century, many who took up land envisioned

FIGURE 0.1 Granite outcroppings characterize much of Muskoka's landscape, 1908. Frank W. Micklethwaite. *John Harold Micklethwaite fonds, PA-159325, Library and Archives Canada*

their place in an agrarian society. Instead, they encountered a heavily forested and poorly drained landscape characterized by numerous small lakes and granite outcroppings. Its thin, acidic soil was largely unsuited to farming (see Figure 0.1). Few thrived as farmers. They did, however, live permanently, year-round on the Shield. To do so, like other rural inhabitants throughout North America, they embraced occupational pluralism, which R.W. Sandwell describes as a combination of "self-provisioning, waged work, and the sale of commodities."[2] Within the first years of resettlement, visitors from cities to the south began showing up, and settlers quickly incorporated tourism as a central pillar of their survival strategies.

Through their temporary, but annual, presence in various places in the region, the Anishinaabeg acquired knowledge and skills related to the Shield environment, which they used to construct, maintain, and reproduce their Indigenous identity. The communities that inhabited the lands at the southern edge of the Canadian Shield in the mid-nineteenth century understood the Shield's material realities and lived in Muskoka for part of every year. Over hundreds of years prior to colonization, First

Nations followed a seasonal cycle between defined resource sites, which included fishing locations next to Lake Simcoe and Georgian Bay, and hunting grounds in Muskoka. After 1850, Euro-Canadian settlement, discriminatory hunting and fishing restrictions, and authoritarian paternalism under the Indian Act seriously constrained their lifeways. To support their communities and cope with the pressures of colonization, they repurposed their skills and knowledge of the Shield environment to sell crafts to tourists and guide fishing and hunting parties in Muskoka. In this way, they returned each year to protect their Indigenous identity.

Tourists visited Muskoka to escape the city, rejuvenate their minds and bodies, and experience the wilderness. Their seasonal presence provides an interesting parallel to that of the Anishinaabeg, since they too spent only part of the year in Muskoka. During the first generation of Euro-Canadian settlement between the 1870s and 1890s, as a strategy to support year-round living on the Shield, settlers who lived near Lakes Muskoka, Rosseau, and Joseph aligned many elements of the local economy with the needs and wants of summer visitors (see Figure 0.2). At resort hotels

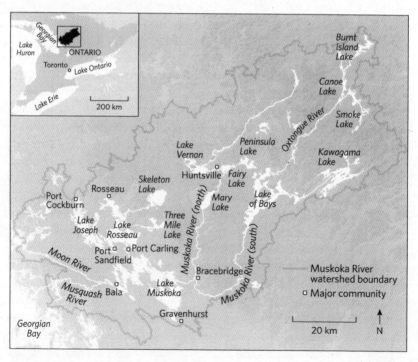

FIGURE 0.2 Muskoka River watershed. *Adapted by Eric Leinberger*

Introduction

and privately owned cottages beside the water, tourists relied on them to do the physical work and provide food and fuel. Tourists had expectations regarding style, taste, and quantity, but settlers were the ones who built and maintained the hotels and cottages, produced the fresh food, chopped the wood, cut the ice, and maintained the landscape aesthetic that visitors demanded each summer.

As was the case nearly everywhere that Euro-Canadians resettled the Shield, agroforestry contributed to the construction of rural identity in Muskoka. The government licensed large logging companies to cut timber and extract incredible wealth from the forests, only a small portion of which benefitted settlers in the form of wages and payment for goods and services to support the winter logging camps. Large-scale logging also degraded aquatic and terrestrial ecosystems, pulled men away from families for months at a time, and declined by the end of the century. Three large leather tanneries consumed enormous quantities of bark from the region's hemlock trees, with similar social, economic, and environmental consequences. Many settlers, however, pursued more sustainable alternatives by selling relatively small quantities of logs to sawmills, and hemlock bark to tanneries, at a scale that moderately altered the local ecology, limited social dislocation, and provided important income. Compared with tourism, agroforestry presented a less sustainable basis for settlers to construct a rural identity.

During the last two decades of the nineteenth century, tourism provided the most sustainable basis for constructing and reproducing a distinct rural identity in Muskoka, because settlers maintained a relatively high degree of control over the goods and services that visitors needed and wanted. After 1900, however, the rise of consumer culture and fossil fuels pulled Muskoka's local economy into new networks of distant market exchange over which settlers had no control. In particular, mail-order catalogue shopping and fossil-fuel technologies created new patterns of life in Muskoka, which eroded the demand for locally produced food and fuel. Tourists continued to rely on many local goods and services, but the opportunities for settlers to turn the material realities of the Shield environment to their advantage diminished when local merchants and farmers competed with large urban retailers for tourists' business, and when local sources of organic energy competed with exogenous sources of mineral energy. By the 1920s, tourism had become a less sustainable feature of rural identity in Muskoka than it had been at the turn of the century.

Scholarship on the history of tourism in North America tends to focus on the visitors, rather than the permanent residents whose lives, labour, and land structured the tourism economy. This is particularly true for Muskoka.[3] Only a few works have concentrated on its rural inhabitants.[4] Historical studies of tourism elsewhere in North America typically explore its cultural meanings, the desires and mentalities of tourists, the efforts by local governments and development agencies to promote various regions, and the points of potential contention between tourists, locals, and Indigenous communities.[5] As a result, histories of tourism tend either to privilege an urban perspective or to treat tourism as an imposition and a detriment to rural communities. In North America, the idea of wilderness that dominated the tourist imagination during the late nineteenth and early twentieth centuries has heavily influenced the perspective of historians. The most popular places to experience the wilderness were national, state, and provincial parks, which governments protected from farming, lumbering, and mining. As William Cronon and Jocelyn Thorpe point out, the trouble with wilderness is that it imagines rural places as being devoid of people and history. Invariably, protected places dispossessed Indigenous peoples, and in most cases they excluded non-Indigenous residents as well.[6]

Of course, North Americans also took holidays in settled rural locations. In areas with a long history of European resettlement and agriculture, residents turned to tourism to supplement their farm economies when commodity prices fell in response to surplus crop production in the American West and the Canadian Prairies at the end of the nineteenth century. As Dona Brown argues in her study of New England, though very few farmers felt "that the work of boarding tourists was essentially different from ordinary farm work," tourism nevertheless "reflected a contest over the farm family's identity and over the meaning of the farm."[7] Blake Harrison shows that farmers and other residents of rural Vermont adopted a strategy of "reworking" to redefine how farmers engaged in new types of farm work to accommodate leisure activities and tourism.[8] In rural locales that were unsuited to agriculture, tourism often followed after periods of fishing, mining, logging, and unsuccessful farming.[9] Ironically, the same limitations that made places such as the northlands of Maine, Michigan, Wisconsin, Minnesota, and Washington unsuited to agriculture also made them desirable wilderness holiday destinations for tourists. Unlike similar places, Muskoka's community and economy co-evolved with tourism, which resulted in a distinct rural identity during the first generation of resettlement.

Rural historians often take for granted that the places, people, and ways of life they investigate are distinct from urban ones. Inspired by the work

Introduction

of Raymond Williams, many simply explain rural people and their life-ways as contrasting with those of urban centres.[10] Generally, they treat "rural" and "agricultural" as interchangeable. As American agricultural historian David B. Danbom states explicitly, "the vast bulk of the rural social, economic, and political history produced in the past generation has focused on farm people."[11] The same is true of the Canadian literature, where rural historians have devoted much more attention to the residents of agrarian communities than to those in hinterland resource communities, where farming was combined with, or supplemented, waged labour.[12] R.W. Sandwell explains what it meant to be rural during the late nineteenth and early twentieth centuries. In Canada, "the *dominance of life lived out-of-doors,* the *enormous amount of hard labour,* and the *pervasive presence of the household*" structured the rural experience. These three features, Sandwell insists, "not only identify for us what it meant to be rural then but also gave coherence and identity to rural Canadians themselves."[13] Understanding the commonalities among rural people across the country acknowledges that "not all farmers relied exclusively on selling farm produce to make a living" and that "many rural dwellers were not really farmers at all." But it does little to help us understand the distinctions between rural people and their ways of life in different places. As early as 1990, geographer Keith Hoggart argued that "researchers have assumed that [rural] places are equivalent to one another when they are dominated by very different causal processes." As a result, "research on rural areas has tended to adopt a theoretically undifferentiated approach to what is 'rural.'"[14] Elsewhere, Sandwell points out that historians must regard the rural "as a place whose meaning and significance is both variable and negotiated on geographically – and historically – specific terms."[15] The concept of rural identity can help historicize and differentiate what it meant to live a rural way of life in discrete places.

Accepting that a wide variety of meaningful similarities and differences in socially constructed categories of identity, such as gender, class, ethnicity, religion, and politics, existed in rural places, this study seeks to understand specifically how more materialist categories of analysis shaped rural identity in Muskoka. Drawing on the work of neo-materialist historian Timothy J. LeCain, I demonstrate that rural identity became constructed, in part, through a creative process that included the influence of the environment and interactions with that environment through work. I treat both ideas and activities as evidence of people's expression of identity. In other words, I accept that we can discern aspects of people's identity in the past through both the discourse they used to signal their inclusion in a particular social group and the physical performance of work and interactions with the material world that they, perhaps subtly and non-discursively, undertook to indicate their commitment to a particular role within their family and community.

Because identity is so malleable, it is a useful tool to aid in understanding change over time, but it also presents some potential risks. Sociologist Rogers Brubaker and historian Frederick Cooper suggest that identity "tends to mean too much (when understood in the strong sense), too little (when understood in the weak sense), or nothing at all (because of its sheer ambiguity)."[16] As a theory of social psychology and sociology, the risk with using identity as a tool for historical analysis is that the ideas, decisions, behaviours, and actions of people in the past (categories of practice) could be used uncritically by the historian to develop broad, reified typologies of groups of people (categories of analysis). Part of this risk, however, stems from the fact that scholars have tended to think of identity as entirely, or perhaps exclusively, *socially* constructed. As sociologists Sheldon Stryker and Peter J. Burke note, identity theory seeks to "understand and explain how social structures affect self and how self affects social behaviors."[17] These postmodernist and poststructuralist approaches to understanding and explaining identity present ample opportunity for researchers, including historians, to treat highly abstracted categories of social roles or belonging as sufficient criteria to evaluate the salience of a particular identity.

Postmodernist and poststructuralist scholars have, LeCain contends, "put far more effort into analyzing the abstract and textual than in trying to discern the real world that was also supposed to be contiguous with that text."[18] They ignored "the possibility that human ideas emerged at least in part from their engagement with [the material] world and could not be accurately understood apart from this engagement."[19] Avoiding the temptation to explain rural identity as the product of a universal consciousness, "entire world view," or *mentalité* requires recognizing that "there was a direct relationship between the material environment, on the one hand, and the consciousness and activity of the population on the other," as historian James A. Henretta maintains.[20] Insisting that identity was shaped by the environment and people's interactions with it should not be an argument in favour of environmental determinism. "From a neo-materialist perspective," LeCain states, "our environments are a powerful influence over this historical process [development of individual cognitive systems] but in a creative rather than a determinative sense."[21] Some of the work by rural studies scholars, and rural sociologists in particular, reveals how environment and occupation have influenced the social construction of

Introduction

identity.[22] And many environmental historians have begun to grapple with the ways that the material world shaped identity in a wide variety of settings, including the Canadian forest-prairie edge, China's borderlands, Black Amazonia, the Adirondacks of Upstate New York, and Washington's Pacific Northwest Coast.[23] On the Shield, most settlers identified as farmers, but they also modified their rural identity to accommodate a plurality of occupations, including many that supported tourism.

Muskoka provides a contrast to studies that equate rural and agrarian or that present resource extraction as the only viable alternative in places unsuited to agriculture. Euro-Canadian resettlement in Muskoka occurred at the height of what historian John Weaver terms "the great land rush."[24] Immigrants from Europe, most of whom were British Protestants, relocated to temperate regions of the globe, where they expected to take up arable land and live as farmers. In 1871, over 93 percent of the 3,756 settlers who lived in the fifteen Muskoka townships included in this study identified as being of English, Irish, or Scottish ancestry. Thirty years later, in 1901, this pattern had not changed: more than 90 percent of the 11,101 permanent residents had British ancestry. Similarly, in 1881, more than 85 percent identified as Methodists, Presbyterians, Baptists, or Anglicans. In 1901, Protestants still constituted more than 80 percent of the population.[25] Central to this project of colonialism were Lockean "ideas about private landed property that were supported by the law; a popular and correct belief that privately held land was a source of freedom and power; and the juxtaposition of improvement and wilderness," which settlers inherited from Britain and spread throughout the Anglo-American world.[26] These "shared cultural traits" justified the dispossession of Indigenous peoples and informed the settler colonial desire "to apply labour and capital, so as to boost the land's carrying capacity and hence its market value."[27] However, land-hungry immigrants were forced to adjust their expectations when the great land rush reached the Shield.

As a bellwether of modernity, tourism presented an alternative path to improvement. Visitors from the city desired to experience the wilderness, which meant uncleared, forested landscapes. And, ironically, settlers in Muskoka found that clearing their land did not necessarily improve it, because the soil was so poor. Those who took up land between the 1870s and 1890s either moved on once they discovered this fact or constructed a rural identity that reflected its realities. The blend of strategies they pursued challenges the idea that rural life in the late nineteenth century was either traditional and insular or destroyed by modern, capitalist economic structures. Using the Saguenay region of Quebec as his case study,

Gérard Bouchard argues that rural people practised "co-integration" whereby "the farming economy maintained numerous, close and regular ties with the extra-regional (and even international) capitalist economy but did so without converting to its specific ways and means."[28] In Muskoka, settlers included tourism as part of their co-integration strategy within the first generation of resettlement and remodelled ideas of improvement into a negotiation between the limited agricultural potential of the Shield and the aesthetic expectations of visitors who paid settlers to accommodate their needs and wants.

To evaluate how tourism and the Shield environment shaped the rural identity of those who resettled Muskoka, I compare the first generation of settlers in Muskoka with three baselines. First, rural identity must be understood in terms of the private property, agrarian ideal that inspired so many immigrants to come to Muskoka. Second, the history of tourism in Muskoka must be understood in contrast to that of similar places, where tourism emerged *after* resettlement and resource extraction. Third, the influence of tourism on rural identity in Muskoka must be understood by comparison with the Indigenous identity of the Anishinaabeg. First Nations lived in Muskoka for hundreds of years prior to Euro-Canadian resettlement, and their lives on the Shield represent an important baseline for understanding how tourism enabled settlers to adjust to the region's material realities. Treating Indigenous occupation of Muskoka as a baseline for comparison risks reifying First Nations people as "ecological Indians" who lived in harmony with the environment simply by virtue of being Indigenous.[29] I avoid this trope by examining the relationships that Euro-Canadian settlers and Indigenous people built and maintained with the Shield. This study highlights the similarities in the process, while also making clear that settler colonialism, including tourism, dispossessed and discriminated against Indigenous people.

Throughout this book, I use the concept of sustainability to characterize and evaluate how rural identity changed in Muskoka because it enables me to consider the constantly evolving circumstances of economy, society, and environment, rather than the static conditions of their interaction. In the chapters that follow, "sustainability" refers to the *potential* for a society, or a particular feature of a society, to reproduce patterns of economic exchange, social relationships, and environmental conditions. This definition asserts that nothing is completely sustainable, only more or less sustainable. The potential is enhanced when the arrangements become more sustainable and is diminished when they become less sustainable. When life in Muskoka became more sustainable, people were better able

Introduction

to construct, maintain, and reproduce their identity than when it became less sustainable.

Defining sustainability in historical terms is complicated by the temporal and spatial variables that must be considered, as well as the technical and ethical ones. Moreover, many definitions of sustainability are not useful for historical inquiry, because they involve certain goals and ways of thinking about the world that were extremely uncommon in the past. Finding value in the concept of sustainability involves reconciling the benefits of a heuristic tool for evaluating change with the risks of anachronism posed by analyzing the past in ways that might not have made sense at the time.[30] The *Berkshire Encyclopedia of Sustainability* defines sustainability as "the capacity to maintain some entity, outcome, or process over time."[31] However, socioecological conditions never remain static, so sustainability can never be an exact science, and therefore, comparison and change become critical to defining, assessing, and understanding it.[32] As sustainability expert Richard Heinberg puts it, "*sustainability* is a relative term."[33] Robert Costanza and Bernard C. Patten argue that "because we can only assess sustainability after the fact, it is a prediction problem more than a definition problem."[34] In other words, changing circumstances and conditions, not identifying indicators, are the real challenge (and opportunity) in using the concept of sustainability. For John Ehrenfeld, sustainability is only a "possibility," not a measurement.[35] Likewise, McMichael, Butler, and Foulke see sustainability as maximizing the chances that any given condition can be maintained indefinitely.[36] Acknowledging these realities, sustainability expert Daniel Lerch suggests that sustainability "is best thought of as a process, not a goal."[37] The sustainability concept's capacity to assess change over time (a central axiom for historians) makes it a useful device to compare a community (Muskoka), or a particular feature of a society (tourism), relative to itself at an earlier or later point, or relative to a similar unit of analysis at the same point in time.[38]

Environmental historians have grappled with the concept of sustainability as either a category of intellectual history itself or a tool to help explain change over time. A number of recent works have investigated the origins of the concept and its influence on land use, resource management, and environmental change over the last several hundred years, particularly in Western Europe and North America.[39] Important scholarship by environmental historians has also demonstrated how it can be used for rigorous comparative historical analysis. In his study of agriculture in colonial Massachusetts, Brian Donahue asks "could Concord's system of husbandry, once established, continue to deliver the desired level of natural products and ecological services to its human inhabitants more or less indefinitely, or did it undermine itself?"[40] Given the pre-industrial realities of farming in the seventeenth and eighteenth centuries, he argues, "the colonial husbandry systems could have gone on supporting the community for a long, long time."[41] But even this particular socioecological system, which demonstrated a high potential for sustaining itself, succumbed to pressures that it could not resist. It "was bound up in and deeply committed to a broader world of European economic growth that ultimately led it to move in a new, arguably *less* sustainable direction as it encountered its limits ... But this should not blind us to what was achieved during the era when, partly by choice and partly by necessity, those constraints prevailed."[42] In his work on Great Plains agriculture, Geoff Cunfer makes a similar case for understanding the contingency of sustainability in the past. "Human adaptation to environment is never permanent," Cunfer states, "because people change and environments change. No system is ever 'sustainable' forever. Sustainability, at its best, can only mean a temporary state of equilibrium and a willingness and ability to change again in the future."[43] As Donahue and Cunfer demonstrate, sustainability is not a template for explaining features, characteristics, and typologies of the past. Instead, it helps to explain changes in the past. Specifically, it allows historians to identify changes that shaped the potential for societies to maintain or reproduce particular economic, social, and environmental arrangements over time. In the case of Muskoka, it provides a methodology for analyzing changes to the relationship between identity and environment found in Indigenous lifeways, Euro-Canadian resettlement, resource extraction, and tourism.

There is no single narrative of sustainability in the history of Muskoka. Instead, sustainability is assessed in multiple comparative terms. Economic, social, and environmental arrangements may have become more sustainable for one group of people in a certain way while simultaneously becoming less so for a different group in another way. For example, during the 1880s and 1890s, tourism made life more sustainable for settlers living near Lakes Muskoka, Rosseau, and Joseph but did not have the same impact in the backwoods. When consumer culture and fossil fuels eroded local control over tourism after about 1900, life became less sustainable for all permanent residents. Likewise, in the 1870s and 1880s, economic opportunities provided by logging camps made settler life more sustainable than it would have been without them, but after about 1900 household-based logging presented more sustainable opportunities. And the Anishinaabeg repurposed their skills and knowledge to pursue opportunities in Muskoka

Introduction

and make their lives more sustainable even as colonization made their lives less sustainable everywhere else. In each case, sustainability provides a useful tool to evaluate how identities changed in Muskoka between 1870 and 1920.

The District of Muskoka is located approximately 150 kilometres north of Toronto and is situated at the southern edge of the Precambrian Shield, east of Georgian Bay and west of Algonquin Park. The origins of the name "Muskoka" are not clear, but early historians have suggested the name derived from Chief Misko-Aki, who spoke for several Anishinaabeg nations in the region during the early nineteenth century and was known to the British as "William Yellowhead."[44] During the 1850s and 1860s, the Government of Canada West created Muskoka as a distinct political territory in an effort to settle the Ottawa-Huron Tract, a swath of land north of the St. Lawrence lowlands between Georgian Bay and the Ottawa River as far north as Lake Nipissing. Township and district borders made Muskoka legible to government agencies, but this study takes a "bioregional" approach to delimiting its geographic scope.[45] In Muskoka, the watershed exerted important influences on people's lives that did not conform to the arbitrary political spaces created by government mapmakers.[46] For this reason, in this book, Muskoka primarily refers to the watershed of the Muskoka River. Many primary sources refer to and organize information according to the township and district borders created by government surveyors during the third quarter of the nineteenth century. But in many ways, the people who lived in Muskoka thought about their geography in different terms.

The geography of the Muskoka River is almost entirely a product of the combined forces of geology and glaciation.[47] Younger than the rock of the Shield farther north, the gneiss granite bedrock across all of Muskoka was created roughly one billion years ago when metamorphic rock thrust upward to form the mountainous Algonquin Dome. These mountains were once as tall as the Rockies, but after eons of ice, water, and wind erosion only their base remains. Approximately one million years ago, the climate cooled and the northern portion of North America experienced cycles of glaciation, the most recent of which began to subside around twenty thousand years ago. This process occurred across most of southern Ontario, including Muskoka, between eleven and twelve thousand years ago. Glaciers scoured the bedrock of its soils and softer sedimentary rock, such as limestone, producing a barren landscape of granite. As they melted, enormous volumes of water flowed out of the Algonquin Dome, forming Lake Algonquin, which at its greatest extent covered the basins of Lake

Michigan and Lake Huron, including Georgian Bay and the western half of what is now Muskoka.

The force of these meltwaters eroded billions of tons of rock and deposited them downstream as glacial till (clay, silt, sand, gravel). As the meltwaters subsided and Lake Algonquin drained out to form the Great Lakes, the region underwent isostatic rebound, and the basins carved by glaciation and erosion formed the lakes that remain today. The outwash of glacial till, the receding of Lake Algonquin, and the deposition of organic matter that accumulated over the last twelve thousand years created the soil arrangements present in Muskoka when Euro-Canadians colonized it after about 1860. Meltwaters carried glacial till downstream to the irregular shoreline and archipelago of Lake Algonquin's eastern coast. Over roughly eight hundred years, it settled to form a layer of lacustrine clay in the low-lying areas along the eastern shore of the lake. As the lake receded, this deposit formed Muskoka's only pockets of fertile soils that were somewhat suitable for farming. However, because Lake Algonquin existed for a relatively short time, little or none of the outwash settled

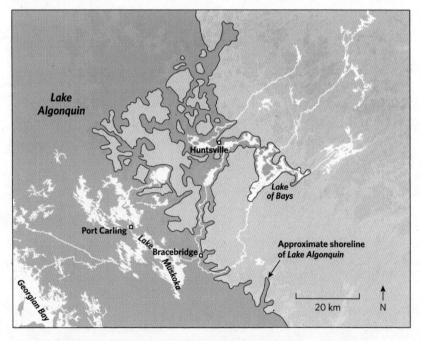

FIGURE 0.3 Muskoka River watershed 11,000 years ago. *Gary Long, This River the Muskoka (Erin, ON: Boston Mills Press, 1989), 25. Adapted by Eric Leinberger*

Introduction   17

along its bottom in deeper water. Thus, like the areas that remained above the level of Lake Algonquin, the landscape west of Lakes Muskoka, Rosseau, and Joseph received very little meltwater deposition, which meant that its thin soils were accumulated solely via organic processes during the next several thousand years (see Figure 0.3).

By almost any measure, Muskoka was unsuited to commercial agriculture. The Canada Land Inventory categorizes soil capability for agriculture according to seven classes and fifteen additional subclasses. Classes 1–4 "are considered capable of sustained use for cultivated field crops, those in Classes 5 and 6 only for perennial forage crops, and those in Class 7 for neither."[48] The vast majority of Muskoka features Class 7 soils, which have no capability for crop use or permanent pasture and are dominated by stoniness and shallowness to bedrock. East of Lake Muskoka between the vicinity of Bracebridge and Three Mile Lake, tucked into the pockets that formed next to the eastern shore of Lake Algonquin, settlers found patches of Class 4 soils, with low natural fertility and deficient moisture that restricted the range of crops. They also encountered larger swathes of Class 5 soils, with severe limitations and adverse relief, as well as Class 6 soils, with undesirable soil structure, low permeability, and shallowness to bedrock. Similarly, farther east, along the old post-glacial lakeshore between Mary Lake, Lake Vernon, Fairy Lake, and Peninsula Lake, settlers found Class 4 and 6 soils, featuring characteristics that resembled those east of Lake Muskoka. By comparison, much of the most fertile regions of southern Ontario, such as Wellington and Middlesex Counties, overwhelmingly possessed Class 1, 2, and 3 soils, with either no or only moderate limitations for crops. Even the Saguenay region of Quebec, which featured many socioecological similarities with Muskoka, contained arguably much better soils, including several pockets of Class 2 and 3 around Lac Saint-Jean, interspersed with lower-quality areas of Class 4, all surrounded by vast stretches of Class 7 farther away from the lake and the Saguenay River.[49]

I opened this introduction with Fanny Potts's insect analogy comparing tourists and settlers. Her comment captures well the distinctions and the relationships between consumers and producers, urban and rural dwellers, temporary and permanent residents. "The tourists we may liken to the butterflies," she continued, "because they flock in upon us with the summer sunshine and flowers. The hard-working settlers are like the bees, because they gather their honey with busy toil in the hot sun and store it away for the cold winter days." Potts was careful not to romanticize the relationship between tourists and settlers, and she acknowledged that "between these two classes there is a great gulf fixed. It seems to come naturally to the pleasure-loving tourist to look down with a kind of pity on the hard-working settler, and it seems just as natural for the hard-working settler to look down on the giddy tourist." It matters greatly, however, from her experience, "One thing is sure, each class would be very badly off without the other. If the busy little brown bees of settlers had not these lovely 'tourist blossoms' from which they gather their honey, where would their winter supply come from?" With these opening lines of a chapter entitled "Settlers and Tourists," Potts articulated, almost perfectly, a key feature in the construction of a rural identity that was distinct in North America.[50]

I

Rural Identity and Resettlement of the Canadian Shield, 1860–80

In the spring of 1878, seventeen-year-old Frederick de la Fosse journeyed on his own from southern England to the small community of Ilfracombe in Muskoka. His uncle, and sole guardian, Colonel Montague Ricketts, had arranged for him to learn backwoods farming at the Harston Agricultural School in Stisted Township, on the shores of Buck Lake northeast of Huntsville. Ricketts had agreed to pay the school £100 per year for three years to lodge and feed his nephew as well as teach him to farm in the wilderness. After that, de la Fosse would be free to take up his own land. In reality, the Harston Agricultural School was simply the homestead of a retired British army officer, Captain Charles G. Harston. A recent settler himself, Harston had no credible agricultural knowledge suitable to frontier farming on the Canadian Shield, with its thin acidic soils, cool climate, and short growing season.[1]

On the final leg of his journey, de la Fosse spent the night at the British Lion Hotel in Bracebridge. In the sitting room, a group of rough-worn settlers attempted to impress upon him the realities of farming life in Muskoka. After learning of his uncle's arrangements, the group had a laugh "to hear a boy whose weight was just one hundred pounds talking glibly of clearing a farm in the woods, but more excruciatingly funny was the fact that he was actually paying out what appeared to most of them a fortune for the privilege of helping a man to clear his farm and attend his cattle."[2] By 1878, most settlers had been in Muskoka for less than a decade and were still learning the difficult lessons of how to live on the Shield. The men at the British Lion understood that de la Fosse had little hope of succeeding as a farmer in Muskoka. These facts on their own were not particularly humorous. But the idea of paying somebody else to improve one's own chances of success seemed farcical.

During the late nineteenth century, North American settler colonial societies extended into places with low agricultural potential, such as Muskoka. What distinguished its settler society during this period were its extraordinarily poor soils and the co-evolution of tourism alongside agriculture and logging. The arrangements made by Ricketts for his nephew reveal assumptions widely shared by settlers in places where governments treated agricultural settlement as the key to continued colonial expansion and state formation. Arriving pioneers expected that environmental conditions would be similar to those of more populated regions with established farming communities. Where the material realities of resettled land precluded a predominantly agricultural society and economy, rural inhabitants pursued a combination of subsistence activities, market exchange, and waged labour. They experimented with various agricultural land uses and practices while simultaneously engaging in the agroforestry economy and earning income through market exchange.[3]

This chapter examines the suite of adjustments first-generation settlers made to construct rural identities that reflected the region's environmental limitations and occupational opportunities. After the first generation, those living closer to the lower lakes (Muskoka, Rosseau, and Joseph) had begun to construct a more sustainable rural identity than those living in the backwoods. Poor soils and limited transportation options left settler households struggling to support themselves and isolated from the wider economy of Southern Ontario and northeastern North America. Compared to regions south of the Shield, Muskoka's agricultural potential was uniformly poor, but settlers living closer to the lower lakes enjoyed opportunities not available to those located in the backwoods. Pioneer households everywhere in Muskoka experimented with various crops and strategies for subsistence, including hunting and fishing. Many pursued opportunities in the logging industry by selling their labour and that of their draught animals, along with the produce of their land, to logging camps in the winter. And, notably, an increasing number quickly seized on the opportunities to provide accommodations, goods, and services to tourists from cities to the south. When confronted with an environmental reality they did not expect, many, including de la Fosse, gave up, abandoned their land, and moved away. By the 1880s, transportation networks linking steamboat navigation and railways alleviated many of the problems associated with isolation closer to the lower lakes, but settlers living in backwoods

FIGURE 1.1 Muskoka Colonization Road, c. 1873. *George Harlow White, 1873. Baldwin Collection of Canadiana, Pictures-R-331. Courtesy of the Toronto Public Library*

locations around the upper lakes continued to struggle and abandoned their land at higher rates.

The Euro-Canadian resettlement of the Muskoka District took place within what John Weaver calls "the great land rush," and, in particular, the mid-century exodus of land-hungry immigrants and farmers' sons from southern Ontario to the American West.[4] Although the rich mineral deposits of the Shield initially attracted the government's interest, the 1850 Robinson-Huron Treaty, which was signed with seventeen Ojibwe (Anishinaabeg) First Nations, also enabled settlers to take up land under the terms of the 1853 Act to Amend the Law for the Sale and Settlement of the Public Lands.[5] An agricultural panic over collapsed wheat prices in 1857 placed pressure on the government to construct the Muskoka Colonization Road, which it completed in stages using mainly local labour (see Figure 1.1). In 1859, the road connected Orillia and Gravenhurst. It was extended to Bracebridge two years later and reached the future site of Huntsville in 1863. At the same time, a series of trunk roads extended laterally into surveyed townships, opening more than half a million acres to resettlement by the end of the century. The 1853 act allowed the government to sell hundred-acre plots at fixed prices and to grant hundred-acre plots of free land to settlers who were willing to locate next to the public road. The government hoped that opening Muskoka to colonization would encourage settlers to stay in the province rather than move to the American West.

This development sparked plenty of optimism. The government sold the first plots in July 1859 and issued the first location tickets for lots along the Muskoka Road in October.[6] In February 1860, Commissioner of Crown Lands P.M. Vankoughnet reported that 54 settler households had officially taken up, or located, free grant lots along the Muskoka Road. The following January, the number of lots had dipped slightly to 48, with a population of 190. Nearly two years later, in December 1862, the number of located lots stood at 283, with a population of 1,012.[7] In his report that year, land agent R.J. Oliver felt "the general progress of the settlement is very gratifying." Although "considerable belts of rock intersect the country," he added that "good farming lands abound, especially on the upper Roads," and that "other townships of good land will soon be added." Sensitive to "the race now existing between the United States and ourselves [Canada West] for securing the tide of Emigration," Oliver understood that "most of the emigrants, with families, leave their homes with a view to farming" and insisted that "to the Immigrant, this settlement [in Muskoka] will offer advantages in the extension of Free Grants."[8] Yet, his cautious optimism overlooked the fact that in a year when 743 people settled in Muskoka, 71 people also left.[9]

At least during the earliest years, Muskoka pioneers did not abandon their land because of low yields. During the mid-nineteenth century, most Ontario farmers placed great importance on wheat, and Muskoka settlers devoted slightly more than a third of their cropland to wheat, producing yields that were just shy of the provincial average.[10] Their much more pressing challenge was inadequate transportation and communication. The environmental realities of the Shield posed ongoing obstacles to the movement of people and goods in and out of Muskoka. Historian Florence Murray points out that "straight lines were impossible; lakes, rivers, and hills caused wide deviations. Numerous rivers and creeks required bridges, swamps required causeways, and parts of the country were so rough that no practical road line could be obtained."[11] In the spring of 1858, Crown surveyor David Gibson encountered "many obstacles to overcome" while exploring possible options for the Muskoka Road. He eventually laid a line that required "deviating slightly from the course where it is crossed by [granite] ridges."[12] Where rock outcroppings presented themselves, routes deviated from the line, and where the line met rivers, streams, or swamps, crews built wooden trestled or cribbed bridges and corduroy

Rural Identity and Resettlement of the Canadian Shield   23

roads.[13] Government contractors and local settlers worked to keep the roads in good repair, but seasonal freezing and flooding, as well as heavy use, took their toll.

Settlers could be forgiven for thinking that the roads served other interests before their own. In 1861, even as local crews worked to extend colonization roads through their areas, the Crown licensed timber berths in five surveyed townships.[14] Ironically, the roads that settlers built to improve settlement conditions actually ended up benefitting mainly loggers whose heavy use caused significant and repeated damage. In November 1866, the commissioner of Crown lands, Alexander Campbell, wrote to J.W. Bridgland, superintendent of colonization roads, to complain that

> in scarcely a single instance has any new road we have made had time to settle into a compact state before it had been ploughed into the deepest ruts and mudholes by the heavy provision loads of lumbermen, so that the roads have not only been mainly used by them, but most unfairly made to suffer in their tenderest condition.[15]

Campbell urged Bridgland to force the "lumberers" to pay for their share of road maintenance, but his letter also reveals that Muskoka's settler economy suffered due to poor road conditions.

By the early 1870s, the roads had become a bottleneck in moving people and goods into and out of Muskoka, inhibiting its economic growth. In 1869, Kivas Tully, chief engineer for the Muskoka Road, claimed that the critical stretch linking the Muskoka District with southern Ontario, between Washago and Gravenhurst, was "in a very bad state, and under the most favourable conditions, an ordinary passenger stage wagon, with a good team, takes three hours to perform the 14 miles; in fact there are few places ... where the horses can go beyond a walk and the difficulties for loaded wagons are still greater."[16] According to a local newspaper that year, the stagecoach ride from Washago to Gravenhurst comprised 20 percent of the total cost of the two-hundred-kilometre journey from Toronto to Gravenhurst.[17] Even the most important section of the road network proved inadequate for settlers' requirements.

During these early years, Muskoka's future seemed to rest on overcoming the isolation that characterized rural life. Settlers continued to leave after only a short stay. Some took up land on speculation only to abandon it after cutting and selling the merchantable pine. Others bought land, built a house, cleared a few acres, and sold their property to incoming settlers. But many wished to farm and left only after they discovered the difficulty of doing so. Regardless of their intentions, the steady departure continued to alarm local officials. At a settlers' association meeting, held in Orillia in November 1867, the district's first member of Provincial Parliament, A.P. Cockburn, commented that "very often people had come [into Muskoka] with exaggerated ideas of the country and had left in consequence of the disappointments they had met with."[18] Prior to his election in Muskoka, Cockburn had run a general store and was reeve of Victoria Township to the south. By 1867, he had already realized that transportation improvements were essential to enhance the standard of living in Muskoka (see Figure 1.2). Two years earlier, he had journeyed through Muskoka by canoe and "was much impressed with the beauty and importance of these lakes."[19] After assessing the navigation potential of the three largest lakes (Muskoka, Rosseau, and Joseph), he wrote a proposal to Minister of Agriculture D'Arcy McGee. If the government promised to make a series of "road and other improvements," he would introduce a steamboat service on the three lakes, which he did the following spring. The arrival of the *Wenonah* had an immediate effect on settlers' lives by dramatically reducing the cost of shipping goods. Freight rates per hundredweight dropped from $0.75–$1.00 to just $0.40, the price of salt fell from $4.00 a barrel to $1.35, and a keg of nails went from $7.00 to $3.50.[20] The *Wenonah* brought in nearly everything that settlers needed, including "lumber, cement, lime, bricks, tools, machinery, grain, groceries, dry goods, furniture, fodder, even livestock."[21] In launching his steamboat business, Cockburn recognized a profitable opportunity but also the means to alleviate some of the burdens produced by inadequate overland transportation.

The Ontario government fulfilled its bargain with Cockburn, making road and navigation improvements in the early 1870s. In 1870, the Department of Public Works built a macadamized and plank road between Lake Couchiching and Gravenhurst.[22] The wooden sections lasted less than three years before rot or fire destroyed them, but the improvements to this fifteen-mile stretch of the Muskoka Road greatly enhanced connections with southern Ontario. Thomas McMurray, author of a promotional tract on Muskoka and editor of its first newspaper, the *Northern Advocate,* called the new road "a great boon to the settlers."[23] It had undeniably become more reliable and comfortable, but the bottleneck persisted. In December 1868, Cockburn organized a petition from residents in three townships to remind the new provincial government about the need for navigation improvements. The petition insisted that "inland navigation ... is so constituted by nature that ... a little government aid [i.e., a lock between Lake Rosseau and Lake Muskoka] will supply a high

FIGURE 1.2 Early artistic impression of Lake Joseph, c. 1880. *Schell and Hogan, artists, R.M. Smart, engravers.* George Munro Grant, Picturesque Canada: The Country as It Was and Is *(Toronto: James Clarke, 1882), 610. Courtesy of the Thomas Fisher Rare Book Library, University of Toronto*

way for 7 months of the year, for Transportation of freight and passengers." In addition to the Port Carling lock, the petition asked for "the removal of certain obstructions in the River between Lakes Muskoka and Rosseau."[24] The government commissioned both projects within a year. In the spring of 1869, the Department of Public Works excavated a channel across the narrow section of land separating the two lakes and built a lock to negotiate the difference in water levels.[25] It also dredged the river below the rapids. In November 1871, steamboats could pass between Lakes Rosseau and Muskoka, and less than a year after that, by July 1872, all three lakes became internavigable when the government built a channel between Lakes Rosseau and Joseph at Port Sandfield. In anticipation of these improvements, Cockburn introduced two more steamers in 1869 and 1871 (see Figure 1.3). After the three lakes became internavigable in 1872, Cockburn had steamboat service running to several ports of call, greatly enhancing the transportation and communication network for settlers.

FIGURE 1.3 Steamer *Nipissing*, c. 1879. *Seymour Penson, artist. John Rogers et al.,* Guide Book and Atlas of Muskoka and Parry Sound Districts *(Toronto: H.R. Page, 1879), 18. Courtesy of the Thomas Fisher Rare Book Library, University of Toronto*

The steamboats eased some of the burdens of isolation, but settlers felt the benefits differently depending on how close they lived to the lower lakes. For example, in May 1871, as the Ontario government finished improving the Muskoka Road between Washago and Gravenhurst, settlers in Chaffey Township, north of what eventually became Huntsville, petitioned to have the road extended. "We have endured very great hardships during the past winter for want of a road," read the petition, "having had to carry in our provisions for miles through the bush." The petition insisted that "unless a road is made ... [we] will have to throw up our lands and beg our way out of the country completely ruined."[26] Later that month, a Chaffey Township resident, identified only as "One of the sufferers," wrote to the Toronto *Globe* to describe the hard conditions of pioneer life in the Muskoka bush. According to the writer, there were "two hundred immigrants now in Muskoka looking for land, and that from ten to twenty intended settlers are leaving the district every day, because we have no road."[27] During the pioneer years, settlers near the lower lakes could avail themselves of the steamboat service in addressing their transportation problems, but this option was unavailable to backwoods settlers, who were forced to endure the inadequate roads.

The first decade of Euro-Canadian resettlement in Muskoka was anything but a land rush. After Confederation, however, it took on new energy in the context of Ontario's 1868 Act to Secure Free Grants and Homesteads to Actual Settlers on the Public Lands. During the 1870s, settlers registered over 3,200 free grant locations, approximately 55 percent of all locations registered before 1907.[28] On taking control of Crown Lands, the new provincial government sought to revitalize settlement efforts in the Ottawa-Huron Tract by increasing the amount of free grant lands. Now, instead of being restricted to lots beside a colonization road, homesteaders could take up free land on any lots in surveyed townships. Modelled after similar legislation in the United States, the 1868 Homestead Act granted hundred-acre parcels to anyone over the age of eighteen.[29] However, the government did not issue patent to the land until five years had elapsed. During that time, the locatee was obliged to build a house, reside in it for at least six months a year, and have fifteen acres cleared and under cultivation, with at least two acres cleared each year to secure title.[30] To prevent the timber speculation that had plagued the 1853 Sale and Settlement of the Public Lands Act, the government withheld the right to sell timber from their land until settlers obtained patent. For homesteaders, making timber off limits effectively placed their chances of success squarely on the agricultural potential of their land.

By the 1870s, experiences with Muskoka's poor soils began to play an increasingly significant role in determining who stayed and who left. The offer of free land attracted many people, but glowing reports of the region's agricultural potential undoubtedly heightened their expectations. In his 1871 booklet *The Free Grant Lands of Canada from Practical Experience of Bush Farming,* newspaper editor and area booster Thomas McMurray gushed about the advantages of Muskoka. Describing its climate as "perfect summer and perfect winter," he assured prospective settlers that "in summer there is more moisture here than further south, owing to the greater elevation and vicinity to the lakes ... [and thus] freedom from drought which is so mischievous below." "If we have somewhat more snow," McMurray justified, "we can fairly claim that, almost as soon as the snow is gone, the land is dry for the plough, and soon ready for the seed." As for the soil, it was "mostly of a loamy nature" but with "clay deposits ... in many places." Two-thirds of it was "fit for cultivation."[31] McMurray reserved his most glowing praise for the crops. The wheat yields were "splendid," "large," and "superior," oats "grow luxuriantly and pay well," and "the grasses are eminently successful."[32] Boosters hoped to lure settlers, but they also offered practical advice. Choosing a lot was obviously the most important decision any settler would ever make. In his pamphlet, McMurray recommended that settlers "make a thorough examination of the land before locating." "Some take almost the first lot they see, without proper examination," he warned, "and after a time get discouraged. The plan is to take time, in the first instance, and make a wise selection, then begin and work with a will."[33] This caution seemed to contradict McMurray's extravagant praise. Nevertheless, this basic truth – that cleared land did not necessarily translate into good *farm*land – anticipated the experience of many pioneers in Muskoka during the 1870s. Prospective settlers were encouraged to expect quite favourable conditions for farming based on selective and often exaggerated information. In fact, they had few options to improve the material realties of the Shield for agriculture and many ways of making them worse.

One of the first people to take advantage of the Homestead Act was John Lacey Oldham. A forty-year-old immigrant from Nottingham, England, Oldham arrived in Muskoka during the fall of 1868 with his three young sons, John Jr., Charles, and William.[34] The family took up a lot several kilometres east of Lake Rosseau in Watt Township and immediately began clearing the land and establishing a farm. The Oldhams made the most of their well-wooded land by using cedar logs for fences and shingles, white pine for planking, maple for sugaring, and a variety of hardwoods for fuel. In the spring, Oldham burned piles of logs and slash cleared during the winter in preparation for sowing. This practice saved a great deal of labour and added soil nutrients for the first crops. During the 1870s, such fires were a common sight in Muskoka. One newly arrived settler recalled seeing "at least one hundred of these great heaps of logs blazing up high into the air" as he made his way along the Muskoka River in 1875.[35] Oldham probably had little idea whether his land would be suitable for farming. With the trees removed, however, he discovered patches of relatively decent farmland. He and his sons experimented with a variety of crops, including peas, wheat, rye, potatoes, oats, barley, corn, beans, and turnips. Although he did not record their yields, his journal suggests that these crops turned out reasonably well in the first season. Oldham also made good use of the diversity of his land, harvesting hay from two beaver meadows, which he called Hill and Home Fields. Naturally occurring beaver meadows provided, in the words of observers, "green gems of prairie, relieving the monotomy [sic] of the forest." Farmers

Rural Identity and Resettlement of the Canadian Shield   29

relied on the meadows to "furnish a useful food for cattle in the 'blue joint,' a nutritious wild grass."[36] By holding back streams that flooded in the spring and began to dry out by the end of the summer, beaver dams locked nutrients into fertile, yet slightly acidic, seasonal meadows. Without needing to modify the environment, households realized the potential of the meadows to support animal husbandry and mixed farming. In 1869, Oldham built on his luck by taking up two more plots of some of the best land in Monck Township, a little south of his homestead. Only a portion of each was arable, so as Oldham's sons came of age, they took up their own free grant land. In each case, they selected lots with limited agricultural capability, though comparatively fertile by the standards of Muskoka.[37] John Oldham died suddenly at the age of forty-seven in 1875, leaving his three sons with two three-hundred-acre parcels between them by the end of the 1870s. The Oldhams toiled during their first years in Muskoka, and in this regard, their experience was typical of pioneers on the Shield. Unusual, however, was their location of several lots whose soils were almost as good as could be hoped for in Muskoka.

Closer to the lower lakes, Harriet Barbara King and her extended family struggled with the material realities of life in the backwoods. The pensioned widow of a British army officer, King emigrated from her home in France during the Franco-Prussian War and joined her son and daughter, and their young families, in Stephenson Township. In 1870, King's son took up three hundred acres under his own name and the maiden name of his wife. Less than a year later, in the summer of 1871, King's daughter and her husband took up two hundred acres. King herself arrived in the fall of 1871 with an unmarried daughter and located a hundred acres directly between her son and daughter, thereby bringing the total area occupied by the family to six hundred acres. All of this land was unsuited to agriculture.[38]

In a series of letters published in 1878, King described "the miseries of Bush life" that plagued her family's pioneer experience. During her first year, she "considered Muskoka ... as the *Ultima Thule* of civilization," and after several years she observed that "many of the settlers themselves bear in their faces the unmistakable signs of hard work, scanty food, and a perpetual struggle for existence."[39] A sense of isolation and claustrophobia pervades her account. "The very sight of the dense forest circling us all round," she wrote on arriving at her new home, "with hardly any perceptible outlet, gave me a dreadful feeling of suffocation."[40] Her perceptions of Muskoka's "immense forest which closes round the small clearings like a belt of iron" reflected a shared cultural history of cleared or pastoral landscapes, which informed the way that many British and Western

FIGURE 1.4 Isolated farm in Stephenson Township, 1875. *George Harlow White. Baldwin Collection of Canadiana, Pictures-R-462. Courtesy of the Toronto Public Library*

European immigrants reacted to New World environments.[41] The King family's remote setting also presented very practical challenges. "For a long time after our arrival in the 'Bush,'" King recounted, "we were in imminent danger of starvation from ... the difficulty of procuring [food] from a distance."[42] The six miles of road leading to the closest village was "nothing but a narrow track with frightful stumps."[43] After three years in Stephenson Township, King wrote that "none but those who have experienced it can ever realise the utter weariness and isolation of Bush-life."[44] Indeed, she recognized that "few of the better class of settlers would remain, but for the near prospect of Government granting roads in the township."[45] Settlers everywhere in Muskoka understood that their success relied on improved transportation networks (see Figure 1.4).

The material realities of the Shield structured the fate of settler colonial society, and the construction of rural identity, in the backwoods. In 1872, King felt cautiously optimistic about the agricultural potential of her family's land. Her son's land was "good, and prettily situated, with plenty of beaver meadow and a sprinkling of rock." Her own was "good flat land for cultivation," which others envied for "the absence of rock."[46] Unfortunately, during her first spring, a late thaw significantly shortened the growing season, and "drenching rain" and "thunder-storms" hampered efforts to clear more than three-quarters of an acre. From the four-and-a-half acres her son had cleared the previous year, the Kings harvested eighty bushels of potatoes, along with "a good average crop" of peas, French beans, vegetable marrows, and cabbages.[47] In the late summer, King's son "was occupied for many weeks in making hay ... in the beaver meadow, a large one and very productive."[48] The family planted "no crops of golden grain" until the fall.[49] A "burst of temporary enthusiasm" during the spring harvest was short-lived when the winter wheat "was found to be wizened, shriveled, and discoloured, and fit for nothing but to feed poultry."[50] Over the next two years, the situation deteriorated. In the fall of 1873, the daughter's family moved to Toronto after the husband became an Anglican minister, though they later returned to Muskoka when the church posted him to Bracebridge.[51] By 1875, her "son's health and strength were visibly decreasing," with nothing to show for it other "than the very uncertain prospect of a bare living at the end of many years more of daily drudgery."[52] By then, the Kings had obtained the patent to four hundred of their original six hundred acres. Finally, Harriet King gave up and moved into Bracebridge, whereas her son's family continued to farm until sometime during the 1880s. Stephenson Township contained some of Muskoka's best soil, but the Kings had not located on it. The material realities of farming on the Shield, combined with the isolation of backwoods life, took their toll.

Pioneers shared many experiences throughout Muskoka, but the likelihood of abandonment increased the deeper one went into the backwoods. The land rises as one moves east along the Muskoka River into the backwoods townships that border the upper lakes. There, despite the addition of steamboats during the 1870s and 1880s, inadequate government roads created transportation bottlenecks like those in townships farther west. Settlers took up hundreds of lots of free grant lands in these areas during the 1870s. The promise of free land also attracted squatters who hoped to clear it, build a home, and plant crops in anticipation of locating their lots once the government opened additional townships for settlement. William Osborne and his family squatted in Franklin Township at almost the same time that Harriet King left her homestead and moved to Bracebridge. And like the Kings, the Osbornes chose poor land. In the winter of 1875, William Osborne purchased the squatter's rights to a parcel of cleared land and a log cabin from a Polish squatter who had preceded him. Osborne originally emigrated with his young family from Nottingham to Philadelphia in 1864. Disappointed with opportunities there, he acted on a tip about free land in Muskoka. The following spring, his teenaged sons, Thomas and Arthur, joined him.[53] Like King, Thomas Osborne recalled the isolation caused by rough roads, infrequent transportation services, and the "dense woods ... on each side of us."[54] On arriving at the clearing for their

32 — Making Muskoka

homestead, he expressed concern to his father about the "stone and burnt-over ground, which close by us showed more stone than ground."[55] During their first two years, 1875 and 1876, the Osbornes cleared land during the winter and planted small subsistence plots of peas, beans, potatoes, and corn. They purchased flour until their third year when, in addition to adding turnips, they experimented with wheat, which they had ground into flour at a mill on the far side of Peninsula Lake.[56] In 1878, Thomas Osborne turned eighteen and became eligible to take up free grant land under the Homestead Act. The government still had not opened Franklin Township to settlement. In anticipation of this development, Thomas laid claim to a section of land to the east of his father. By the end of winter, the Osbornes "had cut down about five acres of almost level land ... [that] proved to be good ... [and] planted it in wheat that grew well, with fine, long heads. It was a heavy crop." The following spring, when the government opened the land, William and Thomas each registered their lots, a total of nearly four hundred acres lying between Peninsula Lake and Lake of Bays.[57] Thomas estimated that roughly half of his land was fit for cultivation, and over the next year he reported respectable crops. Unfortunately, the Osbornes could not subsist solely from the sale of their produce, for which the only markets were local settlers and merchants. Thomas worked a variety of temporary jobs for cash, learned to trap from a neighbouring squatter, and relied on fish and game for a large part of the family diet. In the fall of 1879, he returned to Philadelphia to work for his older brother's hosiery business. He tried to convince his father and brother to join him. "I can't see anything for the future for me," he told his father, "and nothing but a hard, solitary life for you and Arthur."[58] In the end, William and Arthur remained in Muskoka, and Thomas transferred his title to Arthur in 1881.[59] The Osbornes appear to have fared rather well compared to their neighbours, many of whom followed Thomas's example and left Muskoka. In the first five years that Franklin Township was open for settlement, settlers located 212 lots, but only 1 received patent and fifty-five people abandoned their land.[60] Thomas Osborne did not technically desert his land, but the hardships of backwoods life in Muskoka finally convinced him and many others to move on.

But what of Frederick de la Fosse, whom we met at the start of this chapter? As he journeyed to the Harston farm on Buck Lake, he passed the King family lands, and his earliest memories of the Shield shared the same impressions of isolation that Harriet King had reported several years earlier. "The farther we advanced north the scarcer grew the clearings," he recalled, "until at last we entered on an unbroken stretch of forest that

FIGURE 1.5 Captain Harston's second home on Buck Lake, c. 1900. *Fred Hopcraft*

continued for miles."[61] He soon learned for himself what the more experienced men already knew. Harston had used his "Agricultural School" as a scheme to acquire both capital and labour to help him clear his land and establish a farm.

Harston had attracted three other young men. Thirty-four-year-old Aemilius Baldwin came from Toronto, whereas eighteen-year-old Richard Tothill and twenty-three-year-old William Garrett were both from England. By the time de la Fosse arrived, Harston and his three "pupils" had cleared just three acres, "but it was strewn with blackened logs and burnt branches. Where there were no logs, large boulders were the chief visible features." The Canada Land Inventory classifies the vicinity of the Harston farm as some of the best soil in Muskoka, but according to de la Fosse, their efforts uncovered "no arable land at all." When he expressed skepticism, Harston replied that "inside of two years you will see this wilderness flourishing ... The barns will be bursting with grain, and the cattle with fatness." Harston's optimism and conviction buoyed the young men, who became "so imbued with his enthusiasm that we believed in all his rosy dreams of coming prosperity."[62] They carried on, hoping that by clearing the land they would inevitably improve it (see Figure 1.5).

Unfortunately, even the best soils in Muskoka made little difference when efforts to clear the land also destroyed the root structure of the vegetation that prevented erosion. In July 1872, an article in the Toronto

FIGURE 1.6 Cleared land at Buck Lake, c. 1900. *Fred Hopcraft*

Mail, entitled "Farming in Muskoka," warned that "in too many instances the settlers have made the mistake of clearing off the timber from the rocks ... The result has been that the soil being no longer held by the fibrous roots of the trees, is readily washed away by the rains, so that the rocky protuberances look and really are more marked and bare than ever."[63] Indeed, the use of fire risked destroying the soil entirely. The hilly topography of Harston's farm presented ideal conditions for erosion. As de la Fosse wrote, "on that particular part of the clearing there was no soil fit to grow anything. Whatever earth there may have been originally had been either burnt up when the fallow was set fire or washed into the lake during the heavy rains. The good old granite bobbed up serenely everywhere."[64] In showing his students how to improve the land by clearing it, Harston also inadvertently taught them a hard lesson about farming on the Shield (see Figure 1.6).

In 1880, the village of Ilfracombe where Harston and the others lived possessed a church, a sawmill, a post office, two stores, and a newly completed government bridge spanning Buck River.[65] After their first year with Harston, Baldwin and Garrett took up their own free grant lands – the former directly adjacent to Harston in Stisted Township and the latter across Buck Lake in McMurrich Township. Tothill and de la Fosse remained with Harston. After their first year, despite becoming "fairly strong and expert woodsmen," both "were as far as possible from knowing anything about farming or raising stock."[66] By the spring of 1881, they had worked together to clear fifteen acres of Harston's land, as well as five for Baldwin and ten for Garrett. After three years, Tothill and de la Fosse also took up their own land on opposite sides of Buck Lake, very close to the others.[67] De la Fosse's land featured "a generous mixture of rock and swamp," whereas Tothill "obtained his beautiful view but found he had no soil."[68] For the next year, they cooperated in clearing one another's land, "working on more or less aimlessly but with absolutely no idea of how to form a fixed plan of living." By the spring of 1882, "it began to dawn upon some of us that we were not making much progress." De la Fosse "realized the necessity of breaking away from a life where there seemed no possibility of improvement."[69] Like the Osbornes, the settlers around Ilfracombe found it difficult to extend their economy beyond the small community and earn an income. Under such circumstances, many saw little future in the backwoods. Harston joined the Canadian military and left Muskoka in 1885 to help suppress Louis Riel's Northwest Métis Resistance. Around the same time, Baldwin moved to Toronto, Garrett returned to England, and Tothill relocated to Barrie, Ontario.[70] De la Fosse left Muskoka in the spring of 1882 to survey townships in Alberta. He returned in 1884, further improved his farm at Buck Lake, married in 1886, and spent the next thirteen years moving back and forth between Toronto and Muskoka with his young family. At the age of thirty-eight, he moved to Peterborough, Ontario, where he remained until his death in 1950.[71] All five of these men obtained patents to their land, but their departure from Muskoka reflects a pattern of abandonment.

The deeper into the backwoods people settled, the more likely they were to abandon their land. During the 1870s, Watt and Monck Townships possessed the most advantageous combination of proximity to transportation networks and pockets of decent farmland. Settlers located 366 free grant lots in these townships, representing 10.6 percent of the total number of lots located in Muskoka.[72] Between 1875 and 1879, 71 settlers abandoned their land (representing just 7.1 percent of total abandonments), whereas 154 (21.3 percent of total) fulfilled the terms of the Homestead Act and obtained patents (see Figures 1.7 and 1.8). Farther inland, settlers in Stephenson and Brunel Townships enjoyed comparable, or slightly better, soil conditions on average but remained relatively isolated. During the 1870s, incoming settlers took up 682 lots in these townships (19.7 percent of total). Between 1875 and 1879, settlers in Stephenson and Brunel obtained 30 more patents than those in Watt and Monck but abandoned 114 more lots. Settlers in Stephenson and Brunel obtained patents to almost

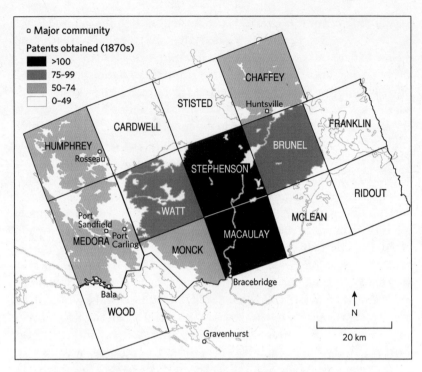

FIGURE 1.7 Patents obtained by township, 1875–79. *Annual Report of the Department of Crown Lands from 1870 to 1879*, Ontario Sessional Papers. Adapted by Eric Leinberger

exactly the same number of lots as they abandoned, whereas those closer to the lower lakes in Watt and Monck Townships obtained patents to more than twice as many lots as they abandoned.

Compared to other Muskoka townships, Stephenson and Brunel possessed good farmland. By any other objective standard, however, this conferred no meaningful advantages during the early years of resettlement. Isolation remained a problem. Homesteaders in the upper lakes townships, such as Thomas Osborne and Frederick de la Fosse, did occasionally manage to grow crops and raise livestock. But in the deep backwoods, isolation exaggerated the Shield's harsh material realties, and turned "minor evils" into "a life which seemed to be full of them."[73] In Stisted and McMurrich Townships, where Charles Harston and his pupils located, settlers took up 670 lots during the 1870s (19.4 percent of total). In the last five years of the decade, settlers in these townships obtained patents to 148 fewer lots than those in Stephenson and Brunel, and 118 fewer than those in Watt and Monck. Even more significantly, however, they abandoned 37 more

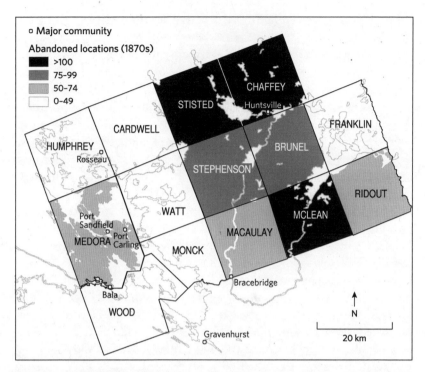

FIGURE 1.8 Abandoned locations by township, 1875–79. *Annual Report of the Department of Crown Lands from 1870 to 1879*, Ontario Sessional Papers. Adapted by Eric Leinberger

lots than settlers in Stephenson and Brunel, and an astounding 151 more than those in Watt and Monck.[74] By 1880, settlers living close to the lower lakes enjoyed greater advantages than those who took up land in the backwoods.

Over time, as they confronted the material realities of life on the Shield, settlers pursued various strategies that contributed to divergent rural identities. Most settlers took up land in Muskoka with the intention of farming. Many left when poor soils and isolation challenged their expectations. Settlers who stayed developed various strategies to cope with the material realities of life on the Shield. The strategies settlers adopted reflected the non-agricultural opportunities available to them. The identity that emerged around the upper lakes reflected backwoods subsistence and waged labour in logging camps. Around the lower lakes, settlers constructed an identity more heavily influenced by tourism.

Regardless of where one took up land, or what strategies one pursued to construct one's rural identity, settlers who had no cash or financial support from elsewhere struggled to establish themselves. Writing five decades after his first year in Muskoka, Frederick de la Fosse acknowledged that he did not quite fit the mould of the typical pioneer. He and his peers at the Harston school "felt the same cold and the same heat, and we entered fairly thoroughly into the settler's work," he recalled, "but we were always assured of three good meals a day and thus escaped the privations and anxieties that were the common lot of those around us."[75] What assured him and his mates but caused privation and anxiety for many of their neighbours was cash or a lack thereof. Captain Harston received £100 per year from each of his four students. The average pioneer household struggled to generate even a fraction of this sum, but establishing a farm in Muskoka would not succeed without cash.[76] The land was free, but nothing else was.

In the years after the government passed the 1868 Homestead Act, prospective settlers wrote to Muskoka newspaper editor Thomas McMurray to inquire about the region. A December 1870 letter asked McMurray to furnish details about "the amount of capital that would be required to work a farm." In his reply, published in a promotional booklet, McMurray estimated that a two-hundred-acre lot with forty cleared acres and a log cabin could be purchased for £400, but £148 would be required annually to operate the farm. A decade later, it was clear that settlers continued to arrive in Muskoka without sufficient funds to establish a farm and support themselves. Anxious about the rate of land abandonment, the Department of Agriculture published a pamphlet for intending settlers in 1880. In addition to providing information about climate, geography, and soil, it warned that "the question of funds is one that should be well considered by the settler." It included a list of provisions and necessities that a family of five would need "while waiting, at all events, for [their] first crop." This catalogue included eight barrels of flour, two barrels of pork, twenty bushels of potatoes, three of wheat, and ten of oats for seed, tools, housewares, blankets, and livestock, totalling $247.40, or roughly £50 sterling.[77] And, even if the family managed to clear enough land and determined how best to harness its potential, their produce was rarely sufficient to cover their cost of living. As Canadian agricultural historian Peter Russell points out: "It took a lifetime for anyone lacking either a large family, or sufficient capital to clear a farm ... and so provide a comfortable living."[78] Settlers in Muskoka faced even greater hardships. In many cases, no amount of capital investment could compensate for the poor soil, especially in places that were prone to erosion, dominated by surface granite, or inundated with poorly drained swamps. The King, Osborne, and Harston households had access to wealth outside of Muskoka. But even settlers with means were commonly forced to abandon or sell their land after only a few years.

Like other Euro-Canadians who resettled forest regions, Muskoka households relied on a number of subsistence strategies to supplement farming and make ends meet. The Department of Agriculture's pamphlet for intending homesteaders attempted to strike a delicate balance between encouraging them to focus on farming and ensuring that they exploited other opportunities afforded by nature's plenty. Of course, "the concentration of the mind on the farm exclusively will pay best in the long run," but hunting and fishing "comes in handy in a pinch." Apart from seasonal restrictions, the pamphlet assured settlers there were "no game laws to preserve [fish and game] for the exclusive use of particular persons." It listed moose, caribou, deer, bears, swans, geese, ducks, partridges, quails, woodcocks, wild turkeys, hare, foxes, otter, marten, mink, muskrat, raccoon, wolves, salmon trout, white fish, trout, herring, muskellunge, bass, pickerel, pike, and many other wildlife species to be had by hunting, trapping, and fishing.[79] Published more than a decade after the 1868 Homestead Act, the pamphlet reflects the government's efforts to claim and profit from more than a decade of knowledge accumulated by settlers about the material realities of life on the Shield.

Isolated households made the most of an overwhelmingly forested environment by exploiting its game and fish resources, but initially many seem to have perceived wild animals as sport rather than a subsistence resource. In his 1871 book addressed to incoming settlers, Thomas McMurray mentioned game and fish as objects of sport, never discussing their usefulness for subsistence.[80] Perhaps having read McMurray's book, Harriet King arrived in Muskoka with "a vague notion that passing deer might be shot from one's own door, that partridge and wild-duck were as plentiful as sparrows in England, and that hares and rabbits might also be caught with the hand." Indeed, she referred to game in terms of "a day's leisure for the gentlemanly recreation of shooting," and her sons "now and then shot a chance partridge or wild-duck, but had to look for them."[81] Once they learned the skills, however, settlers relied on hunting, trapping, and fishing to put food on the table during lean times. The Osbornes included fish as a regular and vital part of their diet, and occasionally sold a portion of their catch in Huntsville or traded it for seed, clothing, and other food.[82] At times, the family also ate muskrat, rabbit, squirrels, partridge, deer, and porcupine, which Thomas Osborne referred to as "good eating and looks nice like chicken; it is just as juicy and tender. We found it very good for a change and, lots of times, were glad to get it."[83] Hunting and fishing could potentially over-exploit wildlife, but pioneer households had few other options when farming did not provide enough.

The relationships between households represented the strongest and most sustainable feature of Muskoka's backwoods rural identity. Even at the best of times, or in the best of locations, no household could provide for all its own needs. This was especially true during the toilsome and uncertain years of the 1870s, when settlers were transforming the landscape and learning how to subsist in their new environment. Despite the pretensions of the Harston Agricultural School, Harston and his four pupils consistently depended on the help and kindness of their neighbours as they established the farm. In turn, many neighbours relied on de la Fosse and the others. Often, this meant working in cooperation. During his first year, de la Fosse and his mates spent several days underbrushing and piling logs to burn, which involved considerably more work than they could handle alone. Thus, "Captain Harston gave it up as a bad job and decided to have a 'bee.'"[84] Work bees were popular forms of collective labour in rural communities, which tied neighbours together socially and formed the basis for reciprocity within the local economy.[85] De la Fosse and his companions managed to round up about twenty men and their wives. While the men worked in the field, the women cooked. "There had not been one refusal," stated de la Fosse, "it being an unwritten law of the woods that everyone must help his fellow man."[86] He and the Harston household maintained strong relationships with other families in the Ilfracombe community. "Everywhere we were most hospitably received," he recalled, "for if there is one thing more than another that can be said for the pioneer, it is that no matter how poor his resources or how attenuated his means of subsistence, he greets you warmly and gives or lends fully and freely of anything that he possesses."[87] In some cases, such as when Mrs. Harston and a neighbour shared laundry duties, interdependencies developed between neighbours.[88] And cooperation bridged distance, as was the case when de la Fosse made long journeys through the woods to obtain butter and eggs from other settlers.[89] Homesteaders invariably found themselves short on labour, with too much of a particular crop and not enough of certain essentials, so they sought ways of sharing the burden of bush life with their neighbours.

The agroforestry economy emerged as a defining feature of identity in the backwoods. Because the 1868 Homestead Act prohibited settlers from selling their timber until after they had obtained patent, they found other ways of earning an income from the destruction of the white pine forest. On arriving in Muskoka, Harriet King was dismayed to learn about this "new law (a most unjust one)," which "at once lost me the power of selling my pine-trees."[90] Instead, the government sold the timber rights to logging interests. As H.V. Nelles shows, timber dues and ground rents from the lumber industry accounted for a large percentage of provincial government revenues during the late nineteenth century.[91] In November 1871, the Ontario government held a public auction for timber berths in several Muskoka townships.[92] And as it opened new townships to settlement, it held additional timber auctions in 1877 and 1881. As Gérard Bouchard argues, the co-integration approach of combining subsistence agriculture and waged labour in logging camps proved remarkably stable for similar rural communities, such as the Saguenay region of Quebec.[93] Indeed, throughout the Great Lakes and in many forested hinterlands across North America, settlers relied on agroforestry, which provided a market for settlers to sell some of their produce, paid them to work in logging camps, and hired their oxen and horses. Muskoka fit this pattern well. These opportunities generated vital income for struggling households, but the benefits proved ephemeral as the logging frontier pushed farther inland each year and eventually declined with the exhaustion of the pine forests.

Selling produce offered the most appealing way to earn an income from the agroforestry economy. Everywhere in Muskoka, farmers attempted to grow wheat during the 1870s and early 1880s, but by the early 1890s they had mostly concluded that it would not become an important staple. Instead, they grew foodstuffs to sell to logging camps, which were much closer to them than markets outside the region. In 1871, when lumber companies bought licences to timber in Muskoka, settlers were growing small amounts of oats and modest amounts of potatoes. Ten years later, they had dramatically increased their output. Between 1871 and 1881, the combined production of oats in Monck, Stephenson, Brunel, Stisted, and McMurrich Townships rose by more than 500 percent, and that of potatoes increased by nearly 80 percent.[94] By the 1890s, however, backwoods settlers produced a greater share of logging camp provisions than those who lived closer to the lower lakes. The logging frontier had moved farther upstream, and the tourism economy assumed a more prominent position closer to the lakes. Thus, settlers in these locales shifted from provisioning the camps, whereas their backwoods counterparts placed greater emphasis on it. Between 1881 and 1891, the production of potatoes in Monck Township declined by 32 percent, while in Stephenson and Brunel it declined by 29 percent. Over the same period, production of oats in Stisted and McMurrich Townships increased by almost 150 percent, while production of potatoes increased by 36 percent. As the logging frontier moved east, and tourism presented lucrative opportunities, settlers adjusted their land use to capitalize on these changes.

At first glance, the relationship between settlers and logging camps seems ideal.[95] The camps needed large quantities of potatoes and meat to feed the men, as well as oats and hay to feed the horses and oxen. Many of their provisions came from outside Muskoka, but homesteaders could expect camp bosses to buy most of what they offered at relatively high prices. In this way, they exchanged some of their crops, and perhaps a few of their animals, for much-needed cash to purchase supplies, clothing, furnishings, and farm equipment. For those who lacked sufficient capital to establish a farm, however, market exchange and sales to the camps were not viable options, and subsistence strategies, such as hunting and fishing, barter, and reciprocity with neighbours, simply could not support the household. In these cases, settlers worked for wages in the logging camps during the winter.

Unfortunately, the camps proved less sustainable for backwoods settlers than tourism did for people who lived closer to the lower lakes. During the winter, farm work diminished, sap ceased flowing in the white pine, and snow cover eased the movement of logs to streams where they were stacked until the spring thaw when meltwater freshets carried them downstream to mills on the lower lakes. During the 1860s and 1870s, logging took place in settled townships, and men returned home each night. But, as operations moved farther upstream during the 1880s, working in the camps took them away from their families for as much as a third of the year.[96] As Graeme Wynn shows with a similar situation in New Brunswick earlier in the century, "in some cases, home and work were separate in the extreme."[97] Thus, many backwoods farmers associated a significant part of their rural identity with their time spent in the woods with other loggers.[98] Regardless of whether the men returned home each night or stayed away for months, commercial logging relied on socioeconomic power structures that created what Wynn calls "a full-time lumbering proletariat."[99] Wages earned from work in the camps supplemented household incomes, but they would not be available unless men were willing to travel farther and farther each year.

By the turn of the century, agroforestry, which had kept many settlers from abandoning their land, declined in tandem with the stands of ancient white pine. In some cases, the opportunity to engage in logging came too late for backwoods settlers who abandoned their land before the government sold timber licences in their townships. During the summer of 1878,

Thomas Osborne took a group of timber cruisers through Franklin Township, north of Lake of Bays. Lumber companies decided not to buy a licence that year, Osborne recalled, "so we didn't have any lumber camps."[100] Most backwoods settlers, however, enjoyed short-lived benefits. The camps worked quickly because companies needed to remove the pine before settlers cleared the land or obtained patents and the rights to the timber. In almost all cases, lumber companies succeeded in removing the pine before settlers could. As a result, the logging frontier moved quickly, providing only ephemeral opportunities for sedentary households.

During the crucial period of the 1880s, backwoods homesteaders relied on agroforestry to make up for the region's poor soils. In Stisted, Franklin, and Ridout Townships, the ratio of abandoned to patented locations dropped significantly. During the 1870s, settlers in these four townships abandoned 364 lots and obtained patents to just 92. The following decade, they obtained patents to 477 lots and abandoned 407. But as lumber companies depleted the timber, employment opportunities shrank. As historical geographer Geoffrey Wall argues, the lumber "industry was essentially of a transitory nature and did not promote settlement to any great degree."[101] During the 1890s, the ratio had swung back in response to the decline of commercial logging. Settlers in the same townships abandoned 180 lots and obtained patents to 101. Once lumber companies removed the merchantable timber, and the logging camps moved on, maintaining a sustainable relationship with the agroforestry economy became difficult. When that happened, backwoods settlers tended to abandon their land and their rural identity on the Shield.

For all the many hardships that confronted them, however, isolation placed the greatest burdens on backwoods settlers in Muskoka. Throughout the 1870s and 1880s, many first-generation settlers expected the railway to deliver their salvation by connecting them to what John Stilgoe terms the "metropolitan corridor" and its opportunities for communication and trade with the city. The completion of the Northern Railway to Gravenhurst in 1875 and its extension north to Bracebridge in 1885 and Huntsville in 1886 removed the transportation bottleneck that had plagued Muskoka's economy.[102] But the railway did much more for the region's tourism industry than it did for its agricultural economy. As a result, it stifled the rural identity of many backwoods settlers even as it privileged the construction of a distinctive rural identity on the shores of the lower lakes.

By the time of Confederation, governments in Canada and the United States saw both urban and rural futures unfolding along the continent's railway networks.[103] Between 1852 and 1859, companies laid more than

1,400 miles of track in Canada West. The three largest railways in 1860 were the Grand Trunk, the Great Western, and the Buffalo and Lake Huron. Fourth largest, with 95 miles of track laid between Toronto, Barrie, and Collingwood, was the Northern Railway. Built during the early 1850s and originally conceived as the Toronto, Sarnia and Lake Huron, and later the Ontario, Simcoe and Lake Huron, the Northern Railway connected freight and passenger traffic between Lake Ontario and Georgian Bay on Lake Huron. By 1870, the Northern was generating considerable revenue, mainly through lumber and fish shipments, as well as passenger service.

Between Confederation and the First World War, another 2,783 miles of railway were built in Ontario.[104] Among the first lines built during this period was a route running north from Barrie, through Orillia and Washago, and onto the Precambrian Shield as far as Gravenhurst. By the late 1860s, politicians, lumber companies, business interests, and other area boosters sought to attract the Toronto, Simcoe and Muskoka Junction Railway Company (TSMJ). In August 1869, at a ratepayers meeting in Gravenhurst, prominent members of the Muskoka community voiced their support for the railway and its benefits for the local economy and society. A.P. Cockburn, who had recently added a second steamboat on the lower lakes, served as the district's member of Provincial Parliament. He highlighted the need for a railway, "with a view to the more rapid development of the vast tracts of agricultural, mineral and pine timbered lands contained in and to the north of The District of Muskoka." Others in attendance commented on the "inducements to an enterprising Railway Company," which Muskoka offered.[105] In December, when it became obvious that the owners of the TSMJ had no plans to build a line into Muskoka, many of the same businessmen successfully petitioned the government to construct it themselves, albeit with generous government subsidy.[106] Less than a year later, in October 1870, at the Muskoka Union of Townships Agricultural Society Show, amid congratulations to the community on its progress and success, Cockburn and his federal counterpart MP John Morrison encouraged both the government and local residents to assist the TSMJ financially. Albert Spring, who had located on several lots in Draper Township, not far from Bracebridge, claimed that "he was a poor man; but knowing the advantages of railroad communication, he would willingly subscribe $200 to assist the enterprise."[107] The TSMJ ran into financial problems during the early stages of construction and was ultimately absorbed by the Northern Railway in June 1875.[108] Once it reached Gravenhurst that November, the railway resolved the transportation bottleneck caused by the Muskoka Road.

In bypassing the road network, however, the railway benefitted some more than others and restructured features of the local economy and patterns of rural identity. In a *Northern Advocate* editorial of January 1871, Thomas McMurray wrote that "settlers here are alive to the importance of [the railway]." Once it was completed, "thousands would flock hither, and in a short time the country would be settled by a loyal flock of industrious people."[109] The promise of a railway enhanced Muskoka's appeal to land-hungry settlers. During the five years before the tracks reached Gravenhurst (1870–74), settlers in Monck and Watt Townships took up an average of thirty-four new lots each year, while settlers in Stephenson and Brunel Townships took up an average of sixty.[110] During the early 1870s, Harriet King had "seldom met with a settler [in Muskoka] ... who was not full of hope that the coveted railway would certainly pass through his lot."[111] Farther north, Frederick de la Fosse's neighbours in Stisted Township also grew hopeful when surveyors took measurements for prospective rail corridors. Had the tracks gone through its location, the "thriving little village" of Hoodstown promised to become "an important centre, transcending Huntsville in importance." According to de la Fosse, "rumours of the railway passing through brought others to the place," but the decision to run the line through Huntsville "sounded the death knell of the budding village."[112] Backwoods settlers enjoyed the benefits of the railway unevenly.

After 1875, the logic of Muskoka's economy followed the rails of the iron horse instead of the muddy, rutted road of the horse-drawn wagon. Unfortunately, as we have seen, the railway did not arrive soon enough to prevent a high rate of abandonment among backwoods settlers. In the ten years before it reached Huntsville in 1886, settlers in Stephenson and Brunel Townships abandoned an average of 14.5 lots per year, while settlers in Stisted and Chaffey abandoned an average of 23.5 lots. In the decade after the train came to Huntsville, however, the average number of lots abandoned per year dropped to 3.5 in Stephenson and Brunel and 5.9 in Stisted and Chaffey.[113] The railway helped stabilize the population turnover in the backwoods.

The introduction of steamboats to the lakes and the advent of the railway also made Muskoka accessible to residents from cities to the south, including Toronto, Hamilton, Buffalo, and Pittsburgh. The arrival of tourists at the same time as settlers took up land presented important opportunities to align the local economy with the needs of summer visitors. In July 1860, eighteen-year-old James Bain Jr. and twenty-year-old John Campbell of Toronto took the Northern Railway to the south shore of

46 Making Muskoka

Lake Simcoe, boarded a steamer that carried them to Orillia, and rented a rowboat to travel up Lake Couchiching. After spending the night near Washago, the pair walked the remaining fourteen miles north along the recently completed Muskoka Road to Gravenhurst. They stayed only a short time, commenting on the undisturbed shoreline and the presence of two "wigwams" on the beach. Bain and Campbell returned every summer, bringing friends with them. They explored the area by water and camped on islands. In 1864, they named their group the Muskoka Club, and the following year they hauled enough lumber across Lake Joseph to erect a cooking shelter on an island. Before the end of the 1860s, a few women, including Campbell's three sisters, had joined the hitherto all-male group. In 1872, the three lower lakes became internavigable for steamers, and the Muskoka Club established a permanent base of operations on Yoho Island, Lake Joseph, where members and their guests came and went each summer. After the railway reached Gravenhurst in 1875, a few members and their acquaintances purchased islands nearby and inaugurated a summer cottage community at the north end of Lake Joseph. Other like-minded urbanites had the same idea. By the 1880s, tourists and cottagers purchased accommodations, food, goods, and services during the summer. They typically stayed next to the water, and most never ventured beyond a thin strip of land surrounding the lower lakes. The money they spent also tended to stay close to the shore. As a result, the rural identity of settlers living close to the lower lakes diverged from that of their backwoods neighbours around the upper lakes.

John Oldham, Harriet King, Thomas Osborne, and Frederick de la Fosse all arrived in Muskoka after James Bain and John Campbell. In fact, members of the Muskoka Club squatted on islands more than a decade before Osborne's father purchased squatter's rights to land in Franklin Township. And Campbell built a cottage on Yoho Island at the same time as King's family built its cabins in the woods. The tourism industry co-evolved with farming and logging as the defining features of rural identity in Muskoka. Settlers near the lower lakes had not expected this, as their intent was to help found an agrarian society. But the material realities of the Shield environment, and Muskoka's particularly poor soils, precluded a rural identity based exclusively, or even primarily, on farming.

In the late 1920s, nearly twenty years after he last set foot in Muskoka, Frederick de la Fosse returned to his old community of Ilfracombe. "It was a depressing pilgrimage," he wrote. The village had all but disappeared. The railway had bypassed it, and a once-hopeful community had gradually given up. De la Fosse discovered that "clearings which had once borne more or less of a crop were grown up again, and their wildness was the wildness of the forest primeval." Even the village cemetery was overgrown and "presented so clear an illustration of the state of abandonment into which the settlement had fallen." In the 1870s, settlers attempted to construct an agrarian society next to the shores of Buck Lake, but by the late 1920s, "it was essentially a byway of civilization."[114] To de la Fosse, the "desolation" of the backwoods stood in stark contrast to the "hundreds of palatial summer homes, catered to by supply boats and commodious steamers." The "older generation of Muskoka settlers," he thought, "might well imagine themselves on some other planet."[115] Indeed, a very different kind of life unfolded next to the lower lakes, one that allowed settlers to construct a more sustainable rural identity.

2

Indigenous Identity, Settler Colonialism, and Tourism, 1850–1920

In 1911, several members of Chippewa (Anishinaabe) First Nations at Rama, Georgina Island, and Christian Island testified to their ancestral rights to hunt, trap, and raise gardens in a large territory that included the Muskoka River watershed. Fifty-six-year-old Henry Simon of Christian Island stated that around 1867 "I made my first hunting trip in the territory referred to accompanied by my father the late Mr. Andrew Simon who had a limit of his own ... located at the Township of Proudfoot where a number of lakes are lying together called Ma-Mah-gah-be-shaong an Indian name."[1] Similarly, Joseph Yellowhead of Rama said that "when I was at the age of fifteen [1848] I made my first hunting trip in the territory referred to Accompanied by my father the late Chief Yellowhead who had a hunting limit of his own ... between the following Lakes, Ox-tongue Lake and Canoe Lake." Several other men from these reserve communities provided formulaic testimony that described the location of their hunting limits, the routes they took to access them, what they did there, and the number of years they and their fathers and uncles exercised their rights to them. A.K. Goodman, a lawyer hired by seven Chippewa and Mississauga First Nations, recorded the testimony to press their claims for compensation for the loss of access to their hunting territory.[2] The testimony formed the central evidence of a 1923 federal-provincial joint inquiry known as the Williams Treaties Commission, which established Crown recognition of, and compensation for, the Chippewa and Mississauga rights to hunting grounds at the southern edge of the Canadian Shield. The testimony demonstrates that throughout the second half of the nineteenth century, members of several First Nations spent part of every year in the Muskoka River watershed. It also helps explain how, for the Anishinaabeg, the maintenance and reproduction of their Indigenous identity partially relied on their continued temporary occupation of and relationship with the Shield environment.

Tourism enabled the Anishinaabeg to translate their knowledge of the Shield environment into valuable opportunities, including selling crafts and guiding hunting and fishing parties. Indigenous and non-Indigenous adjustments to life on the Shield during settler colonialism happened simultaneously. Remarkably, both settlers and First Nations capitalized on tourism as a viable alternative to less sustainable social and economic arrangements. Whereas settlers employed their *acquired* knowledge of the Shield to align their rural identity with the seasonal cycle of tourism, the Anishinaabeg *repurposed* their knowledge in the context of tourism. In the late nineteenth century, settlers came to understand what the Anishinaabeg had long known. The environmental limitations of the Shield made sedentary life there complicated, and necessitated a temporary occupation, including the seasonal movement of people and resources between the Shield and regions to the south.

Indigenous people negotiated and resisted colonization by finding means of continuing traditional ways of life, and by maintaining or reproducing their identity during periods of significant change. As American Indian studies scholar Jill Doerfler argues, adjustments made in response to settler colonialism do not "equate with loss" and are not a negation of Indigenous identity. Rather, families and communities make "changes in order to continue being Anishinaabe." For the Anishinaabeg, "identity is based on actions and loyalties, rather than [colonial concepts of] race or pseudoscientific measure of blood," and is created, maintained, and reproduced "through respectful and reciprocal behavior and relationships."[3] Settler colonialism, government restrictions on fishing, and paternalism on reserves forced the Anishinaabeg to adjust their way of life without necessarily losing their key values. Racial discrimination in Euro-Canadian society and restrictions on their mobility and access to traditional hunting grounds obliged the Anishinaabeg to pursue what historian John Lutz refers to as a "moditional economy," which combined a "traditional mode of reproduction and production" with "new modes of production for exchange in a capitalist market."[4] For example, game laws made it illegal to hunt without a licence, but working as a guide for white hunters allowed Indigenous men to use traditional knowledge and skills to acquire resources and income in a new way. The result is a history that accounts for evidence of what archaeologist

Neal Ferris calls "the nonlinear nature of changed continuities."[5] Understanding the nature of change and continuity experienced by the Anishinaabeg attends to Indigenous survivance. Accounting for the tensions between change and continuity also provides insight into how the effects of colonization and state control were somewhat mitigated by the particular environmental realities of the Precambrian Shield.

With each new wave of colonization during the nineteenth century, the context within which the Anishinaabeg reproduced their identity became increasingly less sustainable. The Williams Treaties negotiations took place approximately fifty years after settlers and tourists began showing up in Muskoka and roughly a century after the British Crown began imposing a settler colonial framework on the lives of Indigenous peoples. Prior to the War of 1812, the British Crown demonstrated far more respect for Indigenous rights than it and its Canadian successors did during the remainder of the nineteenth century and after. During the eighteenth century, the British established "treaties of peace, friendship, and alliance" with several Indigenous nations, which informed what Rani Alexander calls networks of "symmetrical exchange" and "cultural entanglement."[6] During the first half of the nineteenth century, the importance of military alliances and the fur trade waned, and the willingness to reconcile Indigenous lifeways with imperial interests dissolved under the demands of colonists who wished to extend resettlement into new lands. The Crown increasingly pressured its former allies to sign "territorial treaties," which granted British subjects the right to establish transportation corridors, extract valuable natural resources, and resettle Indigenous lands.[7] With each new cohort of government officials responsible for managing relations with Indigenous peoples, and each generation of land-hungry Euro-Canadians, the original intent of the early treaties (to share the land) fell victim to the colonizing prerogatives of alienation and dispossession. As the century unfolded, settler colonial interests came up against Indigenous ways of living, and bureaucrats manipulated, interpreted, and legitimated the treaties as "technologies of occupation."[8] Colonization brought repeated waves of disruptive change, which fractured and redefined Anishinaabe social organization, restricted and denied their rights and access to resources, and dispossessed them of their land.

First Nations came under successive and cumulative pressures to surrender their land and adopt a sedentary, Christian, and "civilized" way of life. An early, failed attempt of the 1830s led to the self-imposed dispersal of four closely related Anishinaabe bands into separate communities, forming the basis for later reserves at Rama, Christian Island (Beausoleil),

Georgina Island (Snake), and Parry Island. Government officials assumed that all Indigenous rights to the region had been extinguished when seventeen Ojibwe First Nations signed the 1850 Robinson-Huron Treaty, covering a huge portion of south central Ontario, including Muskoka. This assumption was grounded in a purposeful project to dispossess Indigenous peoples of their land and rights, and a fundamental misunderstanding, over multiple generations, of Chippewa-Mississauga-Ojibwe kinship, historic Indigenous relationships with the Shield environment, and Anishinaabe identity. Indeed, the categories "Chippewa," "Mississauga," and "Ojibwe/Ojibwa" – derivations of the same word, meaning "people of the puckered seam," referring to the seam sewn into deer skin footwear and clothing – reflect useful Euro-Canadian distinctions more accurately than they do Anishinaabe self-identification.[9] Since the documentary record often applies these names to Anishinaabe communities, I follow suit when discussing individual reserves but use "Anishinaabe" when referring to events that included people from more than one of them.

The 1857 Fisheries Act restricted access to the most critical Anishinaabeg resource, and after Confederation and the British North America Act (1867) it became nearly impossible for the federal and provincial governments to reconcile settler interests with Indigenous ways of living. Ottawa maintained paternalistic responsibility for Indigenous peoples through its Department of Indian Affairs (DIA), and the provinces assumed control over Crown lands and resources. As a result, Ottawa effectively lost the authority to defend Indigenous treaty rights, and provincial governments were not obligated to recognize them. The 1876 Act to Amend and Consolidate the Laws Respecting Indians (commonly known as the Indian Act) replaced self-governance on reserves with the paternalistic authority of the DIA. After 1876, the DIA tightened its control via the reserve system, which persecuted Indigenous people who used traditional knowledge or ventured outside the borders of their reserve.

In 1881, thirty-two Mohawk (Haudenosaunee) families left Quebec and moved to a reserve in Gibson Township, Muskoka. They do not enter the story until near the end of this chapter, but they were also subject to restrictions, paternalistic policies, and discrimination. As a result of social and political disputes between the Mohawk of Kanesatake and the Sulpician Church at Oka, Quebec, the federal government granted permission for the families to move to Gibson. For more than two hundred years before this event, the Mohawk had lived in close proximity to Euro-Canadians in New France and Quebec. Their long experience with Euro-Canadians and a market economy prepared them for life in Muskoka.

During the late nineteenth and early twentieth centuries, none of the Anishinaabe communities at Rama, Christian Island (Beausoleil), Georgina Island (Snake), and Parry Island or the Haudenosaunee one at Gibson had a population of more than a few hundred people (see Figure 2.2). The home territory of the Anishinaabeg of south-central Ontario included the land north and south of the Shield's edge, which somewhat constrained its carrying capacity compared to places farther south and supported a higher population density than places farther north. In the 1871 Canadian census, three communities (Beausoleil Island, Snake Island, and Rama) were enumerated together as "Rama," with a population of 904. In September 1884, a memorandum sent to the DIA deputy minister listed 703 people who were eligible for annuities at Beausoleil Island (318), Snake Island (137), and Rama (248). By the turn of the century, the census listed the population of Rama, which still encompassed all three communities, at 1,618. The population of Parry Island is more difficult to determine, since the census always combined it with that of the town of Parry Sound, which included both Indigenous and non-Indigenous people. Nevertheless, the Parry Island community was probably never larger than a few hundred individuals during this period. In 1891, the census lists the combined population for Baxter, Gibson, and Freeman Townships as 700 people made up of 143 families, which suggests that the Mohawk living on the Gibson reserve (later renamed Wahta) also never numbered more than a few hundred. Altogether, the Indigenous population that relied on Muskoka consisted of slightly fewer than 1,000 people in 1850 and not more than 3,000 by 1920.[10]

For many hundreds of years, the Algonquian-speaking peoples from whom the Anishinaabeg of south central Ontario descend relied on more fertile regions to the south for access to trade goods and Indigenous crops. The coasts of Lake Simcoe and Georgian Bay featured abundant fisheries. Upstream territories on the Shield provided many important resources, most of which were obtained through hunting and trapping. Archaeological and historical records reveal that Indigenous people tended to focus their seasonal occupation of Muskoka around a handful of major catchment areas along the Muskoka River watershed.[11] This type of seasonal mobility and presence in the landscape should not be confused with nomadism. Instead, as Neal Ferris argues, it exhibits "intimate personal and community knowledge of the resources and landscape within a home territory."[12] Despite the environmental limitations of the Shield, places such as Muskoka were crucial components in the economic and cultural lives of the Algonquian-speaking peoples.

By the early seventeenth century, Algonquian-speaking peoples occupied an enormous swath of territory in what later became Canada and the northern United States, from the Rocky Mountains to the Atlantic Ocean. The southeastern extent of this area shifted according to the hegemony of the Iroquoian-speaking Wendat, Petun, and Neutral, who controlled what is now southwestern Ontario.[13] French records from the seventeenth century contain far more references to the Wendat, Nipissing, and Odawa than to the Anishinaabeg living on the east shores of Georgian Bay. These nations enjoyed relatively peaceable relations and trade with one another. Coastal fisheries and inland hunting grounds could not provide for all their needs, so the Anishinaabeg relied heavily on their relationship with the Wendat.[14] In the mid-seventeenth century, the Five Nations Haudenosaunee invaded this territory and dispersed the Wendat and their Algonquian-speaking allies. By the end of the century, the Anishinaabeg from regions north of Lake Superior had invaded the region and pushed the Haudenosaunee south of Lake Ontario. By the start of the eighteenth century, the Anishinaabeg occupied most of southern Ontario. The Great Peace of 1701 between the French and several First Nations, including Algonquian- and Iroquoian-speaking peoples, provided enough stability for the Anishinaabeg to establish seasonal patterns of subsistence and band structure that persisted into the nineteenth century.[15]

Historian J. Michael Thoms refers to the pattern of moving between defined resource sites as "multi-modal."[16] During the eighteenth century, the Anishinaabeg of south-central Ontario followed a seasonal "river mouth/inland pattern" of subsistence, in which the spring and summer were spent trading and fishing at coastal lake sites, whereas the fall and winter were characterized by trips inland to hunt and trap.[17] In the late 1920s, anthropologist Diamond Jenness provided a rough overview of this cycle. The "variety and seasonal nature of their foods" Jenness wrote, "kept the Indians in constant motion." During certain times of the year, "a whole band might camp together for a few days or weeks" before dispersing "into small groups of perhaps four or five families each." This pattern matched the rhythms of "the hunting and the fishing grounds, the maple groves, the patches of wild berries, and of wild rice, [which] lay scattered in different places often many miles apart."[18] Mid-winter was spent in medium-sized camps comprised of several families located along the shores of inland waterways, where conditions were somewhat milder than on Georgian Bay and Lake Simcoe. Occasionally, they moved the winter camps and men fished through the ice, but they embarked on hunting only in rare years when fish or corn reserves did not last until spring.

In late winter and early spring, families collected maple sap for syrup and sugar. Depending on how long and how much sap flowed, they either remained in larger camps or dispersed into family-specific sugar bush territories, which elders occasionally reorganized to reflect demographic realities in the band.[19] Signs of fish spawning runs in spring instigated a move by nearly all the families in the band to fishing camps on Georgian Bay, Lake Simcoe, and Lake Couchiching.[20] According to Thoms, these communal camps were the hubs of the seasonal cycle.

The logic of the cycle stemmed from the centrality of the fishing grounds. At these sites, families caught abundant fish beyond their immediate needs to preserve for the leaner months. The cycle also served important social and political functions. Seasonal mobility and resource availability restricted large gatherings only to certain times of the year. Periods of abundance, particularly during the spring and fall fish runs, marked an important point when many families came together in large camps. In addition to eating well and preparing stockpiles for winter, people socialized, traded, told stories, arranged marriages, and solidified bonds between groups. South of the Shield, next to the Narrows between Lake Simcoe and Lake Couchiching, where the soil was much better for agriculture, the Anishinaabeg cleared large fields. In late spring, families planted corn, squash, and potatoes in close proximity to spring fishing grounds, where soil conditions, frost-free days, and fire prevention were optimal. Present-day Parry Sound was traditionally a preferred planting site. In hunting grounds on the Shield, planted areas were much smaller and were intended only to supplement small family groups between the late summer and early winter. Midsummer was a popular deer-hunting season. Fall fish runs coincided with the harvest of field crops, and men hunted and trapped for meat, skins, and furs before the rivers and lakes began to freeze up, at which point families moved to their winter camps, and the cycle started all over again.[21]

The seasonal movement between sites was neither haphazard nor entirely controlled. Instead, the Anishinaabeg derived their system from long-standing, consensus-style customs made credible by *doodem*/clan-based band organization. Doodems are patrilineal identities associated with animal spirit guardians that determined patterns of reproduction and hunting territories within and between bands. They lay at the heart of Anishinaabeg culture and informed the most sustainable approaches to the variable circumstances of life on the Shield. Unlike the Haudenosaunee farther south, the Anishinaabe formed bands whose members were related to other bands through marriage and doodem affiliation.[22] As

Indigenous Identity, Settler Colonialism, and Tourism 55

Thoms states, through the doodemic system, the Anishinaabeg "developed a sense of a 'chain' between themselves, their environment, their past, their ancestors, and their creator."[23] According to Darlene Johnston, doodems were "the glue that held the Anishnaabeg Great Lakes world together."[24] Members of these First Nations "believed that if they faithfully followed their ancestor's traditional resource use customs, which had proven successful through long practice, that the lakes would continue to abound in fish, and the forests retain plenty of game."[25] Each band included members who were affiliated with a variety of doodems. Leadership fluctuated between doodems depending on the demographic composition of the band and the quality of leadership.[26] Chiefs earned their authority by demonstrating suitable leadership abilities through "hunting and sharing, handling crises, making decisions, orating and shamanistic ability."[27] Legitimized through consensus, their authority depended on the large annual springtime gatherings where abundant food resources provided a critical opportunity to reproduce the individual, the family, the community, and the nation. To allocate limited inland resources fairly among all band members, hereditary chiefs divided up family hunting grounds in Muskoka according to doodem. Defined by geographic boundaries and landscape features, such as heights of land or blazed trees, doodem territories centred on a lake or river in the Muskoka River watershed.[28] As with most elements of the seasonal cycle, it is likely that despite the preference for, and claims of, continuity related to hunting grounds among the Anishinaabeg, changes over time would have forced realignments as certain doodems became too large or small for their particular grounds.[29] Doodemic affiliations with specific hunting territories were a purposeful strategy to avoid competition between band members and to structure a more sustainable access to scarce resources. They created the basis for extensive trade and political arrangements between communities that did not spend all year, or even much of their lives, in close contact. Despite their stability or variability over time, in any given year, members respected the boundaries between doodem hunting grounds.[30]

Over the course of the nineteenth century, the British colonial government, and later the Canadian Dominion government, sought to simultaneously "civilize" the Anishinaabeg, resettle their territory, and restrict access to their traditional resources. British and Canadian authorities justified these goals by insisting that Indigenous people put the land to only limited use and by criticizing their refusal to adopt a sedentary life. The pressure to assume a more civilized lifestyle did not come all at once. Instead, First Nations experienced the settler colonial project in successive waves. From the start, Crown representatives knew little about Anishinaabe kinship affiliations or the seasonal cycle. With each wave of colonization, and each new generation of colonial bureaucrats, these misunderstandings compounded, became institutionalized, and sometimes involved outright hostility. The Anishinaabeg responded by employing a variety of strategies for not being governed that repurposed long-standing patterns of seasonal mobility of which colonial administrators seemed virtually unaware.[31]

Under the leadership of Chief Misko-Aki (known to the British as William Yellowhead), members of Anishinaabe First Nations living between Georgian Bay and the Kawartha Lakes helped defend York in 1813 and signed treaties with the Crown in 1795, 1815, and 1818.[32] The intent of the treaties was to allow the Crown to maintain communication routes and settle British subjects in the region, but the Anishinaabeg saw them as ensuring their rights to hunt, trap, and fish for resources according to their own patterns of subsistence. As Robin Brownlie writes: "First Nations people had never intended to surrender control of their lives to the government or any other outsiders – on the contrary, by signing the treaties they had sought to retain a measure of self-determination."[33] The Anishinaabeg understood the treaties as ceding only upland areas that were suitable for farming, not the low-elevation areas where they themselves relied on sugar bushes, berries, and fisheries.[34] And nothing in the treaties ever mentioned their hunting territories in Muskoka. Changing public sentiment and demands from colonists for land, however, caused successive Crown administrations to lose sight of the original meaning and spirit of the treaties. As the nineteenth century progressed, colonial and dominion authorities interpreted them as an effective extinguishment of Indigenous title.[35]

The colonial government pressed the Anishinaabeg to abandon seasonal migrations in exchange for sedentary lives as farmers. In 1826, as part of the earliest British attempts to "civilize" Indigenous peoples in Upper Canada, Lieutenant Governor John Colborne established model villages for the Anishinaabeg at Sarnia, Credit River, and Coldwater. In 1830, after control over Indian Affairs passed from military to civil administration, three Anishinaabe bands, headed by Chief William Yellowhead Jr. (Misko-Aki's son), Joseph Snake, and John Aisance, agreed to participate in the Coldwater experiment.[36] The model community extended from the Narrows at Lake Couchiching (the site of present-day Orillia), where Yellowhead and Snake settled their bands, to Coldwater approximately twenty kilometres northwest, where Aisance settled his band (see Figure 2.1).

Indigenous Identity, Settler Colonialism, and Tourism

FIGURE 2.1 Two First Nations men at Coldwater River, September 1844. T. Hibbert Ware. Baldwin Collection of Canadiana, Pictures-R-208. Courtesy of the Toronto Public Library

These bands had no intention of remaining permanently in their villages, and they consistently left for long periods to exploit fisheries on Lake Simcoe and Georgian Bay, and hunting grounds in the southern Shield, including Muskoka. In September 1830, five chiefs, including Yellowhead, agreed "that our children will be kept at school" but made it clear that "we wish to hunt this fall, & get some meet [sic] & deerskins against the cold winter." They were "glad of the money [the government] sent us for our work this season," but they wanted to know when they would receive the balance of their pay because they intended to leave for their "huntings in about two weeks, & should be glad of the money before we go."[37] Five years later, the superintendent of the villages at Coldwater and the Narrows, Thomas G. Anderson, reported that "each Indian with a Family has now a little Farm" and that "hunting has in many Cases been altogether abandoned, and in none appears, as formerly, to be resorted to as the only Means of Subsistence." At the end of his report, Anderson admitted that "a few Individuals still pursue their Winter's Hunt."[38] Indeed, most reports on Coldwater acknowledged that its members continued to spend part of the year hunting. The government paid the Anishinaabeg annuities and in return expected them to settle down, raise crops, and pursue a Christian way of life.[39] From the Anishinaabeg's perspective, however, their agreement to reside between the Narrows and Coldwater represented a compromise with Euro-Canadian resettlement that aligned with their seasonal cycle. They happily planted crops at the Narrows and at Coldwater but refused to discontinue their migrations to fishing sites and hunting grounds.

By the end of the 1830s, it had become apparent to both sides that the Coldwater experiment was not working. In 1836, the Crown purchased the settlement to make the land available to colonists, and the Anishinaabeg under Yellowhead split into four bands. Before the War of 1812, the Anishinaabeg did not distinguish between the subgroups that the British later identified as Mississauga, Chippewa, and Ojibwe. After the war, the significance of military alliances in Upper Canada declined and pressure to surrender land for Euro-Canadian resettlement intensified. In an effort to determine which groups held rights to which lands, the Crown began using bureaucratic distinctions between the Mississauga, who were centred on the Kawartha Lakes and the north shore of Lake Ontario, the Chippewa west of Lake Simcoe and south of Georgian Bay, and the Ojibwe east and north of Georgian Bay on the Shield. The added pressures arising from the Coldwater experiment prompted a further dissolution of the Chippewa into four distinct bands during the 1830s and 1840s: Rama, Snake Island (later renamed Georgina Island), Beausoleil Island (who later moved to Christian Island), and Sandy Island (later renamed Parry Island) (see Figure 2.2).[40]

Despite their treatment by colonial administrators, the Anishinaabeg appear to have navigated early pressures to conform on their own terms. In 1836, with money from the sale of the Coldwater reserve, Yellowhead's band purchased 1,600 acres at Rama on the northeast shore of Lake Couchiching (see Figure 2.3).[41] It moved to the site in 1839, and by 1845 had built twenty homes and four barns, and had cleared approximately 300 acres for farming. A little more than a decade later, 201 people were growing mainly corn and potatoes but also kept a handful of horses, cows, and pigs. In 1858, Superintendent General of Indian Affairs R.T. Pennefather recorded contradictorily that members of the Rama band "were given to hunting and basket making, consequently avoiding tilling the soil, and are dragging through a life disgraceful to humanity," yet were still "able to dispose of their surplus agricultural produce to the surrounding settlers."[42] As Sarah Carter argues for the case of prairie reserve farmers, these kinds of reports reveal Euro-Canadian assumptions that "Indians and agriculture are incompatible."[43] The Anishinaabeg had a great deal of experience with cultivating domesticated plants, and they

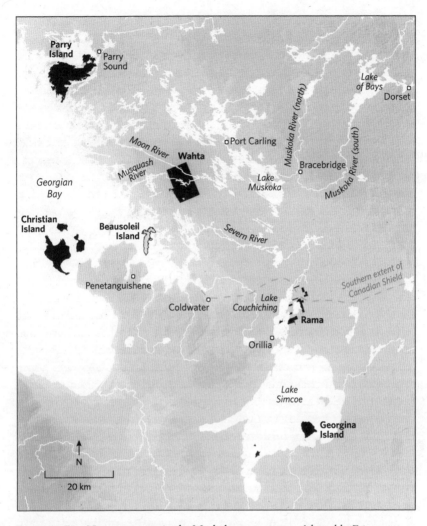

Figure 2.2 First Nations reserves in the Muskoka area, c. 1900. *Adapted by Eric Leinberger*

grew food for their own needs, rather than to meet the expectations of government bureaucrats.

Joseph Snake's band established itself on Snake Island at the south end of Lake Simcoe and had cleared thirty-nine acres for planting by 1858. It raised a comparable number of livestock and harvested almost exactly the same amount of corn, potatoes, wheat, and oats as the Rama band.

FIGURE 2.3 The village at Rama, Lake Couchiching, September 1844. *T. Hibbert Ware. Baldwin Collection of Canadiana, Pictures-R-211. Courtesy of the Toronto Public Library*

By 1842, John Aisance's band had established itself on Beausoleil Island on Georgian Bay. Unlike the Methodist bands under Yellowhead and Snake, Aisance and his followers practised Catholicism. An 1857 census reported that they were clearly putting the most effort into agriculture, with approximately three hundred acres cleared, yielding more than ten times the output of corn grown at Rama or Snake Island and a comparable quantity of potatoes. By this date, the Beausoleil band had also begun to engage in commercial fishing, producing 150 barrels of dried fish from Georgian Bay. A year later, Pennefather recorded that the band had begun to move to Christian Island. It likely decided to move because Christian Island was better suited to farming but also because of its proximity to more plentiful fisheries.[44]

The Sandy Island band is hardest to summarize, mainly because its leadership was more fluid and its social structure more fractious than that of the other bands, but also because it engaged the least with agriculture and spent the most time on the Shield beyond the purview of the state. At the time of the Coldwater experiment, Yellowhead nominally spoke for the Sandy Island band, but it did not participate in the settlement. Instead, some of its members chose to avoid the colonial government and appear to have moved onto the Shield, occupying an area between Georgian Bay and the Muskoka lakes.[45] Fleeting references to the Sandy Island band between the 1830s and 1860s suggest that it lived most of the year, if not all of it, on the Shield.[46] In 1835, while mapping the Muskoka lakes for the

Royal Navy, John Carthew encountered six families that were led by Chief Pamosagay. They took him to their village "on an island in the Lake [Rosseau]," where he "was surprised to find about 40 acres of good clearing, planted with corn and potatoes." According to his report: "They appear to reside here all year round, taking plenty of white fish and trout."[47] More than thirty years later, in 1868, Provincial Lands Surveyor Albert Fowlie visited the same island and described its new growth and young shoots, which suggests that the families Carthew met had not occupied the camp or maintained the gardens for a few years.[48] In the intervening years, the Sandy Island band leadership had split between a branch under Chief Muckata Mishoquet at Shawanaga and a branch under Chief Muskato (Peter Megis) at Parry Island. Both signed the 1850 Robinson-Huron Treaty, along with sixteen other bands farther north along the shore of Lake Huron. The treaty formalized a reserve for each branch at Shawanaga and Parry Island, and the British Crown reclassified them as Ojibwe.

After they signed the Robinson-Huron Treaty, members of the Parry Island branch continued to occupy sites in Muskoka during much of the year. In 1858, Pennefather reported that "the Sandy Island Indians are Heathens, and live alternatively on the borders of Lake Huron, about 50 miles north-west of Penetanguishene, and in the interior north of that place [where] they cultivate very small patches of Corn and Potatoes."[49] By this time, members of the Parry Island branch had established Obajawanung, a small village next to the Baisong Rapids, which empty Lake Rosseau into Lake Muskoka.[50] In 1860, another lands surveyor, Vernon Wadsworth, described Obajawanung as "beautifully situated," with twenty log homes and "a good deal of cleared land about it used as garden plots."[51] Members of the Parry Island branch felt conflicted. On the one hand, they had negotiated with the Crown to have their island reserved because of its proximity to critical fisheries.[52] On the other hand, the land at Obajawanung was better suited to growing crops, more hospitable during the winter months, and closer to their hunting grounds. In 1862, four years after becoming chief of the Parry Island branch, Pegahmegahbow asked the government to have the reserve moved from Parry Island to Obajawanung. With the aid of Lands Surveyor John S. Dennis, he sent a petition to the Department of Indian Affairs:

Father
Our feelings have changed.
This place [Obajawanung] is beautiful in our eyes, and we found we could
    not leave it.

62   Making Muskoka

> Many winters have passed since we settled here and began to cultivate our gardens.
>
> We have good houses and large gardens where we raise much corn and potatoes.
>
> Our children have grown up here and cannot make up their minds to go to a new place. We are not so fortunate as some of your Red Children who have large farms cleared and plenty of cattle.
>
> We live by hunting and taking furs – and our hunting grounds are all near here. Were we to go to Parry Island we should have to clear new Gardens and our hunting grounds would be far off.
>
> *Father*
>
> We wish that you would take back Parry Island, our Reserve on Lake Huron, and instead of it give us our Reserve of three miles by six miles at this place ...
>
> We hope you will grant the wish of your Red Children, and do it soon, because the whites are coming in close to us and we are afraid that your Surveyors will soon lay our lands here into lots.[53]

The DIA never responded to this petition.

For their part, settlers seemed blissfully unaware of the impact of their presence on the Sandy Island band. Many spoke in terms of co-existence, mutual respect, and exchange.[54] Thomas M. Robinson, a settler near Gravenhurst during the early 1860s, recalled rowing twenty kilometres in the spring to Obajawanung to buy corn seed.[55] Elizabeth Penson, granddaughter of settlers living not far from Obajawanung (which settlers called "Indian Gardens") remembered that "local Indians brought [her grandparents] food in exchange for flannel. They were good kind neighbours."[56] At the north end of Lake Joseph, members of the Muskoka Club, the area's first tourists, remembered Pegahmegahbow as "our old friend Peg."[57] Elders at Wasauksing First Nation (formerly Parry Island First Nation) remember this period somewhat differently. According to Carleen Partridge, "the Indians didn't like living with white people."[58] Band members relocated to new spots whenever settlers encroached too closely. Obajawanung quickly became a hub of settler activity. With the introduction of Muskoka's first steamboat in 1866, outsiders easily reached Indian Gardens. The commencement of a government project to build a set of locks to bypass the rapids at Obajawanung in 1870 appears to have been the final straw for Pegahmegahbow and the Parry Island branch. They moved away from what Euro-Canadian settlers had renamed Port Carling.[59]

Indigenous Identity, Settler Colonialism, and Tourism 63

During the first half of the nineteenth century, the government imposed distinct political identities on the Chippewa of Rama, Christian Island, and Snake Island, as well as the Ojibwe at Parry Island. These bands were subject to differing pressures from Euro-Canadian society, but they continued to use Muskoka as a strategy for adjusting to hardships. The formation of reserve communities did not result in the complete isolation of bands from one another. Chief Muckata Mishoquet and Chief Megis of the Sandy Island band signed the 1850 Robinson-Huron Treaty, whereas Yellowhead, Snake, and Aisance did not. As the Crown understood the treaty, the Sandy Island band had surrendered its rights to the Shield. But it was unaware that the same rights of the Chippewa at Rama, Snake Island, and Christian Island were never subject to the treaty. Members from all four bands continued to interact through trade, social gatherings, and intermarriage throughout the nineteenth century. As the colonial government, and subsequently the Dominion government, restricted their mobility, denied them access to critical resources, and discriminated against communities on reserves, they continued to pursue their traditional seasonal cycle as a means of reproducing their Indigenous identity and adjusting to colonization.[60]

After 1850, the Anishinaabeg in south-central Ontario occupied formal reserve locations. Because fish were the most critical component of their yearly cycle, they selected significant fishing grounds, particularly islands, when they were forced to choose their reserves. Each year, they spent the most time at these sites.[61] The Rama band located next to an ancient fishing weir at the Narrows, where Lake Simcoe empties into Lake Couchiching. The Snake Island band took up an island at the south end of Lake Simcoe, which was surrounded by a large fishery. The Christian Island band initially chose Beausoleil Island but moved to Christian Island just north of Penetanguishene on Georgian Bay, perhaps the most advantageous location of the four in terms of access to fisheries. The Sandy Island band's location farther north on Parry Island provided similar advantages.

At precisely the same time as the Anishinaabeg established reserves at important fisheries, the Government of Canada West came under increasing pressure from Euro-Canadian fishing interests to introduce a formal licensing system for commercial operations. Along with later federal-provincial jurisdictional disputes, the Fisheries Act denied Indigenous rights, imposed legal restrictions on access to fisheries resources, and facilitated an expansion of Euro-Canadian commercial fishing. Replicating earlier attempts by the colonial government to cajole the Anishinaabeg into a sedentary life, commercial fishermen and the government justified usurping Indigenous fishing rights in terms of a civilizing mission. Euro-Canadian fishermen accused Indigenous fishermen of hiding behind treaty rights to employ "lazy" or "unsportsmanlike" methods of overfishing.[62] The perception that Indigenous fishing methods were both unfair and more efficient than non-Indigenous ones led to new laws, which required band members to obtain leases and licences from the Crown to use fisheries that had never been included in any of the treaties signed during the first half of the nineteenth century.[63] In effect, the Fisheries Act introduced a bureaucracy that transferred fisheries rights from Indigenous to non-Indigenous people.

This development made life much less sustainable for the Anishinaabeg. After 1867, the bands pressed the federal and provincial governments to have their fishing rights recognized. Even their Indian agents, William Plummer (Rama, Christian Island, and Georgina Island) and Charles Skene (Parry Island), argued vehemently that the Chippewa bands had never discontinued their fishing activities in these locations and "when making the Surrenders of their territories retained the Islands [as reserves] especially for privileges of fishing, on what they have always regarded as their own property."[64] In a March 1876 letter to the DIA office in Ottawa, Plummer explained that "the aged and very young cannot resort to [hunting] as a means of livelihood and during the Winter and Spring they suffer much destitution" without secure access to their fisheries at the Narrows. Similarly, on Christian Island, "old men and women and children fish [the channel facing the village] when the able bodied men are absent."[65] In 1882, Plummer insisted that Anishinaabeg fishermen "have been greatly interfered with by white fishermen" and reminded his superiors that "their rights and privileges in this respect should be strictly guarded."[66] The Anishinaabeg never agreed to relinquish their rights to waterways or fish. British law provided the justification, however, because treaties did not make such rights explicit.[67]

The opinions of Indian agents did not influence government officials in Ottawa, who asserted that restrictive policies were in the interests of Indigenous and non-Indigenous people alike. In 1876, the deputy commissioner of Marine and Fisheries articulated this perspective clearly, writing "these restrictions really involve nothing inconsistent with the spirit of any treaties entered into with the Government." He added, "in fact, they are designed to render more valuable the privileges which Indians are entitled to enjoy in common with their fellow subjects by virtue of the reservations contained in such treaties."[68] Echoing the views of white commercial fishermen, sportsmen and anglers characterized Indigenous fishing as unsportsmanlike and pushed for stringent conservation laws at the end of the century.[69] By 1890, DIA reports on Christian Island no longer mentioned commercial fishing, reflecting the impact of restrictions on fishing activity. Regardless of the justification, or the efforts of certain Indian agents to recognize and defend Indigenous rights, the government retained its harsh restrictions, which created the least sustainable social, economic, and environmental circumstances these bands had ever experienced.

Under the terms of the 1876 Indian Act, the DIA in Ottawa, and specific Indian agents in the field, took control of reserve governance. After this date, all decisions made by band councils had to receive DIA approval before they could take effect, including the use of band funds. As Brownlie states, "the Indian Act superseded the treaties, becoming the sole legal document by which the department was guided in its relations with First Nations."[70] The act had serious implications for each community's economic opportunities and its political autonomy in addressing its concerns and material needs. Since the Indian agent represented the community's only source of redress and social assistance, band members approached him for many of the same reasons they had previously sought help from their chief. In some cases, band members sought a relationship based on reciprocity, but even well-intentioned agents nearly always treated the relationship in paternalistic terms.[71] The Parry Island band's fractious social structure and multiple nodes of leadership complicated this dynamic. In August 1888, Chief James Pegahmegahbow and two second chiefs, Peter Megis and Charles Sinebah, wrote to their Indian agent, Thomas Walton, on behalf of the band council to request two wagons. Walton justified the need to Ottawa because "the band consists of two communities living about six miles apart. Consequently, when one community needs anything the other claims an equivalent. In this case each community desires to have its own waggon."[72] The DIA attempted to control even the most basic of band affairs and manipulated the challenges of consensus by controlling funds and decision making on reserves.

Authoritative, and in many cases racist, Indian agents and DIA representatives frustrated attempts by band members to pursue new strategies for generating income on reserves. In some instances, without the band's consent, the DIA allowed non-Indigenous people to expropriate valuable resources from reserves, which could have generated more sustainable economic, social, and environmental opportunities for members of the community. In 1856, Crown surveyor W.H.E. Napier reported to R.T.

Pennefather, superintendent general of Indian Affairs, that the coasts of Parry Island were "high and rocky timbered with pine and hemlock." There were, Napier went on, "many very excellent flats of open hardwood, beech, maple, elm, ironwood birch and ash interspersed with occasional groves of large pine of good quality." By using words such as "timbered" and "quality," Napier expressed a certain colonial, and commercial, perception of the trees on reserve land, particularly the white pine.[73] In September 1871, the Parry Island band under Chief Pegahmegahbow sold the rights to the island's merchantable timber to a lumberman named Alvin Peter, who operated a sawmill in Parry Sound. Sixteen years later, in 1887, Chief Peter Megis wrote to the Governor General in Council to request assistance in preventing hardwood timber from being cut on the island. According to this petition, Megis and the Parry Island band understood that the agreement with Alvin Peter applied only to pine. Initially, both Peter and the band leadership had agreed that "merchantable" referred to pine alone, which was Peter's sole interest.[74] But in 1887, the company's definition of "merchantable" differed from that of 1871. It had expanded to include several other tree species that now enjoyed a market with the Standard Chemical Company factory in Parry Sound. By addressing the letter to the governor general, Megis followed a long tradition of expecting the Crown to uphold its treaty promises. It illustrates that Indigenous and non-Indigenous understandings of formal agreements continued to differ, just as colonial government representatives had reinterpreted treaties during the first half of the nineteenth century. Twenty-five years later, Chief Megis and the band council were still insisting they had not surrendered the rights to any timber other than pine. In August 1912, Crown timber inspector George L. Chitty dismissed claims made by Megis and others that band leaders had been intoxicated and induced to sign the 1871 surrender. He stated categorically that "the right [of Alvin Peter] is undeniable as the license he holds includes the right to cut Ash, Elm, Birch, Beech, Hickory, & Oak."[75] For over forty years, DIA understandings of agreements with the Parry Island band effectively eliminated logging as a viable strategy for generating income on the reserve.

In the context of restrictions, denial, and marginalization on- and off-reserve, Muskoka provided tangible and stable opportunities for communities whose traditional way of life was changing dramatically. During the second half of the nineteenth century, the government opened up Muskoka for Euro-Canadian resettlement, conceptually and physically transforming Muskoka's environment from an overlapping and fluid set of doodem territories into a rigidly organized and permanent collection

Indigenous Identity, Settler Colonialism, and Tourism 67

of freehold private properties. Reorganizing the landscape into cadastral spaces suitable for freehold private property implied an empty land belonging to no one. Ironically, it was settlers, not First Nations, who left the Shield largely uninhabited and unused during the late nineteenth century. Since the Shield was unsuited to agriculture, settlers left more than 80 percent of the landscape as forest, and the Anishinaabeg found many places, and numerous ways, to continue visiting their traditional hunting territories.

Returning to Muskoka annually was critical to reproducing Anishinaabe and doodem identity during these years. Failing to do so could have serious intergenerational consequences that went beyond one's ability to provide for the family. According to oral tradition as told by Elisabeth Shilling of Rama, the health of her doodem members was proportional to time spent in their doodem lands. In her story, an old woman went to Lake Joseph each summer to feed her serpent. She knew that if she missed one summer, a cousin would die. Sure enough, as access to Lake Joseph became restricted, she was unable to visit her serpent and her cousins died, followed by her son and daughter. Eventually, having failed to return, she died as well.[76] Members of each band believed that returning to Muskoka every year was important, not only as a strategy for acquiring material resources, but also as an essential element of reproducing their identity. In the context of colonial pressures and restrictions elsewhere in their home range, visits to the Shield took on even greater importance.

The government's incomplete understanding of their seasonal cycle enabled the Anishinaabeg to hunt and trap, repurpose their knowledge and skills, and take advantage of the opportunities presented by tourism. The Williams Commission testimony that opens this chapter reveals that settler colonialism did not entirely disrupt their access to, and use of, hunting territories in Muskoka. Band members from Christian Island journeyed to Muskoka by canoeing across Georgian Bay to the mouth of the Musquash River and upstream from there to hunting territories. Georgina Island and Rama band members made the trip north from Lake Couchiching, over a series of portages to Lake Muskoka, and then upstream to hunting grounds. In 1862, James Nanigishkung began making the trip from Rama to his father's hunting limits in what is now Algonquin Park near the headwaters of the Muskoka River watershed. Doodem members planted gardens at Lake of Bays, "where we raised our corn, potatoes and pumpkins." Nanigishkung "hunted regularly in these limits for fifteen years in succession" and "made our regular camping grounds at Canoe Lake where we dried our Furs," which he sold to "Alexander Bailey (Bee-to-beeg his Indian name) who was camped at the point where the Town of Bracebridge now stands."[77] In the same year, John Bigwin from Georgina Island also started travelling with his father to hunting grounds between Lake of Bays and Kawagama Lake. For over forty-five years, Bigwin took the same route as Nanigishkung, relied on the same gardens, and consumed a lot of "wild meat – meat of the fisher and mink and otter."[78] Also from Georgina Island, George Bigcanoe and his family hunted deer for food and trapped "beaver, otter, muskrat, fisher, marten and mink," selling the furs to Alexander Bailey at Bracebridge.[79] During the 1860s, Wesley Monague from Christian Island travelled to his uncle's hunting grounds around Trout Lake, just beyond the headwaters of the Muskoka River watershed at the height of land now included in Algonquin Park.[80] Members from Christian Island also trapped but sold their furs to Alfred Thompson at Penetanguishene.[81] Throughout the late nineteenth and early twentieth centuries, at exactly the same time as Euro-Canadians were moving into the region, the Anishinaabeg still came to Muskoka to hunt and trap.

The Anishinaabeg understood the Shield environment in terms of their seasonal cycle and cultural identity, and consistently reproduced that knowledge and their identity over multiple generations and waves of colonization. Members from each band respected doodem limits, avoided trespassing on one another's hunting grounds, and recognized a flexible system of governance overseen by chiefs. Until the 1880s, Chief John Aisance and his sons made the trip from Christian Island to hunting limits around Lake Muskoka. According to testimony provided by eighty-four-year-old Thomas Kadegegwon, John Aisance controlled the territory "in the centre of all the hunting grounds" through which others passed on their way to and from their own limits farther upstream. Gilbert Williams from Rama recounted his father's warning "to not go over the boundary, this west boundary [outside the watershed], and I never went over it, I just went near there and come back into lake Joseph and Rosseau lake and Skeleton lake."[82] During the Williams Commission hearings, Charles Bigcanoe drew an analogy with the sanctity of private property to help explain boundaries between hunting territories: "They [band members] were very attentive of keeping their limits, like a farmer would be. They don't want anyone to hunt in their grounds."[83] Defined mainly by geographical features, such as lakes, rivers, heights of land, and blazed trees, the boundaries between hunting limits were treated as seriously as settlers treated the separation between plots of private property.

In 1881, Muskoka also became a Haudenosaunee place when thirty-two Mohawk families from Kanesatake moved to a newly created reserve in Gibson Township. Once there, they encountered colonizing pressures much like the Chippewa and Ojibwe bands. But their much longer experience of living near Euro-Canadians enabled their quick adaption to conditions in Muskoka. At Kanesatake, the Mohawk were embroiled in an ongoing land conflict with the Sulpician Order, who possessed the neighbouring seigneury.[84] In 1880, their Indian agent John McGirr reported that their non-Indigenous neighbours destroyed their sugar bushes and "dispose of all the most valuable timber on this reservation."[85] At some point in the 1870s, following the lead of Chief Louis Sahanatien, many band members converted to Methodism, possibly as an act of defiance against their Sulpician seigneurs.[86] These spiritual and material disputes with the Sulpicians prompted the Mohawk to request a new reserve from the Crown.

According to Philip Laforce, one of the first generation born in Muskoka, Ottawa permitted the band to choose between three locations: Rama, Sault Ste. Marie, or Gibson Township.[87] To make room for the Mohawk, it removed a community of twenty-four francophone loggers who had been squatting along the Musquash River.[88] It also obliged the Sulpicians to purchase the reserve lands from the Ontario government, compensate the Mohawk families who left Kanesatake for improvements they had made to their land, provide material assistance in the form of food for the first fourteen days, and cover the costs of a log house for each family at Gibson.[89] The reserve did not become the property of the Mohawk but rather was placed in a trust for the band by the federal government.

Hardships characterized the early years, but the Mohawk recognized and pursued a new set of moditional economic opportunities. During the first year, they brought in supplies by foot from Bala, and approximately 50 percent of their diet in the early years came from venison and other game meat.[90] Despite many challenges, the Mohawk received glowing DIA reports. In September 1883, just two years after they arrived in Muskoka, Indian Agent William Scott visited the reserve and described "land of the very best quality," with "several full fields of oats, or turnips, and of potatoes." "There are fine chances for fishing and hunting," he wrote, "but they said: 'We have no time for that sort of thing. Our own farms take up our time, and when not engaged at home, we have profitable employment at the mills or in the lumber shanties.'" Probably telling Scott what he wanted to hear, band members stated, "'We are quite satisfied with Gibson - nothing could induce us to go back to Oka; we have peace; we are without fear when we go into the woods to cut timber.' One said: 'I am as happy as if I were born here.'"[91] The following year, Indian Agent Thomas Walton reported 220 acres cleared, and for the next fifteen years agents noted that "members of this band depend chiefly on agriculture."[92] Yet, Walton's 1884 report also noted that residents had earned $773.50 from selling tanbark, $1,700 from making lacrosse sticks, and $1,200 from work at a local sawmill.[93] These strategies, which resembled those pursued by the Anishinaabeg at the same time, earned a considerable income for a community of only a couple of hundred people.

Anishinaabe and Haudenosaunee band members did not remain confined to their reserves during the late nineteenth century, as the DIA would have preferred. Instead, many took advantage of various market-oriented and waged labour activities elsewhere, including jobs in local sawmills and factories, selling crafts to summer tourists, and working as guides for sportsmen, anglers, and hunters from the city. Logging camps, sawmills, and factories provided the earliest entries into the moditional economy in Muskoka. During the early 1870s, band members from Christian Island and Parry Island took jobs in mills at Penetanguishene and Parry Sound.[94] In the 1880s, they worked "contracts to load lumber [on and off ships] at saw mills on the 'North Shore' [at Manitoulin Island]," and mills, timber yards, and docks throughout Georgian Bay hired Indigenous people as stevedores during the summer months.[95] Located along the Musquash River, which raftsmen used to float timber downstream, the Wahta Mohawk were ideally situated to "obtain remunerative employment" at places such as the Muskoka Mill and Lumber Company at the mouth of the river on Georgian Bay.[96] In 1884, Indian Agent Thomas Walton reported that Wahta members earned $1,200 from their sawmill employment, and by the 1890s they had generated a fairly regular seasonal cycle of planting their crops in the spring, working at Muskoka Mill for $30 per month in the summer, and returning to cut hay in the autumn.[97] In 1896, Indian agents began to report that members from Parry Island and Wahta were hired to work on logging crews and timber drives during the winter and spring.[98] After the Parry Sound, Arnprior and Ottawa Railway reached Parry Sound in 1897, several Parry Island band members were employed to load and unload the trains. After the turn of the century, Rama band members found work at the Standard Chemical Works at Longford, just south of the reserve.[99] The number of opportunities for waged labour continued to expand as Ontario's economy industrialized during the early twentieth century.

At the same time, tourism offered the Chippewa, Ojibwe, and Mohawk important, yet complicated, opportunities to repurpose their skills and traditional knowledge of the Shield. By the 1890s, thousands of people from the cities to the south visited Muskoka each summer to escape the heat and health risks of the urban environment, relax and socialize next to a lake, and experience the "wilderness."[100] As was the case elsewhere in North America, romantic ideas about wilderness imagined Muskoka as devoid of people and excluded the Anishinaabeg and the Haudenosaunee from its history. In fact, many tourists relied directly on the knowledge, skill, and labour of Indigenous people while simultaneously erasing them from their imagined wilderness experience. As Paige Raibmon shows, engaging as "authentic Indians" by selling crafts or guiding tourists contributed to cultural stereotypes and, ultimately, the government's justification for restrictive game laws and elimination of Indigenous rights.[101] Indeed, by the end of the century, it became very difficult for band members to hunt, trap, and fish in Muskoka, unless they did so as guides for tourists. Conservationists urged the provincial government to adopt a restrictive environmental ethos. When applied to hunting and fishing, conservation laws effectively overwrote Indigenous rights, as laid out in the Robinson-Huron Treaty.[102] In 1892, the Act for the Protection of Game and Fur-bearing Animals prevented Indigenous people in the province from hunting and trapping out of season and without licences. The following year, the Province of Ontario established Algonquin Park to preserve timber and protect the headwaters of several watersheds, including the Muskoka River. The ancestral hunting grounds of several band members from Rama, Georgina Island, and Christian Island lay within the new park's borders. Tourism, therefore, had a rather deliberate hand in denying Indigenous people their rights in Muskoka.

Band members from each of these First Nations found ways of negotiating the restrictions imposed on them in Muskoka. They repurposed skills and traditional knowledge of the Shield environment, and simultaneously used tourism as an opportunity to return to ancestral doodem territory and reproduce their Indigenous identity (see Figure 2.4). Tourists sought out crafts and services, such as guiding, provided by "authentic Indians." As Raibmon explains, "authenticity was a structure of power that enabled, even as it constrained, [Indigenous people's] interaction with the colonial world."[103] Members from all five bands typically sold craftwork to tourists every summer. Members from Georgina Island and Christian Island rarely travelled to Muskoka for this purpose, preferring instead to sell to tourists on Lake Simcoe and Georgian Bay. But women from Rama and Wahta sold a wide variety of items to tourists in Muskoka, including bows and arrows, moccasins, snowshoes, axe handles, beadwork, quill boxes, sweetgrass baskets, splint baskets, birchbark baskets, and birchbark canoes to name just the most common (see Figure 2.5).[104] According to Joyce Tabobondung, an elder at Wasauksing First Nation, craftwork created an opportunity for two, three, or even four generations of women to spend time together, the older generations passing on stories, as well as the necessary skills for work with beads, quills, and birchbark.[105] In the late spring, when tourists started arriving, women dressed themselves and their daughters in regalia and travelled to central locations, such as Port Carling, where their crafts were guaranteed to sell. Indian agents for Parry Island, Wahta, and Rama all reported that the women "found ready sale during the tourist season" for "large quantities of fancy work." They earned "a considerable amount [of money] by the manufacture and sale of Indian fancy work and baskets."[106] Families realized an important income from the sale of these seasonal crafts. However, this required a connection with the past and the land. Mothers and grandmothers passed on knowledge and skills to the next generation at the same time as they sought out new opportunities in a changing world. Indeed, as these women returned year after year into the 1930s, they "would tell their cottaging clients how, each year, they needed to walk in the footsteps of their ancestors."[107]

By the 1880s, parties of sportsmen from the city, as well as hotel and resort guests, relied on Indigenous men to act as guides for their hunting and fishing excursions. Tourism did not afford Indigenous people the power to resist colonization to any great extent, but as Brownlie argues, "a reasonably respectable role for Indigenous skills was integrated into the local Euro-Canadian economy ... [and] created a market for the sale of wilderness skills."[108] Moreover, the ability to maintain and pass on the knowledge and skill employed as guides allowed some men to retain an identity as hunters. In 1874, members of the Muskoka Club hired John Moses, George and Richard Snike, and Joseph Yellowhead from Rama as guides for the season.[109] In 1889, Indian Agent D.J. McPhee remarked that "during the summer months a number of the Indians are constantly employed as guides to tourists and pleasure-seekers, by whom they are well paid, some of them earning as much as $60 per month."[110] This pay rate was considerable, and it appears to have held up through the 1890s, when members of the Wahta band were also hired as guides, despite the fact they had lived in Muskoka for barely a decade.[111] Men from Wahta and Rama employed "their thorough knowledge of Muskoka" as guides in the region, and men from Parry Island were hired by tourists

Indigenous Identity, Settler Colonialism, and Tourism 73

FIGURE 2.4 First Nations camp near Royal Muskoka Hotel, Lake Rosseau, 1904. *Frank W. Micklethwaite. John Harold Micklethwaite fonds, PA-067351. Courtesy of Library and Archives Canada*

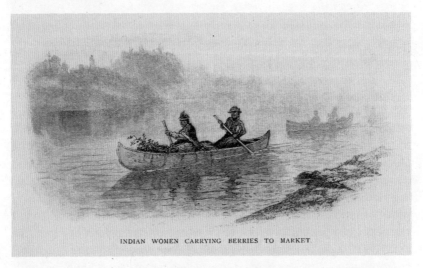

FIGURE 2.5 Indigenous women bringing berries to market, c. 1880. *A. Irwin, engravers. George Munro Grant,* Picturesque Canada: The Country as It Was and Is *(Toronto: James Clarke, 1882), 591. Courtesy of the Thomas Fisher Rare Book Library, University of Toronto*

visiting Georgian Bay.[112] After the turn of the century, guides were in high demand.

Ironically, Indigenous people worked as guides for the same anglers and hunters who were instrumental in getting conservationist legislation passed to restrict Indigenous hunting and fishing, denying them the very identity they could reproduce through guiding. Unlike their traditional seasonal rounds, which brought the Anishinaabeg into Muskoka to hunt and trap during the late fall and early winter, the tourism season bridged the summer months. The same tourist groups repeatedly booked the best months ahead of time, and guides quickly filled their calendars between May and November.[113] Sometimes, close relationships emerged between affluent hunters and their perennial guides. According to Joyce Tabobondung, whose father was a guide, "a lot of them [from the hunting party] would come to the [guide's] house. And, you know, meet his family."[114] Indian agents frowned on this type of association and worried that being treated like equals by their clients would have "a detrimental effect on their sense of humility," as Brownlie puts it.[115] DIA annual reports feature mainly positive assessments of Indigenous participation in the tourist industry, but their knowledge and skills could often be discounted. In 1909, D.F. MacDonald, the Indian agent at Parry Sound, who was also responsible for the Wahta band, referred to "canoemen" and "boatmen" instead of guides, suggesting that their role was simply as labourers rather than as knowledgeable and skilled men.[116] The government perceived their roles as guides separately from their identity as hunters. Indigenous guides, however, conflated the two roles by hunting during their trips with tourists. Equality was not a characteristic of these arrangements, but they created options, which band members used strategically. As Paige Raibmon notes, "survival under colonialism required compromises, but these compromises were not necessarily symptoms of decline and could be signs of resiliency."[117] Indigenous men used guiding as a means of employing and passing on traditional knowledge and skills, as well as supporting their families on-reserve, regardless of the contradictions involved.

Several First Nations called Muskoka home during the nineteenth and early twentieth centuries. At the southern edge of the Shield, Indigenous people hunted game and trapped furs, overwintered, cultivated small garden plots, taught their children traditional knowledge and skills, avoided government control, generated income when few other options were available, and reproduced their Indigenous identity at a time when settler colonialism tried to destroy it. For the Anishinaabeg, Muskoka was only a *part* of a home range that also included Lake Simcoe, Lake Couchiching, the Severn River, Georgian Bay, all the smaller lakes and rivers that connected them, and the land that lay in between. In this area, a flexible seasonal-cycle built resilience into their way of life. But that resilience was eroded throughout the nineteenth century, as Euro-Canadians systemically dispossessed them and the government reinterpreted the treaties to justify violent acts of colonization. In the 1850s, the government formally assigned the Anishinaabeg reserve lands to which they were expected to remain confined. The Chippewa and Ojibwe negotiated locations in close proximity to Indigenous fisheries, but the government worked consistently to deny access to those fisheries in favour of white commercial fishing interests. Confederation (1867) and the Indian Act (1876) institutionalized Indigenous dispossession by separating responsibility for First Nations and Crown lands between the federal and provincial governments, and imposing a disenfranchising, racist, and paternalistic authority over reserve administration. Provincial game laws restricted hunting and trapping off-reserve, while the DIA controlled band funds and resources on reserve.

By the time of the Williams Commission in 1923, the efforts by the bands to share the land with non-Indigenous people had resulted only in its theft. They could no longer hunt and fish in Muskoka without incurring penalty. The Parry Island Ojibwe had signed the Robinson-Huron Treaty in 1850, but the Wahta Mohawks had no treaty related to Muskoka. As early as 1881, the Rama, Georgina Island, and Christian Island bands had insisted that no treaties acknowledged their rights in Muskoka. Lacking an accurate understanding of the Anishinaabe seasonal cycle, the government believed that the Robinson-Huron Treaty had extinguished all Indigenous rights to the Shield. For the next forty years, as white loggers, settlers, and cottagers poured into their hunting grounds, the government rebuffed or ignored pleas, petitions, and lawyers representing Chippewa claims. Annual reports from the DIA demonstrate that band members from Rama still travelled to Muskoka as guides, and testimony given to Chippewa band lawyers in 1911 and evidence heard during the Williams Commission in 1923 reveal that several members from all three reserves consistently returned to Muskoka during the late nineteenth century. Muskoka had provided a variety of strategies for alleviating some of the most intense colonizing pressures, particularly the restrictions placed on their reserve resources and assets, the denial of their fishing rights, and the marginalization of their reserve communities as settlers and cottagers moved in to occupy their ancestral hunting grounds. That the Anishinaabeg were able to continue to rely on Muskoka in this way during the late nineteenth century has a great deal to do with the fact that it was unsuited to agriculture. With less pressure to clear and occupy the land, Euro-Canadians left the landscape largely forested. Its unsuitability for agriculture meant Indigenous people could return to Muskoka on a seasonal basis to reproduce their identity and access resources in much the same way generation after generation. Muskoka could never entirely compensate for the hardships they experienced during the late nineteenth century, but without the opportunities it supplied, life would have been even less sustainable.

3

Rural Identity and Tourism, 1870–1900

In the spring of 1871, Sarah and Enoch Cox, and their six children, left Warwickshire, England, for Ontario. In the spring of 1873, after spending two years in Toronto, Enoch rented land in Muskoka. A few years later, he took up approximately two hundred acres of his own on the shores of Lake Joseph in Medora Township. For several years, Sarah and their daughters ran a boarding house in Toronto while Enoch and their teenage son cleared land in Muskoka. Enoch arrived only a year after the Ontario government finished interconnecting the lower lakes for steamboat travel and more than two years before the Northern Railway finished its line to Gravenhurst. Like thousands of others, the Cox family arrived at the height of the free grant land rush in Muskoka. Over the next several years, Enoch and his son struggled to establish a farm on the poor soils of the Precambrian Shield. In 1880, Sarah recognized a much better use of her family's land and labour. Increasingly large numbers of visitors from the city had been coming to Muskoka every summer, looking for adventure, relaxation, and a wilderness experience. Sarah proposed building a small hotel to offer accommodation, meals, and recreation, believing that "in the near future there would be more money made in Muskoka by boarding the summer visitors than by farming."[1] The next year, she moved to Muskoka, and over the following two decades, the family built additions, transforming their summer boarding house into Prospect House, a resort hotel that could accommodate two hundred guests.

This chapter uncovers how a growing number of homesteaders adjusted to the poor agricultural potential of the Shield by turning the region's environmental limitations to their advantage to construct a rural identity based on tourism. In the late nineteenth century, tourism emerged in a variety of rural North American settings, but its co-evolution alongside agriculture and logging during the first generation of Euro-Canadian resettlement made Muskoka distinct. As the great land rush swept through the region, settlers in Muskoka adjusted to life on the Shield by combining subsistence farming, hunting and fishing, market exchange, and waged labour. Attracted by the chance to take up free grant land, incoming settlers struggled to transform the Canadian Shield into a Neo-Europe. Poor soils presented significant hardships to settlers even on the region's best land, and inadequate transportation networks caused isolation, especially in the backwoods. Unable to establish an agrarian way of life, hundreds of settlers abandoned their lots each year when the promise of free land met the material realities of the Shield. At the same time as many engaged in the agroforestry economy, settlers closer to the lower lakes (Muskoka, Rosseau, and Joseph) aligned the local economy with tourism opportunities. Many provided accommodations by turning their homes into hotels and the productive potential of their land and labour toward the needs of summer visitors. Some of the larger hotels became nodes of activity where the local economy met the social spaces of tourism. In some cases, year-round residents invited friends and family to join them each summer at their lakeside homes, which became the nuclei for small tourist colonies over time. The earliest cottages appeared on islands that rich folks from the city bought from the Crown starting in the 1870s. Over the next three decades, settlers also sold chunks of their shoreline property to people from the city. At first, cottagers erected modest structures, but by the end of the century, affluent visitors were building opulent summer homes. Settlers who did not sell accommodations or land to summer visitors found other ways of benefitting from the tourism economy by providing services, including cutting cordwood for stoves and ice for icehouses, building and repairing cottages, or provisioning lakeside households with supplies and fresh groceries. In every case, tourism relied on the presence, knowledge, labour, and land of local residents in Muskoka.

Tourism provided permanent residents closer to the lower lakes with a seasonal, but consistent, component of their rural society and economy, which paralleled the traditional, seasonal cycle of Indigenous occupation on the Shield. Those who resettled Muskoka during the late nineteenth century quickly discovered something that the Anishinaabeg had long understood: the Shield could not provide for all of their material or cultural needs, and a sedentary, agrarian society was highly unsuited to the

Rural Identity and Tourism

environment of the Canadian Shield. The Anishinaabeg called Muskoka home, but few ever lived there year-round. Within the first generation of resettlement, Euro-Canadians learned about Muskoka's environmental limitations the hard way. A number of subsistence strategies resembled Indigenous uses of Shield resources, but never supported the region's thousands of permanent rural inhabitants. The agroforestry economy provided meaningful income for many households, but declined at the end of the nineteenth century. Tourists, however, returned each summer, in growing numbers, and brought cash and credit into Muskoka, which they used to purchase accommodation, meals, goods, and services from settlers. In order to live sedentarily in Muskoka, settlers relied on the seasonal visits of thousands of tourists each summer. By embracing tourism, without even realizing it, settlers constructed a rural identity that adjusted to a fundamental principle of Indigenous life on the Shield: seasonal, temporary occupation.

In the late nineteenth century, the most popular form of tourism among rich folks from cities in northeastern North America involved the wilderness experience. Hoping to escape congested and unhealthy city conditions, tourists sought divine, romantic, primitive, and curative imagery in landscapes that seemed unaltered by humans.[2] The most iconic examples were national, state, and provincial parks, which governments established on lands that were unsuited for lumbering, mining, farming, or other "productive" purposes. Tourism in these types of places relied on romantic notions of a pristine wilderness that had no private property, human inhabitants, or history. As Patricia Jasen and Claire Campbell show, wild places in Ontario, including the Thousand Islands on the St. Lawrence River, Niagara Falls, Toronto Island, Georgian Bay, and Muskoka, attracted thousands of visitors a year by the 1870s. Muskoka's appeal certainly rested on the idea of wilderness, but its popularity also derived from the presence of year-round settlers who owned their land and sold accommodations, meals, goods, and services to visitors.

In locales with a long history of farming, such as Prince Edward Island, Vermont, and New York, several generations passed between colonization and the development of tourism. In these places, tourism supplemented an economy that was still based predominantly on commercial agriculture, which experienced a decline due to falling commodity prices during the late nineteenth century.[3] In Muskoka, agriculture was an important component of rural identity well into the twentieth century, but in the late 1870s and early 1880s, homesteaders close to the lower lakes quickly aligned their farming activities to support the needs of the tourism economy. In the Great Lakes hinterland regions of northern Michigan, Wisconsin, and Minnesota, tourism often followed as the third wave of settler colonialism. The first wave involved resource extraction (logging and mining), and agriculture either supported it or replaced it when settlers attempted to farm cut-over lands.[4] Mining never occurred in Muskoka, but farming, logging, and tourism all developed at the same time. In the backwoods, settlers constructed a rural identity that blended subsistence activities into the agroforestry economy. Closer to the lower lakes, rural identity featured small-scale agriculture, household-based approaches to logging, and tourism within the first generation.

The same material realties that made Muskoka unsuited to agriculture attracted large numbers of visitors from the city. Settlers left a great deal of the landscape forested, which satisfied visitors' desire to view it as ideal for a healthful rest cure or as a backdrop to reinvigorate their moral well-being. In 1871, forests covered 99 percent of the Muskoka townships considered in this study. Ten years later, as tourism gained momentum, approximately 94 percent remained forested. And thirty years after that, in 1911, settlers had cleared only 9 percent of the landscape. Muskoka was home to some very large logging and sawmilling operations during the late nineteenth century, and though these had measurable environmental impacts on forest and aquatic ecology, clear-cutting did not come to the area until the mid-twentieth century. The tourist preference for forests appears to have influenced settlers near the lower lakes, who by 1891 had cleared 22 percent less of the land than those in backwoods townships.[5] By this time, much of northeastern North America had been either cleared of its forests or spoiled by resource extraction. For most tourists, the remaining uncleared or undeveloped areas seemed too remote. By contrast, Muskoka lay only about two hundred kilometres north of Toronto and was relatively accessible by rail.

Muskoka's earliest tourists arrived almost as soon as it was opened to Euro-Canadian resettlement. In 1860, James Bain and John Campbell made the arduous journey from Toronto by train, steamer, rowboat, and foot to the future site of Gravenhurst. Returning the next year, they stopped at the Freemason's Arms, where the owner, Mrs. McCabe, asked what they were doing in Muskoka. She guessed that they were either surveyors or preachers. According to an account of their trip, "their protests that they were on pleasure bent simply did not register with Mother McCabe."[6] At a time when many struggled to carve out an existence on the Shield, the thought that anyone would actually seek it out for pleasure was largely incomprehensible.

FIGURE 3.1 Muskoka Club, 1866. *Baldwin Collection of Canadiana, Pictures-R-606. Courtesy of the Toronto Public Library*

As transportation improved, tourism increased steadily and contributed to the divergence of rural identities in the backwoods and closer to the lower lakes. In 1866 and 1867, A.P. Cockburn launched the region's first steamboats on the lower lakes. He hosted New York entrepreneur William H. Pratt, who envisioned building a grand resort hotel that would attract visitors who were interested in a wilderness experience but were not willing to compromise on luxury and comfort. Pratt had Rosseau House erected in 1870, and two years later the Ontario Department of Public Works made all three lakes internavigable. Cockburn repeated his tour of Muskoka with a second entrepreneur, Hamilton Fraser of Brampton, Ontario, who purchased land at the north end of Lake Joseph and had a resort hotel built there, which he named Summit House.[7] The seeds of cottage culture developed at the same time. Bain and Campbell continued to visit Muskoka each year, bringing a group of friends who called themselves the Muskoka Club (see Figure 3.1). By the end of the decade, several club members had purchased islands from the Crown and built cottages of their own. In 1875,

Cockburn's steamboats connected with trains arriving at lakeside Northern Railway stations, ferrying passengers to various locations around the lakes, including Rosseau House and Summit House. These major transportation improvements during the 1870s increased the ease with which Muskoka could be reached by residents from cities, such as Toronto, Buffalo, and Pittsburgh, all of which had populations of more than 200,000 by the late nineteenth century. Visitors had been arriving in small numbers since the early 1860s, but after the railway arrived, the trickle turned into a steady stream and eventually became a flood.

As the settler land rush unfolded, the doubling, and later almost tripling, of the summertime population in six townships surrounding the lower lakes transformed the economic activity, social lives, and rural identity of Muskoka's settler community (see Figure 3.2). Almost three dozen boarding houses, small hotels, and grand resorts opened during the last two decades of the nineteenth century. In 1895, approximately 400 cottages dotted the shores of the lower lakes. By the turn of the century, tourism had exploded. In 1903, there were 57 hotels, and by 1909 there were 76. The largest, such as Summit House, the Beaumaris Hotel, and Prospect House, could host about 200 guests, though the average hovered around 65. At their combined maximum occupancy, the hotels could take in approximately 5,000 people. By 1915, the number of summer residences on the lower lakes had climbed to 720. If an average of five people stayed at each of these cottages at any one time, the total cottage population approached 3,600. In 1895, the combined cottage and hotel tourist population of the lower lakes roughly equalled the settler population of the adjacent six townships. By the First World War, the number of summer visitors at any given time nearly doubled that of permanent residents.[8] They came from affluent backgrounds. Most travelled from urban areas in southern Ontario, but many were from the United States, and a few even came from as far away as Britain. The addition of so many rich folks significantly increased the rural population, temporarily altered the class structure along the lakeshore, flooded the local market with cash and credit, and allowed settlers near the lower lakes to distinguish themselves from their backwoods neighbours.

Settlers understood that their reliance on wealthy visitors involved certain compromises, but their control over the tourism industry also made life more sustainable than in the backwoods. Sarah and Enoch Cox's eldest daughter, Fanny, was thirty-one when her parents opened Prospect House in the summer of 1880. By the turn of the century, Fanny and her husband, Edwin Potts, also rented out nearby cottages. During the 1880s and 1890s,

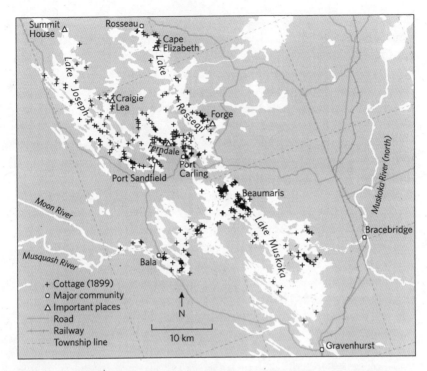

FIGURE 3.2 Cottages on the lower Muskoka lakes, 1899. *G.W. Marshall, Map and Chart of the Muskoka Lakes: Rosseau, Joseph, Muskoka (Toronto: Self-published, 1899). Adapted by Eric Leinberger*

however, Fanny and her sisters spent part of each summer helping their parents run the hotel. During those two decades, Fanny realized that "the population of Muskoka has been gradually dividing itself into two classes – tourists and settlers, otherwise capital and labor, pleasure and toil, butterflies and bees, whichever you like to call them." In comparing the visitors to butterflies and the settlers to bees, she conveyed the importance of the seasonal cycle and the fact that part of many settlers' rural identity was connected to tourism. Drawing on a blend of biblical verse and Marxist rhetoric, she also recognized the social consequences of constructing a rural identity that was so heavily influenced by tourism. "Between these two classes," she remarked, "there is a great gulf fixed." She observed that "the pleasure-loving tourist" treated settlers with contempt, while at the same time it seemed "just as natural for the hard-working settler to look down on the giddy tourist." The irony, as she saw it, was that "each class would be very badly off without the other." Many settlers depended on the income they earned from the summer visitors. Tourists figuratively consumed the wooded landscape and the rugged shoreline of the lakes, but they also physically consumed fresh vegetables, dairy, eggs, and meat grown and raised by settlers, and they occupied hotel bedrooms, dining rooms, verandahs, docks, and boats. From the perspective of the busy settler bee, they were lucrative, renewable resources, "lovely 'tourist blossoms' from which [settlers] gather their honey." Without "these American orchids and roses, these English violets and pansies, these Canadian lilies and daffodils," Fanny asked, "where would their [settlers'] winter supply come from?"[9] During the 1880s and 1890s, tourism accentuated class issues in Muskoka, but settlers were able to control the industry and thus turn the tensions toward their benefit.

This high degree of control informed many settlers' decisions to align their household economies with tourism. Early cottagers on islands and the extraordinary hotels, such as Rosseau House and Summit House, may have seemed odd during the 1870s. But after a decade, the consistent influx of visitors helped convince people like the Coxes to take advantage of tourism. Not far from the Cox family, on Lake Rosseau, Richard and Eliza Penson and their seven children took up two hundred acres in Medora Township in 1869. According to their granddaughter, "innumerable pockets of soil of some depth over the rock shelves ... contained enough workable land that it was worth clearing." During the 1870s, the Pensons "managed to sustain themselves" and "produce excellent wheat, [and] vegetable[s] and fruit trees." As the family established the farm, folks from the city turned up each summer. Cottagers "often came to the Penson farm asking to purchase produce, eggs and so on." As early as 1875, Eliza sensed an opportunity. In 1880, the same year that the Coxes built Prospect House, she and Richard hired a local carpenter to erect a small hotel on their property, which they named Ferndale House (see Figure 3.3).[10] During the 1870s, the Pensons and Coxes struggled to produce enough from their farms to support their families through subsistence and market sales. Once the hotels opened, however, both families added value to their produce by selling it to their guests as meals. Demand was immediate. According to Fanny, "visitors began to arrive at a rapid pace." In the case of Prospect House, they appeared before the Cox family could even finish preparing the new building. "As soon as a bedroom was cleaned and made ready," she wrote in her memoirs twenty years later, "it was occupied by some new arrival." In their first summer, without any advertising, the Coxes hosted fifteen guests at Prospect House. The following summer, "things were in better shape," and "for a short time the house was fairly packed

FIGURE 3.3 Ferndale House, Lake Rosseau, c. 1890. *Frank W. Micklethwaite. John Harold Micklethwaite fonds, PA-068306. Courtesy of Library and Archives Canada*

with visitors." As a result, it "did a much larger business during the season." In these early years, the land and labour of settler households structured the tourism economy, and "people visiting Muskoka were thankful for small mercies and did not look to find all the comforts and conveniences of the large city hotels."[11] The hotels served as oases in the wilderness, a base for camping and fishing excursions, and the kernels of a distinctive rural identity in North America.

Over time, successful hotels became nodes on the routes of A.P. Cockburn's Muskoka Navigation Company. They evolved into important settler-tourist communities, and formed the nuclei that blended homesteads, hotels, camps, and cottages. In the late nineteenth and early twentieth centuries, the waterways were tourism's primary transportation corridors. Until the rise of the automobile, urbanites rarely travelled by land in Muskoka. In 1888, when the Grand Trunk Railway of Canada absorbed the Northern Railway, most tourists disembarked at Muskoka Wharf in Gravenhurst, where they boarded one of three steamboats depending on their final destination.[12] During the summer months, passengers represented a large share of the Navigation Company's business, and steamers made daily stops at several locations, including popular hotels, such as Prospect House and Ferndale House. In 1872, two couples, Mary and Edward

FIGURE 3.4 Solid Comfort Camp, near Beaumaris on Lake Muskoka, 1900. *Frank W. Micklethwaite. John Harold Micklethwaite fonds, PA-068400. Courtesy of Library and Archives Canada*

Prowse and Catharine and John Wilmott, bought Tondern Island, Lake Muskoka, from a settler named Paul Dane and split it between their young families. After almost a decade, Prowse had built a 350-foot-long bridge to the mainland, cleared additional land, and established a relatively successful farm. In 1883, recognizing the same trends as the Cox and Penson families, Edward and Mary erected a three-storey resort (named the Beaumaris Hotel), repurposed the farm to support it, and added a small general store.[13] In July 1887, the *Toronto World* published an article titled "The Muskoka Country," which included a detailed description of the budding settler-tourist community at Beaumaris. By this date, the hotel could accommodate 150 people and fed its guests from "a garden the like of which we have not seen elsewhere [in Muskoka], a veritable triumph of Adam's trade, its trim beds and forcing boxes filled with luxuriant vegetables for the benefit of the coming man and his wife." The Prowse farm totalled 515 acres, split between the island and the mainland, where the family also kept a "herd of blooded milch cows," which was "tended on the farm land near and their lacteal product stored in a cool dairy house for the exclusive use of guests." By the late 1880s, however, Beaumaris had become more than just the hotel.

In addition to his hotel business, Prowse sold shorefront lots to vacationers who had fallen in love with Muskoka. To capture the revenue potential of his new neighbours, he also opened "a store where the campers and cottagers from surrounding islands can purchase groceries, stationery, fishing tackle, canned goods, butter, bacon, eggs and like sundries, as well as that prime comfort, ice."[14] American tourists from Buffalo, Detroit, Cleveland, Chicago, and particularly Pittsburgh purchased most of the properties from Prowse. Railways connecting these cities to Toronto made trips by train relatively quick and easy for Americans who sought a genuine wilderness experience. So popular was Beaumaris with the crowd from Pittsburgh that several members of a camping party from Mercer, Pennsylvania (a suburb of Pittsburgh), known as the Solid Comfort Camp, bought individual properties on Tondern Island from Prowse (see Figure 3.4). By the 1890s, friends of the Solid Comfort Camp had also bought properties from Prowse, and cottagers and settlers alike dubbed the tiny community centred at Beaumaris "Little Pittsburgh." In about ten years, summer residents at Beaumaris had transformed the collection of modest plank-and-batten structures, which comprised the original cottages, into opulent mansions and summer homes famously known as

Millionaire's Row.[15] Just as Sarah and Enoch Cox had done with Prospect House, and Eliza and Richard Penson had with Ferndale House, Mary and Edward Prowse aligned their land and labour to take advantage of the tourism industry. Each of these locations became a node in the Muskoka waterway transportation network and attracted a variety of social and economic activities, which distinguished them from the Muskoka backwoods. But by combining the hotel business with the sale of goods and services to nearby cottagers, Beaumaris represented a further evolution of the tourism economy.

During the 1880s and 1890s, settlers on the lower lakes made tourism a central feature of their household economies. In doing so, they created a rural identity that embraced the seasonal presence of rich urban tourists. In some cases, private homesteads, not resort hotels, served as nuclei for settler-tourist communities, which blurred the lines of Fanny Potts's butterflies and bees dichotomy. In 1876, fifty-five-year-old retired Toronto auction house owner Frederick Coate and his son Harry took up several hundred acres in Cardwell Township on the shores of Lake Rosseau.[16] Frederick's wife, Hannah, remained in Toronto with their four other adult children. Harry took his role as a farmer seriously. He participated and won prizes in the agricultural fair each year and hired men to help him clear land, cut cordwood, and work a sizeable farm. Frederick helped him during the first years but could be most accurately described as a gentleman farmer, since his efforts mainly satisfied his hobbyist pursuits. By the mid-1880s, he was devoting most of his time to cultivating a variety of fruits, including raspberries, strawberries, and blueberries, and he had a small vineyard that did remarkably well considering the cool climate and short growing season.[17] Frederick and Harry grew a diversity of crops, vegetables, and fruits, raised chickens, sheep, pigs, and cattle, and kept a number of cows for dairy and hens for eggs. They sold some of their produce to merchants in Rosseau, as well as to Rosseau House and two other nearby hotels called Monteith House and Maplehurst Hotel. Most of what they grew and raised, however, supplied their own household when the extended Coates family and their friends gathered during the summer at the homestead, which the Coates called Cape Elizabeth.

For several years during the early 1880s, Cape Elizabeth served much the same function as Prospect House, Ferndale House, and even the Beaumaris Hotel. The only real difference was that the exchange between the butterflies and the bees took place within a single extended family. The arrival of the Coates each summer enlarged the household to well over a dozen people. As time passed, the addition of grandchildren and friends meant that dozens of guests could be staying at Cape Elizabeth during the summer – many coming from as far away as New York, Memphis, New Orleans, and Liverpool.[18] These visitors purchased many goods and services from local merchants and tradesmen, but they also relied on the family's land and Harry's labour to provide for many of their needs. Likewise, Harry relied on financial support from his family.

During the mid-1880s, in much the same pattern as at Beaumaris, Frederick started selling lots to friends and family to build cottages. In 1886, he leased a parcel of land to J.P. Brown, the owner of Maplehurst Hotel, to build a cottage. Over the next few years, Frederick's daughter and son-in-law (who was also his business partner in Toronto), and another of his sons, built cottages at Cape Elizabeth. After Frederick's death in 1893, his children sold property to friends and business associates, who also erected cottages. At the end of the century, Cape Elizabeth was a veritable summer colony of tourist butterflies, with six separate, but closely related, cottages. Whereas the settler-tourist community at Beaumaris was a mix of paying guests at the hotel and owners in the cottages, the visitors to Cape Elizabeth consisted entirely of friends and family occupying summer residences.

The Cape Elizabeth cottages joined hundreds of others, and dozens of hotels, on Lakes Muskoka, Rosseau, and Joseph. Hotels offered full service and appealed to a variety of tourist types, including new visitors, those who stayed only briefly, parties looking for a base of operations for camping, hunting, and fishing excursions, or families whose wives and mothers had no desire to spend their holiday time cooking and cleaning. In some cases, cottages clustered around hotels and steamboat wharfs, but just as many popped up in more isolated spots (see Figures 3.5 and 3.6). Islands or points of land provided greater privacy, and owners could more easily maintain the illusion of being surrounded by wilderness. By situating themselves in remote places, rather than near a hotel or public wharf, these cottagers decoupled themselves from the orbit of any particular group of settlers.

Settlers close to the lower lakes experienced the benefits of tourism unevenly. Those who did not take in paying guests needed to work harder to capitalize on the tourism economy. Settlers with good farmland enjoyed access to hotel and cottage markets through the sale of fresh vegetables, fruits, eggs, dairy, and meat. Those whose soil was poor sold other goods and services, such as cordwood, ice, construction, and repairs. Tourists who stayed at a boarding house or hotel were a more lucrative source of cash than the individuals who bought land, had a cottage built, and purchased supplies regularly. In 1898, for example, Louis Martin of Newtonbrook,

FIGURE 3.5 Cottage on Cedar Island, Lake Rosseau, c. 1908. *Frank W. Micklethwaite. John Harold Micklethwaite fonds, PA-159368. Courtesy of Library and Archives Canada*

FIGURE 3.6 Cottage on the east shore of Lake Joseph, 1895. *Frank W. Micklethwaite. John Harold Micklethwaite fonds, PA-068378. Courtesy of Library and Archives Canada*

Ontario, bought Star Island on Lake Joseph for $250 from Charles Corbould, who had bought it for $25 from its first Euro-Canadian owner, Samuel Robinson, who had paid only $5 to the Crown for the five-acre island. The same year, a Toronto family of five who stayed for four weeks at Prospect House would have spent roughly the same amount for their holiday. The round trip from Toronto to Port Sandfield (including steamboat from Gravenhurst) cost $6.05 per person or $30.25 for the family. Prospect House charged anywhere from $10 to $15 per person per week. If we assume that a typical family paid $60 each week, a four-week vacation in Muskoka would cost approximately $270.[19] Settlers who operated a hotel arguably benefitted the most from tourism.

Isolated cottagers were also a consistent and growing source of income for settlers, who sold a variety of goods and services. Summer visitors rarely built their own cottages. Instead, they relied on the local knowledge, skill, and labour of settlers, such as George Croucher, who emigrated with his parents and siblings from Aldershot, England, in 1874 and took up land on the east side of Lake Joseph in Medora Township. In 1880, George married Ruth Webb and moved in with her family near Craigie Lea on Lake Joseph. Their land was extremely unproductive, but the family managed to grow vegetables and raise pigs, cattle, and chickens for eggs, dairy, and meat. Like many settler households, they supplemented swings in the agricultural calendar with subsistence hunting and fishing. Yet, the absence of good soil did not present a serious problem to the Croucher family. A respected carpenter, George Croucher built several of the earliest cottages on Lake Joseph.[20] In 1885, James Maclennan hired him to build a steamboat wharf on Wegamind Island (see Figure 3.7). With the help of the young men in the Maclennan family, who camped on the island that summer, Croucher cut pine logs to build the cribs and filled them with rocks hauled out from along the island's shoreline. He also helped the Maclennans survey the site of their cottage, which he built the following summer. On Yoho Island, John Campbell (founder of the Muskoka Club) paid Croucher to repair, renovate, and caretake the cottage that Campbell had built himself years earlier. According to his daughter Mabel, Croucher "was fortunate enough to work for this man [Campbell]." When Mabel turned twelve, Campbell hired her as a maid for the summer, paying "$2.00 a month, two dresses, and a pair of shoes."[21] Croucher owned a small steam sawmill, which he used to cut pine trees into lumber to build cottages. Logging company tugboats delivered logs to his mill or to cottage construction sites where he fabricated many building materials onsite, including timber frames and shingles.

FIGURE 3.7 Maclennan cottage on Wegamind Island, Lake Joseph, 1907. *Frank W. Micklethwaite. John Harold Micklethwaite fonds, PA-158596. Courtesy of Library and Archives Canada*

Elsewhere around the lower lakes, summer property owners hired several contractors to build cottages, including the Brown Brothers, J.J. Knight, Harry Sawyer, C.A. Young, Alex Cameron, Robert Rogers, Norman Kaye, George Leask, and Peter Curtis. City folks used their cottages only during the summer, and designs tended to ignore the problem of heating the interior, which settlers confronted in their homes. According to local historian Graham Smith, a view of the lake was the primary design consideration until the end of the century, when affluent owners began to demand comfortable and spacious summer homes with ornate features and enough room to accommodate more than a dozen people. Owners also hired contractors and carpenters to build pre-designed cottages chosen from pattern books, which included floor plans and instructions to erect large two-storey buildings. In 1889, the *Bracebridge Gazette* advertised catalogues for architectural plans, mainly for year-round homes, and many cottages built during the next twenty years replicated these designs with minor alterations. Around 1900, architect Sidney R. Badgley designed four nearly identical cottages for wealthy families near Beaumaris. Later carpenters built cottages using plans sold by Aladdin Homes of Toronto. Designs called "The Parry" (cottage design) and "The Carling" (boathouse

Rural Identity and Tourism 93

design with sleeping quarters above) were intended specifically for seasonal residents.[22]

Settlers also built sleeping cabins, boathouses, outhouses, ice houses, and woodsheds for cottagers. Each year, these buildings required specific labour, which cottagers paid settlers to undertake. For example, ice houses needed to be restocked every year, their contents having melted or evaporated during the summer months. Each winter, Croucher and one or two neighbours refilled them, taking a team of horses to cut ice from the frozen lake. Sometime in late January or early February, when the ice was more than two feet thick, Croucher and his team worked for roughly two weeks, using special ice saws to cut 150- to 200-pound blocks of ice eighteen inches wide and thirty inches long. The blocks were pulled out of the water with tongs and loaded onto a sleigh resembling a rock sled, and the horses drew the loads to various ice houses, often up steep inclines, where Croucher packed and covered them with sawdust for insulation. According to Mabel Croucher Ames, cottagers paid five dollars to have their ice house replenished each year. In about 1900, Croucher and his men performed this job for as many as twenty cottages, earning between thirty and forty dollars per man for two weeks of work. Croucher's winter labour not only kept the cottagers' food cool but their stoves hot enough to cook it as well. He and his neighbours cut cordwood for cottages, which they hauled out of the woods and across the frozen lakes by horse-drawn sleigh. By the turn of the century, his team cut roughly one hundred cords each year to supply cottages with sufficient fuel to last the summer season. Cutting ice out of the lake or attempting to get the final loads of wood across it before the spring melt often involved risks to settlers and their animals. In some cases, "a warm spell would come before this job was done, and the ice would weaken." The men understood the hazards, but occasionally their gamble proved disastrous. In her memoirs, Ames recalled that "many a good team of horses was lost by falling through the ice ... The horses would start to panic and get all tangled up in the harness, play themselves out, and drown."[23] The labour performed by settlers in constructing these rural linkages provided badly needed income but also posed risks that sometimes outweighed the rewards.

Cottagers were especially attracted by islands and other remote locations, but these locales were difficult and dangerous for settlers to integrate into the tourism economy. Settlers provided a variety of vital cottage goods and services during the winter, but the majority of activity related to the cottage economy took place during the summer. By 1904, when she published her memoir, it had become quite apparent to Fanny Potts that each summer "the 'tourist' has taken possession of the land." Referring to the rapid increase in cottages during the 1890s, she pointed out that "they appear to be springing up like mushrooms on every island and point." In addition, the season itself seemed to be expanding. "It used to be ... tourists were scarce in the early springtime," Potts noted, "but now you may find them as early as May-day, and in June there is quite a good showing."[24] Longer seasons and expanding numbers of visitors gave settlers more opportunities to generate income. Cottagers brought (or more often had delivered) a store of dry goods when they arrived but relied on settlers to meet many of their day-to-day needs and wants. Most dry goods and processed foods originated in the city, but fresh foods came from farms in Muskoka. During the 1890s, as tourism grew, the Swift and Armour meatpacking firms pioneered cost-effective methods of keeping fresh meat cold during long hauls between the Midwest and eastern urban markets.[25] Unfortunately, using this technology to ship fresh foods from southern Ontario farms to Toronto, and then from Toronto to Gravenhurst by train, and then from Gravenhurst to various points by steamboat did not enjoy the same cost-benefit. As a result, campers, cottagers, and hotel guests all depended on settlers for locally grown and raised vegetables and fruits, eggs, dairy, and meat.

To take advantage of the tourist demand for fresh vegetables and fruits, settlers near the lower lakes consistently expanded the size of their market gardens and orchards. In Monck Township (where Beaumaris was located), these grew from an average of just 0.07 acres per household in 1871 to 0.34 in 1881 and 0.55 in 1891. Similarly, households in Medora and Wood Townships increased their gardens and orchards from 0.02 acres in 1871, to 0.21 in 1881, and to 0.6 in 1891. By contrast, settlers living farther away from the lower lakes in Stephenson and Brunel Townships enlarged their gardens and orchards from 0.05 acres per household in 1871, to 0.23 acres in 1881, and to 0.43 acres in 1891. Even farther into the backwoods, in Stisted and McMurrich Townships, settlers cleared only 0.02 acres for gardens and orchards in 1881 and just 0.36 in 1891.[26] As the number of tourists grew, the demand for fresh foods increased, and settlers aligned their labour and land to take advantage of it.

Throughout the late nineteenth and early twentieth centuries, tourists and settlers depended on general stores to facilitate the exchange of many goods and provisions. Several Canadian historians have used the meticulous records kept by merchants to show how general stores served as important sites of market activity and social life.[27] The isolation of many cottages, however, presented settlers with important challenges in the summer. In

Rural Identity and Tourism

some locations, such as Beaumaris, cottagers bought property near hotels, steamboat wharves, farms, and general stores, which offered consistent, easy access to a steady supply of provisions. But most preferred to build several kilometres from the nearest general store or farm. Equally problematic, most settlers did not live next to the shores of the lower lakes, where they might expect to sell their produce directly to hotels and cottages. They solved their problem by creating a sophisticated network to link their farms with merchants and cottagers in remote spots. Recognizing that cottagers had little enthusiasm for time-consuming and arduous trips by rowboat or costly steamboat fares into town to purchase groceries, settlers devised a delivery strategy to connect them with fresh produce and supplies.

To establish the commercial exchange between cottage households and year-round residents, farmers and merchants used supply boats to convey goods out onto the lakes and into the homes of summer visitors. As Fanny Potts explained to the city people who rented one of her cottages, "the stores come to you instead of you going to the stores; they float up to your very doors, bringing ... 'everything we mortals can possibly need in Muskoka.'"[28] Cottagers experienced limited mobility in Muskoka prior to the First World War. The railway brought them into the region, and steamboats dropped them off at their final destination (or close to it), but after that, they had few comfortable and convenient ways of reaching the closest farm or general store. Taking a steamboat entailed added expense and restricted them to the route and schedule of the company. Using a rowboat or canoe involved significant labour and the risk of getting caught in bad weather (see Figure 3.8). Like Sarah and Enoch Cox, who realized that building a hotel would enable them to profit from summer visitors, several entrepreneurial settlers saw the economic potential in supply boats that linked tourists with the merchants and farmers who sold fresh foods and provisions.

Frank Forge emigrated from Yorkshire, England, in the early 1860s and moved to Muskoka with his wife a few years later, where they took up two hundred acres in Watt Township on Lake Rosseau. By the time Richard and Eliza Penson settled across the lake in 1869, the Forge property boasted a log shanty and "about 25 to 30 acres of nice land well cleared and fenced."[29] Like many other first-generation homesteaders in Muskoka, the Forges struggled to establish a rural identity based on agriculture. Around 1880, however, Forge had an innovative idea. Witnessing the campers and cottagers who rowed across the lake to ask settlers, such as the Penson family, for fresh foods, Forge decided to start marketing vegetables, fruit, eggs,

FIGURE 3.8 Contrasting modes of water transport. Two canoes and the steamboat *Muskoka*, near Bala, c. 1881. *Grace E. Shabaeff, photographer.* Toronto Star *Photograph Archive, TS-2-124-GO-079. Courtesy of the Toronto Public Library*

dairy, and meat by bringing them directly to customers. Loading a rowboat with his own produce, along with what he bought or bartered from his neighbours, Forge worked as "a kind of distributing agent." According to Richard Penson's son, Forge also "bought from [other] settlers, for he could not raise nearly all that he could sell. And he sold to the islanders at almost any price he liked to ask."[30] In this way, Forge became Muskoka's first supply boat operator. In 1888, he purchased a small steamboat, which he used for three years to extend his services to Lake Joseph, before selling it and resuming his business by rowboat once again.[31] His brief foray into steam power was probably inspired, and ultimately thwarted, by more successful local merchants and entrepreneurs.

As the number of cottagers and their material needs increased, supply boats greatly expanded the scope of local economic exchange on the lower lakes and occupied a central place in rural life during the summer. In 1860, William Hanna settled with his parents and siblings in Draper Township. During the 1870s, he worked as a general store clerk in Bracebridge, and in 1883 at the age of thirty-five, he, his wife, and young family moved to Port Carling, where he opened his own store. At the time,

Rural Identity and Tourism

Port Carling enjoyed a steady flow of local commerce but also a growing number of summer visitors who changed steamboats at the locks. Realizing that his store captured their business for only a short period as they travelled into and out of Muskoka, and conscious that most cottagers preferred not to row into town for supplies, Hanna hired a steamboat in 1887 to connect his store more effectively with the summer tourism market. During that year, in an article that no doubt interested many readers who were contemplating a trip to Muskoka, the *Toronto World* described his Port Carling store. In addition to installing a "special oven ... to supply a fresh home-made bread," Hanna had also made "arrangements with farmers for supplies of fresh butter, eggs, milk, as well as vegetables and fruits in season." "To facilitate the transaction of business," Hanna had "arranged with Mr. Acton Lowe of the steamer 'Lady of the Lake,' who will make regular trips upon certain days of each week to take orders, and or the delivery of goods."[32] Hanna purchased a larger boat and added a second in 1909.[33] During the 1890s, as cottages proliferated, other merchants and farmers also introduced supply boats. Located near the mouth of the Muskoka River, John James (J.J.) Beaumont owned several hundred acres of the best farmland in Muskoka.[34] In 1894, he purchased a steamboat to market farm produce to cottagers and lakeside residents during the summer months.[35]

In 1887, George Henry Homer opened a general store in Gravenhurst, which stayed in business for more than twenty years. Building on its success, he launched a second general store in Rosseau, in 1890 (see Figure 3.9).[36] An accounts ledger kept between 1896 and 1901 reveals its importance to the surrounding community, as well as the differing relationships that seasonal and permanent residents held with Muskoka general stores.[37] Homer kept store accounts with over four hundred permanent residents, several churches and sawmills, the Navigation Company, the Muskoka Leather Company, and eight hotels. His ledger does not distinguish between permanent residents and cottagers, but cross-referencing it with the 1915 *Muskoka Lakes Bluebook* directory reveals that twelve cottagers maintained store accounts with Homer, including four at Cape Elizabeth.[38] The number of cottage accounts are so few because Homer also ran a supply boat, and the accounts of most cottage customers would have been recorded in its ledger, which has not survived. In 1896, Homer bought a small steamer from Enoch Cox and converted it into a supply boat to serve as an extension of his store in Rosseau (see Figures 3.10 and 3.11). Eight years later, he switched to a larger vessel and advertised that it "calls at all Cottages, Camps and Hotels on Lakes Rosseau and Joseph, and is stocked with a complete assortment of fine 'Groceries, Fruits, Confectionary, Vegetables,

FIGURE 3.9 Overlooking the town of Rosseau at the head of Lake Rosseau, c. 1890. *Frank W. Micklethwaite. John Harold Micklethwaite fonds. Courtesy of PA-068379, Library and Archives Canada*

FIGURE 3.10 Homer and Company supply boat *Constance*, c. 1900. *Micklethwaite Photo. Courtesy of Muskoka Steamship and Historical Society*

FIGURE 3.11 Interior of the *Constance*, c. 1900. *Micklethwaite Photo. Courtesy of Muskoka Steamship and Historical Society*

Fresh Meats, etc.'"[39] Supply boats disrupted the usual pattern in which individuals visited a store to stock up on provisions. Instead, this rather novel method of buying groceries, which involved the store moving between various cottages and lakeside residences, became an ordinary part of rural life in Muskoka. Not only did families, such as the Hannas and the Homers, as well as the people who worked for them, benefit directly from tourism, but many others also stood to gain indirectly by producing goods sold through the general stores – and their supply boats – to tourists and cottagers. From about 1880 to 1900, supply boats made it possible for settlers to construct a rural identity based on tourism by using the waterways transportation corridor to connect mainland farms and general stores with isolated lakeside consumers.

Accomplishing this supply network entailed significant labour. According to Fanny Potts, supply boats "commence their trips as soon as the ice breaks up in the spring, and continue running till the ice forms thickly enough to stop them in the fall."[40] Most tourists visited Muskoka in July and August, with increasing numbers coming in June and September after the turn of the century. But many settlers also relied on supply boats throughout the navigation season. Thus, most boats made stops once a week during the spring and fall, and twice a week during the height of the tourist season.[41] Their service was initiated during the 1880s, but as Potts noted in 1904, "their trade has gradually grown to meet the demand, which is increasing every year, and in consequence they seem nearly always able to supply just what is needed."[42] Muskoka's tourist population doubled the permanent population during the 1890s, and tripled it during the summer before the First World War. To make the most of what Potts referred to as "their harvest time," supply boat owners put in long hours six days a week and "in the rush of the season ... scarcely [got] any rest at all."[43] At J.J. Beaumont's farm, for example, butchers were up at 2:00 a.m., butchering and dressing lambs to have them in the iceboxes aboard the boat by cast off at 7:00 a.m. William Hanna's employees loaded his boat each morning at 4:30. During a busy summer, it averaged approximately sixty stops per day and often did not return to Port Carling until 10:00 p.m., when any unsold cargo had to be unloaded. On Lake Rosseau and Lake Joseph, the situation became so competitive that Hanna and Homer agreed not to run their boats on the same days.[44] Stops not only made supplies available to customers, but also made the market available to settlers looking to sell their produce. Occasionally, a stop included an exchange with "an active young fellow trundling a big wheelbarrow laden with garden stuff, monster cabbages, bunches of onions and lettuces, baskets of peas and beans, for all is grist that comes to the supply boat's mill."[45] Through their labour, boat owners and operators facilitated the construction of a rural identity based on tourism among settlers who might not otherwise have interacted directly with summer visitors.

Steamboat historian Harley Scott argues that supply boats also assumed the important role of "a social institution."[46] The exchange of local produce for badly needed cash created the space for neighbours to gather on a regular basis (see Figure 3.12). As the boat moved up and down the lake, its three-toned whistle warned of its approach. Settlers or cottagers who wanted it to stop raised a white flag to signal to the captain to pull into the closest wharf. "No sooner is their whistle heard in the distance," Fanny Potts wrote, "than the people begin to gather at the wharf, expectant."[47] The presence of the supply boat (or any steamboat for that matter) docked at one's wharf denoted social standing. Scott points out that "large docks became a status symbol, which everyone just had to have." In many cases, however, the differences of rank and privilege dissolved, because "when a prosperous cottager built a suitable dock then all his neighbours rowed over to shop on the supply boat."[48] Mabel Croucher Ames recalled

FIGURE 3.12 Crowds on the dock next to the *Mink,* Hanna's supply boat, c. 1910. Frank W. Micklethwaite. John Harold Micklethwaite fonds, PA-158130. Courtesy of Library and Archives Canada

that when "the boat would land at your dock, you would step on board, and there you would be in a small grocery store. There would be meats in the cold locker, fresh vegetables, canned goods, and all the staples." To reduce shopping times in the cramped space below the main deck, the boats compartmentalized departments, with the butcher in the bow, fresh articles in the centre, and dry goods toward the stern. Children arrived at the boat "in a perfect fever of anxiety to exchange [their five-cent pieces and coppers] for the coveted candy." Ames remembered: "It was always a big thrill for us children when the boat came in." Mothers and servants prepared lists ahead of time, and if the boat did not carry an item or had run out, they placed orders for the following visit. Ames's mother "would always buy salt pork, prunes, raisins, and sugar, along with the week's supply of flour."[49] At the same time, parents tasked older children with particular responsibilities when the boat stopped, such as refilling the coal-oil or replenishing the syrup and vinegar. Despite the flurry of activity, supply boats functioned according to an informal order, which extended beyond the floating store to manage the exchange of goods between settlers and tourists.

On the lakes, supply boats not only collapsed time and space to connect settlers and cottagers, but they often did so in such a way that all cottagers

FIGURE 3.13 Interior of the *Mink,* date unknown. *Photographer unknown. Courtesy of the Muskoka Lakes Museum Archives*

had somewhat equitable access to local produce. Cottages and hotels that were nearest to the eastern shores of the lower lakes were, generally, closest to good farmland. Thus, they potentially had first choice of the fresh produce and meat each week, thereby denying more distant households the most popular types of fruit, vegetables, and cuts of meat. In practice, however, this rarely occurred, because grocers and butchers made every effort to distribute high-demand items as fairly as possible (see Figure 3.13). As Potts recounted, Homer's supply boat butcher told one customer: "I can't give you a hind-quarter of lamb to-day, you'll have to take the forequarter. You had the hind-quarter last week. Everybody has to take their turn, for we can't grow lambs with four hind-quarters even in Muskoka."[50] Cottagers often put in special orders, but this system made it more likely that the most popular items were evenly distributed throughout the lakes.[51] Plenty of social occasions, including dances, day trips, and regattas, punctuated the summer schedule, but a visit by the supply boat was an event in and of itself.

During the last two decades of the nineteenth century, tourism had an important impact on the construction of rural identity in Muskoka near the lower lakes. The Shield frustrated settlers' efforts to construct a rural identity based on agriculture, but after 1880 tourism presented opportunities closer to the lakes that were not available in the backwoods. Visitors from cities to the south began arriving at the same time as homesteaders began living in Muskoka permanently. During the 1860s and 1870s, a few ambitious entrepreneurs opened hotels, but most settlers took little notice. During the 1880s, the trickle of summer visitors had turned into a steady flow, and the Coxes, Prowses, Crouchers, and Hannas recognized a way to make their lives on the Shield more sustainable. Working independently, but pursuing very similar arrangements, lakeside settlers aligned their household economies with the opportunities presented by tourism. By harnessing the flow of cash and credit introduced by tourists and cottagers each summer, settlers turned the Shield's environmental realities to their advantage. In some cases, they sold visitors accommodation and meals prepared with the produce from their otherwise relatively unsuccessful farms. In other cases, settlers sold their knowledge, expertise, and labour to build and repair cottages, cut ice and firewood, and provide services. The most novel approach to controlling some share of the tourism economy came from farmers and general store owners who used supply boats to link settlers' produce with cottage consumers. Many settlers also sold their land, but this provided only limited benefits. The meaningful opportunities derived from the annual, seasonal exchange with tourists and cottagers who visited every summer.

By about 1900, the stream of summer visitors had become a flood, and settlers living close to the lower lakes succeeded in constructing a rural identity based on tourism. Ironically, the environmental features of the Shield that had discouraged so many settlers during the 1870s turned out to be the same ones that attracted rich folks from the city. Settlers chose not to continue clearing their land, or did so strategically, once they discovered the region's poor soils. This seemed to satisfy urban desires for a wilderness experience, which many associated with a forested landscape. Equally ironic, the seasonal pattern of tourism in Muskoka paralleled very closely the Anishinaabe seasonal cycle of occupation. The Anishinaabeg understood the limitations of the environment for year-round habitation, and spent only part of each year on the Shield. Tourism allowed settlers to cope with this material reality by relying on the seasonal cycle of visitors with money each summer. After the turn of the century, however, settlers began to lose control of the tourism economy. Tourists still visited Muskoka and spent their money, but consumer culture, urban retailers, and fossil fuel energy steadily eroded local economic exchange in Muskoka and in many cases replaced it entirely.

4

The Promise of Wood-Resource Harvesting, 1870–1920

Weird monarchs of the forest! ye who keep
Your solemn watch betwixt the earth and sky;
I hear sad murmurs through your branches creep.
I hear the night-wind's soft and whispering sigh,
Warning ye that the spoiler's hand is nigh:
The surging wave of human life draws near!
The woodman's axe, piercing the leafy glade,
Awakes the forest-echoes far and near,
And startles in its haunts the timid deer,
Who seeks in haste some far-off friendly shade!
Nor drop ye stately Pines to earth alone.
The leafy train who shar'd your regal state –
Beech, Maple, Balsam, Spruce and Birch – lie prone,
And having grac'd your grandeur – share your fate!

–Harriet Barbara King, Letters from Muskoka

During the last three decades of the nineteenth century, as settlers discovered the region's limited agricultural potential and took advantage of tourism close to the shores of the lower lakes, many also harvested white pine lumber and hemlock bark from Muskoka's old growth forests. Alongside farming and tourism, wood-resource harvesting shaped rural identity in Muskoka. Like tourism, it generated a meaningful income and offered

The Promise of Wood-Resource Harvesting

settlers an important strategy for sedentary life on the Shield. But as is made clear in the above poem by Harriet King, whose family settled in Muskoka during the 1870s, not everyone saw the benefits of "the woodman's axe." Important distinctions existed, however, between the large-scale approach, which dominated logging in Muskoka between 1870 and 1900, and the household-based alternative, which became more important afterward. The former relied on settlers who sold their labour and farm produce to large companies and spent months felling trees in timber berths across the watershed. In the latter, settlers cut smaller quantities of trees on their own land and sold the wood resources directly to local sawmills and leather tanneries.

This chapter closely examines the small-scale approach to wood-resource harvesting performed by individual settler households in Muskoka, compares that with the large-scale commercial-industrial approach, and demonstrates that the direct sale to sawmills and tanneries of relatively modest amounts of wood resources provided year-round residents with a much more sustainable basis for constructing a rural identity on the Shield. Many settlers practised household-based logging that relied on the sale of sawlogs and tanbark to local mills and tanneries. As was the case with farming that supplemented tourism, household-based logging represented a value-added alternative to a traditional staples economy. Most of the value of the wood resources sold by settlers to sawmills and tanneries still left Muskoka, but the household-based approach reserved a greater share of the value in each tree for the person who cut it down. Men who sold trees they cut on their own land could also stay at home with their families, along with the money they earned. Individual households cut fewer trees per capita each year than logging companies, and the impact was more dispersed, resulting in less stress on the local ecosystem. By the 1920s, however, both white pine and hemlock were commercially exhausted in Muskoka and logging occupied a less prominent place than it had a generation earlier. Ultimately, the scale and kind of approach taken by lumber and tanning industries undermined a rural identity shaped by wood resource extraction, despite evidence that a more sustainable arrangement for extracting value from the region's forests existed at the household level.

Many Canadian settlers engaged in occupational pluralism.[1] They may have identified primarily as farmers (and most did in the census), but they also developed some version of the co-integration strategy discussed by Gérard Bouchard.[2] It was common for settlers to combine agricultural activity with resource extraction work in rural industries to satisfy subsistence needs and accumulate sufficient capital to support the household into the next generation. Without much else to do during the winter, or with time to spare between seeding and harvest in the summer, they generated income by selling some of the wood resources growing on their land. Rural historians, particularly those who examine New England, demonstrate that small-scale woodland exploitation provided resources, particularly for local consumption, which did not necessarily involve destructive methods or exhaustive outcomes for socioecological systems.[3] Compared with those who sold their labour to camps, Graeme Wynn argues, "those who worked [cutting trees] independently could derive even larger profits from their winter's work."[4] In the case of Ontario, Ian Radforth acknowledges that "a small proportion of the cut was made by settlers who supplied the industry from their own woodlots or homesteads," but little study has been made of this alternative approach to logging.[5]

The large-scale commercial exploitation of Muskoka's forests proved an unsustainable basis on which to construct a rural identity. It did bring some wealth into the region, but most companies eventually left and did not provide lasting economic, social, and environmental arrangements for residents. As settlers felled the trees, and the camps moved on, maintaining a sustainable relationship with the companies became increasingly difficult. The men who worked in the camps left their families to live in rough conditions for a third of the year. The removal of almost every mature tree of two key species in Muskoka – pine and hemlock – had serious impacts on the ecology, altering the composition of the forest and the nutrient levels of the lakes.

Whether Canada's trees were consumed in Britain, the American Midwest, or only a short distance from where they fell, commercial logging was rapacious.[6] It took all it could, with outcomes that generally benefitted the political and economic centres of Ottawa, Montreal, and Toronto far more than they did resource hinterlands, such as Muskoka.[7] Repeating a main argument of Harold Innis's staples thesis, Daniel Drache points out that for people living in the hinterland, "the wealth from resources, the revenues from markets, and the benefits from production flowed largely to others."[8] This was an organizing principle of a staples economy. Moreover, as Arthur Lower noted in his 1938 history of the lumber trade between Canada and the United States, "staple trades are precarious." Staples, according to Lower, "may bring great wealth quickly, they may as suddenly bring calamity. Canada has known and knows both extremes." Because Canada had limited arable land, Lower continued, its population was sparse, "and consequently the country will always have an economy that is out of balance – a large production of primary commodities and a comparatively small population. Hence it will always be dependent on outside markets. This is the key to its history and will be the key to its future."[9] Historians have debated this assessment of Canada's reliance on the staples economy, but staples production did play a major role in shaping the history of Canada.[10] In Ontario, the wealth generated by pine timber and hemlock bark contributed to a political economy that reinforced resource extraction as a primary means of social and economic development.[11] In Muskoka, however, the commercial exploitation of white pine and hemlock was entirely out of balance with the region's economic, social, and environmental arrangements. According to Lower, white pine was the focus of commercial logging during the nineteenth century "because of the quantity available but also because of its qualities. Its wood is soft and easily worked, light yet strong. It has been used ... as building timber, for ordinary lumber, for flooring, for doors and windows, for ship-building."[12] Hemlock trees were less desirable for lumber. Instead, the main purpose for commercially logging hemlock was to derive an extract from the bark, which contained a high concentration of tannins used to chemically transform animal hides into finished leather. In both cases, Muskoka lumber companies and tanneries, operating with licences from the provincial government, took as much white pine and hemlock as they possibly could for as long as it remained profitable to do so. The results were more or less the same everywhere that North Americans waged their assault on the Canadian forests.

In the early nineteenth century, commercial logging companies established themselves in Ontario along the St. Lawrence River, the lower stretches of the Ottawa River, and the north shores of Lake Ontario and Lake Erie. By the 1840s, considerable logging occurred throughout southern Ontario, including the Trent and Grand River Valleys. Logging commenced on Georgian Bay and the lower reaches of the Muskoka River watershed a decade later, when the Crown issued the first timber licences along the Moon and Musquash Rivers. Throughout the first half of the nineteenth century, logging was carried out primarily for square timber and British markets. American interest in Ontario's forests emerged during the 1850s, around the same time as logging commenced in the states bordering the Great Lakes. Consequently, timber barons built the earliest mills in Muskoka as part of a general trend to develop timber resources along eastern Georgian Bay from the Severn River to Parry Sound. In 1861, the Crown licensed timber berths in five of the surveyed Muskoka townships where access was easiest. By the end of the 1860s, even before the introduction of steamboats to the lower lakes, all the white pine greater

FIGURE 4.1 A steam tug tows a log boom across Lake Joseph, c. 1900. *Frank W. Micklethwaite. John Harold Micklethwaite fonds, PA-068422. Courtesy of Library and Archives Canada*

than a foot in diameter was gone from the shores of Lake Muskoka. However, because removing logs from the district was so difficult, very little additional logging occurred until the 1870s.[13]

The provincial government licensed timber berths in several more of Muskoka's centrally located townships during the 1870s, most of which it auctioned off in November 1871.[14] Of the 845 square miles encompassing thirteen centrally located townships, 582 square miles (roughly 69 percent, including lakes) were under licence as of the winter of 1871–72.[15] Of that area, 93 percent was controlled by two firms: the Cook Brothers (227 square miles) and Hotchkiss, Hughson and Company (315 square miles), with the rights to the other 7 percent controlled by three others.[16] A prolonged recession limited the amount of logging in Muskoka during the 1870s, but increased market demand after 1880 initiated a timber rush there. When Ontario Public Works projects connected Lakes Muskoka, Rosseau, and Joseph in the early 1870s, logging companies were able to tow enormous log booms of two hundred feet wide and five hundred feet long, some containing as many as twenty thousand logs, across the lakes to Bala Falls, where they were sent downriver to Georgian Bay (see Figure 4.1). As logging moved upstream, the cut greatly exceeded what had been available on the lower lakes.[17] Accurate statistics for Muskoka alone are

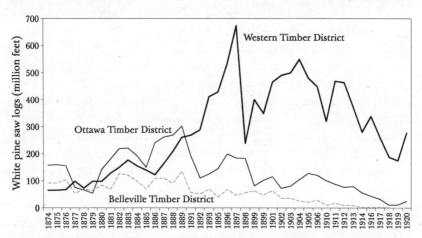

FIGURE 4.2 Feet of white pine sawlogs cut in Ontario, 1874–1920. *Ontario Sessional Papers*, 1874–1920

not available, but those for the entire Western Timber District (of which Muskoka was a major part until the end of the century) demonstrate a meteoric rise in white pine exports. In 1874, almost 400,000 white pine sawlogs were counted, amounting to almost 65 million board feet. Less than ten years later, more than three and half times as many were counted. Indeed, the general trend suggests that the companies took as much as they could as fast as they could. By about 1900, however, this was clearly on the decline, as the pine was logged out (see Figure 4.2).[18]

The Ontario government had a financial incentive to facilitate commercial logging and discourage household-based approaches. Even before it opened Muskoka for Euro-Canadian resettlement, it passed laws that privileged the large-scale commercial model and disincentivized alternatives. The Crown Timber Act of 1849 allowed private interests broad rights to dispose of timber on licensed lands but vested overall control of the land itself with the colonial government, rather than transferring those rights as private property. Maintaining control of the land allowed the Crown to regulate the industry but more importantly to retain a financial stake in the profits accruing from exploiting its forests.[19] After Confederation, this arrangement continued when the provincial government assumed control over Crown lands. By this time, however, both farmland for new immigrants and timber had become scarce in southern Ontario. As a solution, the government opened Muskoka for both colonization and commercial logging.[20]

The government received payment from logging companies for the right to cut timber on Crown lands in three ways. The first was the licence, which a company bought at auction, and for which it usually paid a bonus to outbid its competitors. The second was an annual ground rent that was calculated according to the area held under licence. And the third consisted of dues paid according to the amount of timber cut. The licence constituted a one-time fee, but the ground rents and timber dues fluctuated from year to year. The rents doubled each year that a licence holder did not use the timber berth, and the dues depended on how many trees were cut each season. The system was designed to make the provincial government a great deal of money, and it encouraged the rapid exploitation of licensed berths. As H.V. Nelles points out, in the last three decades of the nineteenth century, "bonuses, dues and ground rent from the lumber industry produced in excess of $29 million, or approximately 28 per cent of the total provincial revenue. Only the federal subsidy brought in a larger sum."[21] The Province retained the rights to forest resources and occasionally sought to regulate their exploitation, but it always treated commercial logging interests and its own governing interests as closely tied.[22]

The 1868 Act to Secure Free Grants and Homesteads to Actual Settlers on the Public Lands committed the Province to opening new lands based on the principle of private property ownership. To avoid confusion and conflict over who owned the timber rights, the Homestead Act stipulated that "all Pine trees growing or being upon any land so located ...

The Promise of Wood-Resource Harvesting

shall be considered as reserved from said location, and shall be the property of Her Majesty," with the caveat that locatees would be allowed to "cut and use such trees as may be necessary for the purpose of building, fencing, and fuel," as well as clearing land for farming.[23] Intending to derive as much public income as possible from the sale of licences, the government did not want settlers to engage in land speculation and sell the resources to which the logging companies had purchased rights. Settlers who took up free grant land were not eligible to obtain the patent to it until five years had elapsed, during which time they needed to satisfy certain requirements. Until they obtained patent, logging companies had the right to cut as many trees as they wished. In 1871, when she and her family arrived to take up land, Harriet King discovered that the sale of timber licences had "at once lost me the power of selling my pine-trees."[24] Historian Florence Murray notes that "under these regulations a law-abiding settler had little hope of reaping much profit from his [or her] pine."[25] Throughout the 1870s and 1880s, companies had rights to cut pine trees on the land where settlers located. By the time homesteaders acquired patent, most of the mature white pine was gone.[26]

By the start of the 1880s, settlers had begun to work in logging camps as a way of supporting their families. Companies generally built camps next to rivers and streams and pushed farther up the watershed as the timber was cut. Camps usually consisted of a stable for the horses, a series of buildings for the blacksmith, foreman, and cookhouse, and cambooses for sleeping.[27] Logging was a winter activity because sap stopped running and it was easier for men, oxen, and horses to move logs when snow covered the ground. The foreman and a skeleton crew set up camps at the end of September, and the rest of the logging gangs arrived not long after the agricultural harvest at the end of October. Until the first months of winter, twenty- or thirty-man crews cut down and prepared an average of sixty logs per day. By the beginning of February, the snow was usually deep enough for the focus to switch from log cutting to log hauling, skidding, and piling. When the ice began to break up in late April or early May, crews dumped the logs into the water, and rivermen floated them downstream to the open lakes, where steamers collected them into booms and towed them to mills in Gravenhurst (see Figure 4.3).[28]

With few other options to generate income, wages earned in logging camps became an important part of the local economy and shaped the rural identity of Muskoka settlers for more than a generation. This was especially true in the backwoods, where the opportunities from tourism emerged much later, if at all. Logging operations were ephemeral, however,

FIGURE 4.3 Logs blocking the South Muskoka River, 1918. *John Boyd. John Boyd fonds, PA-071083. Courtesy of Library and Archives Canada*

and they placed burdens on families even as they provided income. Initially, logging took place in or close to settled townships, and men could return home for visits. But, as operations pushed farther upstream, wage labour in camps pulled men away from their families for as much as a third of the year and immersed them in all-male environments.[29] "In some cases," writes Graeme Wynn, "home and work were separate in the extreme."[30] In early-nineteenth-century New Brunswick, husbands and wives might not see each other for as much as ten months. Thus, a significant part of each logger's identity involved spending time with other loggers. Harriet King, who settled with her family in Stephenson Township in 1871, conveyed the hardships endured by wives and children in this situation. Even before the first snowfall, King recalled, the typical settler hired by the camps "starts for the lumber-shanties, and receiv[es] from twenty to twenty-five dollars a month and his food." Equally arduous was the "very hard and anxious life for the wife and children, left to shift for themselves throughout the long dreary winter, too often on a very slender provision of flour and potatoes and little else."[31] Regardless of how families felt about the absence of the men, working in logging camps and earning wages posed constant challenges.

Commercial logging relied on socioeconomic power structures that created what Wynn calls "a full-time lumbering proletariat."[32] For most loggers across North America, as historian Joseph Conlin reveals, "wages

The Promise of Wood-Resource Harvesting   113

were not good, well into the twentieth century. Employment was unsteady; job security did not exist. Bunkhouse conditions appalled the roughest of outsiders."[33] Wages earned from camp work supplemented household incomes but rarely provided enough for families to live on.[34] According to a Department of Labour report titled *Wage Rates and Salaries,* choppers in Ontario received $26 (including board) per month in 1914, barely more than what King says men were paid forty years earlier.[35] In Muskoka, a chopper's wages were often less than what a settler could earn by selling logs cut from his own land. Moreover, husbands and fathers often spent a portion of their wages on equipment and gear, and occasionally squandered their earnings on alcohol. During the 1870s, several roadside taverns popped up that catered to labourers.[36] Working for pay far from home meant that wages did not always make it home.

The work itself was among the most, if not *the* most, labour-intensive jobs in Muskoka. The various tasks involved in commercial logging required between eight and twelve calories of muscle energy per minute, between one and a half to six times more than was needed to perform other jobs in North America. Drilling coal, for example, used four calories per minute.[37] Depending on the length of the work day, loggers required six to nine thousand calories every day to sustain the energy necessary for chopping, trimming, squaring, hauling, skidding, and piling logs. This required what Conlin refers to as "vast *fueling*."[38] For most of the nineteenth century, apart from the occasional serving of game meat or fish, loggers ate very little fresh food. Diets began to change into the twentieth century (even as white pine and logging began to wane in Muskoka), but during the 1870s and 1880s, camps had little or no vegetables, fruit, eggs, or milk.[39] Throughout a season, a camp of thirty men and their horses consumed approximately thirty-six barrels of pork, ten barrels of beef, thirty-four barrels of flour, seventy-six bushels of potatoes, twenty tons of hay, four hundred bags of oats, and four hundred bags of chop.[40] Given that dozens of camps were scattered throughout the region, the scale of provisions was immense.

At first, local produce failed to meet the needs of the camps. Overtime, however, it became harder and less profitable for the same settlers to sell their produce to camps. In 1862, an average Muskoka household produced less than seven bushels of oats, an important staple that fed men and horses in the camps.[41] In 1866, the supervisor of colonization roads, J.W. Bridgland, observed that "the whole market produce of all the settlers on one of these roads [along which logging companies brought in their provisions] would very little exceed (and in some instances it would fall below) the amount required to supply the united gangs of the adjacent lumberers."[42] Even by 1871, when the census first captured Muskoka's agricultural production, farmers were barely growing enough oats and hay to meet the needs of logging camps. Townships closest to the lower lakes produced twenty-eight bushels of oats per household, whereas the average backwoods township household produced just thirteen. Likewise, hay production near the lower lakes averaged 3.8 tons per household, but backwoods households produced less than half a ton each. By 1891, settlers were producing far more than the camps needed, and as the logging frontier moved east, backwoods settlers now enjoyed more opportunities to sell their potatoes, oats, and hay.[43] Perhaps for a few years, the camps provided an excellent market for local produce, but this did not persist. Shortly after the turn of the century, this option was largely eliminated as commercial logging exhausted the merchantable pine forests.

Large-scale commercial logging also affected the way in which people imagined the landscape. Many settlers perceived the forest as an impediment to farming. But as Claire Campbell shows for Georgian Bay, the opening of the region for settlement coincided with, and in many ways made possible, the establishment of the white pine as a symbol of the rugged beauty of the Ontario wilderness.[44] In 1871, as Harriet King observed the hardships that logging imposed on her neighbours, she also presented the pine as a symbol of untouched nature and a victim of exploitation. She did not find the Canadian forest "half as beautiful as I had been led to expect," but she could not help noticing that "there are certainly some very tall pines, and they are of a considerable girth."[45] In her 1878 memoir, King included the "Sonnet to the Muskoka Pines" that opens this chapter and laments the impact of logging. In it, she describes pine trees as "monarchs of the forest" that were under threat from "the spoiler's hand," "the surging wave of human life," and "the woodman's axe."[46] The emphasis on the pine reveals that for King, and many others like her, this species was the most appealing feature of the forest, and its steady decline was a nostalgic signal of humanity's destructive effect on the natural world. As Seymour Penson, the son of an original settler, noted in 1910, picturesque images of Muskoka conveyed no memory of "the great white pines that sprang up higher [on the islands] than their neighbours on the shores, or towered majestically upon the highest ridges inland."[47] The fate of the white pine became a warning about the decline of valuable resources that forestry experts and government officials had previously thought inexhaustible.

The Promise of Wood-Resource Harvesting

Change is normal in all ecosystems, including the Great Lakes–St. Lawrence forest. They are dynamic and they experience a variety of significant and unpredictable influences from fire, insects, diseases, and weather, which affect their composition to varying degrees over time and from place to place.[48] In some cases, these disturbances are equal to, or greater than, those caused by humans. Approximately 4,800 years ago, for instance, an unknown pathogen decimated the hemlocks in eastern North America.[49] Major events, such as the hemlock decline, produce carry-over effects, including a sharp reduction in evapotranspiration, increased catchment erosion, and greater nutrient deposition in lakes. But the risk of fundamental shifts in forest ecology as a result of anthropogenic disturbances is much greater than from natural events, which background variability smooths.[50] For example, after stripping trees of their branches and canopies, logging gangs discarded the slash, which greatly increased the risk of catastrophic forest fires.[51] In the summer, many months after they had removed the timber, slash acted like "a powder-train in igniting the whole region."[52] Because loggers typically selected the most mature trees, the probability of good seed years diminished significantly. Seedlings that did take root required twenty-five disturbance-free years before they could produce seeds of their own. Under these conditions, large conflagrations often followed logging, which sterilized entire landscapes and prevented the forest from regenerating or altered its composition.[53] On the Precambrian Shield, a new forest complex dominated by hardwood deciduous species typically followed the removal of softwood trees, such as pine and hemlock.[54] Pine grows well in areas that are disturbed by windblow rather than logging, but it usually does not return where forest fires destroy conditions for regrowth.[55] Hemlock tends to do well on shallow, wet soils, is intolerant of burning, and may take centuries to recover its former abundance after intense fires.[56]

Logging altered more than the terrestrial components of the forest. Historical geographer J. David Wood points out that "timber exploitation had perhaps an even greater effect on the waterways ... through the scouring and gouging of river banks, by rolled or dragged logs; damming and diverting streams to expedite the logrush; and sedimenting of lakes and streams with eroded soil, 'deadheads,' and debris from felled trees."[57] Forests are critical to the hydrological cycle. They regulate watershed flow rates by slowing run-off during and after large rainfall events. Leaves, decaying vegetation, and the root structures of living plants absorb much of the water, obstructing the flow into rivers and streams. Tree cover on the banks of streams and rivers also provides shade, keeping the water cool and preventing nutrient loading from run-off and erosion. Both water temperature and nutrient levels are critical components of water quality that shape habitat conditions in the nutrient-poor lakes on the Shield.[58]

Analysis of the diatoms in a core sample taken from one of Muskoka's larger lakes displays the low nutrient levels that were characteristic of oligotrophic lakes on the Shield until about 1870, when Euro-Canadian resettlement and logging commenced in the area.[59] Around this date, phosphorous concentrations approximately doubled, significantly changing nutrient availability in the lake and reducing deep water oxygen and water quality. In another study, limnologist R.L. France examined the effects of logging on the habitat of aquatic organisms called macrophytes that consume woody debris. The author determined that macrophytes struggled to survive during the years after intensive logging, adding pressure to lake system health.[60] Yet both the diatom and macrophyte studies also suggest that aquatic ecosystems in Muskoka, and the Shield more generally, did not suffer in a consistent or irreversible way due to commercial logging. Indeed, a study of its impact on thirteen Muskoka lakes revealed that phosphorous concentrations (a measure of the nutrient content of lakes) generally went down, not up, after the arrival of European settlers. They declined in seven lakes, rose in four, and remained unchanged in two. When settlers and loggers removed the trees, less organic material was available to contribute to phosphorous loading in the lakes, and concentrations decreased relative to those after the Second World War, when regrowth began to introduce more leaf litter into the nutrient cycle.[61] During colonization, phosphorous concentrations in Muskoka lakes tended to spike, before declining to below pre-industrial levels owing to a reduction in the total biomass available as a result of land clearance and large-scale commercial logging.

In the space of roughly fifty years, from the late 1850s to the turn of the century, logging removed much of Muskoka's merchantable white pine. Logging had been the primary reason for the introduction of the first steamer in 1866, the interconnection of the lower lakes in 1871–72, and the construction of the Northern Railway to Gravenhurst in 1875. These developments benefitted residents and supported the region's economy, but the harvests of Muskoka's forests left few lasting economic, social, or environmental arrangements. This approach provided settlers with only short-lived opportunities to sell their labour or farm produce to camps, and pulled fathers and husbands away from their families in the process. In altering forest composition and lake system ecology, large-scale logging had detrimental impacts on the environment. At the same time, however, many households practised alternatives to the commercial approach, which created more sustainable opportunities.

As larger numbers of settlers acquired patents to their land, and logging camps moved deeper into the backwoods, sawmills began purchasing a greater share of logs from local households.[62] Beyond Muskoka, as Béatrice Craig and Graeme Wynn demonstrate, sawmills played "a pivotal role in integrating the agricultural and the lumbering sectors of the economy."[63] Because individual settlers were exempt from the licensing system, logging became an unrivalled "means for the ordinary man to acquire capital."[64] Unfortunately, no records survive that could illuminate the relationship between Muskoka sawmills and local households during the first generation of Euro-Canadian resettlement. But a ledger from the Snider Lumber Company, kept between 1902 and 1907, sheds light on the household-based approach to logging in Muskoka.

In 1877, brothers Elias and William Snider, both prominent businessmen and politicians in Waterloo, Ontario, purchased land and built a sawmill near the north end of Lake Rosseau. In partnership with Peter Mutchenbacker, who had taken up a nearby lot, they started the Snider Lumber Company. Around 1895, the Sniders sold their share of the mill to Mutchenbacker's two sons, Asa and Herman, who consolidated their business in Gravenhurst, where they owned another larger mill. The Mutchenbackers and Sniders maintained a close business relationship until 1903, when the Mutchenbacker brothers sold the mill to their father, who eventually sold it to the Kaufman Furniture Company of Berlin, Ontario. At its height, the mill cut as much as 1.5 million board feet of lumber every year and employed fifteen to twenty men (see Figure 4.4).[65]

The Snider Lumber Company accounts reveal that selling logs cut from their own land or from their neighbours' land provided individual households with a measure of economic stability. For settlers, this relationship established more sustainable economic, social, and environmental arrangements than those that arose from selling their labour and supplies to logging camps. Snider held accounts with approximately six hundred people and companies from all over Muskoka, southern Ontario, and a few locations in Upstate New York. In addition to timber acquired from berths in Muskoka, Snider purchased many logs from households around the lower lakes and sold the finished lumber by railcar to businesses and individuals throughout southern Ontario, via the head office in Waterloo. Between January 1902 and April 1907, Snider purchased nearly $67,000 worth of logs from 158 people in seven Muskoka townships. Not every location of

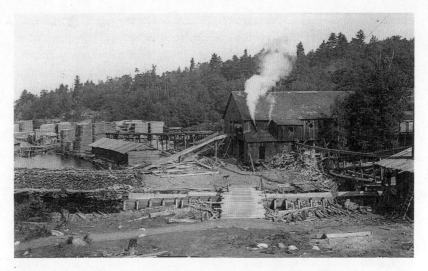

FIGURE 4.4 Kaufman sawmill, c. 1908. *Frank W. Micklethwaite. John Harold Micklethwaite fonds, PA-158659. Courtesy of Library and Archives Canada*

these individuals can be identified, but 75 households emerge when the Snider accounts are cross-referenced with census returns and the 1879 *Guide Book and Atlas of Muskoka*. During the sixty-four months for which records exist, 84 percent of the 75 households sold an average of $172 logs each, totalling just 16 percent of the amount spent by Snider. Over the same period, the other 16 percent of households sold an average of $1,374 logs each, totalling 25 percent of the amount spent by Snider. Thus, households that were capable of producing large quantities of logs each season could earn a significant income, but most sold just a handful of logs from their property.

General store accounts from the time reveal that log sales covered a significant portion of household expenditures. For example, in January 1906, Snider purchased $65.82 of hemlock logs from Julius Grenkie in Cardwell Township.[66] Nine years earlier, in 1897, Grenkie purchased $93.46 worth of goods from Homer's general store in Rosseau.[67] If Grenkie's 1897 account with Homer is typical of his expenses in later years, his 1906 sale of logs to Snider amounted to 70 percent of a year's expenses at the store. Similarly, Alex Phillips of Humphrey Township sold Snider $282.53 of pine and hemlock logs in the winter of 1902.[68] Four years earlier, in 1898, Phillips bought a total of $105.97 worth of goods from Homer.[69] His sale of logs to Snider amounted to more than 250 percent of his household's

The Promise of Wood-Resource Harvesting   119

annual expenses at the store. Had these men been working as choppers in a logging camp, Grenkie would have needed more than two months, and Phillips more than two years, to earn what they received from selling logs to Snider.[70] Equally important, households could have continued this scale of cutting on hundred-acre lots almost indefinitely. Assuming that the logs sold to Snider were eighteen inches in diameter and forty feet long, and that each log equalled one tree, Grenkie would have required approximately sixteen hemlocks for his sale in 1906, and Phillips would have required about twenty-one pines and thirty-four hemlocks for his sale in 1902.[71] Even just a few logs cut from private lots each season contributed substantially to a typical settler's annual household budget, while placing little pressure on the local forest ecology.

The combined total of all the logs that Snider acquired from households put only a modest demand on the forest ecology of Muskoka (see Figure 4.5). Of the seventy-five households identified in the ledger, fifty-one sold fewer than 100 logs to Snider between 1902 and 1907, requiring an average footprint of 2.27 acres each. At the upper end, only ten households sold between 150 and 500 logs (an average footprint of 16.0 acres), and just three sold more than 500 logs (an average footprint of 51.6 acres). A majority of sales came from settlers who cut only a few trees on their land; very few came from those who were engaged in significant logging operations. Snider bought mainly hemlock logs from these households because the pine was almost completely exhausted. In the winter of 1903–4, the company purchased approximately 1,114 thousand board feet (mbf) of hemlock, equal to roughly 2,102 logs, from local settlers. The following winter, that number rose to 2,922 mbf from 5,513 logs, before declining to 1,309 mbf from 2,470 logs in 1905–6.[72] This was a large amount of hemlock, but when the impact is spread over the entire area from which the company obtained logs, it placed fewer pressures on the ecosystem than large-scale commercial logging, which removed all mature pine timber from entire swathes of the forest.

Environmental factors, particularly soil quality, also influenced how many logs settlers sold during these years. Sixty-four percent of the money Snider paid to these seventy-five individuals went to purchasing logs in two townships (Watt and Medora) with a considerable shoreline on the lower lakes.[73] Although 49 percent of the individuals who sold logs to Snider lived in Watt Township, their sales represented only 29 percent of the total value of the logs it purchased from households. By contrast, 19 percent of households were in Medora Township, where 35 percent of the value of logs originated. With some of the best farmland in Muskoka,

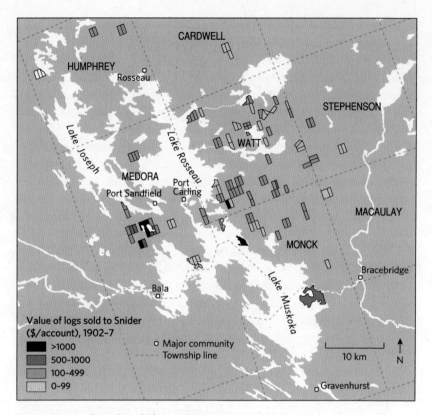

FIGURE 4.5 Settlers who sold logs to Snider, 1902–7. *"Accounts Ledger for Gravenhurst Sawmill of Snider Lumber Company, 1902–1907."* Archives of the Muskoka Steamship and Historical Society. Adapted by Eric Leinberger.

settlers in Watt probably earned a sufficient income from farming and so had less need to sell logs to Snider. Watt also contained two large lakes that emptied into Lake Rosseau, where settlers must have found it relatively easy to transport logs downstream to sell at Snider's mill on this lake. In Medora Township, the soils were poor, making the average household there somewhat more dependent on selling logs to make ends meet than their neighbours in Watt Township. Households generated meaningful income from the sale of logs, but the environmental impact of this practice appears to have been smallest and most dispersed in places with better soils.

Unfortunately, there are no reliable sources to show how small-scale, household-based logging fared after 1910. The census includes useful data for forest products from farms, but in 1901 these data are available only at the aggregate district level, and the fifteen Muskoka townships under study here are split between three districts, each of which included many townships that were not in Muskoka. Comparing the 1911 and 1921 censuses is made almost impossible by the fact that forest products are listed in cubic feet of timber and board feet of logs for lumber in 1911 and then simply as logs for lumber in 1921.[74] Nevertheless, it is safe to conclude that settlers found it increasingly difficult to sell logs to local sawmills. After commercial logging exhausted the merchantable white pine, sawmills purchased greater quantities of hemlock for a short time. Between 1903 and 1907, hemlock represented anywhere from one-third to three-quarters of the logs bought from the seventy-five households identified in the Snider ledger. However, hemlock logs brought fewer profits for the industry, and the switch to hemlock signalled its decline in Muskoka. The Snider Lumber Company, for example, closed its sawmill in Gravenhurst in 1910.[75] During the first decade of the twentieth century, the dwindling volume and size of merchantable timber could no longer support the large operations that characterized the industry, and sawmilling in Muskoka shrank by 75 percent.[76] New demand for hardwood sawlogs emerged during the early twentieth century, which supported smaller enterprises, such as the Muskoka Wood Product Company. It is tempting to interpret the general waning of the industry as a sign that household-based approaches to logging were no more sustainable than their large-scale counterparts. However, we must not confuse the potential for the former to maintain these arrangements over time with the decision by the companies to leave Muskoka when the pursuit of profit demanded that they move elsewhere. Had the provincial government allowed settlers, rather than large companies, to cut the pine on their own land, the household-based approach might have emerged earlier and lasted longer than it did. Commercial logging accounted for a much larger proportion of Muskoka's economy by extracting the region's white pine as quickly as possible, but individual households tended to log in a much more sustainable way. The people who cut and sold their own trees were able to remain with their families during the winter, received a greater share of the value of each tree, and dispersed the effects of their cutting over a bigger area.

The exploitation of hemlock bark by Muskoka's leather-tanning industry also lent stability to a rural economy and identity that were heavily reliant on agroforestry, but it proved just as ephemeral as pine logging, given its scale and pace of exploitation. In 1877, George Beardmore established Muskoka's first tannery, in Bracebridge. Originally from Liverpool, Beardmore arrived in Canada in 1843, built a tannery in Hamilton in 1844, and later bought another in Acton, Ontario. Disappearing forests in southern

FIGURE 4.6 Muskoka Leather Company tannery, Bracebridge, 1910. *Phillips and Wrinch, Ltd. Baldwin Collection of Canada, PCR-175. Courtesy of Toronto Public Library*

Ontario around the mid-century also meant disappearing tannin supplies. Hemlock bark contains 8–10 percent tannin, a chemical that is used in processing animal hides into leather. Consequently, Beardmore looked north to Muskoka, where hemlock was abundant. Attracted by Bracebridge's offer of $2,000 and a ten-year tax exemption for his company, Beardmore located his new tannery (later renamed the Muskoka Leather Company) near the region's extensive stands of hemlock. Raw hides were shipped into Muskoka by rail, processed into rough leather, and transported to factories in Acton and, later, Toronto (see Figure 4.6).[77]

In the late 1880s, another prominent leather manufacturer, Shaw, Cassils and Company, toured Muskoka, looking to benefit from the same arrangements that Beardmore had secured a decade earlier. From Massachusetts, the Shaws moved part of the family business to Montreal, and at the company's height operated sixteen tanneries in Quebec and Ontario.[78] In 1891, the company built a tannery in Huntsville, having received a ten-year tax exemption.[79] Shortly afterward, it acquired a second tannery in Bracebridge.[80] In 1905, the Shaws renamed it the Anglo-Canadian Leather Company. Thus, at the beginning of the twentieth century, two tanneries operated on opposite sides of the Muskoka River in Bracebridge, with a third in Huntsville. Like logging, the tanning industry contributed meaningfully to the construction of rural identity in Muskoka, but it had similar economic, social, and environmental consequences.

The Muskoka tanning industry operated year-round and processed a considerable number of hides.[81] In 1906, Anglo-Canadian tanned approximately 313,000.[82] One local historian estimates that the three tanneries together could have processed as many as 10,000 hides per week, and the *Bracebridge Gazette* claimed that Muskoka Leather put out "750 sides per day."[83] Muskoka supplied the hemlock, but it certainly could not supply the hundreds of thousands of cowhides processed by these factories every year. The need for so many hides embedded Muskoka's economy in a transnational flow of resource commodities from all over the world, including China, India, South America, the United States, western Canada, and Ontario. One former employee estimated that the hides came from Toronto packing house plants (25 percent), western Canadian packing house plants (25 percent), the United States (20 percent), South America (20 percent), and New Zealand, northern Italy, Switzerland, and Germany (10 percent combined).[84] Processing so many hides consumed a tremendous volume of hemlock bark.

In many ways, the destruction of the region's hemlock resembled that of the pine. It supplemented household incomes at a critical time during the agricultural calendar. Between the middle of May and the start of August, four-man teams known as "bark gangs" harvested tanbark when the bark was most supple and farmers had time between seeding and harvest. This arrangement still took them away from home for extended periods, but wives and children experienced fewer hardships than when the men spent the winter months in the logging camps, especially since provisions were generally easier to obtain in summer. According to local historian Gail Smith, hemlock bark was cut in four-foot lengths and could be anywhere from one to three and a half inches thick. Each tree usually supplied between ten and fifteen lengths of tanbark. Assuming an average diameter of eighteen inches per hemlock, each cord of tanbark (four feet high by four feet wide by four feet long) required roughly 9.1 trees. Herbert Hergert, a historian of the tanning industry in the United States, estimates that two and a half cords of bark were required to process a hundred hides.[85] In 1879, the Beardmore tannery in Bracebridge processed approximately 160,000 hides (about 3,000 per week) using 4,000 cords of bark, which would have required an estimated 36,400 hemlock trees.[86] Twenty-seven years later, in 1906, at the height of the tanning industry in

Muskoka, Anglo-Canadian processed an astonishing 313,000 hides at its Huntsville tannery. At a broad estimate, between 1879 and 1891 (when the Huntsville tannery was built), an average of 53,800 hemlocks was cut each year to feed the single tannery in Bracebridge.[87] Between 1892 and 1895 (when Anglo-Canadian opened a second tannery in Bracebridge), an average of 107,600 hemlocks was required every year to supply the two tanneries. And, after 1895 until some time after the First World War, when production began to falter in Muskoka, an average of 161,400 hemlock trees was felled each year to tan leather.[88] At a rough estimate, the three tanneries consumed bark from over 4.5 million hemlocks between 1879 and 1918.

Few sources shed light on the pattern of hemlock bark harvesting practised by the gangs, and no contracts with the tanneries have survived to provide reliable details. But a ledger from Muskoka Leather, listing accounts between July 1905 and August 1906, gives some clues. Every week, an entry was made under the heading "Bark Ticket a/c [account]," indicating the number and price of cords bought by the company. Bark gangs purchased tickets, which entitled them to cut hemlock on company lands and timber berths. The gangs then sold the tanbark to the company at a price slightly above the going rate for tanbark purchased from local households.[89] In the year between 17 August 1905 and 18 August 1906, Muskoka Leather bought 2,021 cords via the bark ticket account, approximately 27 percent of its estimated needs.[90] The company made nearly two-thirds of the purchases during the winter months, suggesting that most of the tanbark obtained through the bark ticket account was cut inland – rather than close to the lakeshore, where company scows could retrieve it during the summer – and brought to the tannery only when snow made overland transport by sleigh easier. According to its ledger, Muskoka Leather also owned sixteen hundred-acre lots spread through six townships. All but two were well back from the water. Muskoka Leather also held rights to timber berths in the unoccupied portions of Medora and Freeman Townships, west of the lower lakes, and shared an agreement with the Conger Lumber Company for the rights to hemlock trees in the licensed parts of Conger Township, also west of the lower lakes.[91] A typical gang cut about six and a half cords of tanbark per day, requiring fifty-nine hemlocks.[92] In 1879, a local newspaper advertisement announced that Muskoka Leather would pay $3.00 per cord if the bark were delivered to the tannery in Bracebridge and $2.25 per cord if it were delivered to a lakeshore location where a company scow could collect it (see Figure 4.7).[93] If all of Beardmore's tanbark (four thousand cords) came from the gangs,

The Promise of Wood-Resource Harvesting

FIGURE 4.7 A group sitting next to the shore at Lake Rosseau, with the town of Rosseau in the background, c. 1908. At the right, a scow is piled with hemlock tanbark. *Frank W. Micklethwaite. John Harold Micklethwaite fonds, PA-158653. Courtesy of Library and Archives Canada*

he would have paid between $9,000 and $12,000 to thirty-two men, with each man earning between $280 and $375, depending on where the cords were delivered.[94] This model was relatively intensive, since the gangs had an incentive to cut as much bark as they could during the brief period between mid-May and the end of July. They worked long hours, and until a market developed for hemlock timber after 1900, the logs themselves were left in the woods.[95] The inevitable result was a rapid depletion of hemlocks in Muskoka by the early 1920s.

The detrimental effects of tanning operations were not limited to the forests. Large-scale tanneries also produced great volumes of waste, the sheer scale of which must have had a deleterious effect on the aquatic environment downstream. Tanning leather involved transforming the collagen proteins of hides into insoluble material through the absorption of tannic acid. The companies produced the acid by dissolving the tannins from vegetable matter, in this case hemlock bark, in warm water – much like steeping tea. The hides, which first underwent a week-long process to remove hair and flesh, were suspended in vats of tanning liquor, after which the leather was bleached, oiled, and dried before being rolled, pressed, graded, and shipped to factories, where it was turned into finished products. The entire process took between sixty and eighty days.[96] Other methods used chrome or resin extracts to produce soft leather suitable for clothing, bags, and shoe uppers. Hemlock tannins produced a hard, reddish leather used in shoe soles, mechanical belts, harnesses, and upholstery. Once the tanneries were finished with the bark, its disposal presented problems. Some was loaded onto scows and sold to cottagers and resorts as a lining for paths and walkways.[97] But even greater quantities often found their way into the water. As late as 1919, a board member of the Muskoka Lakes Association witnessed tannery employees dumping "a deposit [of bark] a foot deep on one of the Bark Scows into the water."[98]

After tanbark had been brought in and leather sent out, the tanneries were also left with liquid waste by-products. In Pennsylvania, heavy tanneries produced an average of 730 gallons of effluent for every hundred hides processed.[99] If this ratio applies in the Muskoka tanneries, Anglo-Canadian generated approximately 2.3 million gallons of effluent in 1906, the equivalent of 44,000 gallons every week. According to New York City merchant Jackson Smith Schultz, whose father operated a Pennsylvania tannery during the second half of the nineteenth century, exhausted lime and sodium sulphide solution (used to remove the hair and flesh from hides) and all the "sweepings and scrapings" were combined with spent tanning liquor in large reservoirs and spread on farmers' fields as fertilizer.[100] However, there is no evidence that this occurred in Muskoka.[101] Enormous amounts of wastes were held onsite in vats and pits before being simply dumped into the river, releasing a toxic soup of animal fats, biodegradable organic matter, heavy metals, and poisonous chemicals that flowed downstream.[102] The ongoing anaerobic activity necessary for microbial decomposition of the organic waste – the most benign by-product dumped into the river – meant that aquatic organisms suffered significantly from drastically reduced oxygen levels in the water.[103] Surprisingly, local histories do not mention the pollution, and no scientific studies have been carried out to determine its impact on the local ecology. Since the Muskoka River flows relatively swiftly, much of the waste from the Bracebridge tanneries would have been carried downstream. Like the logging industry, tanning seriously damaged a single species of the Great Lakes–St. Lawrence forest in Muskoka, and the toxins it poured into the river resulted in ecological damage downstream.

Just as with logging, large-scale tanbark collection had a more sustainable alternative. Muskoka Leather and Anglo-Canadian both purchased some bark from settlers who worked on their own. Households generally produced fewer cords each season than the average member of a gang, and the volume never accounted for a majority of the bark procured by the companies. Still, their sale generated important family income even as it

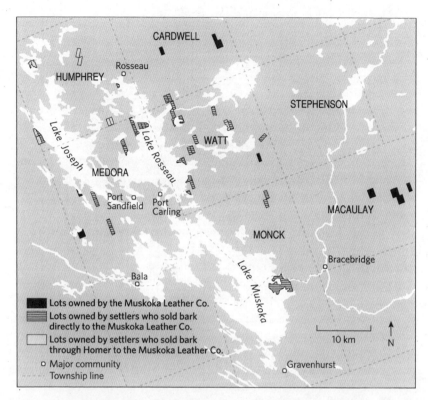

FIGURE 4.8 Locations where the Muskoka Leather Company sourced tanbark, 1886–1906. *"Muskoka Leather Company Ledger, July 1905–August 1906." Courtesy of Muskoka Lakes Museum Archives. Adapted by Eric Leinberger*

reduced the scale and dispersed the environmental impact of the industry. According to a tannery journal, between July and October 1886 Muskoka Leather bought tanbark from seventeen households around the lower lakes, totalling 741 cords, roughly 13 percent of its bark needs that year (see Figure 4.8).[104] Two households sold more than 100 cords, and nine sold fewer than 30.[105] Similarly, between 1897 and 1899, the Homer general store in Rosseau served as a middleman for sales of tanbark from local households to Muskoka Leather.[106] In 1897, nine households sold 264 cords, an average of 29 each. In 1898, nine households sold 271 cords, an average of 30 each. And, in 1899, the average dropped to 20 when twelve households sold 197 cords. Over these three years, only six households sold more than 50 cords through Homer to Muskoka Leather, and eleven sold fewer than 10. Much more bark not mentioned in these sources came in from other settlers, but this sample provides a glimpse into household-based approaches to bark cutting in Muskoka during the late nineteenth and early twentieth centuries.

During an 1899 trip through Muskoka, G. Mercer Adam learned that "the bark of the [hemlock] is to the settler no inconsiderable source of revenue at the hands of the tanner."[107] If the price paid by Beardmore in 1879 is taken as the price paid by Muskoka Leather seven years later (perhaps a slightly low estimate), the average household earned approximately $102 by selling bark in 1886. Between 1897 and 1899, the average household earned between $58 and $99 per year by selling tanbark. In 1899, Joseph Paisley sold 13.5 cords of bark through Homer to Muskoka Leather for $47.25. This amount covered almost a third of Paisley's entire $165 account with Homer's store that year. The same year, Louis Phillips sold 55 cords of bark for $192.50, more than enough to cover his $134 debit with Homer.[108] Rather than committing all their energies to cutting as much bark as quickly as possible, individual settlers cut a portion from their property to supplement their household economies. If 1886 and 1897–99 are indicative of their tanbark collection patterns at the turn of the century, it is safe to say that they typically cut anywhere between 161 and 355 hemlock trees each year that they engaged in the trade.[109] When compared to the 500 cords (approximately 4,550 trees) cut every season by the average gang, these are considerably smaller totals. Moreover, whereas the gangs removed all the hemlock in an area, the household-based approach spread out the impacts of tanbark harvesting across multiple locations around the lakes. As these examples demonstrate, without having a devastating impact on the forest, settlers supplemented their budgets very nicely by cutting down a few dozen hemlock trees and selling the bark to a tannery.

Eventually, however, the tanning industry in Bracebridge and Huntsville exhausted the hemlock, just as the logging industry had the pine. In 1906, a *Huntsville Forester* article reported somewhat naively "the glad realization ... that there is no probable limitation to [hemlock's] continued existence and usefulness. Unlike the lumbering industry, there is no possibility of the supply of raw material failing."[110] Between 1901 and 1911, the tanbark cut throughout Muskoka declined by 75 percent.[111] In and of itself, this does not necessarily mean that the hemlock was running out, but other evidence suggests that was the case. Three maps of Anglo-Canadian tanneries, one for Bracebridge and two for Huntsville, illustrate a move away from hemlock after the turn of the century. An 1896 map of the Bracebridge tannery shows nineteen tanbark sheds. Fifteen years later, in Huntsville, there were just four. And ten years after that, the Huntsville factory had removed the sheds (see Figures 4.9, 4.10, and 4.11).[112] Shortly after the end of the First World War, the tanneries began switching to mineral-based (particularly chromium-based) and high-concentrate imported vegetable-based tannins, presumably in response to rising costs associated with the increasing scarcity of hemlock bark.[113] With insufficient hemlock bark coming from the forest, the company removed the sheds and repurposed the space. The hemlock was the reason for locating the tanneries in Muskoka. Once it ran out, the purpose for being in Muskoka

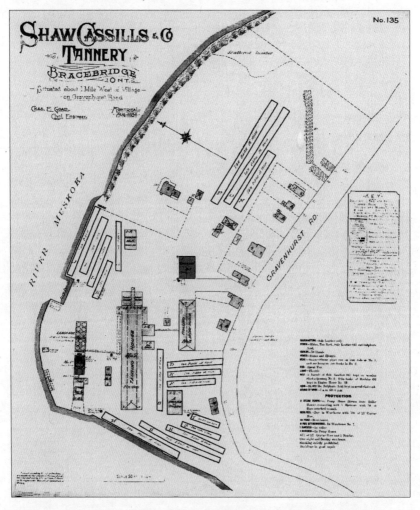

FIGURE 4.9 The Anglo-Canadian Leather Company tannery in Bracebridge, 1896. Sheds indicated in bold outline. *Author's private collection*

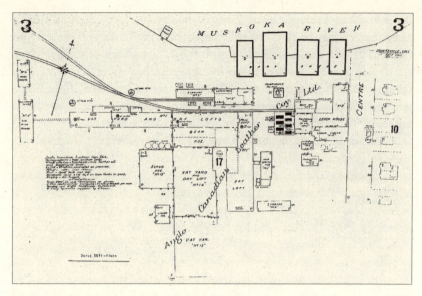

FIGURE 4.10 The Anglo-Canadian Leather Company tannery in Huntsville, 1911. Sheds indicated in bold outline. *Anglo-Canadian Binder, Muskoka Heritage Place Archives*

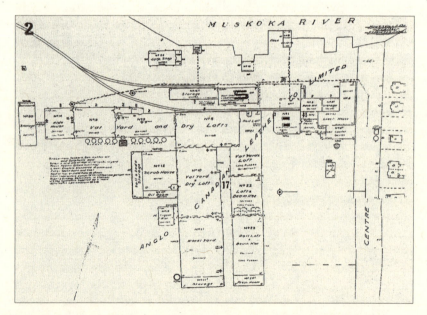

FIGURE 4.11 The Anglo-Canadian Leather Company tannery in Huntsville, 1921. *Anglo-Canadian Binder, Muskoka Heritage Place Archives*

The Promise of Wood-Resource Harvesting 131

expired too. Although the Huntsville tannery remained in business until the 1960s, both hides and tannins were imported. After the 1920s, Anglo-Canadian needed Muskoka solely to serve as a sink for its waste.

Individual settlers located on free grant land during the late nineteenth century could not sell the pine they cut on their land. But large logging companies could, and did. Aided by the provincial government, which saw the profits of these companies as a vehicle for generating public revenues, the logging industry promptly entered Muskoka's forests and quickly cut as much pine timber as it could. Since settlers were prohibited from selling their own trees, they were forced to sell their labour to logging camps instead. They cut trees for the companies if they hoped to benefit at all from the commodification of the region's extremely valuable pine. Throughout the late nineteenth century, white pine was Muskoka's most important staple export. Shortly after 1900, by which time settlers had obtained the patents to their land and were legally allowed to sell it, the pine was gone. The logging and tanning industries removed most mature trees of two species, but the scale and kind of logging employed also had serious economic, social, and ecological effects on the environment and people living in Muskoka. Large forest fires, substantial erosion, and post-harvest mortality all followed the intensive logging methods of these companies. To generate income during the winter, men left home to work in logging camps.

Despite this relationship with logging operations, many households also demonstrated a different pattern of timber extraction, which offered more sustainable arrangements and contributed more meaningfully to the construction of rural identity in Muskoka. After the turn of the century, many households sold relatively modest amounts of timber directly to sawmills, obtained a larger share of the profits on each log, remained with their families over the winter, and limited the damage done to the local ecosystem. A household-based approach to wood-resource extraction existed in the tanbark trade as well. Settlers could not sell pine, but they could sell hemlock bark. Two companies established three tanneries in Muskoka between 1877 and 1895, specifically because Muskoka had ample supplies of hemlock. Almost immediately, households found a market for hemlock trees growing on their land. Bark gangs also cut hemlock trees from timber berths and property owned by the tanneries, and just like the logging companies, the objective of the bark gangs was to quickly extract the resources. The camp, or gang, model of taking every useful tree had more detrimental consequences for the environment, and fewer economic and social benefits at the local level, than the household approach.

Household-based harvesting targeted only a few dozen trees on privately owned land. This approach was much more sustainable than the model imposed by the commercial prerogatives of the logging and tanning industries. Had the household-based approach been followed exclusively, had timber and tanbark been harvested at a scale and pace similar to that of the average household, the wood resource economy would have had a greater and more lasting influence on the construction of rural identity in Muskoka.

5
Fossil Fuels, Consumer Culture, and the Tourism Economy, 1900–20

In the spring of 1905, John James (J.J.) Beaumont issued the tenth annual circular for his supply boat service on Lake Muskoka. Supply boats did business with many settlers, but cottagers were their primary market. Beaumont felt it necessary to emphasize that "our long experience in the supply boat business has made us acquainted with the requirements of our customers, and they will find this year a more up-to-date stock than in previous years in every department." His circular listed many canned and dry goods, and its cover page described "Meat of the best quality and variety. Butter, Milk, Cream, Fresh Eggs, Poultry (of which this season we have reared close on to a thousand) and vegetables of all kinds, fresh from our own farm." A separate line on the cover page mentioned "Bread and Confectionary by a first-class City baker on the premises." Beaumont promised that "we are doing our utmost to cater to the wants of our increasing business." He thanked his customers for their patronage and outlined the many advantages of obtaining goods from his boat. The cover also featured an appeal – almost a plea. "Before ordering supplies from outside," it asked customers, "give us a trial as we feel sure that we can in every department, supply as good quality, and at as reasonable price as they can purchase elsewhere."[1] Beaumont did not elaborate on what he meant by "outside" and "elsewhere," but his comment suggests that he was concerned about the ease with which cottagers could obtain all sorts of goods through mail order, and the implications that increased competition from urban retailers would have for the future of his supply boat business.

Over the first two decades of the twentieth century, urban retailers and mineral energy began to erode the high degree of control over the tourism economy that formed an important component of settlers' rural identity. Permanent residents never lost complete control over tourism. Indeed, tourists continued to rely on them for many goods and services. But new networks of exchange, which connected households in Muskoka with urban consumer culture and distant sites of fossil fuel extraction, emerged alongside, and grew in proportion to, local exchange and organic energy use. Specifically, settlers began to lose control over the food and fuel dimensions of the tourism economy, and in turn, their ability to turn the environmental limitations of the Shield to their advantage by selling high-value local goods and services. During the 1880s and 1890s, settlers in Muskoka cornered the market for fresh fruits, vegetables, meat, dairy, and eggs, because major urban retailers did not ship fresh food. Likewise, settlers met the energy requirements of the region's many steamboats, as well as household cooking and heating needs (including hotels and cottages), with local biomass energy, mainly fuelwood cut from Muskoka's forests. Shortly after the turn of the century, mail-order catalogues from department stores, such as Eaton's in Toronto, began selling a wide variety of foods, including many fresh items, in addition to the latest fashions, home furnishings, and outdoor recreation gear. At almost the same time, Navigation Company steamboats switched from cordwood to coal, new gasoline motorboats provided personal forms of mobility, and cottagers and hotels installed coal and gasoline power plants to generate steam heating and hot water. The steady integration of these exogenous foods and fuels into Muskoka disconnected certain features of tourism from the local economy and the environmental realities of the Shield, and linked them with distant commodity hinterlands, abstract urban-commercial networks of exchange, and rhythms of life that resembled life in the city.

Some features of rural identity shaped by tourism survived the rise of consumer culture and mineral energy, but not the most sustainable ones. Settlers living next to the lower lakes (Muskoka, Rosseau, and Joseph) continued to combine farming, wood-resource harvesting, and tourism. What made tourism so important to rural identity, however, was that for many settlers it was tied closely and actively to their identities as farmers and wood resource harvesters. In fact, what gave settlers control over tourism was the demand for local fresh foods and fuelwood. When mail-order delivery and mineral energy competed with local foods and fuels, they also threatened the rural identity that settlers had constructed based on tourism's demand for local goods and services.

Fossil Fuels, Consumer Culture, and the Tourism Economy   135

In the first decade of the twentieth century, a culture of conspicuous consumption enveloped the Muskoka lakes. Thorstein Veblen introduced the concept of conspicuous consumption in his highly influential and critical sociological study *The Theory of the Leisure Class* (1899), published just as consumer culture began to alter the relationship between tourism and the Muskoka economy. Veblen argued that the leisure class (those who were wealthy enough to take time away from work), having determined that labour was "intrinsically unworthy," engaged in the possession, use, and ingestion of high-value goods and services with the express purpose of demonstrating their social (or "honorific") standing.[2] Canadian humourist Stephen Leacock, who studied under Veblen at the University of Chicago, took a satirical look at the leisure class in his 1914 novel *Arcadian Adventures with the Idle Rich*. Midway through the story, the main character, Peter Spillikins, is invited to "rough it" in the "simplest fashion" at Castel Casteggio, the posh woodland summer retreat of Margaret and Edward Newberry, a nouveau riche couple. A "beautiful house of white brick with sweeping piazzas and glittering conservatories, standing among great trees with rolling lawns broken with flower-beds as the ground sloped to the lake," Castel Casteggio would not have been out of place in Muskoka. Spillikins, who has roughed it before, knows what to expect, so he brings the necessary gear: "two quite large steamer trunks ... together with his suit-case, tennis racket, and golf kit." A car picks him up at the train station and takes him to the house, where the dress code consists of "plain white flannel trousers, not worth more than six dollars a leg, an ordinary white silk shirt ... that couldn't have cost more than fifteen dollars, and ... an ordinary Panama hat, say forty dollars."[3] Inspired by Veblen's critique of the leisure class, Leacock's novel is a satirical commentary on a pattern of consumption that was no longer limited to the idle rich. By 1914, conspicuous consumption and the leisure class encompassed an overarching culture that permeated a rather wide segment of society.

The most pronounced consequences of consumer culture unfolded in cities, where physical stores served as catalytic sites of social, economic, and cultural change. And the literature on its history tends to focus mainly on the social impacts of mass merchandising and department stores in urban places, particularly on women, the working and lower middle classes, and immigrant and racial minorities. Historians have detailed the rise of big businesses based on mass merchandising, the adjustments that the burgeoning middle class made in its shopping patterns, and the consequences for independent shopkeepers and merchants who struggled to compete with the new scale and modes of market exchange between 1890 and 1940.[4] Historian Donica Belisle defines consumer culture as a predisposition toward economic activity in which individuals pursue, purchase, or use commodities.[5] She argues that between the 1880s and 1920s, department stores and "mass merchandising changed Canadian life," "brought Canadians into modernity," and transformed the country into a consumer society.[6] In the process, consumer culture contributed to the creation of a Canadian national identity by establishing common experiences, expectations, behaviours, and practices across the country.

It did not take long for all of this to be felt in rural places as well. Hal Barron contends that the arrival of consumer culture in rural areas of the northern United States represented "a second great transformation" comparable to "the initial spread of industrial capitalism earlier in the [nineteenth] century."[7] According to Barron, for rural people, consumer culture "challenged their identities as producers and their assumptions about the moral superiority of rural life by introducing new standards of value that were defined and embodied in material possessions that emanated from and reflected urban culture."[8] Department stores used mass merchandising to establish high standards for quality, consistent product availability, uniform service, and competitive prices. In both the city and the country, independent retailers and merchants attempted to resist the trends that lent significant advantages to large retailers and chain stores. As David Monod shows, they survived by emulating the marketing strategies, operational efficiencies, and branding of their department store competitors.[9] But during the first two decades of the twentieth century, they also had trouble negotiating consumer expectations, not only for certain products, but also for the right to purchase them regularly and consistently. And, unlike for a generation earlier, a personal connection to independent merchants and retailers did not generate customer loyalty. These expectations quickly extended into the countryside, where "thanks to the [mail-order] catalogue, there was no escape for rural merchants because even the most isolated shoppers could now buy with abandon."[10]

Tourists were not alone in their embrace of consumer culture; rural residents also made mail-order purchases from urban department stores and joined the modern era along with the rest of Canada. Rather than causing these social, economic, and cultural changes in Muskoka, tourism accelerated and exaggerated them. However, the consumer choices of tourists had a significant impact on its economy. As Belisle demonstrates, department stores played on fears about comfort, convenience, health, and lifestyle to encourage consumption.[11] Shoppers placed their trust in department stores, a trust that extended to food purchases – even if they bought packaged and processed food, as well as fresh items.[12] Year-round and summer residents bought a wide variety of things, including clothing, home furnishings, tools, and toys, but the purchase of manufactured goods did not present the same challenge to rural identity as that of food. Regardless of who made the purchases, the choice to order goods from the city, rather than locally, undermined the Muskoka economy to some extent. When cottagers ordered food via a catalogue, settlers not only lost control over an important feature of the tourism economy, but their identities as farmers became threatened as well.

This chapter also focuses on how tourism facilitated the rapid spread of fossil fuels in Muskoka and on how this process weakened the ability of settlers to control the local economy and reproduce their rural identity. In doing so, it adds new insights on the transition from organic to mineral energy that occurred between about 1900 and 1920. Even as many Canadians self-consciously entered the modern era by embracing a consumer culture, they also reached a turning point in the energy transition.[13] In Muskoka, it spanned more than three decades, was never complete (even to this day), and involved significant overlap between energy regimes. In the 1890s, settlers provided for most of tourism's energy needs from their farms and forests. By the 1920s, fossil fuels from distant places such as Pennsylvania and Ohio met a large proportion of those needs. As was the case with consumer culture, tourism did not introduce fossil fuels to Muskoka, but it did hasten the adoption of coal and petroleum in many ways that undermined settler control of the flow of energy. As the transition unfolded, mineral energy enabled tourists and cottagers to assume new rhythms of mobility, standards of living, and patterns of social and economic exchange that depended less on the goods and services of settlers, and more on urban-commercial networks and distant sites of mineral energy resource extraction.

Histories of tourism have emphasized the importance of railways, steamboats, and automobiles in connecting urbanites with scenic and wilderness locations during the early twentieth century, but they tend to take fossil fuel energy largely for granted and have not investigated tourism's role in its impact on rural culture and identity.[14] Historians of the rural transition to mineral energy typically concentrate on the adoption of fossil fuels for trucks and tractors, the effect of those technologies on labour productivity, and the social changes that accompanied greater mobility and the introduction of modern energy carriers in the home. They have generally ignored the impact on the organic energy producers in rural communities.[15] As R.W. Sandwell reveals, Canada's transition to a mineral energy economy occurred somewhat later than in Britain and the United States, during the first decade of the twentieth century.[16] The most remarkable social, cultural, and economic changes from fossil fuels happened in the city, but important developments took place in the countryside as well. Consumer culture and the mineral energy transition had much in common and reinforced one another. Fossil fuels became both an object of consumer culture and the chief energy source underpinning its mode of production and network of distribution. Together, they helped transform tourism in Muskoka.

Even as consumer culture and fossil fuels took hold in Muskoka, and settlers lost control over some important features of the tourism economy, the most sustainable elements of their rural identity continued to revolve around local exchange networks. For many who lived near the lower lakes, the ability to derive a livelihood from farmland contributed to the reproduction of their identity. Fresh food and fuelwood were important items that settlers sold to tourists because the resulting income enabled them to support themselves through modest farming. Indeed, tourism became vital in Muskoka precisely because it enabled settlers to include farming as a key part of their identity.

In Port Carling, the Medora and Wood Agricultural Society Fall Fair reinforced the importance of the agrarian livelihoods that maintained the community's relationship with tourism. Farmers and rural communities organized agricultural fairs to gather, share expertise, celebrate culture, and reaffirm the foundations of their economy.[17] An essential feature of the fairs were the contests that showcased the quality of local farms. Between 1907 and 1912, more than a hundred people won prizes in the Medora and Wood Fall Fair. During these years, nineteen people won prizes every year, and forty-four people won prizes in at least three years.[18] Each year, an average of forty-eight men and women split two to three hundred prizes in dozens of categories, including grain crops, garden vegetables, fruit, livestock, maple syrup, preserves, baked goods, and flowers. Those who won on a regular basis, such as Port Carling butcher Joseph McCulley, took prizes in many, sometimes dozens, of categories worth between fifteen and twenty dollars every year. The average entrant, however, generally went home with between five and six dollars in prize money. These sums were obviously not enough to live on, but given that a dozen eggs or a pound of butter cost about fifteen cents and a bag of flour cost two to three dollars in Muskoka, they were not insignificant either.[19] The fall fair celebrated the talent, hard work, and quality of local farmers. It also demonstrated that many settlers in Muskoka included farming as an important component,

Fossil Fuels, Consumer Culture, and the Tourism Economy   139

perhaps the most important component, of their rural identity. At a time when they were losing control over the market for groceries consumed by cottagers and tourists, they still prided themselves on their capacity to produce fresh foods.

In the townships close to Port Carling, next to the lower lakes, many members of the Medora and Wood Agricultural Society turned their farming skills and knowledge of the environment into goods and services, which they sold to summer visitors from the city. In the 1870s, Charles Riley and his family settled in Monck Township. By about 1900, their farm, Brooklands, had become reasonably successful and was comparable in many respects to others near the lower lakes (see Figure 5.1). But, it was not *on* the lake. As a result, Charles Riley, his wife, Emma, and their eight children did not benefit directly from tourism the way lakeside settlers did. However, their farm was only a short distance from three hotels on Lake Muskoka, as well as the Beaumaris cottage community. On Tondern Island, the Beaumaris Hotel formed the nucleus for one of Muskoka's earliest cottage colonies, and local settlers, including the Rileys, undoubtedly benefitted *in*directly from being so close to this hub of social and economic activity. Around 1900, at age twenty-five, the Rileys' second-youngest child, Charles (Charlie) Walker Riley, bought a piece of lakeshore property near both Beaumaris and his parents' farm.[20] The land included a home, which Charlie converted into a boarding house named Scarcliff (see Figure 5.2). During the next few years, his two unmarried sisters, Mary (called Hettie) and Julia (called Leena), moved in with him to run the hotel and take care of the household. Between October 1909 and May 1914, Leena Riley's diary reveals that, though several new social and technological forces were influencing her life, many of the most sustainable features of Muskoka's society and economy still operated in ways that were critical to the success of Scarcliff.[21]

Like many settlers, Charlie understood that tourism provided a useful means of earning income from his family's land and labour. The land around Scarcliff sustained a vegetable garden, pasture for sheep, pigs, and dairy cows, and a sizeable woodlot for fuel. Hettie and Leena shared some farm responsibilities with their brother but were almost entirely responsible for running the hotel during the summer. In fact, the sisters became so busy with the hotel in July and August that, unfortunately, Leena stopped writing in her journal during those months. In addition to his farm work, Charlie scaled logs for a local lumber agent and sold farm products to merchants and neighbours. In the spring, he bought piglets in Bracebridge, which he fattened over the summer to slaughter in the fall.[22] In June, he

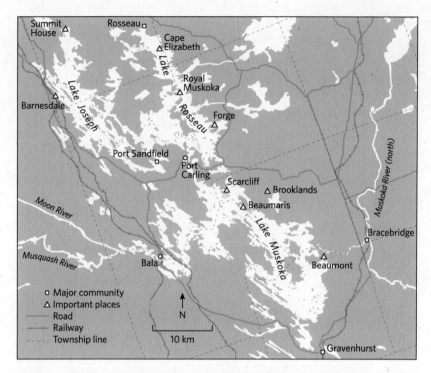

FIGURE 5.1 The lower Muskoka lakes, c. 1913. *Adapted by Eric Leinberger*

usually sold spring lambs; one of his customers was J.J. Beaumont, who operated a supply boat.[23] Charlie and his sisters, as well as their parents at Brooklands, kept dairy cows, which produced large quantities of milk, cream, and butter that the family regularly sold to, or traded with, neighbours. Hettie and Leena frequently obtained eggs from Brooklands or a neighbour and borrowed horses from their neighbours, the Kayes and the Huttons. The Rileys and their neighbours continued to rely on each other to help make ends meet, on tourism to generate income, and on the farms themselves to support their hotel businesses.

Hotels simply could not operate without local labour, food, and fuel, even as mail-order catalogues made it possible for large urban retailers to compete with local producers. Most hotels advertised a variety of amenities, including shaded verandahs, tennis courts, and fine dining, and their promotional material often mentioned their gardens and farms. In 1915, for example, of the seventeen hotels that advertised in the *Muskoka Lakes Bluebook*, six referred to their farms (see Figures 5.3 and 5.4). Summit House, at the north end of Lake Joseph, noted a "Dairy and Vegetable

FIGURE 5.2 Advertisement for Scarcliff on Lake Muskoka, 1918. John Rogers, Muskoka Lakes Bluebook, Directory and Chart, 1918 *(Port Sandfield, ON: Self-published, 1918), 105.* Courtesy of Muskoka Lakes Museum Archives

Farm in connection [with the hotel]," whereas Ernescliffe on Lake Rosseau assured guests that a "large farm supplies eggs, poultry, milk, vegetables, etc."[24] In the 1918 *Muskoka Lakes Bluebook,* thirteen of the thirty-three hotels that took out advertisements featured gardens and farms. Elgin House on Lake Joseph boasted that its "table is liberally supplied from the farm and garden belonging to the house," and the Rileys highlighted Scarcliff's "200 acres of Farm and Forest Lands." Paignton House on Lake Rosseau advertised that "we have our own milk supply, raise our vegetables and poultry on our own farm."[25] Not all hotels started out as farms; nor did all of them operate a farm. However, the fact that those who did chose to promote their farms and gardens in their publicity demonstrates an understanding that guests valued fresh foods from a local source.

FIGURE 5.3 A view of the grounds at Summit House on Lake Joseph, c. 1907. Frank W. Micklethwaite. John Harold Micklethwaite fonds, PA-067336. Courtesy of Library and Archives Canada

When they could not obtain what they needed from their own farm, or from their neighbours, hotel owners went to the general store merchant – and sometimes the merchant delivered goods by supply boat. Importantly, the boats helped ensure that settlers retained a high degree of control over tourism. Unfortunately, the account books from the numerous Muskoka supply boats no longer exist, so it is impossible to reconstruct the details of an average transaction. But the main ledger from George Henry Homer's general store in Rosseau provides a glimpse into the relationship between the boats and hotels or cottages. In 1896, Homer bought the steam yacht *Edith May* from Enoch Cox, the proprietor of Prospect House in Port Sandfield, and converted it into a supply boat. Once a year, Homer carried over the total of Cox's annual supply boat account into the main store ledger, something he did not do for any other supply boat customer.[26] In 1896, the amount was $173.55, or 86 percent of Cox's total account with Homer that year. The following two years were similar, with Cox spending $223.33 (or 87 percent of his total account) in 1897 and $274.67 (or 77 percent of his total account) in 1898 on the supply boat. By performing

Fossil Fuels, Consumer Culture, and the Tourism Economy 143

FIGURE 5.4 Advertisement for Ernescliffe on Lake Rosseau, 1918. *John Rogers, Muskoka Lakes Bluebook, Directory and Chart, 1918 (Port Sandfield, ON: Self-published, 1918), 99. Courtesy of Muskoka Lakes Museum Archives*

the work of connecting merchants and farmers with the demand from hotels and cottagers, supply boats, such as the *Edith May*, ensured that hotels could accommodate tourists, and cottagers could avoid costly and inconvenient trips into town during their holiday.

Consumer culture did not immediately overwhelm, displace, or eliminate the local exchange networks that settlers had assembled in Muskoka. Between about 1900 and 1920, however, mail-order retail and fossil fuels slowly, almost imperceptibly, weakened settlers' control of tourism's food and fuel needs. Writing in 1904, Fanny Potts described supply boats as "Eaton's in miniature."[27] Potts and her husband lived near Port Sandfield and rented cottages to tourists in the summer. That she chose to compare supply boats with a mail-order department store in Toronto suggests that Muskoka residents saw the boats as offering a surprisingly wide array of provisions. At the same time, her comparison reveals the belief that goods purchased from Eaton's were almost as easy to acquire as potatoes or milk from across the lake. Indeed, over the next two decades, tourists in Muskoka embraced a culture of consumption and new fossil-fuelled technologies, even as resilient settlers worked to satisfy their needs from local farms and forests. By the time Potts made her comparison, Eaton's had become a regular part of life in Toronto and was fast becoming so across the country.

Timothy Eaton opened his first department store in Toronto in 1869, which printed its first catalogue in 1884. By the 1890s, Eaton's was distributing its catalogues to customers across Canada, including Muskoka.[28] Thus, rural residents could gain access to basic supplies and provisions, hardware, clothing, home furnishings, and new consumer products that had previously required either a special trip to the city or a third party to prepare the shipment. Once mail orders became available, people of all classes throughout rural Canada were encouraged to order whatever they pleased. Interestingly, Muskoka seems to have played a role in the development of the Eaton's catalogue. In 1896, Timothy Eaton purchased a summer estate of four and a half acres on the east shore of Lake Rosseau from Francis Forge (ironically, Muskoka's first supply boat operator).[29] He probably noted the affluence of the cottage and vacation community and endeavoured to target its increasingly conspicuous consumption. Thus, even as Eaton's began shaping consumer culture in Muskoka, leisure time spent at the lake in Muskoka also appears to have influenced its marketing.

The pattern of urban-rural commerce made possible by mail order added a new layer of material consumption and siphoned off some portion of local exchange. It is not possible, given the aggregated provincial sales records available, to provide a thorough analysis of exactly what Muskoka households ordered from Eaton's. The records provide product breakdowns but do not specify where in Ontario they were shipped. The catalogues, however, give a glimpse into mail-order consumer culture and hint at how Muskoka cottagers in particular altered their purchasing habits. In 1899, Eaton's released a *Summer Needs and Outing Goods* supplement to its summer catalogue.[30] Judging from the products and illustrations in its twenty-six pages, the intended market was Toronto's middle class, who might spend the day at a park or beach in the city. Eaton's had not yet turned its attention to cottagers. The next year's summer supplement came closer. Entitled *Campers' Supplies,* the booklet included a variety of photographs and sketches depicting people, landscapes, and activities that may very well have been inspired by Muskoka. It devoted fifteen pages to food, such as canned vegetables, biscuits, coffee, fresh and dried fruit, salted and smoked meats, preserves, and condiments. The last page featured an illustration of the rural setting that Eaton's both serviced and competed with (see Figure 5.5). "No matter how far away from Toronto you may be this summer," the catalogue concluded, "this store's goods and its unequalled

Fossil Fuels, Consumer Culture, and the Tourism Economy 145

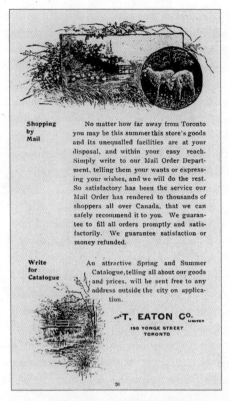

FIGURE 5.5 The final page of Eaton's *Campers' Supplies* supplement, 1900. Campers' Supplies, 1900, 26, T. Eaton Company fonds, F229–5-0–58, no. 2, AO. Courtesy of Sears Canada Inc.

facilities are at your disposal, and within your easy reach. Simply write to our Mail Order Department, telling them your wants or expressing your wishes, and we will do the rest."[31] By framing its products as "within your easy reach," Eaton's claimed the same advantage that local farmers, merchants, and supply boats had offered each summer for the previous two decades.

Over the next several years, Eaton's refined its marketing to target tourism in Muskoka. In 1902, it took out a full-page advertisement in the Muskoka Lakes Association (MLA) Yearbook, the annual membership publication of an organization that represented the interests of hundreds of cottagers and prominent year-round residents.[32] The ad proclaimed that "the pleasure and comforts of your summer outing in Muskoka will be greatly increased if you have easy access to the things you want or would like to have. Shopping by mail is the secret." Cottagers simply needed to "write to us for anything you want – for things to eat, things to wear, things for the house and things for pleasure or sport." Even though the MLA had only 182 members in 1902, it was the perfect market because the cottager demographic continued to grow in size and buying power. The cover of the Eaton's 1903 *Summer Holiday Needs* catalogue reflects the influence that Muskoka consumers had on Eaton's marketing. The cover shows three scenes that could have been set in Muskoka (see Figure 5.6).[33] In the first, three young men work beside a tent on a smooth carpet of grass under a canopy of pine trees. In the second, a woman reclines in a hammock next to a lake, a nearby stump suggesting a recently cleared landscape. In the third, a man and woman engage in a bit of fishing, while in the background a steamboat makes its way across the lake. In a 1905 advertisement for "Canada's Greatest Store," Eaton's featured an image of a "Moonlight Scene Muskoka."[34] In the 1906 *Outing Supply Catalogue*, the company assured its customers that "special deliveries will be made to boats and trains" and that "our Depositors' Account Department is a convenience for Summer Cottagers."[35] Eaton's tried to tailor its advertising to appeal to various regions of the country, but as Donica Belisle documents, Muskoka – and the southern Ontario urbanites who spent their summers there – often featured prominently in its national advertisements.

Over the span of just a few years, cottagers discovered the convenience and reliability of catalogue shopping, which provided a growing list of reasonably priced food items, an increasing number of which were fresh. In addition to preserved food, the 1901 Eaton's *Summer Catalogue* listed the "finest hand-picked beans," butter, "fresh cream daily," cheese, and fresh fruits in season ("oranges, lemons, pineapples, bananas, cranberries, strawberries, etc"). It offered preserved meats "from our own farms and cured on premises," as well as fresh meats of "the choicest quality and from our own farms."[36] Two years later, in 1903, the *Summer Holiday Needs* catalogue included a "Grocery Department" section and promised customers that in the "Butter and Egg Dept. We keep a supply of the finest butter and eggs possible to procure, and we guarantee quality to the finest." And just in case customers were not entirely convinced, the catalogue added that "we are receiving fresh consignments of new laid eggs daily, and you can always depend on getting them fresh."[37] By repeatedly invoking the freshness of its products, Eaton's moved into consumer territory that had previously been the exclusive preserve of settlers.

Fossil Fuels, Consumer Culture, and the Tourism Economy   147

FIGURE 5.6 Front cover of the 1903 Eaton's *Summer Holiday Needs* catalogue. *T. Eaton Company fonds*, F229–5-0–60, no. 2, AO. Courtesy of Sears Canada Inc.

In Muskoka, the impacts of consumer culture and mail-order shopping unfolded gradually after 1900. The main consequence was a steady erosion of local control over tourist food provisioning, which had been central to rural identity a generation earlier. Settlers who indirectly sold fresh foods to summer visitors continued to enjoy the same type of benefits from tourism in the 1920s as they had during the 1890s. For those whose command of the tourism economy involved direct sales to cottage customers, however, changes occurred more quickly. Supply boat owners experienced this process earliest and perhaps the most acutely.

Once Eaton's could rely on its wholesale economy of scale, along with swift transport by train and steamboat between Toronto and various wharves in Muskoka, local merchants, farmers, and supply boat owners had trouble keeping up. Many improved their service and appealed to their customers' sense of loyalty in an effort to stay in business. But visitors increasingly expected the prompt and reliable service, not to mention high-quality goods and competitive prices, that had become the norm in the city. In its 1906 catalogue, Eaton's promised "the prompt dispatch of orders for groceries" by designated staff who had "special charge of Cottagers' and Campers' orders." Customers in Muskoka could rely on "the work of the special train and boat delivery," which would "get all parcels to the station and wharves."[38] In the 1902 MLA Yearbook, an ad for Homer's general store in Rosseau attempted to appeal to vacationing urbanites who were just getting accustomed to the comforts and conveniences of mail-order shopping. Homer tried to retain their business by encouraging them to "save freight and all unnecessary expense by purchasing your Supplies from our Supply Boat."[39] Throughout the next decade, supply boat owners worked hard to remain viable in the tourism economy and to counter the competition from urban retailers.

This chapter opened with J.J. Beaumont's 1905 appeal to cottagers to give him their business. His efforts capture the variety of strategies that supply boat owners used to maintain some control over the local tourism economy. In 1887, Beaumont and his family bought a 657-acre farm near the mouth of the Muskoka River. When tourism hit its stride on Lake Muskoka during the 1880s, the Beaumont farm already included large vegetable gardens, orchards, pastures, and barns. Having quickly developed a reputation as a supplier of the best lamb in Muskoka, Beaumont began selling meat, vegetables, fruit, dairy, eggs, and other items by supply boat in 1894. By about 1900, the Beaumonts employed "over two dozen people as butchers, bakers and farm hands."[40] In his 1905 circular, Beaumont offered a variety of fresh meat, including beef and pork, dressed chicken and duck, and, of course, his famous lamb. Cream was a "specialty" and butter came from the "best creamery." His boat would be stocked with vegetables, "everything in season," and "all foreign and domestic fruits in season," as well as eggs "strictly new laid." Beaumont knew his market and understood how it was changing.

Aware that they were losing control, local merchants scrambled to retain the loyalty and business of seasonal customers. Beaumont attempted to protect his relationship with cottagers by reminding them that many people had "expressed their satisfaction at the service received last season and intend giving their full business the coming Season."[41] In June 1905, the *Bracebridge Gazette* ran a front-page article titled "Bracebridge Grocers

Fossil Fuels, Consumer Culture, and the Tourism Economy   149

and the Tourist Trade," which raised the alarm about the threat posed by urban retailers. Its unnamed author (probably Beaumont) claimed that local

> merchants wrote, advertised and visited the tourist trade early in the season only to find that Toronto houses had had their representatives earlier over the ground and had been most successful in securing good orders. In short, the general supply of the season had been placed and our merchants returned with saddened countenances and resolved there was no use of the strenuousness of catering longer for the tourist trade.

If local merchants, grocers, and suppliers were to compete with Toronto retailers and conserve "the tourist trade which is fast slipping away," they had to cooperate with one another. "The people of the lakes [tourists]," the writer argued, "will loyally support local enterprise if the same can vouchsafe to them an equal service with that of the outside."[42] Beaumont's message evinced pride in the local farmer as a provider for cottagers and the tourism economy. He improved the goods and services offered by his supply boat while simultaneously appealing to both his customers and other merchants, grocers, and farmers in Muskoka.

In July 1913, the Toronto *Globe* ran an essay by Toronto poet Katherine Hale about her visit to Muskoka. She recounted her day trip aboard a supply boat and her conversation with its captain, who described the difficulties that his father had experienced when he settled in Muskoka. "Twas a different country from that we know to-day," he said. "Then one or two Toronto people came up to camp," and they "liked it, and came again to build cottages, and they brought others. And so Muskoka began." By stating that Muskoka began with tourism, the captain conveyed that the relationship settlers had cultivated with summer visitors out of their own homes, and from their own land, was an important feature of their rural identity. "In the last ten years," he added, "nearly every island and all the best locations on the mainland have been taken up [by cottagers]," who "had to be provided for in the way of food." Proud of the novelty and the work involved, he crowed: "Well, we thought out the regular Supply Boat scheme ... We put in first-class supplies and the market gardening is getting better every year in Muskoka. People can buy fresh vegetables in the country now instead of having to go back to the City for them."[43] In this symbiotic relationship between farming and tourism, both parties benefitted. Settler labour met the needs of tourists, and tourism motivated settlers to improve their farms and market gardens. Tourism was an important part of the captain's rural identity and thanks to his services, to that of many other settlers as well.

Unfortunately, the days of the supply boats were numbered. In 1906, Eaton's began paying the freight charges on orders over twenty-five dollars, and in 1913 it lowered the minimum purchase for free shipping to ten dollars.[44] In 1915, it placed an ad in the *Muskoka Lakes Bluebook*, which stated that its "Mail Order Catalogue offers the best way of buying for Cottage or Camp." Indeed, the store seemed to be settling the contest between mail order and local supplier. "Surely," its ad began, "this is the ideal way to buy for the summer home." Just as cottagers had put in a weekly order with a supply boat, Eaton's encouraged its customers to "get a copy of our Catalogue, and consult it each week, buying from it all you need in the way of Clothing, Furniture, Supplies, Groceries, etc."[45] As it turned out, most supply boats survived less than a decade longer. J.J. Beaumont's *Nymoca* remained in business until 1919. In 1898, Homer had replaced the *Edith May* with a slightly larger boat, the *Constance*, which ran until 1921. Of the top twenty largest supply boats, seven stopped operating in 1910 or earlier, four in 1918 or 1919, and four more by 1925. Only three lasted into the 1930s, including William Hana's *Newminko*, which was the largest. It plied the lakes until 1940.[46] The number of boats declined as consumer culture increased its grip on the tourism economy.

The transition to mineral energy in Muskoka also entailed significant consequences for settler control of the tourism economy and the ability of those near the lower lakes to reproduce their distinctive rural identity. Indeed, the impact of consumer culture was enhanced by the spread of mineral energy, particularly gasoline. Motorboats freed tourists from the constraints of organic energy, including both the labour of rowing across the lake and the network of steamboat transportation that relied on fuel-wood. After about 1900, fossil fuels and motorboats became their own forms of conspicuous consumption in which tourists (and settlers) increasingly indulged. During the summer months, lakeside social occasions typically took place within the distance that one could row. Regular access to provisions and groceries in more isolated locations involved a visit from the supply boat, rather than a trip into town. Travelling farther than one could comfortably row involved a scheduled and expensive trip by Navigation Company steamer. In each case, settlers exercised relatively great control over the flow of energy because their labour and land provided the food and fuel that human bodies and steam engines converted into work. The transition to a mineral energy economy embedded Muskoka in a wider set of industrial processes that connected its consumption of

Fossil fuels with the extraction of coal and petroleum elsewhere, mainly in Pennsylvania. As the mineral share of Muskoka's energy budget grew, the organic share shrank, and settlers lost another important way of engaging with the tourism economy.

The railway was the earliest form of transportation to consume mineral energy in Muskoka. During the mid-nineteenth century, locomotives everywhere in Ontario were fuelled by cordwood. As land clearance removed the trees closest to the tracks, the cost of fuelwood rose compared to that of coal. Running between Niagara Falls and Windsor, the Great Western Railway was the first Ontario railway to adopt coal. In 1858, it experimented with coal, converting twenty-five of its locomotives by 1873.[47] In 1878, a memorandum released by the Grand Trunk Railway of Canada outlined how a shortage of cordwood had contributed to its rising fuel costs. Two years later, company president W.H. Tyler announced that Grand Trunk would begin systematically switching its engines to coal.[48] Ontario has no coal deposits, and importing coal from Britain or the Maritimes was not economical. Close proximity to the Appalachian mines in Pennsylvania meant that coal was available in sufficient quantities and at a price necessary to supply the province's railways.[49] As early as 1855, barges transported 45,692 tons of coal along the Welland Canal.[50] Most of it went to industrial purposes, but more than enough would have been available to power the railways. By 1870, coal imports to Ontario had reached 115,000 tons, climbing quickly to 750,000 tons in 1880 and 2.2 million tons in 1890. Over the next thirty years, imports of American coal roughly doubled each decade.[51] By the time the railway reached Gravenhurst in 1875 and was extended to Bracebridge and Huntsville during the 1880s, trains everywhere in Ontario had access to coal. An exhaustive search through local histories and archival records turned up no mention that railway companies in Muskoka had purchased or consumed cordwood as fuel. Exactly the opposite is true of its steamboats.

Between 1866 and 1907, the steamboats relied entirely on wood cut by local settlers, who sold it directly to the owners or indirectly through general stores. At the turn of the century, their market included lumber company tugboats, supply boat owners, and the Muskoka Navigation Company's eight passenger steamers, which made the largest cordwood purchases.[52] In 1907, however, the company added the *Sagamo* to its fleet and the *Cherokee* the following year (see Figure 5.7). Both boats burned coal. This transition to coal appears to have been motivated, at least partially, by concerns over growing fuel costs. In January 1903, at a company shareholders meeting in Toronto, the Navigation Company board reported that operating "expenses have materially increased ... due in part to operation being extended over a period longer than usual, but chiefly to increase in prices, such as fuel, provisions, etc."[53] Indeed, the company's fuel expenses had risen substantially over the previous five years. In 1897, its seven steamers consumed $5,048 worth of wood. Five years later, in 1902, its eight steamers required $9,435 worth.

Cordwood was abundant in Muskoka, so its price probably did not significantly escalate between 1897 and 1902. Rather, the board's anxiety was probably sparked by the abrupt increase in overall fuel expenses due to the equally sizeable growth in the number of tourists that visited Muskoka each summer. The number of hotels roughly doubled between 1896 and 1903, whereas the number of cottages increased by more than three hundred between 1895 and 1915.[54] In the years before motorboats became widespread, the expansion of tourism placed added pressures on the Navigation Company to transport passengers from wharf-side train stations to dozens of locations throughout the lower lakes. Indeed, the revenue generated by its passenger service more than doubled between 1897 and 1902, from $19,522 to $40,009. To accommodate the demand without adding new routes, and therefore compromising the efficiency of its operations, the company renovated and enlarged several of its steamers. As a result, greater passenger revenue matched the rise in fuel costs. Between 1897 and

FIGURE 5.7 Steamboat *Sagamo* emits heavy coal smoke, 1908. *Frank W. Micklethwaite. John Harold Micklethwaite fonds, PA-158597. Courtesy of Library and Archives Canada*

1898, the *Nipissing* and the *Kenozha* became less efficient in terms of passenger revenue dollars versus the cost of purchasing fuel, but most boats in the fleet became more efficient. The company was concerned about the direct costs of fuelwood, but the continued efficiency of its passenger to fuel cost ratio suggests that other factors influenced the transition as well.

Two such factors were the logistics of supply and the material challenges of refuelling the steamboats. From the perspective of the company, the only real advantages of cordwood were price and access to supply. There was plenty of wood in Muskoka, but moving it from living trees into steamer furnaces presented many challenges. To start with, steamers did not refuel at a single, centralized depot, but rather at numerous locations around the lakes (see Figures 5.8 and 5.9). This was necessary both because settlers tended to pile fuelwood at the closest shoreline location and because steamers often needed to refuel as they traversed a lake. Multiple refuelling sites interrupted service and required coordination between the company and suppliers at the shore. The process of refuelling was also time consuming and labour intensive. At each refuelling stop, crew members had to handle each individual piece of wood to move it from the shore into the ship's hold. When the wood was placed in the firebox, each piece had to be handled again. Coal alleviated both of these problems and included additional advantages. It arrived by train at a centralized

FIGURE 5.8 A small crowd watches a regatta, 1907. Note the cordwood stacked on the wharf. *Frank W. Micklethwaite. John Harold Micklethwaite fonds, PA-158226. Courtesy of Library and Archives Canada*

FIGURE 5.9 Steamboat *Muskoka* moored at a wharf, date unknown. Note the cordwood stacked on the shore, ready to be picked up by the steamer. *Unknown photographer. Courtesy of the Muskoka Steamship and Historical Society*

FIGURE 5.10 Men shovelling coal on the *Sagamo*, date unknown. *Unknown photographer. Courtesy of the Muskoka Steamship and Historical Society*

wharf-side station, where it could be poured out of the car directly into the ship's hold. To add coal to the firebox, crew members used shovels instead of handling it (see Figure 5.10). Moreover, coal is more energy dense than wood. A pound of air-dried wood contains roughly 6,500 British Thermal Units of energy, whereas a pound of coal contains approximately 10,500.[55] Coal's greater fuel-to-weight ratio meant that ships could carry much larger amounts of energy in their holds and therefore needed to stop less frequently. For all of these reasons, coal possessed many more advantages than wood.

Another probable reason for the switch to mineral energy was the influence of the idea, widespread when the *Sagamo* and the *Cherokee* were added to the fleet in 1907 and 1908, that coal represented modern, material progress. Over the previous three decades, southern Ontario had industrialized rapidly, particularly Toronto and Hamilton. In 1905, six of the Navigation Company's eight directors, including the president and vice-president, were businessmen, merchants, or manufacturers who lived in Toronto or Hamilton.[56] Undoubtedly, the board of directors applied the same managerial ethos to the company as they and their class of capitalists and industrialists did to their businesses in the city. Primarily concerned with adding value and generating profit, they understood that economic success required investment in modern, technologically advanced ships. Moreover, the vast majority of their tourist passengers also lived in, or had an intimate understanding of, industrialized cities. In 1902, the Muskoka Lakes Association had 182 members, 63 percent of whom resided in either Toronto or Hamilton.[57] Notably, 12 members lived in the Pennsylvania coal region. In 1915, the *Muskoka Lakes Bluebook* listed 68 cottagers from Appalachia, the largest coal-producing region in North America.[58] Accommodating the increased demand from tourists required modernization. And since coal was the fuel of the modern, industrial era, so too must it power the newest class of steamers plying the Muskoka lakes. It is no surprise, then, that the *Sagamo* and the *Cherokee* burned coal mined in Appalachia, not fuelwood cut in Muskoka.

For settlers, the shift to coal eliminated an important source of income and further eroded their control over the tourism economy. Prior to 1907, they met the entire fuel needs of the Navigation Company by cutting, chopping, and stacking cordwood next to the shores of the lakes. In some cases, they sold it directly to the company, and steamers collected it from their shoreline or wharf. In other cases, merchants served as intermediaries between settlers and the company. In 1896, settlers who sold cordwood to the company through Homer's store in Rosseau earned an average of

$64.47 on the sale of approximately 44 cords each.[59] The next year, the company bought 3,440 cords, which put $5,048.30 in the pockets of approximately 78 settlers.[60] Five years later, in 1902, the company spent $9,435.25 on 6,429 cords supplied by roughly 146 settlers, an increase of 87 percent. For the next several years, it purchased a comparable quantity of wood from settlers.

With the introduction of its two coal-fired steamboats, the company's demand for fuelwood dropped, resulting in less income for fewer settlers. In addition, the company reorganized its routes so that the smaller boats ran shorter trips and served as feeders for its flagship, the *Sagamo,* which handled the longest and busiest trips.[61] As a result, the wood-fired steamers used less cordwood in 1908. Between 1906 and 1908, the company's fuel expenses increased by almost 16 percent, from $9,726.49 to $11,323.01, whereas its consumption of fuelwood declined by 18 percent from 6,627 to 5,444 cords. The sale of cordwood injected $7,989.50 into the local economy in 1908, but this was $1,736.99 less than two years earlier. In 1906, the Navigation Company bought cordwood from an average of 151 settlers, but in 1908 it purchased from 124. Although it remained dependent on settlers to meet more than 70 percent of its fuel requirements, the reduction of 1,183 cords eliminated an important source of income for 27 settlers. Furthermore, the fuel requirements of the *Sagamo* and the *Cherokee* represented a significant lost opportunity for settlers who might have sold the company even more wood had the steamers not run on coal. According to the company's 1908 annual account balance summary, the *Sagamo* and the *Cherokee* together consumed 29 percent of its total fuel expenses. This amounted to approximately 1,449 tons of bituminous coal. A ton (2,000 pounds) of coal contains almost exactly the same amount of energy as a cord of wood. If the *Sagamo* and the *Cherokee* had burned wood, they would have added approximately $2,127.09 to the local economy, or an average income of $64.00 for 33 settlers. Over the next three years, the company's fuel expenses declined while its passenger revenues increased. In 1910, the company purchased just 4,702 cords from approximately 107 settlers – a decline of 29 percent from 1906, when the entire fleet ran on wood. The addition of the *Sagamo* and the *Cherokee* represented a significant incursion of the mineral energy regime into Muskoka. After 1907, mineral energy dislocated the mode of power for water transportation from local to distant environments.

Coal was not the only fossil fuel to displace local organic energy in Muskoka. Gasoline, and the motorboats it powered, had a dramatic effect on tourist mobility and the local economy. The introduction of the motorboat

Fossil Fuels, Consumer Culture, and the Tourism Economy   157

had much in common with that of the automobile. Both technologies emerged and became popular as oil and coal became an integral part of the mineral energy regime. In 1870, Ontario produced 15.6 million US gallons of oil and 41.9 million in 1894, after which its output declined steadily to just 7.6 million in 1920.[62] In the Appalachian region, by contrast, oil production reached 1,524 million gallons in 1900.[63] After that time, as production waned in Ontario, provincial refineries began importing oil from Pennsylvania, so that by 1910 more than half of the petroleum products refined in Ontario were derived from imported oil.[64] As the market for gasoline developed, technological advances enabled refineries to get more end product from each barrel of oil. Around 1900, 5 gallons of gasoline could be refined from one 42-gallon barrel of crude oil. After the cracking method of separating petroleum was introduced in 1913, the gasoline yield per barrel increased to 22.5 gallons. By 1918, gasoline consumption in the United States had reached 3,219 million gallons.[65] Its meteoric rise throughout North America reflected the widespread adoption of the internal combustion engine.

The internal combustion engine had several important applications during the early twentieth century but none more significant than the automobile. However, the car was relatively inconsequential in Muskoka until after the Depression. Car ownership in Ontario remained relatively modest until the second decade of the century, when the number of registered cars climbed from 23,700 in 1913 to 127,860 in 1919.[66] Automobiles transformed towns and cities, but the most dramatic changes occurred in the countryside, where farmers owned between a quarter and a third of all Ontario's cars between the First World War and the Great Depression.[67] In Muskoka, automobiles were comparatively unpopular with year-round residents. In 1920, only 611 were registered there and in 1929 still only 2,363.[68] Compared to the improvements under way farther south in the province, Muskoka's roads remained poor. Between 1889 and 1908, the money that the Districts of Muskoka and Parry Sound spent on roads amounted to just 40 and 21 percent of the provincial average, respectively.[69] Not until the 1920s and the election of the United Farmers of Ontario did the provincial government invest in highways that reached into Muskoka. The rugged terrain of the Shield undoubtedly added expense to building and servicing roads that were suitable for automobiles. In the years before 1920, a small, but growing, number of tourists attempted the adventurous journey to Muskoka by automobile. Overall, cars remained a novelty during the golden age of steamboat navigation in Muskoka.[70] The impact of motorboats, however, was much more profound.

Before motorboats became widespread, several hotels and a few wealthy cottagers had owned small private steam yachts, which freed tourists from the inconveniences of rowboats and mass transportation. In 1902, the MLA Yearbook listed twenty-seven steam yachts belonging to members, and in 1906 it recorded fifty-two owned specifically by cottagers.[71] According to Muskoka steamboat historian Richard Tatley, seventy steam yachts were introduced between 1904 and 1918, although not all existed at the same time.[72] They declined in popularity as the merits of motorboats became clear. In 1918, the *Muskoka Lakes Bluebook* listed twenty-eight steam yachts belonging to cottagers. A variety of factors made them an impractical option. Perhaps the most important was cost. Their engines were so large and heavy that the boats themselves also had to be large and therefore expensive. They were not on-demand modes of transportation. Pressure had to be built up in the engine before it could function properly, which required time. Thus, trips had to be planned ahead. And steamers were complex and potentially dangerous machines, whose inner workings and operation were a mystery to the average cottager. Owners often kept engineers in their employ, which added to the costs. All of these factors made steam launches an unrealistic transportation choice for any but the wealthiest cottagers.

Motorboats presented fewer problems, and their popularity exploded. In 1902, both the McLachlan Gasoline Engine Company of Toronto and the Hamilton Model Works advertised marine engines in the MLA Yearbook. The latter even included a photograph of a motorboat filled with people to demonstrate exactly what a gasoline engine could offer.[73] Local boatbuilders recognized the potential immediately and pioneered watercraft designs to accommodate internal combustion engines. In 1898, Henry Ditchburn began building gasoline launches in Gravenhurst. A decade later, his 1908 catalogue featured a canoe and a rowboat, as well as two motorboats: a small "power skiff" and a larger "cabin day cruiser."[74] Four other boat builders started up in Port Carling around the same time.[75] In 1902, the MLA Yearbook listed no motorboats, and two years later it recorded four.[76] By the First World War, they were ubiquitous on the lower lakes. The 1915 *Muskoka Lakes Bluebook* mentions 407 gasoline motorboats on the three lower lakes, 80 percent of which belonged to cottagers.[77] In that year, Port Carling resident William Johnston built the prototype for the first mass-produced motorboat in North America – the Disappearing Propeller Boat (Dispro, DP, or "Dippy" for short). Initially, he simply added small gasoline engines to modified rowboats, but by 1916 Dippies were factory-produced.[78] The cheapest model sold for $225, roughly

FIGURE 5.11 Advertisement for the Disappearing Propeller Boat, 1918. Manipulating an inboard lever lifted the propeller into a protective housing. *John Rogers,* Muskoka Lakes Bluebook, Directory and Chart, 1918 *(Port Sandfield, ON: Self-published, 1918),* 82. *Courtesy of the Muskoka Lakes Museum Archives*

two-thirds the cost of a Ford Model T. The popularity and price of Dippies inspired owners to compare them to the Model T, and Johnston quickly capitalized on this trend by changing the name of his original model to the "Water-Ford."[79] In 1918, advertisements for the Dippy claimed that it was "safe, economical, convenient" and capable of getting twenty-three to twenty-five miles per gallon (see Figure 5.11).[80] Of the 895 cottagers listed in the 1918 *Muskoka Lakes Bluebook,* 38 percent, or 345 of them, owned a motorboat – exactly the same number of automobiles registered in Muskoka a year later.[81] In 1920, Muskoka still had more automobiles than motorboats, but the numbers of the latter continued to climb.

Motorboats revolutionized water transportation. Like the automobile, they offered new freedom of mobility.[82] Of course, both settlers and tourists embraced them, further entrenching the mineral energy regime in Muskoka. But when tourists did so, they broke free of the constraints of the organic energy regime. Each individual motorboat had very little impact on patterns of exchange, but in aggregate they diminished settler control of the tourism economy. During the early twentieth century, general stores sold small quantities of gasoline. Special orders from Imperial Oil occasionally arrived by train, and the Navigation Company transferred steel barrels aboard scows (fastened to the side of steamers to avoid fire) and shipped them to lakeside destinations.[83] As the number of motorboats increased, specialized distributors, such as boatbuilders and liveries, sold gasoline. By the First World War, rail tankers were delivering gasoline shipments to Muskoka, which suppliers transferred to holding tanks at the water's edge. Firms, such as Ditchburn at Muskoka Wharf or Bastien at Barnesdale on Lake Joseph, portioned out barrels into five-gallon cans and delivered them to customers by scow.[84] Demand grew steadily and piecemeal distribution proved both inadequate and dangerous. In 1919, Imperial Oil introduced the *Motor Queen,* a 2,300-gallon tanker, which delivered gasoline to customers. The fuel was transferred from rail tankers to the *Motor Queen* at the Canadian Pacific Railway station in Bala, shipped throughout the lakes, and pumped into each customer's barrel or personal holding tank. Two years later, in 1921, in an attempt to keep up with demand, the *Motor Queen* was replaced with the larger *Muskokalite.*[85] The Navigation Company and supply boats remained essential services in the tourism economy, but the mineral energy regime dominated water transportation by the 1920s.

Travelling via water was no longer strictly a choice between cramped muscles or crowded steamers. Unlike trips on foot, by canoe, or in wood-fired steamboats, trips by motorboat more effectively hid the relationship between the consumption of energy and its production, which made the decision to take a trip much easier. Motorboat owners found they could make trips more frequently than they did before. Between 1909 and 1914, Leena Riley, who ran Scarcliff hotel with her siblings, noted the presence of motorboats around Port Carling and Beaumaris with increasing frequency.[86] After the war, it was common for people to make trips by motorboat that they would have made by rowboat just a few years earlier. In 1919, dozens of cottagers gathered at the Barnesdale train station to listen to the boxing match between Jess Willard and Jack Dempsey. Brendan O'Brien, whose family spent each summer at the north end of the lake, recalled that the Barnesdale wharf "was an extraordinary sight. Every inch of dock space was occupied with launches tied two and three deep."[87] During regattas, the motorboats that conveyed spectators to the event often outnumbered the canoes that were competing in the race (see Figure 5.12).

Personal mobility for tourists translated into less control for settlers over patterns of consumption. According to Leena Riley, owners relied on their motorboats to meet the train (which had previously required connection by Navigation Company steamer), to collect the mail and socialize with friends (trips usually made by rowboat), and to go shopping in Port Carling (replacing a visit from the supply boat). Once cottagers could hop into

FIGURE 5.12 A crush of motorboats and steamers at the 1909 Muskoka Lakes Association Regatta on Lake Rosseau. *Frank W. Micklethwaite. John Harold Micklethwaite fonds, PA-160410. Courtesy of Library and Archives Canada*

their own motorboats and set out across the lake, perhaps to visit the store in Bala, Port Carling, or Rosseau, supply boat owners lost their control over a vital component of the local exchange network. Cottagers could still buy local dairy, eggs, meat, fruit, and vegetables, but they were no longer tied to the set schedule and limited stock of the supply boat. Now, they placed their mail orders and picked them up at a time of their own choosing. This new fossil-fuelled mode of transportation altered the flow of energy, the mobility of tourists, the influence of consumer culture, and the ability of settlers to connect the needs of summer tourists with local goods and services.

The energy requirements of hotels and cottages also changed. In the years before rural electrification, tourism created additional applications for fossil-fuelled technologies. After about 1900, several large hotels and a few of the most opulent summer estates installed steam power plants to provide electric lighting, steam heating, and hot and cold running water. According to one local historian, Elgin House, at the south end of Lake Joseph, burned wood to generate electricity and steam heat, and its kitchens used approximately two hundred cords each season.[88] But technological requirements and the ethos of modernity that prompted the Navigation Company to switch to coal appear to have convinced at least some owners to follow suit. In the spring of 1918, Charlie Coate arranged for the Navigation Company to deliver "one [rail]car load of anthracite coal" from Muskoka Wharf to his cottage at Cape Elizabeth, presumably to fuel the steam power plant at his cottage.[89] In the same year, the Navigation Company also delivered "a carload of stove coal for use at the Royal Muskoka."[90] Opened in 1902 as a subsidiary of the Navigation Company, the Royal Muskoka Hotel could accommodate 350 guests and immediately became the most luxurious resort on the lake. It was also one of the earliest hotels to offer electric lights, steam heating, and hot and cold running water.[91] Other hotels followed its lead. In 1915, Prospect House was "lighted by electricity," and Monteith House promised "hot and cold running water in every room ... Steam heated; Electric Lights."[92] In 1915, six of the seventeen hotel ads in the *Muskoka Lakes Bluebook* mentioned steam-powered amenities. Three years later, in 1918, fifteen of thirty-three hotel ads featured at least one (an increase of 10 percent), including hot running water, steam heat, electric lighting, and acetylene lighting.[93] Visitors from the city increasingly expected modern conveniences while on vacation in Muskoka, and affluent cottagers and hotel owners used a technology of the mineral energy regime to accommodate their desire for greater comfort. In the process, they disconnected the energy requirements of tourism from the local economy.

Fossil fuels, especially coal oil and kerosene, were regular household commodities in Muskoka before 1900. After that time, however, the consumption of fossil fuels expanded considerably, as new technologies made their use much easier and affordable. A growing number of cottagers experimented with gasoline stationary power plants to generate electricity. In 1902, Toronto's Gasoline Engine Company advertised small engines that could be used as boat motors, "for running an Electric Light Plant, or pumping water at your summer cottage."[94] Similarly, in a 1915 ad that targeted cottagers, the Canadian Fairbanks–Morse Company of Toronto promised that its Residence Lighting and Water System would "eliminate all the drudgery of carrying water and filling oil lamps."[95] It is impossible to determine exactly how many hotels and cottages had gasoline-powered generators installed before 1920, but several local histories make passing references to these types of systems.[96] At least one household at Cape Elizabeth had an oil-fuelled stationary power plant of some sort. In a June 1915 letter to the Navigation Company, an unknown member of the family inquired about an oil heater that was supposed to have been delivered along with a barrel of oil.[97] Two years later, in October 1917, Charlie Coate wrote to the Navigation Company to inquire about a barrel of "Petroleum refined Oil shipped by the Imperial Oil Co. of Toronto."[98] Most cottages

Fossil Fuels, Consumer Culture, and the Tourism Economy 163

and hotels continued to burn wood, and replacing oil lamps with power plants did not create entirely new linkages with distant material and energy flows. But new kinds of household energy consumption were added to more sustainable ones and in some cases replaced them. The use of power plants to lift water from the lake and provide interior lighting and heating expanded the proportion of Muskoka's energy needs coming from elsewhere while simultaneously isolating households from organic fuel supplied locally by settlers.

In roughly two decades, consumer culture and mineral energy established themselves in Muskoka and began to undermine the component of rural identity that was shaped by tourism. Relationships between settlers and tourists that had been so important less than a generation earlier weakened and sometimes dissolved. Tourists now had new choices, and the local economy was subject to enormous pressures and competition from larger networks of exchange. Yet, settlers never entirely lost their control of the tourism economy, especially during the first two decades of the twentieth century. The interdependent relationships between tourists and settlers remained at the heart of the local economy. In fact, the new links with the greater world were overlaid onto, or ran parallel to, pre-existing locally based exchange. Settlers still worked for hotels and cottagers, and continued to supply them with fresh vegetables, dairy, eggs, and meat. But over time and in subtle ways, the resiliency of local interdependencies was eroded, lessening the sustainability of rural identity next to the lower lakes.

Exogenous inputs were nothing new in Muskoka, where reliance on resources and goods from the south had always been an unavoidable fact of life. Like the Anishinaabeg, who had never depended exclusively on the Shield to meet their subsistence needs, settlers and tourists required resources and goods from the south. During the late nineteenth century, however, tourists counted on local farmers and merchants to provide for many of their needs. Fresh food and fuelwood, as well as other goods and services, came from the land and labour of settlers during the 1870s, 1880s, and 1890s. After the turn of the century, however, mail-order consumer culture and the new mineral energy regime largely supplanted this sustainable arrangement, replacing it with exchange networks that lay beyond settler control.

Conclusion

Near the end of his 1936 study *Settlement and the Forest Frontier in Eastern Canada,* Canadian historian A.R.M. Lower concluded that "the future of the Huron-Ottawa tract of the Shield [which includes Muskoka] is ... by no means gloomy." Writing during the Depression, Lower was convinced that one "direction from which the rejuvenation of the southern Shield may come is from the tourist." Recognizing the long history of tourism in Muskoka, and acknowledging that few opportunities were available in the logging industry, he felt that "every year sees more summer hotels erected and more summer cottages built," so that "the summer population of the Shield is growing rapidly and the local market it creates is just as important and likely to be much more permanent than was that created by the lumber trade."[1] More than eighty years later, in 2018, the Muskoka Community Foundation's "Vital Signs" report revealed that despite the popular image of Muskoka as "an affluent cottage/vacation destination, ... this idyllic vision of the region obscures the economic reality among the population. Muskoka, like many rural communities, faces challenges in addressing poverty and helping the community's most vulnerable people."[2] Part of a nationwide program organized by Community Foundations of Canada, the "Vital Signs" reports are intended to "measure the health and vitality of our communities" and to "identify significant trends in a range of sectors and areas that are critical to quality of life and maintaining smart and caring communities."[3] As Daniel Bradbury, chair of the Muskoka Community Foundation, wrote in his introduction to the report, its purpose was "to inform a constructive debate about how

Conclusion

we can work together towards ensuring that Muskoka is an attractive, supportive and sustainable region for everyone."[4] Tourism has been an important part of Muskoka's history since the late nineteenth century, but evaluating that history depends very much on whether one takes the perspective of the visitor or the permanent resident.

Rather than trying to determine whether tourism has been "good" or "bad" for Muskoka, this book insists that understanding its importance requires an evaluation of how its role changed and became more or less sustainable over time. Most historians of tourism, like most popular images of Muskoka, tend to privilege the views and experiences of the visitors. In the preceding chapters, I explored the importance of tourism to the Indigenous and non-Indigenous people who called Muskoka home during the late nineteenth and early twentieth centuries. And, in particular, I considered the sustainability of the rural identity based on tourism that settlers constructed between 1870 and 1920. Neither tourism nor the rural identity it supported in Muskoka has ever been completely sustainable, only more or less sustainable.

To the Anishinaabeg and the Haudenosaunee, tourism was little consolation for the displacement, discrimination, restrictions, and marginalization imposed by settler colonialism. Like Indigenous peoples everywhere, they navigated systems of rule and negotiated space to maintain and reproduce their identity. As new laws limited their critical fishing practices and the Indian Act prevented their own governance on reserves, tourism enabled band members to retain their Indigenous identities and provide for their families by selling crafts or working as guides. Settler colonialism made everyday life much less sustainable for the Anishinaabeg and Haudenosaunee, but tourism presented some of the most sustainable strategies for adjusting to, and coping with, the burdens of colonization.

For settlers, it presented a novel component for constructing a rural identity that was distinct in North America. They arrived in Muskoka as part of the great land rush of the nineteenth century, and quickly discovered that the Shield was unsuited to an agrarian society and economy.[5] However, during the earliest years of Euro-Canadian resettlement, visitors from the city began showing up. Some paid to stay in hotels, many of which grew out of settlers' homes. Others bought land and built cottages on remote points and islands. In all cases, they relied on settlers for locally derived food and fuel, goods and services. In this way, tourism became an important part of what R.W. Sandwell and others refer to as "occupational pluralism," a common survival strategy in most rural places of northern North America at this time.[6] In Muskoka, tourism co-evolved with farming and logging during the first generation of resettlement to become the defining feature of a distinct rural identity in North America.

Tourism did not benefit everyone. For backwoods settlers, it was of little consequence, and agroforestry shaped the rhythms and patterns of their lives. They retained only a small portion of the value of the logs they cut, spent months away from home, and contributed to the degradation of local ecosystems. Unlike tourism, agroforestry was relatively short-lived, but settlers also engaged in small-scale logging that was more sustainable than the large commercial approaches that dominated logging in Muskoka.

After the turn of the century, tourism began to change as well. During the last two decades of the nineteenth century, settlers retained a great degree of control over the tourism economy, because visitors relied on local goods and services they could not acquire elsewhere. During the first two decades of the twentieth century, however, fossil fuels, consumer culture, and distant urban networks of exchange, particularly department stores and mail-order catalogues, began to erode settler control over tourism. Visitors still relied on settlers for many goods and services, but substitutes from elsewhere increasingly took precedence. An identity based on tourism became less sustainable as settlers gradually lost control of the local economy.

Sustainability was never a condition of life in Muskoka, but rather a non-linear process in which certain features became more sustainable as others became less so. Tourism was a more sustainable basis for constructing rural identity on the Shield than either farming or logging. Of course, most settlers engaged in a plurality of occupations, but many took advantage of tourism and found more sustainable opportunities than those who could not. However, tourism also contributed directly to settler colonialism, which dispossessed Indigenous peoples. In this respect, it was much less sustainable than the Indigenous lifeways it displaced, even if it did follow similar seasonal cycles. Nonetheless, it presented the Anishinaabeg and Haudenosaunee with more sustainable opportunities than were available to them elsewhere. After the First World War, tourism remained an important component of the local economy, perhaps the most essential one, but it had become less sustainable for all residents, whether Indigenous or non-Indigenous. Indeed, it would never again be as sustainable as it had been during the late nineteenth and early twentieth centuries.

The general shape of tourism in Muskoka did not change dramatically during the interwar years, but the seeds of change had been sown. On the lakes, motorboats became the most common form of transportation for cottagers, and though the steamboats still ran, their importance steadily

Conclusion 167

declined.[7] Automobiles remained a novelty until after the Depression. Many people drove to the cottage or the resort but mainly to prove that they could, not because it was particularly comfortable or convenient. In the 1920s, road improvements began to make Muskoka easier to access by car. A kind of positive feedback developed in which better roads tempted more people to drive, and vice versa, until, by the end of the Second World War, the car had replaced the train as the chief means of reaching Muskoka.[8] By mid-century, motorboats and cars had eclipsed steamboats and passenger trains. Throughout these years, department stores and urban retailers made continual inroads into the rural economy in Muskoka. Farmers and merchants continued to meet the needs of tourists and cottagers, but they competed directly with mail-order catalogues and the allure of mass-marketed consumer products, including food. After the war, however, these forces combined to greatly alter the character of tourism in Muskoka and its place in the identity of permanent residents.

For the Anishinaabeg and Haudenosaunee, engaging in the tourism economy became a less sustainable strategy for adjusting to, and coping with, settler colonial discrimination during the interwar years. As Robin Jarvis Brownlie shows, life on reserves in central Ontario before the Second World War was tightly controlled by the Department of Indian Affairs.[9] Between about 1900 and 1925, band members from Wahta, Rama, and Georgina Island still sold crafts to tourists or worked as guides for hunting and fishing parties so they could make annual trips to their hunting grounds along the upper reaches of the Muskoka River watershed. As the century proceeded, however, greater enforcement of hunting and fishing laws, especially in Algonquin Park, made this practice increasingly difficult.[10] And after 1923, under the terms of the Williams Treaties, the Chippewa at Rama, Georgina Island, and Christian Island (along with four other First Nations) surrendered their land rights to twenty thousand square kilometres at the southern edge of the Shield, which included Muskoka.

During the interwar years, as Sharon Wall reveals, settler colonialism scrubbed the history of Indigenous peoples from rural landscapes in Ontario, even as resorts and children's summer camps invented rituals and "played Indian" to reinforce popular ideas about wilderness.[11] One resort on Lake of Bays exploited its location on Bigwin Island, near Anishinaabe burial grounds, to generate tourist revenue. In 1920, Charles Orlando Shaw, owner of the leather tannery in Huntsville, purchased the island and built an extravagant resort hotel and a nine-hole golf course, which immediately became one of the most popular tourist destinations in Canada.[12]

168   Conclusion

In addition to fine dining, golfing, cruises on the lake, and many other amenities, Bigwin Inn provided guests with a rare opportunity to meet a real live "Indian Chief." John Bigwin, after whose family both the island and the hotel were unceremoniously named, was a member of the Georgina Island First Nation. At the Williams Treaties Commission hearings, Bigwin had explained that he and his father travelled from Lake Simcoe to their traditional hunting grounds near present-day Dorset, Ontario. During the late nineteenth century, he and other band members tapped maple sap, tended a garden between Kawagama Lake and Lake of Bays, and hunted deer and trapped fisher, mink, and otter along the upper Muskoka River watershed. Throughout the interwar years, they still made the trip to Lake of Bays, but now they entertained guests at the resort by dressing in regalia and performing for payment. Undoubtedly, this income represented an important source of support for their families, as it had for many band members who sold crafts or worked as guides. But it also enabled Bigwin and his kin to return to their hunting territory, where younger generations learned from their elders, and the community could maintain doodem relationships with ancestors buried on the island. After Bigwin died at the age of 102, tourism in Muskoka ceased to provide any meaningful opportunities for the Anishinaabeg and Haudenosaunee. In the first two decades of the twenty-first century, tourists encountered almost no signs of Indigenous history in Muskoka. Things are beginning to change, however, as the Muskoka Steamships and Discovery Centre in Gravenhurst has partnered with several First Nations and Indigenous organizations to add a curated exhibit on the Indigenous culture and history of Muskoka.[13]

During the postwar years, Muskoka experienced what historian Peter Stevens refers to as the "democratization" of cottaging. The economic boom that followed the war, combined with more affordable cars and expanded municipal and provincial road construction, created conditions that saw cottage ownership shift away from being exclusive to the wealthy. In the interwar years, cottage ownership, and tourism more generally, had become an increasingly middle-class experience. After the Second World War, even many working-class families could afford to vacation at the lake in a cabin of their own. On the larger lakes, where the oldest cottages had been built, permanent residents continued to subdivide their land and sell lots for development. But many postwar cottages were built beside smaller lakes on land bought from either the Crown or a developer who had purchased a large tract from permanent residents and subdivided it for individual sale. In most cases, these small lakes had never experienced the impacts of tourism, apart from an occasional hunting or fishing party.

Conclusion   169

Cottages became attainable to more people for several reasons. Cars and improved roads made them more accessible. Increased incomes made owning, maintaining, and accessorizing them more affordable for many white, middle-class families. And, importantly, for the first time, employees were legally entitled to paid vacations. In 1944, the Ontario government passed legislation that entitled all full-time employees to a minimum of one week of paid vacation, which was extended to two weeks in 1968. Many companies granted three or four weeks.[14] The number of cottages rose significantly after about 1950. In 1955, an estimated 8,071 "summer homes" in the District of Muskoka were occupied by approximately 40,355 seasonal residents. By 1973, the "seasonal dwellings" had increased to 18,427 and the seasonal population to about 71,760. In fact, cottages went up so quickly that in 1972, more than two-thirds of them dated from between 1951 and 1971. In 2017, there were 22,879 seasonal dwellings in the District of Muskoka, with a seasonal population of 81,907.[15] A similar trend held true for resorts and hotels. Of the 925 resorts built in the century after 1870, nearly half were added between 1950 and 1970.[16] After 1970, however, overnight accommodation went into decline. In 1957, Muskoka had 554 resorts and hotels. By 1989, that number had dropped to 149, shrinking to just 89 by 2008. Holidays in places all over the world became more affordable relative to a resort vacation in Muskoka. The ones that stayed in business, and most of the new hotels, were large, corporately owned or managed operations. Only a handful of locally and family owned resorts survived into the twenty-first century. These changes in tourism had a significant impact on rural identity in Muskoka.

In the backwoods, other features of occupational pluralism mattered much more than tourism, but residents in those areas undoubtedly felt the new waves of postwar tourism as an imposition and a challenge to the identities that they, their parents, grandparents, and great-grandparents had constructed. As Muskoka residents lost their hold on the tourism economy, the tensions created by the arrival of cottagers in hitherto less accessible areas became more acute. Throughout the region, settlers grappled with the seemingly immense potential of tourism, on the one hand, and its consistent postwar failure to meaningfully support the local economy, on the other.

Ironically, an important dimension of this tension arose from the process of democratization, which Stevens describes. Initially, tourism in Muskoka had been limited almost exclusively to what Stephen Leacock referred to as the "idle rich," who typically spent their holiday time in leisure pursuits.[17] As a result, settlers had many opportunities to earn an income by selling necessary goods and services to these vacationers. After the Second World War, however, democratization of cottaging reduced the types of opportunities permanent residents could expect from tourism. If cottaging were to be attainable for middle- and working-class people, its cost needed to come down. For the cost to come down, cottagers had to take on many chores and projects themselves rather than relying on local residents to do so. Cottage culture embraced greater opportunities to perform a kind of masculinized autonomy over the household, in which men handled maintenance, repairs, and renovations, and possibly even built the cottage and its dock.[18] Lower costs and more do-it-yourself projects deprived permanent residents of income that would have been common half a century earlier.

In the postwar period, as Stevens shows, cottagers imagined themselves as settlers and compared their own maintenance of a second home on the lake with settlers' struggles to carve out a homestead from the forest. Stevens suggests that "pioneers provided a model for people who hoped to recapture what they thought had been lost amidst the headlong rush into postwar consumer society."[19] At the same time, they retained the illusion that their cottage was nestled in a wilderness. Cottagers could certainly play the role of settler by building a cabin in the woods, but this rarely entailed clearing the land or planting a subsistence garden to support themselves. So selective was this mentality that most failed to perceive nearby farms, owned and operated by the descendants of actual settlers, as places where they could potentially obtain food and fuel. Instead, many wives who spent most of the summer at the lake with the children tasked their husbands with buying groceries in the city on their way to the cottage for the weekend. By the 1970s, supermarket chain stores had begun to appear in Muskoka, which made it even easier to obtain groceries, and far less likely that cottagers satisfied these needs from local farmers. The shift from buying fresh local food became all but complete with cottage electrification during the 1950s and 1960s. Before this point, cottagers commonly relied on local sources of ice for iceboxes, fuelwood for the stove, and fresh food, especially milk and dairy, but also fruits and vegetables.[20]

Drawing on the criticisms of the wealthy in F. Scott Fitzgerald's *The Great Gatsby*, scholars such as Peter Stevens and Roy Wolfe label cottages as a "luxury" that meets an "inessential need."[21] Cottages may be inessential to their owners, but they can be an essential part of the local economy and can provide vital income to permanent residents. As fossil fuels, consumer culture, and distant markets of exchange made it easier for more people to own and spend time at a cottage, they became increasingly ignorant of

Conclusion

their impact on the local economy and of the long history of interdependence between seasonal and permanent residents in Muskoka.

For the communities that supported it, tourism was less sustainable during the postwar period than it had been earlier. Nevertheless, if even small proportions of the new cottagers and the older ones had continued to patronize permanent residents, the democratization of cottaging could have supported the local economy and provided additional income. In 1972, approximately 27 percent of the entire labour force in the District of Muskoka worked in the "tourism and recreation" sector, which injected nearly $60 million into local businesses. This sum included approximately $4 million (7 percent) from the construction of new cottages and repairs or renovations to existing ones, more than $16 million (27 percent) from overnight accommodations, and $30 million (51 percent) from retail and service trades, other than overnight stays and construction trades. In 2001, roughly 57 percent of the district's economic base "could be attributed to meeting the needs of tourists or seasonal residents." Fifteen years later, in 2016, the census recorded that 26 percent of the district's labour force worked in sales and service, and 21 percent in trades, transport, and equipment operation – the two sectors most closely connected to tourism.[22] Most retail revenue went toward corporate profits of large chain stores and mainly provided what anthropologist John Michels refers to as "lower-end service-sector jobs."[23] Tourism became less sustainable, not because fewer tourists visited Muskoka each year, but because permanent residents had much less control over the tourism economy.

In 2005, journalist Brett Grainger wrote an article in *Toronto Life* magazine entitled "The Other Muskoka," detailing rural life that seemed hidden to, or perhaps ignored by, the tourist gaze. He reminded his urban audience – many of whom owned summer homes in Muskoka or knew people who did – that their "northern playground of pleasant lakeside cottages and resorts is built next door to grinding poverty, addiction and spousal abuse."[24] Throughout the late twentieth and early twenty-first centuries, permanent residents readily acknowledged the economic importance of tourism. In the same breath, many also remarked on the challenges of what John Michels refers to as "rural gentrification."[25] For her 2017 master's thesis exploring the views of permanent residents regarding cottaging in Muskoka, Ashley Gallant interviewed many people who struggled with the tension between the potential offered by tourism and the reality of its numerous shortcomings. According to a social worker who had lived in the area for five years, seasonal residents "don't understand the underbelly

172   Conclusion

of Muskoka."[26] For another resident who worked in planning and economic development, and had lived in Muskoka for seventeen years, the popular image of the area overlooked "one of the biggest gaps between housing prices and income in Ontario ... [the] homeless people, people who can't find jobs, people with addictions, people with mental health issues."[27] The view from the lake has obscured the various social crises of life in Muskoka.

A major challenge identified by permanent residents and government studies was the seasonality of the tourism economy. In 1972, the average cottager spent 77 percent of their time in Muskoka during the summer months. Since the Second World War, both the number of tourists and the amount of time they spend in Muskoka during the winter have expanded due to new recreational activities, such as snowmobiling and skiing, as well as renovations to winterize cottages. Nevertheless, in 2019, summer tourism still accounted for 60 percent of annual visitors to Muskoka.[28] Between 1870 and 1920, tourism was even more seasonal – until the postwar period, very few people visited during the winter. A century ago, summertime tourism earned settlers a sizeable portion of their annual income. During the winter, they found alternative sources of income, prepared for the next tourist season (by cutting wood and ice), and engaged in a variety of subsistence activities, including hunting and fishing. These days, occupational pluralism is less common because most seasonal income is available only as low-waged jobs during the summer. As a result, employment insurance (EI) has become a form of subsistence. One of Gallant's interviewees, who had lived in Muskoka for twenty-five years, alternated between working one day a week and collecting EI during the winter, and working twelve-hour days for a month or more during the summer. A community advocate who had resided in Muskoka for thirty years told Gallant that "seasonal jobs are hard on a lot of families in Muskoka, we need to find better jobs."[29] The 2018 "Vital Signs" report concluded that in many cases, part-time and seasonal employment was insufficient to meet "the high cost of housing, food, electricity, transportation, and child care" in Muskoka.[30] Nonetheless, nearly all of Gallant's interviewees conceded that "we can't throw tourism out. We need to support it, we need to encourage it, broaden it, we need to convince them to pay better money."[31] Tied up with their acknowledgment that tourism was vital to life in Muskoka was the impression that visitors needed to contribute more meaningfully to the local economy and the welfare of permanent residents.

In the late nineteenth and early twentieth centuries, visitors to Muskoka made a more meaningful contribution to the local economy than they did

Conclusion 173

a century later, because settlers had a higher degree of control over tourism. As Michels points out in his study of rural gentrification just north of Muskoka, free market economics, neoliberal trade agreements, and globalization eroded the control that permanent residents have over the rural economy. Equally important, however, permanent residents in Muskoka significantly lost control over local politics after about 1950, as seasonal residents came to outnumber them. As early as the 1890s, cottagers roughly doubled the population near the larger lakes during the summer months, though they remained a minority in the district as a whole. After the Second World War, their numbers grew more quickly than those of permanent residents, so that by 1972 they owned an estimated 52 percent of private land. In 2017, they constituted 57 percent of Muskoka's total population.[32] As several scholars note, when a seasonal population outnumbers a permanent one, tension and conflict arise over governance.[33] Since the 1970s, second-home property owners in Ontario have been entitled to vote municipally in the ridings of both their properties. In 1973, a report on tourism's impact on the Muskoka economy warned that "with land ownership comes the right to vote in municipal elections, so that the right of franchise is being gradually shifted outside the District."[34] From about 1975 onward, seasonal residents increasingly wielded their political clout as a way of protecting their property rights.

No other issue exemplifies how seasonal residents have used their property rights to extend control over political affairs in rural areas more than environmentalism. In the late twentieth and early twenty-first centuries, environmentalism fuelled a kind of distrust felt by cottagers and tourists regarding permanent residents. In the 1980s, environmental concerns, such as water quality and shoreline development, became increasingly important to second-home property owners in Muskoka.[35] Suddenly, certain types of work and land use, such as short-term cabin rentals or resort and timeshare developments, which generated important occupational opportunities for permanent residents, were perceived by tourists as a threat to their property values and enjoyment of the environment.[36] A century earlier, when they had relied on the land and labour of residents, they would have better understood how their interests aligned. Now, however, they had trouble imagining how the rural identity of residents might complement their own ethos and perceptions of Muskoka.

In the century after 1920, tourism continued to shape the identity of people in Muskoka, and it will continue to do so for many generations to come. But why does this history matter? It matters because it demonstrates that, more than a century ago, tourism contributed in many meaningful ways to the society and economy of permanent residents in Muskoka. It also matters because it offers insights into how tourists and cottagers could more sustainably contribute to the welfare of residents in the twenty-first century. Tourism had important impacts on the identity of people who lived on the Shield, and it still exerts an important influence on how they think about the opportunities for life in Muskoka. But tourists, cottagers, second-home owners, and visitors take for granted that they can enjoy a holiday and ignore the welfare of the people who live there. This history matters because it helps articulate what a more sustainable rural identity might look like in a place that is unsuited to agriculture but where the environmental limitations can be turned to the advantage of residents. It matters because it demonstrates that the most sustainable economic, social, and environmental arrangements for rural communities are those in which permanent residents retain control over patterns of economic exchange, social relationships, and environmental conditions. Tourism was most sustainable when this was the norm and least sustainable when it was not.

In 1936, Arthur Lower stated that "it was a mistake to allow [the Shield's] indiscriminate settlement years ago, a mistake that undoubtedly has entailed much human misery." Lower did not have the Anishinaabeg in mind when he wrote this, but it applies to them even more than it does to the first generations of settlers. Lower predicted that "these exact mistakes are not likely to be made again in this area on any considerable scale."[37] Seventy years later, journalist Brett Grainger visited the site of his great-great-great grandfather's homestead near Huntsville. As he neared the property, he detected "no fields and no houses. Just interminable bush." Contemplating what had once been a farm, he saw "a low wall of stones six feet wide and waist high, covered in rotting branches and leaves," which marked the edge of the clearing his ancestors had carved out of the forest. "Whatever mark the homesteaders left six generations ago," Grainger realized, "had been erased by the land's cruel fecundity. After many fruitful harvests of human misery, the only proof of their labour was a pile of stones."[38] The hope and the expectation that tourism can continue to support future generations in rural Muskoka can become a reality only if those who visit the region every summer recover the history that has been obscured by the wilderness they seek.

Appendix

A Note on Sources

Focusing on what Fernand Braudel refers to as the "structures of everyday life," this study draws extensively from sources that reveal minute and personal details about people's perceptions, struggles, relationships, and interactions with one another and with the Shield environment.[1] Particularly useful were many diaries, journals, and memoirs written by settlers, both men and women, which covered nearly the entire period and a variety of locales in Muskoka. As Virginia DeJohn Anderson states, these types of sources "reveal not only what colonial [or pioneer] farmers were doing but also what they thought about their world."[2] Both published and unpublished, they create a sense of the social fabric of Muskoka, describe the ways that households connected with each other to structure the local economy, and reveal how the environment shaped their everyday lives. I also rely heavily on census records and a variety of ledgers from local businesses and industries to cross-reference quantitative and qualitative source materials in reconstructing people's lives.

Quantitative sources, such as census records, directories, and ledgers, contained vital information that complemented the intimate and more contextual details in other sources. Historic maps provided invaluable information for understanding the spatial component of this research. Using Historical Geographic Information Systems (HGIS), I combine the information from these maps with quantitative data from census records and ledgers to visualize the spatial patterns of settlers' economic activity

175

176 Appendix

at the household level, particularly location patents and abandonment, land use, cottage proliferation, resource extraction, and market activity. Of particular importance was the 1879 *Guide Book and Atlas of Muskoka and Parry Sound Districts,* which mapped and labelled the owner or locatee of every lot in every township in the district, as well as every village, town, road, sawmill, and post office.[3] Ownership sometimes changed, but where it did not, these maps identified where people lived, allowing me to correlate information from other sources, particularly diaries, journals, memoirs, and ledgers. Maps and resident lists, such as the 1899 *Map and Chart of the Muskoka Lakes* and the *Muskoka Lakes Bluebook, Directory and Chart* from 1915 and 1918, were also very helpful in identifying cottages, old steamer routes, and hotel locations that no longer appear on modern maps.[4] A central challenge of studying history through the lens of sustainability is evaluating how particular arrangements became more or less sustainable over time. As historians, including Brian Donahue and Geoff Cunfer, show, HGIS can be useful here.[5] For example, by mapping who supplied sawmills and leather tanneries with logs and bark, I demonstrate how households embraced small-scale wood-resource harvesting as a more sustainable alternative to working in logging camps. Visualizing quantitative information using HGIS supplements the evidence provided in qualitative sources and presents an invaluable method of investigating the fabric of people's material lives and how they changed over time.

To analyze the experiences of First Nations in Muskoka during colonization and the opportunities they pursued through tourism, I relied on a number of ethnographic studies of Algonquian-speaking people prior to contact and colonization, annual Department of Indian Affairs agent reports from the late nineteenth and early twentieth centuries, testimony recorded during the 1923 Williams Treaties hearings, and interviews that I conducted in 2011 with two elders of Wasauksing First Nation (formerly Parry Island First Nation). Sadly, Indigenous history in Muskoka has been mostly left out of the local history literature. In bringing together a wide variety of sources, this book makes the important contribution of rectifying its erasure.

This study draws heavily on published local histories of Muskoka. Written by amateur historians, these decidedly non-scholarly books provide distinct challenges.[6] Their intended readership consists mainly of cottagers and local history enthusiasts, and almost none include citations or list their sources. It is clear, however, that they are based on government documents, newspapers, and interviews. Although I use them with care, I treat their content as reliable on the whole. Less reliable are their interpretations of the past. Typically, they concentrate on the challenges faced and overcome by hardy pioneers or the pleasant experiences of a bygone age – both of which are tinged with nostalgia. Most tend to promote, or defend, a particular view of the past. Many draw on interviews with residents who have since passed away. And many of their authors are themselves Muskoka residents who acquired considerable first-hand knowledge of Muskoka's past, which they use to weave together narrative histories that reflect community understandings of that past. They need to be handled cautiously, but these works are an invaluable source of information without which this story would be incomplete. Reconstructing the relationships that help explain life in Muskoka relies on this type of inherited knowledge of Muskoka as a place.

Notes

FOREWORD: EDGE EFFECTS

1 For Frederic Edward Clements, see Frank N. Egerton, "Homage to Frederic E. Clements, Historian of Plant Succession Studies," *Bulletin of the Ecological Society of America* 90, 1 (2009): 43–79, https://doi.org/10.1890/0012-9623-90.1.43 and John Phillips, "A Tribute to Frederic E. Clements and His Concepts in Ecology," *Ecology* 35, 2 (1954): 114–15, https://esajournals.onlinelibrary.wiley.com/doi/abs/10.2307/1931106. For Aldo Leopold, see Susan L. Flader, *Thinking Like a Mountain: Aldo Leopold and the Evolution of an Ecological Attitude toward Deer, Wolves, and Forests* (Columbia, MO: University of Missouri Press, 1974) and Richard L. Knight and Suzanne Riedel, eds., *Aldo Leopold and the Ecological Conscience* (New York: Oxford University Press, 2002). For a pithy synopsis, see Leslie Ries, "A Brief History of Edge Effects: 100 Years of Research in Four Short Paragraphs," https://science.umd.edu/lries/EERC/EERCbackground.html. The Center for Culture, History and Environment, a cluster in the Nelson Institute for Environmental Studies at the University of Wisconsin–Madison, has adopted "Edge Effects" as the title of its digital magazine. The rationale for this, congruent with that adduced here, is recounted in William Cronon, "Why Edge Effects," *Edge Effects,* 9 October 2014, https://edgeeffects.net/why-edge-effects/.

2 F.E. Clements, *Plant Succession: An Analysis of the Development of Vegetation* (Washington, DC: Carnegie Institution of Washington, 1916).

3 Alfred Russel Wallace is credited with coining the term "ecotone" in 1859 to describe the (sharp) faunal boundary between the Indonesian islands of Bali and Lombok ("Wallace's Line").

4 Aldo Leopold, *Game Management* (New York: Charles Scribner's Sons, 1933).

5 Jan Conn, *Edge Effects* (Kingston, ON: Brick Books, 2012); H.L. Hix, "Jan Conn, On Thresholds and Edges," *In Quire,* reposted at https://031454a.netsolhost.com/inquire/2012/12/16/jan-conn-on-thresholds-and-edges/ For Conn's scientific contributions see https://www.wadsworth.org/senior-staff/jan-conn.

6 Shannon Stunden Bower, "Ecotone Scholarship and Structural Change," *Global Environment: A Journal of Transdisciplinary History* 14, 3 (2021): 639–45.
7 "Southern Muskoka's 'living edge,'" https://www.ontarioparks.com/parksblog/six-mile-lake-living-edge/#more-22269.
8 Graeme Wynn, "Notes on Society and Environment in Old Ontario," *Journal of Social History* 13, 1 (1979): 49–65.
9 P.M. Vankoughnet, cited by Derek Murray, "Equitable Claims and Future Considerations: Road Building and Colonization in Early Ontario, 1850–1890," *Journal of the Canadian Historical Association/Revue de la Société historique du Canada* 24, 2 (2013): 156–88, and noted by John C. Walsh, "Landscapes of Longing: Colonization and the Problem of State Formation in Canada West" (PhD diss., University of Guelph, 2001).
10 T. McMurray, *The Free Grant Lands of Canada, from Practical Experience of Bush Farming in the Free Grant Districts of Muskoka and Parry Sound* (Bracebridge, Ontario, 1871), 14.
11 Murray, "Equitable Claims and Future Considerations." See also the thoughtful work of Derek Murray, "A 'Colony of Unrequited Dreams'? Settler Colonialism and the Failed-Settlement Narrative in the Ottawa-Huron Tract, 1850–1910" (PhD diss., University of Victoria, 2018).
12 Cited in Wynn, "Notes on Society and Environment," 58.
13 Arthur R.M. Lower, "The Assault on the Laurentian Barrier," *Canadian Historical Review* 10, 4 (December 1929): 294–307.
14 Lower, "Assault on the Laurentian Barrier," 302–3.
15 Walter Shanly, *Report on the Ottawa and French River Navigation Project* (Montreal: John Lovell, 1863) 43–44, cited in Walsh, "Landscapes of Longing," 120.
16 The allusions here are to Cole Harris, *The Reluctant Land: Society, Space and Environment in Canada before Confederation* (Vancouver: UBC Press, 2008) and Cole Harris, *A Bounded Land: Reflections on Settler Colonialism in Canada* (Vancouver: UBC Press, 2020). The general argument was also adumbrated in R. Cole Harris and John Warkentin, *Canada before Confederation* (New York: Oxford University Press, 1974).
17 Harris, *Reluctant Land*, xv.
18 The "gigantic geographic growth," and imperialism ideas are threaded through the four volumes of D.W. Meinig, *The Shaping of America: A Geographical Perspective on 500 Years of History* (New Haven: Yale University Press, 1986, 1993, 1998, 2004). See also my "D.W. Meinig and *The Shaping of America*," *Journal of Historical Geography* 31, 4 (October 2005): 610–33. The conception of Canada as an archipelago is from Cole Harris, "Regionalism and the Canadian Archipelago," in *Heartland Hinterland: A Regional Geography of Canada*, ed. Larry McCann and Angus Gunn (Scarborough, ON: Prentice Hall Canada, 1998), 395–421.
19 Walsh, "Landscapes of Longing," 5.
20 In extension of this point see Ian McKay, "The Liberal Order Framework: A Prospectus for a Reconnaissance of Canadian History," *Canadian Historical Review* 81, 4 (December 2000): 616–45; Doug Owram, *Promise of Eden: The Canadian Expansionist Movement and the Idea of the West, 1856–1900* (Toronto: University of Toronto Press, 1980); and A.A. den Otter, *Civilizing the Wilderness: Culture and Nature in Pre-Confederation Canada and Rupert's Land* (Edmonton: University of Alberta Press, 2012).
21 Cited by Carl C. Berger, "The True North Strong and Free," in *Nationalism in Canada*, ed. Peter Russell (Toronto: McGraw-Hill, 1966), 6; see Carl C. Berger, *The Sense of Power: Studies in the Ideas of Canadian Imperialism, 1867–1914* (Toronto: University of Toronto Press, 1970).

180   Notes to pages xv–xxi

22 Wynn, "Notes on Society and Environment"; H.V. Nelles, *The Politics of Development: Forests, Mines & Hydro-electric Power in Ontario, 1849–1941,* 2nd ed. (Montreal and Kingston: McGill-Queen's University Press, 2005).

23 Patricia Jasen, *Wild Things: Nature, Culture, and Tourism in Ontario, 1790–1914* (Toronto: University of Toronto Press, 1995), 121.

24 Jasen, *Wild Things,* chapter 5 is particularly useful here. Quote from page 121. As Jasen points out, such sentiments were widespread at the turn of the twentieth century and had deep and diverse roots, from H.D. Thoreau to Social Darwinism. For developing recognition of urban squalor, see Herbert B. Ames, *"The City Below the Hill": A Sociological Study of a Portion of the City of Montreal, Canada* (Montreal: Bishop Engraving and Printing, 1897; reprint, Toronto: University of Toronto Press, 1972).

25 Jean Graham, "Camping Out," in "Women's Sphere" section of *Canadian Magazine* 31, 3 (1908): 272. Graham was presumably alluding to Caleb W. Saleeby, *Worry: The Disease of the Age* (London and New York: Cassell, 1907).

26 Jasen, *Wild Things,* 118, 105.

27 "The Group of Seven," n.p., available at https://www.theartstory.org/movement/group -of-seven/history-and-concepts/.

28 Elizabeth Prelinger, Edvard Munch, Michael Parke-Taylor, and Peter Schjeldahl, *The Symbolist Prints of Edvard Munch: The Vivian and David Campbell Collection* (New Haven, CT: Yale University Press, 1996), 31–32.

29 For early, middle, and late contributions to the bookshelves of work on the Group of Seven see F.B. Housser, *A Canadian Art Movement: The Story of the Group of Seven* (Toronto: Macmillan, 1926), Peter Mellen, *The Group of Seven* (Toronto: McClelland and Stewart, 1970), and Joan Murray, *Northern Lights: Masterpieces of Tom Thomson and the Group of Seven* (Toronto: Key Porter, 2021). A pointed critique of the Group's failure to acknowledge an Indigenous presence in the areas they painted is found in Jonathan Bordo, "Jack Pine—Wilderness Sublime or the Erasure of the Aboriginal Presence from the Landscape," *Journal of Canadian Studies/Revue d'etudes canadiennes* 27, 4 (1992): 98–128. For the connection with "Canadian identity" see John O'Brian and Peter White, eds., *Beyond Wilderness: The Group of Seven, Canadian Identity, and Contemporary Art* (Montreal and Kingston: McGill-Queen's University Press, 2007).

30 Mark Kuhlberg, *Killing Bugs for Business and Beauty: Canada's Aerial War against Forest Pests, 1913–1930* (Toronto: University of Toronto Press, 2022), chapter 4.

31 Andrew Watson, "Poor Soils and Rich Folks: Household Economies and Sustainability in Muskoka, 1850–1920" (PhD diss., York University, 2014).

32 John R. McNeill, *Something New Under the Sun: An Environmental History of the Twentieth Century World* (New York: W.W. Norton 2000).

33 The quote is from A.D. Fraser, *The Summit House, Port Cockburn, Muskoka Lakes, Canada* (Parry Sound: North Star Press, 1910); this version of the postcard picture carries the caption "You Auto Come ... "; the arrival of this automobile is discussed in Geoffrey Shifflett, "The Evolving Muskoka Vacation Experience 1860–1945" (PhD diss., University of Waterloo, 2012), 232–34, in which the alternate version of the postcard is reproduced.

34 A persistent theme in the environmental history of North America – see William Cronon, *Nature's Metropolis: Chicago and the Great West* (New York: W.W. Norton, 1991) and Kathryn Morse, *The Nature of Gold: An Environmental History of the Klondike Gold Rush* (Seattle: University of Washington Press, 2010).

Notes to pages xxii–8

35 Peter A Stevens, "Getting Away from It All: Family Cottaging in Postwar Ontario" (Unpublished PhD diss., York University, 2010), 72; and Peter Stevens, "Cars and Cottages: The Automotive Transformation of Ontario's Summer Home Tradition," *Ontario History* 100, 1 (Spring 2008): 26–56.

36 See, for example, Julia Harrison, *A Timeless Place: The Ontario Cottage* (Vancouver: UBC Press, 2014); Claire E. Campbell, *Shaped by the West Wind: Nature and History in Georgian Bay* (Vancouver: UBC Press, 2005).

37 The quote is from Stephen Metcalf, "Provence Profound," *The New York Times Magazine*, 18 May 2008, 2, and is found in Shifflett, "Evolving Muskoka Vacation," at 407, where the insider-outsider argument is elaborated on.

38 F. Scott Fitzgerald, *The Great Gatsby* (New York: Charles Scribner's Sons, 1925), 136, and used to slightly different ends in Shifflett, *Evolving Muskoka Vacation*, 409.

INTRODUCTION

1 Ann Hathaway, *Muskoka Memories: Sketches from Real Life* (Toronto: William Briggs, 1904), 143. Potts used pseudonyms for herself and other people mentioned in her otherwise biographical account of life in Muskoka.

2 R.W. Sandwell, *Canada's Rural Majority: Households, Environments, and Economies, 1870–1940* (Toronto: University of Toronto Press, 2016), 5.

3 Roy I. Wolfe, "The Summer Resorts of Ontario in the Nineteenth Century," *Ontario History* 54, 3 (1962): 149–61; Geoffrey Wall, "Recreational Land Use in Muskoka," *Ontario Geography* 11 (1977): 11–28; Elaine A. Boone, "From Hot Streets to Lake Breezes: The Development of Tourism in Muskoka, 1860–1930" (master's thesis, Laurentian University, 1992); Patricia Jasen, *Wild Things: Nature, Culture, and Tourism in Ontario, 1790–1914* (Toronto: University of Toronto Press, 1995); Claire Campbell, *Shaped by the West Wind: Nature and History in Georgian Bay* (Vancouver: UBC Press, 2005); Peter Stevens, "Getting Away from It All: Family Cottaging in Postwar Ontario" (PhD diss., York University, 2010); Geoffrey Shifflett, "The Evolving Muskoka Vacation Experience 1860–1945" (PhD diss., University of Waterloo, 2012).

4 Norman Hall MacKenzie, "The Economic and Social Development of Muskoka, 1855–1888" (PhD diss., University of Toronto, 1943), 77–78; Geoffrey Wall, "Pioneer Settlement in Muskoka," *Agricultural History* 44, 4 (October 1970): 393–400; Andrew Watson, "Supply Networks in the Age of Steamboat Navigation: Lakeside Mobility in Muskoka, Ontario, 1880–1930," in *Moving Natures: Mobility and Environment in Canadian History*, ed. Ben Bradley, Jay Young, and Colin Coates (Calgary: University of Calgary Press, 2016), 79–103; Andrew Watson, "Pioneering a Rural Identity on the Canadian Shield: Tourism, Household Economies, and Poor Soils in Muskoka, Ontario, 1870–1900," *Canadian Historical Review* 98, 2 (June 2017): 261–93; Jessica Dunkin, *Canoe and Canvas: Life at the Encampments of the American Canoe Association, 1880–1910* (Toronto: University of Toronto Press, 2019).

5 Richard W. Judd, "Reshaping Maine's Landscape: Rural Culture, Tourism, and Conservation, 1890–1929," *Journal of Forest History* 32, 4 (1988): 180–90; Ian McKay, *The Quest for the Folk: Antimodernism and Cultural Selection in Twentieth-Century Nova Scotia* (Montreal and Kingston: McGill-Queen's University Press, 1994); Hal Rothman, *Devil's Bargains: Tourism in the Twentieth-Century American West* (Lawrence: University Press of Kansas, 1998); Bill Parenteau, "Angling, Hunting and the Development of Tourism in Late

182 Notes to pages 8–9

Nineteenth Century Canada: A Glimpse at the Documentary Record," *The Archivist* 117 (1998): 10–19; Cindy Aron, *Working at Play: A History of Vacations in the United States* (New York: Oxford University Press, 1999); Karl Jacoby, *Crimes against Nature: Squatters, Poachers, Thieves, and the Hidden History of American Conservation* (Berkeley: University of California Press, 2001); Aaron Shapiro, "Promoting Cloverland: Regional Associations, State Agencies, and the Creation of Michigan's Upper Peninsula Tourist Industry," *Michigan Historical Review* 29, 1 (2003): 1–37; Michael Dawson, *Selling British Columbia: Tourism and Consumer Culture, 1890–1970* (Vancouver: UBC Press, 2004); Camden Burd, "Imagining a Pure Michigan Landscape: Advertisers, Tourists, and the Making of Michigan's Northern Vacationlands," *Michigan Historical Review* 42, 2 (2016): 31–51.

6 Roderick Nash, *Wilderness and the American Mind* (New Haven: Yale University Press, 1967); Robert Craig Brown, "The Doctrine of Usefulness: Natural Resources and National Park Policy in Canada, 1887–1914," in *The Canadian National Parks: Today and Tomorrow,* ed. J.G. Nelson and R.C. Scace (Calgary: National and Provincial Parks Association of Canada and the University of Calgary, 1969), 94–110; Alfred Runte, *National Parks: The American Experience* (Lincoln: University of Nebraska Press, 1979); William Cronon, "The Trouble with Wilderness or, Getting Back to the Wrong Nature," in *Uncommon Ground: Rethinking the Human Place in Nature,* ed. William Cronon (New York: W.W. Norton, 1995), 69–90; Alan MacEachern, *Natural Selections: National Parks in Atlantic Canada* (Montreal and Kingston: McGill-Queen's University Press, 2001); Claire Campbell, ed., *A Century of Parks in Canada, 1911–2011* (Calgary: University of Calgary Press, 2011); Jocelyn Thorpe, *Temagami's Tangled Wild: Race, Gender, and the Making of Canadian Nature* (Vancouver: UBC Press, 2012).

7 Dona Brown, *Inventing New England: Regional Tourism in the Nineteenth Century* (Washington, DC: Smithsonian Institution Press, 1995), 163–64.

8 Blake Harrison, *The View from Vermont: Tourism and the Making of an American Rural Landscape* (Burlington: University of Vermont Press, 2006), 3.

9 Glenn Harris, "The Hidden History of Agriculture in the Adirondack Park, 1825–1875," *New York State History* 83, 2 (Spring 2002): 165–202; James Feldman, "The View from Sand Island: Reconsidering the Peripheral Economy, 1880–1940," *Western Historical Quarterly* 35, 3 (2004): 284–307; Harrison, *The View from Vermont;* Aaron Shapiro, "Up North on Vacation: Tourism and Resorts in Wisconsin's North Woods 1900–1945," *Wisconsin Magazine of History* 89, 4 (2006): 2–13; Jason Pierce, "The Winds of Change: The Decline of Extractive Industries and the Rise of Tourism in Hood River County, Oregon," *Oregon Historical Quarterly* 108, 3 (2007): 410–31; J.I. Little, "Scenic Tourism on the Northeastern Borderland: Lake Memphremagog's Steamboat Excursions and Resort Hotels, 1850–1900," *Journal of Historical Geography* 35, 4 (2009): 716–42; Edward MacDonald, "A Landscape ... with Figures: Tourism and Environment on Prince Edward Island," *Acadiensis* 40, 1 (2011): 70–85; Aaron Shapiro, *The Lure of the North Woods: Cultivating Tourism in the Upper Midwest* (Minneapolis, MN: University of Minnesota Press, 2013); Joseph E. Taylor III, *Persistent Callings: Seasons of Work and Identity on the Oregon Coast* (Corvallis, OR: Oregon State University Press, 2019).

10 Raymond Williams, *The Country and the City* (New York: Oxford University Press, 1973).

11 David B. Danbom, *Born in the Country: A History of Rural America* (Baltimore: Johns Hopkins University Press, 1995), xi; Jeremy Burchardt, "Agricultural History, Rural History, or Countryside History?" *Historical Journal* 50, 2 (2007): 465–81.

Notes to pages 9–12

12 Some important exceptions include Gérard Bouchard, *Quelques arpents d'Amérique: population, économie, famille au Saguenay, 1838–1971* (Montreal: Boréal, 1996); James David Mochoruk, *Formidable Heritage: Manitoba's North and the Cost of Development, 1870 to 1930* (Winnipeg: University of Manitoba Press, 2004); Merle Massie, *Forest Prairie Edge: Place History in Saskatchewan* (Winnipeg: University of Manitoba Press, 2014); Liza Piper, *The Industrial Transformation of Subarctic Canada* (Vancouver: UBC Press, 2009); Mark Kuhlberg, *In the Power of the Government: The Rise and Fall of Newsprint in Ontario, 1894–1932* (Toronto: University of Toronto Press, 2015); James Murton, Dean Bavington, and Carly Dokis, eds., *Subsistence under Capitalism: Historical and Contemporary Perspectives* (Montreal and Kingston: McGill-Queen's University Press, 2016).
13 Sandwell, *Canada's Rural Majority*, 17 (emphasis in original).
14 Keith Hoggart, "Let's Do Away with Rural," *Journal of Rural Studies* 6, 3 (1990): 245.
15 R.W. Sandwell, ed., *Beyond the City Limits: Rural History in British Columbia* (Vancouver: UBC Press, 1999), 6.
16 Rogers Brubaker and Frederick Cooper, "Beyond 'Identity,'" *Theory and Society* 29, 1 (February 2000): 1.
17 Sheldon Stryker and Peter J. Burke, "The Past, Present, and Future of an Identity Theory," *Social Psychology Quarterly* 63, 4 (December 2000): 285; Jan E. Stets and Peter J. Burke, "Identity Theory and Social Identity Theory," *Social Psychology Quarterly* 63, 3 (September 2000): 224–37.
18 Timothy J. LeCain, *The Matter of History: How Things Create the Past* (New York: Cambridge University Press, 2017), 49.
19 Ibid., 59.
20 James A. Henretta, "Families and Farms: *Mentalité* in Pre-Industrial America," *William and Mary Quarterly* 35, 1 (January 1978): 32, 14.
21 LeCain, *The Matter of History*, 103.
22 James C. Malin, *History and Ecology: Studies of the Grassland*, ed. Robert P. Swierenga (Lincoln: University of Nebraska Press, 1984); Berit Brandth and Marit S. Haugen, "Farm Diversification into Tourism – Implications for Social Identity," *Journal of Rural Studies* 27 (2011): 35–44; John R. Parkins and Maureen Reed, eds., *Social Transformation in Rural Canada: Community, Cultures, and Collective Action* (Vancouver: UBC Press, 2013).
23 Massie, *Forest Prairie Edge;* David A. Bello, *Across Forest, Steppe, and Mountain: Environment, Identity, and Empire in Qing China's Borderlands* (New York: Cambridge University Press, 2015); Oscar de la Torre, *The People of the River: Nature and Identity in Black Amazonia, 1835–1945* (Chapel Hill, NC: University of North Carolina Press, 2018); Melissa Otis, *Rural Indigenousness: A History of Iroquoian and Algonquian Peoples of the Adirondacks* (Syracuse, NY: Syracuse University Press, 2018); Taylor, *Persistent Callings*.
24 John C. Weaver, *The Great Land Rush and the Making of the Modern World, 1650–1900* (Montreal and Kingston: McGill-Queen's University Press, 2003); James Belich, *Replenishing the Earth: The Settler Revolution and the Rise of the Angloworld* (Oxford: Oxford University Press, 2009).
25 Census of Canada, 1871, 1881, and 1901.
26 Weaver, *The Great Land Rush*, 95.
27 Ibid., 81.
28 Gérard Bouchard, "Marginality, Co-Integration and Change: Social History as a Critical Exercise," *Journal of the Canadian Historical Association* 8, 1 (1997): 25.

184 Notes to pages 12–15

29 Shepard Krech III, *The Ecological Indian: Myth and History* (New York: W.W. Norton, 1999).

30 Mark A. White, "Sustainability: I Know It When I See It," *Ecological Economics* 86 (2013): 213–17; Sarah E. Fredericks, "Challenges to Measuring Sustainability," in *Berkshire Encyclopedia of Sustainability*, vol. 6, *Measurements, Indicators, and Research Methods for Sustainability*, ed. Willis Jenkins and Whitney Bauman (Great Barrington, MA: Berkshire, 2010), 46; Paul Johnston et al., "Reclaiming the Definition of Sustainability," *Environmental Science and Pollution Research* 14, 1 (2007): 60–66.

31 Willis Jenkins, "Sustainability Theory," in Jenkins and Bauman, *Berkshire Encyclopedia of Sustainability*, vol. 1, *The Spirit of Sustainability*, 380.

32 Helmut Haberl et al., "Progress towards Sustainability? What the Conceptual Framework of Material and Energy Flow Accounting (MEFA) Can Offer," *Land Use Policy* 21 (2004): 199–213; William E. Rees, "Thinking 'Resilience,'" in *The Post Carbon Reader: Managing the 21st Century's Sustainability Crises*, ed. Richard Heinberg and Daniel Lerch (Healdsburg, CA: Watershed Media, 2010), 25–40.

33 Richard Heinberg, "What Is Sustainability?" in Heinberg and Lerch, *The Post Carbon Reader*, 13 (emphasis in original).

34 Robert Costanza and Bernard C. Patten, "Defining and Predicting Sustainability," *Ecological Economics* 15 (1995): 193.

35 John R. Ehrenfeld, "The Roots of Sustainability," *MIT Sloan Management Review* 46, 2 (2005): 24.

36 A.J. McMichael, C.D. Butler, and Carl Foulke, "New Visions for Addressing Sustainability," *Science* 302 (12 December 2003): 1919–20.

37 Daniel Lerch, "Preface," in Heinberg and Lerch, *The Post Carbon Reader*, xxiii.

38 Santiago López-Ridaura, Omar Masera, and Marta Astier, "Evaluating the Sustainability of Complex Socio-environmental Systems: The MESMIS Framework," *Ecological Indicators* 2, 1–2 (2002): 138.

39 Ulrich Grober, *Sustainability: A Cultural History*, translated by Ray Cunningham (Totnes, UK: Green Books, 2012); Jeremy L. Caradonna, *Sustainability: A History* (Oxford: Oxford University Press, 2014); Jeremy L. Caradonna, ed., *Routledge Handbook of the History of Sustainability* (New York: Routledge, 2018); Paul Warde, *The Invention of Sustainability: Nature and Destiny, c. 1500–1870* (Cambridge, MA: Cambridge University Press, 2018).

40 Brian Donahue, *The Great Meadow: Farmers and the Land in Colonial Concord* (New Haven: Yale University Press, 2004), 23.

41 Ibid., xvi.

42 Ibid., 231 (emphasis in original).

43 Geoff Cunfer, *On the Great Plains: Agriculture and Environment* (College Station: Texas A&M University Press, 2005), 6.

44 Florence B. Murray, ed., *Muskoka and Haliburton, 1615–1875: A Collection of Documents* (Toronto: Champlain Society for the Government of Ontario by University of Toronto Press, 1963), 100n18. Murray uses the spelling *Mesqua-Ukee*. More recently, the Muskoka Steamships and Discovery Centre has switched to the spelling Misko-Aki, which translates as "red earth" in Anishinaabemowin and refers to both the colour of the region's pink granite and Chief Yellowhead's name. See https://realmuskoka.com/revitalization/; https://yellowheadinstitute.org/about/.

45 Dan Flores, "An Argument for Bioregional History," *Environmental History Review* 18, 4 (Winter 1994): 5–6.

Notes to pages 15–21

46 Most of the District of Muskoka correlates fairly well with the Muskoka River watershed, except the north ends of Lake Joseph and Lake Rosseau, which were part of the District of Parry Sound, and the very top of the watershed, which lay outside the eastern borders of the District of Muskoka.

47 Gary Long, *This River the Muskoka* (Erin, ON: Boston Mills Press, 1989), 23–30; Jamie Bastedo, *Shield Country: The Life and Times of the Oldest Piece of the Planet* (Red Deer, AB: Red Deer Press, 1994), 38–47.

48 Canada Land Inventory for Ontario, *Soil Capability for Agriculture*, Soil Research Institute, Research Branch, Agriculture Canada, based on maps prepared by the Canada-Ontario Soil Survey, with the support of the Lands Directorate, Environmental Management Service, Environment Canada, Ottawa, Surveys and Mapping Branch, Department of Energy, Mines, and Resources, 1975, https://sis.agr.gc.ca/cansis/publications/maps/cli/1m/agr/index.html.

49 Canada Land Inventory for Quebec, *Soil Capability for Agriculture*, Soil Research Institute, Research Branch, Agriculture Canada, based on maps prepared by the Quebec Soil Survey, with the support of the Lands Directorate, Environmental Management Service, Environment Canada, Ottawa, Surveys and Mapping Branch, Department of Energy, Mines, and Resources, 1974.

50 Hathaway, *Muskoka Memories*, 143–44.

CHAPTER 1: RURAL IDENTITY AND RESETTLEMENT OF THE CANADIAN SHIELD

1 Frederick Montague de la Fosse, *English Bloods: In the Backwoods of Muskoka, 1878*, ed. Scott D. Shipman (Toronto: Natural Heritage Books, 2004), x–xi, 3, 177–78. De la Fosse originally published this book in 1930 under the pseudonym Roger Vardon, using many fictitious names for neighbours, including Harston (called Captain Martin). Shipman suggests that changing the names was intended to avoid embarrassing those involved, but it may also have enabled the author to take liberties with the truth. De la Fosse arrived eight years after the Ontario government opened Stisted Township for settlement. His journey to Muskoka was exceptional, but his experiences as a pioneer were representative.

2 Ibid., 15.

3 J. David Wood, *Making Ontario: Agricultural Colonization and Landscape Re-Creation before the Railway* (Montreal and Kingston: McGill-Queen's University Press, 2000); John Clarke, *Land, Power, and Economics on the Frontier of Upper Canada* (Montreal and Kingston: McGill-Queen's University Press, 2001); Kenneth Kelly, "The Transfer of British Ideas on Improved Farming to Ontario during the First Half of the Nineteenth Century," *Ontario History* 63, 2 (1971): 103–11; J. David Wood, *Places of Last Resort: The Expansion of the Farm Frontier into the Boreal Forest of Canada, c. 1910–1940* (Montreal and Kingston: McGill-Queen's University Press, 2006); Bouchard, *Quelques arpents;* J.I. Little, *Nationalism, Capitalism and Colonization in Nineteenth Century Quebec: The Upper St. Francis District* (Montreal and Kingston: McGill-Queen's University Press, 1989); Neil Forkey, *Shaping the Upper Canadian Frontier: Environment, Society, and Culture in the Trent Valley* (Calgary: University of Calgary Press, 2003), 75–96; Mochoruk, *Formidable Heritage.*

4 Weaver, *The Great Land Rush;* Belich, *Replenishing the Earth;* Murray, *Muskoka and Haliburton*, lxx.

5 *An Act to Amend the Law for the Sale and Settlement of the Public Lands*, No. 209, 1st Session, 4th Parliament, 16 Victoriae (1852–53); J.R. Miller, *Compact, Contract, Covenant: Aboriginal Treaty-Making in Canada* (Toronto: University of Toronto Press, 2009), 110.

186   Notes to pages 22–27

6   Murray, *Muskoka and Haliburton*, lxx, lxxx.

7   Ibid., 243–52.

8   Ibid., 250–52.

9   Ibid., 249.

10 In 1851, Ontario farmers produced an average of approximately sixteen bushels per acre. John McCallum, *Unequal Beginnings: Agriculture and Economic Development in Quebec and Ontario until 1870* (Toronto: University of Toronto Press, 1980), 20; Marvin McInnis, "The Changing Structure of Canadian Agriculture," *Journal of Economic History* 42, 1 (1982): 191–98; R.M. McInnis, "Perspectives on Ontario Agriculture, 1815–1930," in *Canadian Papers in Rural History*, ed. Donald H. Akenson (Gananoque, ON: Langdale Press, 1992), 8: 69.

11 Murray, *Muskoka and Haliburton*, lxviii–lxix.

12 Ibid., 190–91.

13 De la Fosse, *English Bloods*, 21.

14 Richard Tatley, "Timber! The Lumber Trade in Muskoka," in *Summertimes: In Celebration of 100 Years of the Muskoka Lakes Association*, ed. Muskoka Lakes Association (Erin, ON: Boston Mills Press, 1994), 77.

15 Murray, *Muskoka and Haliburton*, 187.

16 Quoted in Richard Tatley, *The Steamboat Era in the Muskokas*, vol. 1, *To the Golden Years; A History of the Steam Navigation in the Districts of Muskoka and Parry Sound, 1866–1905* (Erin, ON: Boston Mills Press, 1983), 61.

17 *Northern Advocate* (Parry Sound), 21 December 1869.

18 Murray, *Muskoka and Haliburton*, 253.

19 Alexander Kirkwood and J.J. Murphy, *The Undeveloped Land in Northern and Western Ontario: Collected and Compiled from Reports of Surveyors, Crown Land Agents, and Others, with the Sanction of the Honourable the Commissioner of Crown Lands* (Toronto: Hunter, Rose, 1878), 72–73.

20 W.E. Hamilton, *Guide Book and Atlas of Muskoka and Parry Sound Districts*, maps by John Rogers, sketches by Seymour Penson (Toronto: H.R. Page, 1879), 22, 25.

21 Tatley, *The Steamboat Era*, 1: 46.

22 Contract between Department of Public Works and J.T. Kirkpatrick for Improvement of Washago and Gravenhurst Road, RG15–55–1, vol. 1, file 29, Archives of Ontario (AO); Tatley, *The Steamboat Era*, 1: 62.

23 Thomas McMurray, *The Free Grant Lands of Canada from Practical Experience of Bush Farming in the Free Grant Districts of Muskoka and Parry Sound* (Bracebridge: Office of the Northern Advocate, 1871), 10–11.

24 Quoted in Tatley, *The Steamboat Era*, 1: 57.

25 Contract between Department of Public Works and John Ginty for a lock between Lakes Muskoka and Rousseau, RG15–55–1, vol. 1, file 10, AO.

26 Murray, *Muskoka and Haliburton*, 195–96.

27 Ibid., 196.

28 "Annual Report of the Department of Crown Lands," *Ontario Sessional Papers*, 1870–1906. This analysis is based on records for fifteen central townships in the Muskoka River watershed: Wood, Monck, Macaulay, McLean, Ridout, Medora, Watt, Stephenson, Brunel, Franklin, Humphrey, Cardwell, Stisted, Chaffey, and Sinclair.

29 The land grant was enlarged to two hundred acres the following year when it became evident that many hundred-acre plots did not contain enough suitable land. *An Act to*

Notes to pages 27–32

Secure Free Grants and Homesteads to Actual Settlers on the Public Lands, Cap. VIII, 1st Session, 1st Parliament, 31 Victoriae (1867); Tatley, *The Steamboat Era,* 1: 53.

30 Peter Russell suggests that settlers at the southern edge of the Shield had "clearing rates consistently below the [provincial] average of one and a half acres per farm per year." Thus, the average locatee in Muskoka would have had difficulty in meeting the conditions for the patent. Peter A. Russell, "Upper Canada: A Poor Man's Country? Some Statistical Evidence," in *Canadian Papers in Rural History,* ed. Donald H. Akenson (Gananoque, ON: Langdale Press, 1982), 3: 137. Neil Forkey found that only a small percentage of families along the Bobcaygeon Road, east of Muskoka in Ontario, were capable of clearing enough land to meet the requirement. Forkey, *Shaping the Upper Canadian Frontier,* 82–83.

31 McMurray, *The Free Grant Lands of Canada,* 4–5.

32 Ibid., 8–9; Graeme Wynn, "Notes on Society and Environment in Old Ontario," *Journal of Social History* 13, 1 (Fall 1979): 57–58.

33 McMurray, *The Free Grant Lands of Canada,* 37.

34 "Farm Journal of John Oldham, 1868–1871," 978.20.1, Muskoka Lakes Museum Archives.

35 Thomas Osborne, *The Night the Mice Danced the Quadrille: Five Years in the Backwoods* (Erin, ON: Boston Mills Press, 1995), 11–12.

36 Kirkwood and Murphy, *The Undeveloped Land,* 57; Osborne, *The Night the Mice Danced,* 15.

37 Canada Land Inventory for Ontario, *Soil Capability for Agriculture.*

38 Ibid.

39 Harriet Barbara King, *Letters from Muskoka, by an Emigrant Lady* (London: Richard Bentley and Son, 1878), 75, 138–39. *Ultima Thule* translates roughly as a "distant place beyond the known world."

40 Ibid., 33.

41 Ibid., 159.

42 Ibid., 38.

43 Ibid., 28.

44 Ibid., 158.

45 Ibid., 114.

46 Ibid., 44–45.

47 Ibid., 86–87.

48 Ibid., 103.

49 Ibid., 110.

50 Ibid., 163–65.

51 Ibid., 157–58.

52 Ibid., 180–81.

53 William's wife and daughters joined them in the fall but stayed less than a year. Osborne, *The Night the Mice Danced,* 5, 10, 30, 46. Osborne does not mention John Oldham, who also left Nottingham around the same time.

54 Ibid., 12.

55 Ibid., 16.

56 Ibid., 18, 21, 22, 33, 60, 93.

57 Ibid., 99, 139–40, 151.

58 Ibid., 99, 124–26, 156, 166.

59 Ibid., 152.

188 Notes to pages 32–39

60 "Annual Report of the Department of Crown Lands, 1870–1906," *Ontario Sessional Papers.*
61 De la Fosse, *English Bloods,* 26.
62 Ibid., 32, 34; Census of Canada, 1881. Harston's strategy appears to have been common in Muskoka at this time, since de la Fosse learned of at least ten other settlers who employed it. De la Fosse, *English Bloods,* 129; Canada Land Inventory for Ontario, *Soil Capability for Agriculture.*
63 Murray, *Muskoka and Haliburton,* 260.
64 De la Fosse, *English Bloods,* 53.
65 Ibid., 115–16. McMurrich Township was located directly north of Stisted Township.
66 Ibid., 94.
67 Ibid., 118, 130, 132.
68 Ibid., 133.
69 Ibid., 140.
70 Ibid., 156–59.
71 Ibid., 140, 146, 170–71.
72 "Annual Report of the Department of Crown Lands, 1870–1879," *Ontario Sessional Papers.*
73 De la Fosse, *English Bloods,* 131.
74 Even taking into consideration that the government opened Watt and Monck Townships for resettlement several years earlier than Stisted and McMurrich, the rate of abandonment remained much higher in the backwoods. In the ten years between 1877, when McMurrich was opened for settlement, and 1886, settlers in Stisted and McMurrich abandoned 473 lots and obtained patent on only 244. "Annual Report of the Department of Crown Lands, 1877–1886," *Ontario Sessional Papers.*
75 De la Fosse, *English Bloods,* 113.
76 Indeed, the need for start-up money, along with the conditions that had to be met under the terms of the Homestead Act, meant that agricultural society still risked becoming hierarchical in Muskoka, as it had in southern Ontario. David Gagan, *Hopeful Travellers: Families, Land and Social Change in Mid-Victorian Peel County, Canada West* (Toronto: University of Toronto Press, 1981), 34; Joy Parr, "Hired Men: Ontario Agricultural Wage Labour in Historical Perspective," *Labour/Le travail* 15 (1985): 92–95.
77 McMurray, *The Free Grant Lands of Canada,* 43–44; *Muskoka and Lake Nipissing Districts: Information for Intending Settlers* (Ottawa: Department of Agriculture, 1880), 17–18. Helen Cowan estimates that £100 was sufficient to clear a farm. Helen I. Cowan, *British Emigration to British North America* (Toronto: University of Toronto Press, 1961), 67–79.
78 Russell, "Upper Canada," 144. Indeed, an overriding consideration regarding settlement during the first half of the nineteenth century was to maintain a socially stratified, hierarchical society by making it difficult for anyone without wealth to own land. Yet by 1871, it was still possible for the majority of those who wanted a farm to eventually secure land somewhere in Ontario. Certainly, the 1868 Homestead Act helped make its acquisition possible, but the costs associated with owning a farm still contributed to some measure of inequality in Muskoka during the late nineteenth century. Cole Harris, *The Reluctant Land: Society, Space, and Environment in Canada before Confederation* (Vancouver: UBC Press, 2008), 318–19, 363.
79 *Muskoka and Lake Nipissing Districts,* 20.
80 McMurray, *The Free Grant Lands of Canada,* 75.
81 King, *Letters from Muskoka,* 42–43.
82 Osborne, *The Night the Mice Danced,* 36, 48, 111, 147.

83 Ibid., 34, 37, 48, 80.
84 De la Fosse, *English Bloods,* 40.
85 Catherine Anne Wilson, "Reciprocal Work Bees and the Meaning of a Neighbourhood," *Canadian Historical Review* 82, 3 (September 2001): 431–64.
86 De la Fosse, *English Bloods,* 48.
87 Ibid., 44.
88 Ibid., 45.
89 Ibid., 75.
90 King, *Letters from Muskoka,* 26.
91 H.V. Nelles, *The Politics of Development: Forests, Mines & Hydro-electric Power in Ontario, 1849–1941,* 2nd ed. (Montreal and Kingston: McGill-Queen's University Press, 2005), 18.
92 Norman Hall MacKenzie, "The Economic and Social Development of Muskoka, 1855–1888," 176.
93 Bouchard, *Quelques arpents;* Gérard Bouchard, "Co-intégration et reproduction de la société rurale: Pour un modèle saguenayen de la marginalité," *Recherches sociographiques* 29, 2–8 (1988): 283–309.
94 Census of Canada, 1871–91.
95 Graeme Wynn, for example, claims that "to a very considerable extent, settler and lumberman in [the Ottawa-Huron Tract] had a complementary relationship." Wynn, "Notes on Society and Environment," 57. And, in Manitoba, James Mochoruk insists that "the thousands of winter jobs provided by tie cutting and lumber camps ... were crucial to the local economy." Mochoruk, *Formidable Heritage,* 160.
96 MacKenzie, "The Economic and Social Development," 206; Wall, "Pioneer Settlement," 398; Ian Radforth, *Bushworkers and Bosses: Logging in Northern Ontario, 1900–1980* (Toronto: University of Toronto Press, 1987), 26. Even when men did not leave home for long periods, many observers also worried that their work in logging camps would make them neglect their farms. There is little evidence to substantiate these claims. In fact, much the opposite appeared to be true. Graeme Wynn, *Timber Colony: An Historical Geography of Early Nineteenth Century New Brunswick* (Toronto: University of Toronto Press, 1981), 83–84.
97 Wynn, *Timber Colony,* 86.
98 Steven Maynard, "Rough Work and Rugged Men: The Social Construction of Masculinity in Working-Class History," *Labour/Le travail* 23 (Spring 1989): 159–69; Ian Radforth, "The Shantymen," in *Labouring Lives: Work and Workers in Nineteenth-Century Ontario,* ed. Paul Craven (Toronto: University of Toronto Press, 1995), 232; Adele Perry, *On the Edge of Empire: Gender, Race, and the Making of British Columbia, 1849–1871* (Toronto: University of Toronto Press, 2001), 29–30.
99 Wynn, *Timber Colony,* 86. Ian Radforth argues that working for pay in logging camps tended to lock households into a dependent relationship in the agroforestry economy. Economic downturn amplified this effect. Radforth, *Bushworkers and Bosses,* 28, 40–43; Radforth, "The Shantymen," 214; Normand Séguin, *La conquête du sol au 19e siècle* (Quebec City: Editions du Boreal Express, 1977); Bouchard, "Co-intégration et reproduction"; Bouchard, *Quelques arpents.*
100 Osborne, *The Night the Mice Danced,* 119.
101 Wall, "Pioneer Settlement," 397; Forkey, *Shaping the Upper Canadian Frontier,* 77.
102 Murray, *Muskoka and Haliburton,* cii; John Stilgoe, *Metropolitan Corridor: Railroads and the American Scene* (New Haven: Yale University Press, 1983).

190   Notes to pages 43–50

103 A.W. Currie, *The Grand Trunk Railway of Canada* (Toronto: University of Toronto Press, 1957); Ian Drummond, *Progress without Planning: The Economic History of Ontario* (Toronto: Ontario Historical Studies Series for the Government of Ontario by University of Toronto Press, 1987); Richard White, *Railroaded: The Transcontinentals and the Making of Modern America* (New York: W.W. Norton, 2011); William Cronon, *Nature's Metropolis: Chicago and the Great West* (New York: W.W. Norton, 1991).

104 Douglas McCalla, *Planting the Province: The Economic History of Upper Canada, 1784–1870* (Toronto: University of Toronto Press, 1993), 200, 311; Currie, *The Grand Trunk Railway*, 260–80; Campbell, *Shaped by the West Wind*, 71; Nelles, *The Politics of Development*, 117.

105 Murray, *Muskoka and Haliburton*, 346–47.

106 The list of provisional directors of the TSMJ included A.P. Cockburn and A.G.P. Dodge, the largest lumber baron in the Western Timber District of Ontario. Ibid., 348.

107 McMurray, *The Free Grant Lands of Canada*, 61.

108 Murray, *Muskoka and Haliburton*, ciii, 348–52; Currie, *The Grand Trunk Railway*, 272–73; Tatley, *The Steamboat Era*, 1: 73–76; "Amalgamation of Toronto, Simcoe & Muskoka Junction Railway Company and North Grey Railway Company as the Northern Extension Railways Company and Lease of Amalgamated Lines to the Northern Railways Company of Canada, June 29, 1871," RG12, vol. 1952, file 3502–5, Library and Archives Canada (LAC).

109 Murray, *Muskoka and Haliburton*, 349.

110 "Annual Report of the Department of Crown Lands, 1870–1874," *Ontario Sessional Papers*.

111 King, *Letters from Muskoka*, 68.

112 De la Fosse, *English Bloods*, 58.

113 "Annual Report of the Department of Crown Lands, 1876–1895," *Ontario Sessional Papers*.

114 De la Fosse, *English Bloods*, 151.

115 Ibid., 14.

CHAPTER 2: INDIGENOUS IDENTITY, SETTLER COLONIALISM, AND TOURISM

1 "Correspondence and reports regarding claims, by the Chippewas and Mississaugas of the Province of Ontario, to compensation for land not surrendered by the Robinson Treaty of 1850," Department of Indian Affairs and Northern Development fonds (DIA fonds), RG10, vol. 2329, file 67071–2, LAC.

2 Peggy Blair, *Lament for a First Nation: The Williams Treaties of Southern Ontario* (Vancouver: UBC Press, 2008), 103.

3 Jill Doerfler, "A Philosophy for Living: Ignatia Broker and Constitutional Reform among the White Earth Anishinaabeg," *Centering Anishinaabeg Studies: Understanding the World through Stories*, ed. Jill Doerfler, Niigaanwewidam James Sinclair, and Heidi Kiiwetinepinesiik Stark (East Lansing: Michigan State University Press, 2013), 182–83; Scott Richard Lyons, *X-Marks: Native Signatures of Assent* (Minneapolis: University of Minnesota Press, 2010).

4 John S. Lutz, *Makúk: A New History of Indigenous-White Relations* (Vancouver: UBC Press, 2008), 23.

5 Neal Ferris, *The Archaeology of Native-Lived Colonialism: Challenging History in the Great Lakes* (Tucson: University of Arizona Press, 2009), 29; *Report of the Royal Commission on Aboriginal Peoples*, 7 vols. (Ottawa: Royal Commission on Aboriginal Peoples, 1996), vol. 1, part 1, chapter 3 (*RCAP*).

Notes to pages 50–53

6 Miller, *Compact, Contract, Covenant*, 5; Rani Alexander, "Afterword: Toward an Archaeological Theory of Culture Contact," in *Studies in Culture Contact: Interaction, Culture Change, and Archaeology*, ed. James Cusick, Center for Archaeological Investigations Occasional Papers 25 (Carbondale: Southern Illinois University Press, 1998), 476–95.

7 Miller, *Compact, Contract, Covenant*, 5; *RCAP,* vol. 2, part 1, chapter 2, section 1; *RCAP,* vol. 2, part 2, chapter 4, section 4.

8 Weaver, *The Great Land Rush*, 139.

9 Blair, *Lament for a First Nation*, 3.

10 Population figures for these communities are difficult to determine, because census enumerators understood neither their kinship interconnections nor the seasonal movements of individuals during the year. As a result, they missed some people and counted others twice. Nevertheless, combined with DIA reports, these records provide some rough measure of reserve populations. Murray, *Muskoka and Haliburton*, lviii; "Correspondence, reports and publication regarding claims to compensation for lands improperly included in the Robinson Treaty of 1850, by the Mississaugas of Mud Lake, Rice Lake, Alnwick & Scugog as well as the Chippewas of Lake Huron and Simcoe," DIA fonds, RG10, vol. 2328, file 67071, pt. 1B, LAC; Census of Canada, 1871, 1891.

11 *Report of the Master Plan of Archaeological Resources of the District Municipality of Muskoka and the Wahta Mohawks*, 3 vols. (Toronto: Archaeological Services, 1994), 2: 97–98 (*RMPAR*).

12 Ferris, *Native-Lived Colonialism*, 38. Hugh Brody explores the inaccuracy of classifying Indigenous cyclical migrations as nomadic. Hugh Brody, *The Other Side of Eden: Hunters, Farmers and the Shaping of the World* (Vancouver: Douglas and McIntyre, 2000).

13 William Arthur Allen, "Wa-nant-git-che-ang: Canoe Route to Lake Huron through Southern Algonquia," *Ontario Archaeology* 73 (2002): 38.

14 Joan A.M. Lovisek, "Ethnohistory of the Algonkian Speaking Peoples of Georgian Bay – Precontact to 1850" (PhD diss., McMaster University, 1991), 151; E.S. Rogers and Flora Tobobondung, "Parry Island Farmers: A Period of Change in the Way of Life of the Algonkains of Southern Ontario," in *Contributions to Canadian Ethnology, 1975*, ed. David Brez Carlisle, National Museum of Man Mercury Series (Ottawa: National Museums of Canada, 1975), 256–57; Diamond Jenness, *The Ojibwa Indians of Parry Island, Their Social and Religious Life*, Department of Mines and National Museum of Canada Bulletin 78, Anthropological Series 17 (Ottawa: J.O. Patenaude, I.S.O., 1935), 13–14.

15 Bruce G. Trigger, *The Children of the Aataentsic: A History of the Huron People to 1660* (Montreal and Kingston: McGill-Queen's University Press, 1987); Bruce G. Trigger, *Natives and Newcomers: Canada's 'Heroic Age' Reconsidered* (Montreal and Kingston: McGill-Queen's University Press, 1986); Peter S. Schmalz, *The Ojibwa of Southern Ontario* (Toronto: University of Toronto Press, 1991); Kathryn Magee Labelle, *Dispersed But Not Destroyed: A History of the Seventeenth-Century Wendat People* (Vancouver: UBC Press, 2013); Gilles Havard, *The Great Peace of Montreal of 1701: French-Native Diplomacy in the Seventeenth Century*, translated by Phyllis Aronoff and Howard Scott (Montreal and Kingston: McGill-Queen's University Press, 2001). It should be noted that there is some controversy over whether the Anishinaabeg who migrated south from the top of Lake Superior during their conflict with the Haudenosaunee were descended from the original Algonquian-speaking peoples who resided along Georgian Bay prior to their dispersal. As Richard White shows, most Algonquian-speaking peoples north of Lake Ontario and east of Lake Huron moved

west into what later became Michigan and Wisconsin. They returned to the region in the aftermath of the War of 1812 and claimed ancestral rights to southern Algonquia. Moreover, Lovisek argues that some portion of the Algonquian-speaking peoples of Georgian Bay were not entirely displaced. Instead, they remained inland and along the coast of Georgian Bay, moving often to avoid detection and confrontation with the Haudenosaunee. Thus, the population of the Anishinaabeg who resided in southcentral Ontario at the time of the Robinson-Huron Treaty in 1850 was very probably an amalgam of two politically separate, yet ethnically related Algonquian-speaking peoples. Richard White, *The Middle Ground: Indians, Empires, and Republics in the Great Lakes Region, 1650–1815* (New York: Cambridge University Press, 1991); Lovisek, "Ethnohistory," 219, 229–32.

16 J. Michael Thoms, "Ojibwa Fishing Grounds: A History of Ontario Fisheries Law, Science, and the Sportsmen's Challenge to Aboriginal Treaty Rights, 1650–1900" (PhD diss., University of British Columbia, 2004), 44. John Lutz's "moditional" pattern of pursuing economic opportunities in the context of dispossession and displacement is similar to Thoms's notion of "multi-modal" but is more purposefully framed as a description of strategies for survival under colonization. Lutz, *Makúk*.

17 Lovisek, "Ethnohistory," 259.

18 Jenness, *The Ojibwa Indians*, 11.

19 Allen, "Wa-nant-git-che-ang"; Ferris, *Native-Lived Colonialism;* Lovisek, "Ethnohistory"; White, *The Middle Ground.*

20 Ferris, *Native-Lived Colonialism;* Allen, "Wa-nant-git-che-ang"; Lovisek, "Ethnohistory."

21 Thoms, "Ojibwa Fishing Grounds"; Lovisek, "Ethnohistory"; Rogers and Tobobondung, "Parry Island Farmers"; Ferris, *Native-Lived Colonialism;* Allen, "Wa-nant-git-che-ang."

22 Heidi Bohaker, *Doodem and Council Fire: Anishinaabe Governance through Alliance* (Toronto: University of Toronto Press, 2020); Heidi Bohaker, "'Nindoodemag': The Significance of Algonquin Kinship Networks in the Eastern Great Lakes Region, 1600–1701," *William and Mary Quarterly,* 3rd ser., 63, 1 (January 2006): 23–52; Allen, "Wa-nant-git-che-ang," 39.

23 Thoms, "Ojibwa Fishing Grounds," 68.

24 Darlene Johnston, "Connecting People to Place: Great Lakes Aboriginal History in Cultural Context" (Prepared for the Ipperwash Commission of Inquiry, 2005), 7, http://www.turtleisland.org/news/ipperwash2.pdf.

25 Thoms, "Ojibwa Fishing Grounds," 68.

26 Lovisek, "Ethnohistory," 282; Janet E. Chute, *The Legacy of Shingwaukonse: A Century of Leadership* (Toronto: University of Toronto Press, 1998), 4.

27 Ferris, *Native-Lived Colonialism*, 38.

28 Thoms, "Ojibwa Fishing Grounds," 39–41.

29 Diamond Jenness observed that heads of families gathered prior to winter dispersal to decide "where each family should hunt during the ensuing winter." Jenness, *The Ojibwa Indians,* 4. However, oral testimony given at the Williams Treaties hearings in 1923 suggests that these limits remained constant over long periods. "Bound volume of testimony given to a commission, chaired by A.S. Williams, investigating claims, by the Chippewas Mississaugas of Ontario, to compensation for land not surrendered by the Robinson Treaty of 1850," DIA fonds, RG10, vol. 2331, file 67071–4B, LAC.

30 Jenness, *The Ojibwa Indians,* 3.

31 James C. Scott, *The Art of Not Being Governed: An Anarchist History of Upland Southeast Asia* (New Haven: Yale University Press, 2009).

Notes to pages 56–61

32 Murray, *Muskoka and Haliburton*, 100n18. The 1795 treaty aimed to secure a transportation corridor for the Crown along the Severn River between Lake Huron and the eastern end of Lake Ontario. The 1815 and 1818 treaties were intended to permit white settlement.

33 Robin Brownlie, *A Fatherly Eye: Indian Agents, Government Power, and Aboriginal Resistance in Ontario, 1918–1939* (New York: Oxford University Press, 2003), 81.

34 Thoms, "Ojibwa Fishing Grounds," 1; Ferris, *Native-Lived Colonialism*, 61.

35 Murray, *Muskoka and Haliburton*, lvi.

36 Blair, *Lament for a First Nation*, 32–33; Lovisek, "Ethnohistory," 297. Thoms argues that the Coldwater reserve was established in an attempt to convince the Chippewa under Yellowhead to forsake their shoreline locations and move into land-locked sites where they could be coerced into becoming Christian farmers. Thoms, "Ojibwa Fishing Grounds," 183.

37 Murray, *Muskoka and Haliburton*, 105–6.

38 Ibid., 109–11.

39 Schmalz, *The Ojibwa*, 148. The lieutenant governor of Upper Canada, Sir Francis Bond Head, also expressed some concern that exposure to white settlement was having an adverse effect on the Chippewa at Coldwater. Murray, *Muskoka and Haliburton*, 112–13.

40 The same year that Lieutenant Governor Colborne established the Coldwater village, in 1830, the United States government passed An Act to Provide for an Exchange of Lands with the Indians Residing in Any of the States or Territories, and for Their Removal West of the River Mississippi. Commonly known as the Indian Removal Act, it forced all Indigenous peoples onto reserves west of the Mississippi. Expecting fairer treatment from the British, many Anishinaabeg from Wisconsin, Illinois, Indiana, and Michigan who had kinship ties with Anishinaabeg communities in Upper Canada and along the eastern shores of Georgian Bay joined their relatives there. Groups of Menominee, Potawatomi, and Odawa joined the four bands considered here, although larger numbers joined the Christian Island and Sandy Island bands. A non-status community also emerged after mid-century and established itself at Moose Deer Point near the mouth of the Moon River on Georgian Bay. It initially joined with the Sandy Island band but later splintered off. Moose Deer Point became a formal First Nations reserve in 1918 but evidence related to it is scarce and difficult to distinguish from the Sandy/Parry Island band. Schmalz, *The Ojibwa*, 200–4; Brownlie, *A Fatherly Eye*, 15; Rogers and Tobobondung, "Parry Island Farmers," 261–63, 275, 278.

41 Murray, *Muskoka and Haliburton*, lvii–lviii. Yellowhead and his group had difficulty obtaining the money they were promised. Their complaints during the early 1840s resulted in a series of investigations and a commission of inquiry in 1842.

42 Ibid., 120.

43 Sarah Carter, *Lost Harvests: Prairie Indian Reserve Farmers and Government Policy* (Montreal and Kingston: McGill-Queen's University Press, 1990), 3.

44 Murray, *Muskoka and Haliburton*, 121–23.

45 *RMPAR*, 2: 9.

46 Lovisek, "Ethnohistory," 44.

47 Murray, *Muskoka and Haliburton*, 108. The island is now called Tobin Island.

48 *RMPAR*, 2: 50.

49 *Report of the Special Commissioners Appointed on the 8th of September, 1856, to Investigate Indian Affairs in Canada* (Toronto: Stewart Derbishire and George Desbarats, 1858), appendix 30.

Notes to pages 61–64

50 Richard Tatley, *Port Carling: The Hub of the Muskoka Lakes* (Erin, ON: Boston Mills Press, 1996), 14–15.

51 Murray, *Muskoka and Haliburton*, 125–26.

52 Michael Marlatt, "The Calamity of the Initial Reserve Surveys under the Robinson Treaties," *Papers of the Thirty-Fifth Algonquian Conference*, ed. H.C. Wolfart (Winnipeg: University of Manitoba Press, 2004), 284, 295–96. Controversy surrounds the decision to choose Parry Island for their reserve and whether the band had actually asked for its reserve to include both the island and the future site of Parry Sound, or whether Crown surveyors made a unilateral decision to create the reserve out of the island alone and leave the more valuable Parry Sound site available for Euro-Canadian resettlement.

53 Quoted in Tatley, *Port Carling*, 14.

54 Unfortunately, most local history on Muskoka pays only cursory attention to, or entirely omits, First Nations. The accounts that do exist, however, tend to romanticize relations between the Indigenous population and white settlers. Despite the somewhat biased memory of these encounters, I have found no indication that physical violence accompanied Euro-Canadian settlement during the 1860s and 1870s.

55 D.H.C. Mason, *Muskoka: The First Islanders and After* (Bracebridge, ON: Herald-Gazette Press, 1974), 10.

56 Joan E. McHugh, *Beloved Muskoka: Diaries and Recollections of Elizabeth Penson* (Port Elgin, ON: Brucedale Press, 2009), 66.

57 Mason, *Muskoka*, 19.

58 Carleen Partridge, author interview, 21 October 2011.

59 Tatley, *Port Carling*, 14–15. Evidence suggests that the entire branch did not relocate to Parry Island right away. Whereas Pegahmegahbow settled there, others, including Mishoquetto (William King), migrated to new sites closer to Georgian Bay, north of the Moon River. Some spent their winters at smaller inland sites, such as Maple Lake, Swan Lake, and Turtle Lake. "Parry Sound Superintendency – Correspondence regarding Certain Indians Reported by Chief Paudash as Living in the Vicinity of Moose Deer Point, Georgian Bay. It was Learned that the John King Family, Non-treaty Indians, Came Under the Control of this Agency," DIA fonds, RG10, vol. 3082, file 272444, LAC; Rogers and Tobobondung, "Parry Island Farmers," 275.

60 The Mississauga also used parts of the southern Shield in their seasonal cycle. But, since their territories were east of Muskoka, in the Haliburton region of the province, they are not considered here. See Blair, *Lament for a First Nation*, for more on the history of the Mississauga around the Kawartha Lakes.

61 Ibid., 25–26; Rhonda Telford, "Anishinabe Interest in Islands, Fish and Water," *Papers of the Thirty-First Algonquian Conference*, ed. John D. Nichols (Winnipeg: University of Manitoba Press, 2000), 415.

62 Blair, *Lament for a First Nation;* Thoms, "Ojibwa Fishing Grounds"; Jean Teillet, "The Role of the Natural Resources Regulatory Regime in Aboriginal Disputes in Ontario" (Prepared for the Ipperwash Commission of Inquiry, 2005); Brownlie, *A Fatherly Eye;* Chute, *The Legacy of Shingwaukonse;* Edwin C. Koenig, *Culture and Ecologies: A Native Fishing Conflict on the Saugeen-Bruce Peninsula* (Toronto: University of Toronto Press, 2005); Tim E. Holzkamm, Victor T. Lytwyn, and Leo G. Weisberg, "Rainy River Sturgeon: An Ojibway Resource in the Fur Trade Economy," *Canadian Geographer* 32, 3 (September 1988): 194–205.

Notes to pages 64–68 195

63 Blair, *Lament for a First Nation*, 38–61. The Fisheries Act was amended in 1859 to allow for bona fide domestic consumption. This did not reduce its impact, however, since the Anishinaabeg had always relied on fish for trade in addition to consumption. Brownlie, *A Fatherly Eye*, 85.

64 Dominion of Canada, "Part I: Reports of Superintendents and Agents," *Annual Report of the Department of Indian Affairs for the Year Ended 31st December, 1883* (Ottawa: MacLean, Roger, 1884), 415.

65 "Headquarters – Reports by various agents on the state of the fisheries under their jurisdiction," DIA fonds, RG10, vol. 1972, file 5530, LAC.

66 Dominion of Canada, "Part I: Reports of Superintendents and Agents," *Annual Report of the Department of Indian Affairs for the Year Ended 31st December, 1882* (Ottawa: MacLean, Roger, 1883), 121–22.

67 Telford, "Anishinabe Interest," 412–14; Blair, *Lament for a First Nation*, 69–73.

68 "Headquarters – Reports by various agents," LAC.

69 Teillet, "The Role of the Natural Resources"; Frank Tough, "Ontario's Appropriation of Indian Hunting: Provincial Conservation Policies vs. Aboriginal and Treaty Rights, ca. 1892–1930" (Paper prepared for the Ontario Native Affairs Secretariat, Toronto, January 1991); David Calverley, *Who Controls the Hunt? First Nations, Treaty Rights, and Wildlife Conservation in Ontario, 1783–1939* (Vancouver: UBC Press, 2018).

70 Brownlie, *A Fatherly Eye*, 10.

71 Ibid., 101.

72 "Parry Sound Superintendency – Requisition of the chiefs and councillors of the Parry Island Band for two lumber waggons," DIA fonds, RG10, vol. 2427, file 88559, LAC.

73 "Ontario – Copy of 'Sir Francis Bond Head's Treaty' signed at Manitowaning in 1836 in the matter of the islands on the north and east shores of Lake Huron. Copies of Robinson Superior, Robinson Huron and Lake Simcoe Treaties and correspondence, reports, memoranda and claims relating to these treaties," DIA fonds, RG10, vol. 2848, file 178978, LAC.

74 "Parry Sound Superintendency – Correspondence regarding the A. Peter Estate Timber License Covering the Parry Island Reserve," DIA fonds, RG10, vol. 2477, file 98011–4, LAC.

75 "Parry Sound Superintendency – Correspondence regarding the surrender of the timber on Parry Island reserve," DIA fonds, RG10, vol. 3082, file 271899, LAC.

76 John Colombo, *Voices of Rama: Traditional Ojibwa Tales from the Rama Reserve, Lake Couchiching, Ontario* (Toronto: Self-published, 1994), 24–25.

77 "Correspondence and reports regarding claims," LAC.

78 Ibid.; "Bound volume of testimony," LAC.

79 "Correspondence and reports regarding claims," LAC; "Bound volume of testimony," LAC.

80 "Correspondence and reports regarding claims," LAC.

81 Ibid. The members of the Rama, Georgina Island, and Christian Island bands seem to have remained somewhat independent of the Hudson's Bay Company (HBC) trading network. Neither Bailey nor Thompson appear to have been employed by the HBC. Joan Lovisek argues that the company was unable to penetrate the lower Georgian Bay fur trade during this period. It is also worth noting that William Benjamin Robinson, who brokered and signed the Robinson-Huron Treaty on behalf of the government, also ran a post on Yoho Island on Lake Joseph during the 1820s. His successful completion of the treaty was

196   Notes to pages 68–71

possible thanks to the relationships he established through his post. Lovisek, "Ethnohistory," 313–15; Murray, *Muskoka and Haliburton*, 117.

82 "Bound volume of testimony," LAC.

83 Ibid.

84 Brenda Katlatont Gabriel-Doxtater and Arlette Kawanatatie Van den Hende, *At the Woods' Edge: An Anthology of the History of the People of Kanehsatà:ke* (Kanesatake, QC: Kanesatake Education Centre, 1995).

85 Dominion of Canada, "Part I: Reports of Superintendents and Agents," *Annual Report of the Department of Indian Affairs for the Year Ended 31st December, 1880* (Ottawa: MacLean, Roger, 1881), 28.

86 Philip Laforce, *History of Gibson Reserve* (Bracebridge: Bracebridge Gazette, n.d.), 2.

87 Ibid., 2. According to Joyce Tabobondung, the band's second choice was Sault Ste. Marie. Joyce Tabobondung, author interview, 21 October 2011. The band had a good reason for choosing Gibson. According to Joan Lovisek, ancestors of the Mohawks who settled at Kanesatake may have been part of the Algonquian-speaking peoples who were dispersed from the Georgian Bay region by the Iroquois in the mid-seventeenth century. Lovisek, "Ethnohistory," 229–32.

88 Laforce, *History of Gibson Reserve*, 7; "Parry Sound Superintendency – Correspondence regarding an inspection of the Indians from Oka Agency located on the Gibson Reserve and a request from superintendent Thomas S. Walton that the band be attached to the Penetanguishene Agency rather than Parry Sound," DIA fonds, RG10, vol. 2788, file 156530, LAC.

89 Dominion of Canada, *Annual Report of the Department of Indian Affairs for the Year Ended 31st December, 1881* (Ottawa: MacLean, Roger, 1882), liv–lv.

90 Laforce, *History of Gibson Reserve*, 3, 5.

91 Dominion of Canada, *DIA Annual Report, 1883*, 19.

92 Dominion of Canada, "Part I: Reports of Superintendents and Agents," *Annual Report of the Department of Indian Affairs for the Year Ended 31st December, 1884* (Ottawa: MacLean, Roger, 1885), 9; Dominion of Canada, *Annual Report of the Department of Indian Affairs for the Year Ended 30th June, 1896* (Ottawa: S.E. Dawson, 1897), 31; Dominion of Canada, *Annual Report of the Department of Indian Affairs for the Year Ended 30th June, 1897* (Ottawa: S.E. Dawson, 1898), 34; Dominion of Canada, *Annual Report of the Department of Indian Affairs for the Year Ended March 31, 1910* (Ottawa: C.H. Parmelee, 1910), 32.

93 Dominion of Canada, *DIA Annual Report, 1884*, 9.

94 Dominion of Canada, "Indian Branch, Report of Deputy Superintendent General of Indian Affairs," *Annual Report of the Department of the Interior for the Year Ended 30th June, 1874* (Ottawa: MacLean, Roger, 1875), 19, 36–37.

95 Dominion of Canada, *DIA Annual Report, 1881*, 4.

96 Dominion of Canada, *DIA Annual Report, 1882*, xxix.

97 Dominion of Canada, *DIA Annual Report, 1885*, 9; Dominion of Canada, "Part I: Reports of Superintendents and Agents," *Annual Report of the Department of Indians Affairs for the Year Ended 31st December, 1890* (Ottawa: Brown Chamberlin, 1891), 9.

98 Dominion of Canada, *DIA Annual Report, 1896*, 27, 31.

99 Dominion of Canada, *Annual Report of the Department of Indian Affairs for the Year Ended 30th June, 1903* (Ottawa: S.E. Dawson, 1904), 5.

100 Cronon, "The Trouble with Wilderness," 69–90; Thorpe, *Temagami's Tangled Wild*.

Notes to pages 71–79   197

101 Paige Raibmon, *Authentic Indians: Episodes of Encounter from the Late-Nineteenth Century Northwest Coast* (Durham: Duke University Press, 2006).
102 Blair, *Lament for a First Nation*, 73–87; Teillet, "The Role of the Natural Resources"; Tough, "Ontario's Appropriation"; Calverley, *Who Controls the Hunt?*
103 Raibmon, *Authentic Indians*, 11; Jasen, *Wild Things*, 80–104; Ruth Phillips, *Trading Identities: The Souvenir in Native North American Art from the Northeast, 1700–1900* (Seattle: University of Washington Press, 1998).
104 Rogers and Tobobondung, "Parry Island Farmers," 322; Diary of F.W. Coate, May–June 1883, Frederick W. Coate family fonds, F720, AO.
105 Joyce Tabobondung, author interview, 21 October 2011; Dominion of Canada, *DIA Annual Report, 1910*, 32.
106 Dominion of Canada, *Annual Report of the Department of Indian Affairs for the Year Ended 30th June, 1895* (Ottawa: S.E. Dawson, 1896), 5; Dominion of Canada, *DIA Annual Report, 1897*, 4; Dominion of Canada, *Annual Report of the Department of Indian Affairs for the Year Ended 30th June, 1904* (Ottawa: S.E. Dawson, 1905), 5; Dominion of Canada, *DIA Annual Report, 1910*, 32; Dominion of Canada, "Part II: Reports of Indian Agents," *Annual Report of the Department of Indian Affairs for the Year Ended March 31, 1914* (Ottawa: J. de L. Taché, 1914), 10.
107 Allen, "Wa-nant-git-che-ang," 45–46.
108 Brownlie, *A Fatherly Eye*, xiii.
109 Mason, *Muskoka*, 29; Jasen, *Wild Things*, 118–19. The name "Snike" is probably a misspelling of "Snake."
110 Dominion of Canada, "Part I: Reports of the Superintendents and Agents," *Annual Report of the Department of Indians Affairs for the Year Ended 31st December, 1889* (Ottawa: Brown Chamberlin, 1890), 18.
111 Dominion of Canada, *DIA Annual Report, 1897*, 4, 30, 34.
112 Dominion of Canada, *DIA Annual Report, 1903*, 5; Joyce Tabobondung, author interview, 21 October 2011.
113 Dominion of Canada, *Annual Report of the Department of Indian Affairs for the Year Ended March 31, 1913* (Ottawa: C.H. Parmelee, 1913), 10; Joyce Tabobondung, author interview, 21 October 2011.
114 Joyce Tabobondung, author interview, 21 October 2011.
115 Brownlie, *A Fatherly Eye*, 129.
116 Dominion of Canada, *Annual Report of the Department of Indian Affairs for the Year Ended March 31, 1909* (Ottawa: C.H. Parmelee, 1909), 30.
117 Raibmon, *Authentic Indians*, 64.

Chapter 3: Rural Identity and Tourism

1 Hathaway, *Muskoka Memories*, 101. Ann Hathaway was the pseudonym of Fanny Potts, eldest daughter of Sarah and Enoch.
2 Runte, *National Parks;* Jasen, *Wild Things;* Cronon, "The Trouble with Wilderness," 69–90; Gregg Mitman, "Hay Fever Holiday: Health, Leisure, and Place in Gilded Age America," *Bulletin of the History of Medicine* 77, 3 (2003): 600–35; Campbell, *Shaped by the West Wind.*
3 Harris, "The Hidden History," 165–202; Jacoby, *Crimes against Nature;* Harrison, *The View from Vermont;* MacDonald, "A Landscape ... with Figures," 70–85.

4 Judd, "Reshaping Maine's Landscape," 180–90; Shapiro, "Promoting Cloverland," 1–37; Feldman, "The View from Sand Island," 284–307; Shapiro, "Up North on Vacation," 2–13; Pierce, "The Winds of Change," 410–31; Shapiro, *The Lure of the North Woods*.

5 In 1871, the backwoods townships were slightly more forested than those closer to the lakes. By 1891, however, settlers in backwoods townships had cleared 10.9 percent of the land, whereas those in townships nearer to the lakes had cleared 8.5 percent. Census of Canada, 1871–1911.

6 Mason, *Muskoka*, 6.

7 Barbaranne Boyer, *Muskoka's Grand Hotels*, ed. Richard Tatley, (Erin, ON: Boston Mills Press, 1987), 19–22.

8 In 1911, the total rural population in Humphrey, Medora, Wood, Cardwell, Watt, and Monck Townships was 4,677. This number does not include Muskoka Township or urban areas, such as Gravenhurst, Bracebridge, and Port Carling. Census of Canada, 1911. In 1915, John Rogers conducted a census on the lower lakes and recorded 720 separate summer residences. John Rogers, *Muskoka Lakes Bluebook, Directory and Chart, 1915* (Port Sandfield, ON: Self-published, 1915). Local Muskoka historian Graham Smith estimates that more than three hundred new summer homes were built in Muskoka between 1895 and 1915, suggesting there were approximately four hundred cottages in 1895. "A Room with a View: Cottage Architects and Builders," in Muskoka Lakes Association, *Summertimes*, 137. Statistics on hotel numbers and occupancy capacity are from Tatley, *The Steamboat Era*, 1: 232; and Boyer, *Muskoka's Grand Hotels*, 53, 66, 100.

9 Hathaway, *Muskoka Memories*, 143–44. The biblical reference is to Luke 16:26. Many thanks to my wonderful copy editor, Deborah Kerr, for drawing my attention to this.

10 McHugh, *Beloved Muskoka*, 66–68.

11 Hathaway, *Muskoka Memories*, 112, 125.

12 Very few connections were made at Bracebridge, because of the time it added to most journeys. Currie, *The Grand Trunk Railway*, 276–80; Tatley, *The Steamboat Era*, 1: 127, 1: 154.

13 Boyer, *Muskoka's Grand Hotels*, 36.

14 "The Muskoka Country," *Toronto World*, 14 July 1887, reprinted in John Denison, *Micklethwaite's Muskoka* (Toronto: Stoddart, 1993), 13.

15 Boyer, *Muskoka's Grand Hotels*, 36; Denison, *Micklethwaite's Muskoka*, 44.

16 Coate co-owned the Toronto auction house Oliver, Coate and Company, also known as "The Mart." In 1880, four years after acquiring his land in Muskoka, he retired, leaving his partner, and son-in-law, J.D. Oliver to take over the company. The Coate household represents an interesting blend of farming and cottaging, and Coate's farm diaries provide rare, critical insights into the nature of late-nineteenth-century settler-tourist communities, for which very few comparable sources exist. Details about Coate's professional life are from two newspaper clippings from the Toronto *Globe*, 31 October 1884, and the *Toronto Mail*, 14 November 1884, which are pasted into the Coate diary on the dates specified. "Diary of F.W. Coate," Frederick W. Coate family fonds, F720, AO.

17 In 1888, Coate finally grew enough grapes to yield twenty gallons of wine. Most years, he produced only a dozen gallons on average. In 1892, however, he bottled forty-seven and the next year twenty-seven. "Diary of F.W. Coate," October 1888–93, AO.

18 Ibid., May, September 1883; Rogers, *Muskoka Lakes Bluebook, 1915*.

19 William M. Gray, *Lake Joseph, 1860–1910: An Illustrated Notebook* (Toronto: Self-published, 1991), 77; Boyer, *Muskoka's Grand Hotels*, 34; Grand Trunk Railway Company of Canada,

Notes to pages 91–100

Picturesque Muskoka: To the Highlands and Lakes of Northern Ontario (Toronto: Grand Trunk Railway System and Muskoka Navigation Company, 1898).

20 "Memoirs of Mabel Croucher Ames, 1884–1977," oral memoirs originally shared with and transcribed by Vera Gross Ames, 1975, presented to Bill Gray by Lynda McClelland Stringer, 10 June 2006, Muskoka Lakes Museum Archives; Gray, *Lake Joseph*, 86, 93, 113; Diary of R.J. Maclennan, "A Few Weeks among the Northern Lakes and Islands, from My Diary," August 1885, author's private collection.

21 "Memoirs of Mabel Croucher Ames," 9, Muskoka Lakes Museum Archives (hereafter "MLM").

22 Smith, "A Room with a View," 129–41.

23 "Memoirs of Mabel Croucher Ames," 19, MLM.

24 Hathaway, *Muskoka Memories*, 144–45.

25 Cronon, *Nature's Metropolis*, 233–35.

26 Census of Canada, 1871–1891.

27 Douglas McCalla, *Consumers in the Bush: Shopping in Rural Upper Canada* (Montreal and Kingston: McGill-Queen's University Press, 2015); Douglas McCalla, "Retailing in the Countryside: Upper Canadian General Stores in the Mid-Nineteenth Century," *Business and Economic History* 26, 2 (1997): 393–403; Elizabeth Mancke, "At the Counter of the General Store: Women and the Economy in Eighteenth Century Nova Scotia," in *Intimate Relations: Family and Community in Planter Nova Scotia, 1759–1800,* ed. Margaret Conrad (Fredericton: Acadiensis, 1995), 167–81; Béatrice Craig, *Backwoods Consumers and Homespun Capitalists: The Rise of a Market Culture in Eastern Canada* (Toronto: University of Toronto Press, 2009), 113–36.

28 Hathaway, *Muskoka Memories*, 218. Potts takes on the voice of a typical settler here, explaining how things work to a new visitor.

29 Seymour Penson, "Seymour Penson and His Muskoka Neighbours, Part I," *East Georgian Bay Historical Journal* 3 (1983): 194.

30 Seymour Penson, "Seymour Penson and His Muskoka Neighbours, Part II," *East Georgian Bay Historical Journal* 5 (1985): 185–86.

31 Tatley, *The Steamboat Era,* 1: 245; Tatley, *Port Carling,* 36; Mason, *Muskoka,* 27–28.

32 "The Muskoka Country," *Toronto World,* 14 July 1887, reprinted in Denison, *Micklethwaite's Muskoka,* 17. The operator of the *Lady of the Lake* was actually named Arthur Lowe, not Acton.

33 Tatley, *The Steamboat Era,* 1: 247–48; Tatley, *The Steamboat Era,* 2: 237.

34 Murray, *Muskoka and Haliburton,* 255.

35 Tatley, *The Steamboat Era,* 1: 245.

36 Ibid., 250.

37 "General Store Ledger of George Henry Homer, 1896–1901" (Homer Ledger), box 35, Gravenhurst Public Library Archives.

38 "Homer Ledger," Gravenhurst Public Library Archives.

39 Tatley, *The Steamboat Era,* 1: 250.

40 Hathaway, *Muskoka Memories,* 219.

41 Ibid., 222; "Memoirs of Mabel Croucher Ames," 8, MLM.

42 Hathaway, *Muskoka Memories,* 226.

43 Ibid., 218, 222.

44 Tatley, *The Steamboat Era,* 1: 245; Tatley, *The Steamboat Era,* 2: 38; Harley E. Scott, *Steam Tugs and Supply Boats of Muskoka* (Lancaster, NY: Cayuga Creek Historical Press, 1987), 11.

200   Notes to pages 100–7

45 Hathaway, *Muskoka Memories*, 220.
46 Scott, *Steam Tugs and Supply Boats*, 10.
47 Hathaway, *Muskoka Memories*, 219.
48 Scott, *Steam Tugs and Supply Boats*, 10.
49 "Memoirs of Mabel Croucher Ames," 8, MLM.
50 Hathaway, *Muskoka Memories*, 221.
51 Ibid., 218–21; "Memoirs of Mabel Croucher Ames," 8, MLM.

CHAPTER 4: THE PROMISE OF WOOD-RESOURCE HARVESTING

1 Sandwell, *Canada's Rural Majority*; R.W. Sandwell, "Notes toward a History of Rural Canada, 1870–1940," in Parkins and Reed, *Social Transformation*, 21–42; R.W. Sandwell, *Contesting Rural Space: Land Policy and Practices of Resettlement on Saltspring Island, 1859–1891* (Montreal and Kingston: McGill-Queen's University Press, 2005); Massie, *Forest Prairie Edge*.
2 Bouchard, "Co-intégration et reproduction," 283–309; Bouchard, *Quelques arpents*.
3 Brian Donahue, *Reclaiming the Commons: Community Farms and Forests in a New England Town* (New Haven: Yale University Press, 1999); Donahue, *The Great Meadow*; David R. Foster and John D. Aber, *Forests in Time: The Environmental Consequences of 1,000 Years of Change in New England* (New Haven: Yale University Press, 2004).
4 Wynn, *Timber Colony*, 82.
5 Radforth, *Bushworkers and Bosses*, 26; Judith Fingard, "The Poor in Winter: Seasonality and Society in Pre-Industrial Canada," in *Pre-Industrial Canada: 1760–1849*, ed. Michael S. Cross and Gregory S. Kealey (Toronto: University of Toronto Press, 1982), 62–78; Craig, *Backwoods Consumers*.
6 Wynn, *Timber Colony*; Mochoruk, *Formidable Heritage*; A.R.M. Lower, *Great Britain's Woodyard: British America and the Timber Trade, 1763–1867* (Montreal and Kingston: McGill-Queen's University Press, 1973); Cronon, *Nature's Metropolis*; Richard White, *Land Use, Environment, and Social Change: The Shaping of Island County, Washington* (Seattle: University of Washington Press, 1980); Jamie Swift, *Cut and Run: The Assault on Canada's Forests* (Toronto: Between the Lines, 1983); Gordon Hak, *Turning Trees into Dollars: The British Columbia Coastal Lumber Industry, 1858–1913* (Toronto: University of Toronto Press, 2000).
7 Donald G. Creighton first introduced the idea that Canadian history can be explained by the relationship between metropolitan centres and hinterland regions. Donald G. Creighton, *The Commercial Empire of the St. Lawrence, 1760–1850* (Toronto: Ryerson Press, 1937); J.M.S. Careless, *Frontier and Metropolis: Regions, Cities, and Identities in Canada before 1914* (Toronto: University of Toronto Press, 1989).
8 Daniel Drache, "Celebrating Innis: The Man, the Legacy, and Our Future," in *Staples, Markets, and Cultural Change: Selected Essays*, ed. Daniel Drache (Montreal and Kingston: McGill-Queen's University Press, 1994), xxii.
9 A.R.M. Lower, *The North American Assault on the Canadian Forest: A History of the Lumber Trade between Canada and the United States* (Toronto: Carnegie Endowment for International Peace, 1938), xx–xxi.
10 Harold A. Innis, "The Importance of Staple Products in Canadian Development," in Drache, *Staples, Markets, and Cultural Change*, 3–23; Kenneth Buckley, "The Role of Staple Industries in Canada's Economic Development," *Journal of Economic History* 18 (1958):

Notes to pages 107–11

439–60; McCalla, *Planting the Province;* Marjorie Griffin Cohen, *Women's Work, Markets, and Economic Development in Nineteenth-Century Ontario* (Toronto: University of Toronto Press, 1988); Serge Courville and Normand Séguin, *Rural Life in Nineteenth Century Quebec,* CHA Booklet 47 (Ottawa: Canadian Historical Association, 1989).

11 Nelles, *The Politics of Development.*

12 Lower, *The North American Assault,* 22; Cronon, *Nature's Metropolis,* 152.

13 Lower, *The North American Assault;* Donald MacKay, *The Lumberjacks,* 3rd ed. (Toronto: Dundurn, 2007), 18; Long, *This River,* 144–45; Tatley, "Timber!," 77; Scott, *Steam Tugs and Supply Boats,* 2.

14 The remaining timber berths in Muskoka were auctioned off on 6 June 1877 and 6 December 1881, as surveys made new townships open for settlement and exhausted pineries pushed logging companies farther upstream. MacKenzie, "The Economic and Social Development," 176.

15 *Ontario Sessional Papers, 1871–72,* 15–18. Note that the 845 square miles is an estimate based on an average of 416 hundred-acre lots in each township.

16 A.G.P. Dodge, a partner with Hotchkiss and Hughson, facilitated an agreement between the two firms to share the timber limits in Muskoka and Parry Sound so as to avoid a bidding war when the territory was auctioned in 1871. James T. Angus, *A Deo Victoria: The Story of the Georgian Bay Lumber Company, 1871–1942* (Thunder Bay, ON: Severn, 1990), 49.

17 Scott, *Steam Tugs and Supply Boats,* 2.

18 *Ontario Sessional Papers, 1874–1920.*

19 Nelles, *The Politics of Development,* 13–14.

20 Part of the reason that logging companies moved so swiftly was because settlement would destroy the trees before they could be cut. Although the government was committed to settling the southern region of the Shield, this tension between settlers and loggers informed much of the legislation that granted logging companies rather than settlers the rights to access forest wealth. A.R.M. Lower, *Settlement and the Forest Frontier in Eastern Canada* (Toronto: Macmillan, 1936); Nelles, *The Politics of Development,* 16; Wynn, "Notes on Society and Environment," 57–58.

21 Nelles, *The Politics of Development,* 18.

22 Lawson, Levy, and Sandberg conclude that the provincial government "saw the long-term interest of business and its own fiscal needs as its priorities." However, there was nothing "long-term" about the business model or policy approach taken by industry and government at this time. Jamie Lawson, Marcelo Levy, and L. Anders Sandberg, "'Perpetual Revenues and the Delights of the Primitive': Change, Continuity, and Forest Policy Regimes in Ontario," in *Canadian Forest Policy: Adapting to Change,* ed. Michael Howlett (Toronto: University of Toronto Press, 2001), 286. The only exception might have been the use of revenues from timber dues in funding road construction in Muskoka. Between 1863 and 1871, the government collected $124,439 in timber dues and spent $79,872 on roads in Muskoka. Paying for these roads would have been challenging without the revenues generated from timber dues. MacKenzie, "The Economic and Social Development," 175.

23 Murray, *Muskoka and Haliburton,* 239–40.

24 King, *Letters from Muskoka,* 26.

25 Murray, *Muskoka and Haliburton,* xcii.

26 In some cases, settlers managed to obtain patent while merchantable pine still remained on their property. When this happened, they often replicated the logging company pattern of large-scale cutting. Some sold the standing timber directly to the companies, whereas

202 Notes to pages 111–13

others hired men to do the work themselves and sell the logs for higher profit. While the environmental impacts of settler logging were similar to commercial logging operations, a greater share of the value remained with the settler. MacKenzie, "The Economic and Social Development," 182.

27 Tatley, "Timber!" 83. As Graeme Wynn contends, "a fundamental functional unity" existed in all pre-industrial Canadian lumbering operations "that transcended local variations in the relationship between lumbering and farming, and in the relative importance of lumbering in the pioneer economy." Wynn, *Timber Colony*, 6. Given this, where information is lacking for logging in Muskoka, research into similar operations elsewhere may be drawn on as representative. For a more detailed discussion on logging camp work and operations, see Robert Pike, *Tall Trees, Tough Men* (New York: W.W. Norton, 1967); Radforth, *Bushworkers and Bosses;* Cronon, *Nature's Metropolis;* and Radforth, "The Shantymen," 214–21.

28 Angus, *Deo Victoria*, 79–80; Wynn, *Timber Colony*, 54–69.

29 Wynn, *Timber Colony*, 83–84; MacKenzie, "The Economic and Social Development," 206; Wall, "Pioneer Settlement," 398; Radforth, *Bushworkers and Bosses*, 26. In *On the Edge of Empire*, Adele Perry shows that gendered work and behaviour challenged, even as it reinforced, the role of the male breadwinner. See also Maynard, "Rough Work and Rugged Men," 159–69; and Radforth, "The Shantymen," 232.

30 Wynn, *Timber Colony*, 86.

31 King, *Letters from Muskoka*, 135–36.

32 Wynn, *Timber Colony*, 86. In *La conquête du sol*, Normand Séguin presents a similar argument for Quebec. Gérard Bouchard suggests that work in the woods did not always result in a dependent economic position for smallholders. In fact, economic plurality, made possible by the agroforestry economy, helped stabilize rural households – especially in marginal environments with low agricultural potential – by providing wage labour opportunities within the context of subsistence agriculture. Bouchard, "Co-intégration et reproduction"; Bouchard, *Quelques arpents*.

33 Joseph Conlin, "Old Boy, Did You Get Enough Pie? A Social History of Food in Logging Camps," *Journal of Forest History* 23, 4 (October 1979): 165. Graeme Wynn suggests that "the communal camaraderie of camp life described in many fulsome accounts of lumbering elsewhere in eastern North America was almost certainly exaggerated." Wynn, *Timber Colony*, 62.

34 As Ian Radforth notes, wage labour in the camps tended to lock households into a dependent relationship within the agroforestry economy. This effect was amplified during downturns in the economy. Radforth, *Bushworkers and Bosses*, 28, 40–43; Radforth, "The Shantymen," 214.

35 Radforth, *Bushworkers and Bosses*, 43; King, *Letters from Muskoka*, 135. Depending on skill, however, other roles in the camp could earn a logger more or less. During the 1870s, hewers made $30–$38 a month, liners $20–$22, scorers $15–$19, and general hands $14–$16. Radforth, "The Shantymen," 217.

36 MacKenzie, "The Economic and Social Development," 206. For more on the prevalence of alcohol in all-male environments, such as those in logging camps, see Perry, *On the Edge of Empire*, 40–42; Hak, *Turning Trees into Dollars*, 143–44; and Craig Heron, *Booze: A Distilled History* (Toronto: Between the Lines, 2003), 84, 285.

37 J.V.G.A. Durnin and R. Passmore, *Energy, Work, and Leisure* (London: Heinemann, 1967), 71–73.

38 Conlin, "Old Boy," 165 (emphasis in original).
39 Ibid., 166–68; Radforth, "The Shantymen," 229; Bob Petry, *Bala, an Early Settlement in Muskoka: A Pictorial History of Bala from the Late 1800s* (Bracebridge: Self-published, 1998), 121.
40 Grant Head, "An Introduction to Forest Exploitation in Nineteenth Century Ontario," in *Perspectives on Landscape and Settlement in Nineteenth Century Ontario*, ed. J. David Wood (Toronto: McClelland and Stewart in association with the Institute of Canadian Studies, Carleton University, 1975), 78–112. On variations on camp provisions, see Wynn, *Timber Colony*, 69–71.
41 Murray, *Muskoka and Haliburton*, 244–45, 248–49.
42 Ibid., 187.
43 Census of Canada, 1871–91.
44 Campbell, *Shaped by the West Wind*.
45 King, *Letters from Muskoka*, 59.
46 Ibid., 55–56.
47 Penson, "Seymour Penson, Part I," 191.
48 Eric A. Bourdo Jr., "The Forest the Settlers Saw," in *The Great Lakes Forest: An Environmental and Social History*, ed. Susan L. Flader (Minneapolis: University of Minnesota Press, 1983), 3–4.
49 Roland I. Hall and John P. Smol, "The Influence of Catchment Size on Lake Trophic Status during the Hemlock Decline and Recovery (4800 to 3500 BP) in Southern Ontario Lakes," *Hydrobiologia* 269–70 (1993): 371.
50 Ibid., 383.
51 For an excellent historical overview on the effects of fire on the Great Lakes–St. Lawrence forest, including Muskoka, see Stephen J. Pyne, *Awful Splendour: A Fire History of Canada* (Vancouver: UBC Press, 2007).
52 G. Mercer Adam, "Georgian Bay and the Muskoka Lakes," in *Picturesque Spots of the North: Historical and Descriptive Sketches of the Scenery and Life in the Vicinity of Georgian Bay, the Muskoka Lakes, the Upper Lakes, in Central and Eastern Ontario, and in the Niagara District*, ed. George Munro Grant (Chicago: Alexander Belford, 1899), 46–47.
53 Clifford E. Ahlgren and Isabel F. Ahlgren, "The Human Impact on Northern Forest Ecosystems," in Flader, *The Great Lakes Forest*, 38–39; Bourdo, "The Forest the Settlers Saw," 14; White, *Land Use, Environment, and Social Change*, 89.
54 R.L. France, "Macroinvertebrate Colonization of Woody Debris in Canadian Shield Lakes following Riparian Clearcutting," *Conservation Biology* 11, 2 (April 1997): 514; Lawson, Levy, and Sandberg, "'Perpetual Revenues,'" 305.
55 Bourdo, "The Forest the Settlers Saw," 9.
56 Foster and Aber, *Forests in Time*, 111; Bourdo, "The Forest the Settlers Saw," 8.
57 Wood, *Making Ontario*, 12.
58 Long, *This River*, 51; David M. Gates, C.H.D. Clarke, and James T. Harris, "Wildlife in a Changing Environment," in Flader, *The Great Lakes Forest*, 62.
59 Saloni Clerk et al., "Quantitative Inferences of Past Hypolimnetic Anoxia and Nutrient Levels from a Canadian Precambrian Shield Lake," *Journal of Paleolimnology* 23 (2000): 325, 327. Diatoms are a major form of algae, one of the most common types of phytoplankton.
60 France, "Macroinvertebrate Colonization."

204 Notes to pages 116–21

61 Roland I. Hall and John P. Smol, "Paleolimnological Assessment of Long-Term Water-Quality Changes in South-Central Ontario Lakes Affected by Cottage Development," *Canadian Journal of Fisheries and Aquatic Sciences* 53 (1996): 13–14.
62 Most small sawmills in Muskoka were built during the 1860s and 1870s and rarely cut more than 1,000 or 2,000 board feet per day during their first years. As single-blade band saws were replaced with turbine-powered circular saws around 1900, several mills expanded their capacity to about 10,000 board feet per day. In 1869, in response to what many saw as a threat to their livelihoods by the licensing system, owners of small sawmills petitioned the government to reserve a certain amount of timber for local purposes. The result was a policy requiring logging companies to leave 50,000 to 100,000 board feet per limit for local use. After 1900, many of the smaller mills were squeezed out of business by larger commercial operations that could easily and affordably deliver lumber anywhere in Muskoka. Others hung on until after the First World War and some even survived to the onset of the Depression. Tatley, "Timber!" 82; Gray, *Lake Joseph,* 15; Long, *This River,* 86–98.
63 Craig, *Backwoods Consumers,* 98.
64 Wynn, *Timber Colony,* 83.
65 In 1903, the Mutchenbacker brothers moved west to Mafeking, Manitoba, where they struggled for a decade to maintain a viable business cutting several million board feet every year. Mochoruk, *Formidable Heritage,* 157–58; Tatley, *The Steamboat Era,* 1: 161; Andrew Hind and Maria Da Silva, *Ghost Towns of Muskoka* (Toronto: Natural Heritage Books, 2008), 33–35.
66 "Accounts Ledger for Gravenhurst Sawmill of Snider Lumber Company, 1902–1907," 688, Archives of the Muskoka Steamship and Historical Society (AMSHS).
67 "Homer Ledger," 117, Gravenhurst Public Library Archives.
68 "Snider Ledger," 762, AMSHS.
69 "Homer Ledger," 192, 227, 298, Gravenhurst Public Library Archives.
70 This calculation is based on an average wage of $26 per month over a five-month period. Radforth, "The Shantymen," 43.
71 These calculations are based on the 1901 and 1911 Canadian censuses, which list $12.76 per thousand board feet of pine and $7.89 for hemlock on average, and the gross board-foot volume equivalent of a tree that was eighteen inches in diameter and forty feet tall. See Figure 6 in Paul Oester and Steve Bowers, *Measuring Timber Products Harvested from Your Woodland,* The Woodland Workbook, rev. ed., Oregon State University Extension Service, 2009, https://knowyourforest.org/sites/default/files/documents/Measuring_timber_products.pdf. My calculations do not take into consideration portions of each log that ended up as milling waste.
72 These calculations are based on the same sources listed in endnote 71, as well as total log purchases by the Snider Lumber Company between October and May in each of the winters listed. "Snider Ledger," AMSHS.
73 The other 7 percent came from three townships that had little or no shoreline on the lower lakes.
74 Census of Canada, 1901, 1911, 1921.
75 Tatley, *The Steamboat Era,* 1: 161.
76 Barry Davidson, "Forest Management Plan for the French/Severn Forest (360)," Ministry of Natural Resources, Parry Sound District, Southern Region and Westwind Forest Stewardship, 2008, 14.

Notes to pages 122–24 205

77 Abbott Conway, *A History of Beardmore and Company Limited and Anglo Canadian Leather Company Limited* (Toronto: Canada Packers, 1990).

78 Abbott Conway, "The Tanning Industry in Muskoka," in *Pioneer Muskoka: Notes on the History of Muskoka District as Presented by Guest Speakers on Behalf of Georgian College (Barrie)* (Parry Sound: Algonquin Regional Library System, 1974), 19, Muskoka Local History Collection, Huntsville Public Library Archives.

79 "The Rise and Fall of the Huntsville Tannery, Part One," *Huntsville Forester*, 19 May 1982.

80 Tatley, *The Steamboat Era*, 1: 158.

81 Conway, *A History of Beardmore*, 5.

82 Tatley, *The Steamboat Era*, 2: 67.

83 Gail Smith, "Chapter Three: The Tanning Industry in Muskoka," T7–8, Anglo-Canadian Leather Company: Tannery and Housing, Concert Band Binder of Collected documents (Anglo-Canadian Binder), 785.06 ANG c. 1, Muskoka Heritage Place Archives; "Bracebridge: The Largest Town in Muskoka and the Judicial Seat," *Bracebridge Gazette*, 26 July 1906, 7. A side is half a hide.

84 Conway, "The Tanning Industry in Muskoka," 22; "Bracebridge: The Largest Town," *Bracebridge Gazette*, 7. Reliable documentation on the source of overseas hides is almost non-existent. Numerous local histories, first-hand accounts, oral histories, and local newspaper articles describe hides coming in from a variety of overseas locations, with South America, especially Argentina, being the most common. The earliest scholarly research on Muskoka lists "South and Central America" as the source of Beardmore's imported hides, but with no primary sources to confirm or deny the claims, suffice it to say that some portion, between a quarter and a third, of the hides processed in Muskoka came from "overseas." MacKenzie, "The Economic and Social Development," 151.

85 Herbert H. Hergert, "The Tannin Extraction Industry in the United States," *Journal of Forest History* 27, 2 (April 1983): 92.

86 Tatley, *The Steamboat Era*, 1: 90.

87 If we use Hergert's ratio of 2.5 cords per 100 hides, this would have required 7,825 cords of tanbark from approximately 71,000 hemlock trees. Without any other aggregate data for the intervening years, and assuming all three tanneries processed comparable amounts of leather, the average between the lowest requirements (from 1879) and the highest requirements (from 1906) may be used as a proxy to calculate the number of trees cut each year to supply the industry.

88 This estimate must be treated as extremely rough, since the 1901 census lists 30,426 cords of tanbark sold in Muskoka that year (the equivalent of 121,704 trees) – approximately 50,000 more trees than this author's estimate. There is no way of knowing how many cords listed in the census were consumed locally, and it is likely that some were shipped to tanneries in southern Ontario and elsewhere.

89 The 1901 census lists 30,426 cords of tanbark sold in Muskoka for $133,518, an average price of $4.39 per cord, well below the approximately $6 per cord paid under "Bark Ticket a/c" in the Muskoka Leather Company ledger. It should be noted that I could not discover exactly what a bark ticket was or how it worked. The explanation offered here is based on the information available. Since weekly "Bark Ticket a/c" entries were almost always accompanied by both the number of cords and the price paid for them, I assumed a company-managed system. Moreover, since the amount purchased during certain weeks is often extremely high and no names are ever associated with any bark ticket entries, I likewise

206 Notes to pages 124–27

assume that these purchases were not made from individual households, but were instead aggregate numbers of purchases from all bark gangs holding tickets.

90 This assumes that Muskoka Leather consumed as many cords as Anglo-Canadian did in 1906: 7,825 cords. "Muskoka Leather Company Ledger, July 1905–August 1906," MLM.

91 James Bay Railway Company and the Canadian Northern Ontario Railway Company, "Regarding Agreement between the Muskoka Leather Company and James Bay Railways for construction of dam and sluice way at Stewart Lake outlet," RG30, file 1046–25–2, LAC; Conway, *A History of Beardmore*, 6.

92 Ex-tannery workers whom Smith interviewed claimed that a bark gang could finish about 35–40 trees per day (1 tree every twenty-five minutes during a fifteen-hour work day). Finishing a tree meant chopping it down, removing the branches and canopy, girdling and stripping it, and stacking the bark into cords. Each man was expected to produce at least 1 cord per day or 4 cords per gang (2.5 trees every sixty minutes per fifteen-hour work day). If 9 cords are taken as the high end of what a gang could complete in a day (equivalent to 82 trees), and 4 cords was the minimum, we arrive at 6.5 cords per bark gang on average. Smith, "Chapter Three: The Tanning Industry," T4.

93 Tatley, *The Steamboat Era*, 1: 90.

94 This assumes a work schedule of seventy-seven days, from 15 May to 1 August. If each gang cut 6.5 cords each day, after seventy-seven days each gang would have cut approximately 500 cords. It would therefore have required thirty-two men, working in teams of four, to cut the 4,000 cords consumed by Beardmore's tannery in 1879. In 1906, the Muskoka Leather Company employed approximately five hundred men to cut hemlock bark during the summer months. "Bracebridge: The Largest Town," *Bracebridge Gazette*, 7.

95 Gray, *Lake Joseph*, 15.

96 "Brief Synopsis of Leather Manufacture," April 26, 1967, Muskoka Local History Collection, Huntsville Public Library Archives.

97 Scott, *Steam Tugs and Supply Boats*, 17–18; Denison, *Micklethwaite's Muskoka*, 40.

98 "Minutes of the Muskoka Lakes Association, August 1919," Muskoka Lakes Association fonds, GA 100, box 1, file 1–14, University of Waterloo Archives and Special Collections.

99 Vagel Charles Keller Jr., "Forgotten Brownfields: Rural Industrial Districts in Pennsylvania, 1870–1930" (PhD diss., Carnegie Mellon University, 2005), 188.

100 Jackson Smith Schultz, *The Leather Manufacture in the United States: A Dissertation on the Methods and Economies of Tanning* (New York: 'Shoe and Leather Reporter' Office, 1876), 153–54. Hair and flesh removed from hides was regularly sold to other industries for use in manufacturing and chemical production. Keller, "Forgotten Brownfields," 181–82; *Huntsville Forester*, 26 July 1906; "The Tanning Process," T7–8, Anglo-Canadian Binder, Muskoka Heritage Place Archives.

101 Keller, "Forgotten Brownfields," 189.

102 Harry Wahl, "A Lesson in the Workings of the Tannery," *Huntsville Forester*, 17 October 2001.

103 Mwinyikione Mwinyihija, *Ecotoxicological Diagnosis in the Tanning Industry* (New York: Springer, 2010), 22.

104 This percentage is based on an average of 23,650 hemlock trees cut in 1886. "The Tannery Journals, Part One," in *Vintage Muskoka*, 17, Muskoka Local History Collection, Leather Industry file, Huntsville Public Library Archives.

105 One household sold 127.5 cords, and five others sold at least 50, but nine sold 25 or fewer. Ibid.

Notes to pages 127–36

107

106 "Homer Ledger," Gravenhurst Public Library Archives.

107 Adam, "Georgian Bay and the Muskoka Lakes," 38.

108 "Homer Ledger," 329, 389, 560, 601, Gravenhurst Public Library Archives.

109 Of course, a few settlers each season cut far more intensively, but they were anomalies in the general pattern. Also, since consecutive records are unavailable, it is impossible to conclude whether this pattern was replicated each season by certain households or whether they engaged in the tanbark trade only periodically.

110 *Huntsville Forester,* 26 July 1906.

111 Census of Canada, 1901, 1911.

112 "Anglo-Canadian Leather Company Tannery Grounds Maps, 1911 and 1921," Anglo-Canadian Binder, Muskoka Heritage Place Archives.

113 Conway, "The Tanning Industry in Muskoka," 19–20; Long, *This River,* 4. A special extract, produced by boiling quebracho hardwood that grew in Argentina and Brazil, contained tannins that could be substituted for those found in hemlock bark. Conway, *A History of Beardmore,* 20.

Chapter 5: Fossil Fuels, Consumer Culture, and the Tourism Economy

1 "Summer Supply Season, 1905: Supply Boat 'Nymoca' Calling tri-weekly at all points on the Muskoka Lake," James Bay Railway Company, General Claims, Claim of JJ Beaumont and Sons, 1905, RG30, file 1046–78–1, LAC.

2 Thorstein Veblen, *The Theory of the Leisure Class,* ed. Martha Banta (New York: Oxford University Press, 2007), 28–69.

3 Stephen Leacock, *Arcadian Adventures with the Idle Rich* (reprint, Toronto: McClelland and Stewart, 1989), 112–16. For more on the parallels between Muskoka and Leacock's chapter on cottaging, see Stevens, "Getting Away from It," 71.

4 William Leach, *Land of Desire: Merchants, Power, and the Rise of a New American Culture* (New York: Pantheon, 1993); Daniel Horowitz, *The Morality of Spending: Attitudes toward the Consumer Society in America, 1875–1940* (Baltimore: Johns Hopkins University Press, 1985); Tracey Deutsch, *Building a Housewife's Paradise: Gender, Politics, and American Grocery Stores in the Twentieth Century* (Chapel Hill: University of North Carolina Press, 2010); Kristin L. Hoganson, *Consumer's Imperium: The Global Production of American Domesticity, 1865–1920* (Chapel Hill: University of North Carolina Press, 2007).

5 Donica Belisle, *Retail Nation: Department Stores and the Making of Modern Canada* (Vancouver: UBC Press, 2011), 9–10; Donica Belisle, "Toward a Canadian Consumer History," *Labour/Le travail* 52 (Fall 2003): 181–206; Joy I. Santink, *Timothy Eaton and the Rise of His Department Store* (Toronto: University of Toronto Press, 1990).

6 Belisle, *Retail Nation,* 3.

7 Hal S. Barron, *Mixed Harvest: The Second Great Transformation in the Rural North, 1870–1930* (Chapel Hill: University of North Carolina Press, 1997), 8.

8 Ibid., 155.

9 David Monod, *Store Wars: Shopkeepers and the Culture of Mass Marketing, 1890–1939* (Toronto: University of Toronto Press, 1996), 101; Belisle, *Retail Nation,* 11.

10 Monod, *Store Wars,* 128.

11 Belisle, *Retail Nation,* 69; T.J. Jackson Lears, "From Salvation to Self-Realization: Advertising and the Therapeutic Roots of Consumer Culture, 1880–1930," in *The Culture of Consumption: Critical Essays in American History, 1880–1980,* ed. Richard Wightman Fox

208   Notes to pages 137–41

and T.J. Jackson Lears (New York: Pantheon Books, 1983), 1–38; Bettina Liverant, *Buying Happiness: The Emergence of Consumer Consciousness in English Canada* (Vancouver: UBC Press, 2018).

12 Gregory Alexander Donofrio, "Feeding the City," *Gastronomica* 7, 4 (Fall 2007): 30–41.

13 The concept of organic and mineral energy is introduced in the context of the Industrial Revolution in England in E.A. Wrigley, *Continuity, Chance and Change: The Character of the Industrial Revolution in England* (Cambridge: Cambridge University Press, 1988).

14 Wolfgang Schivelbusch, *The Railway Journey: The Industrialization of Time and Space in the Nineteenth Century* (Oakland: University of California Press, 1986); Jasen, *Wild Things;* John Armstrong and David M. Williams, "The Steamboat and Popular Tourism," *Journal of Transport History* 26, 1 (2005): 61–77; Little, "Scenic Tourism," 716–42; Dawson, *Selling British Columbia;* Ben Bradley, *British Columbia by the Road: Car Culture and the Making of a Modern Landscape* (Vancouver: UBC Press, 2017).

15 Leo Marx, *The Machine in the Garden: Technology and Pastoral Ideal in America* (New York: Oxford University Press, 1964); Deborah Fitzgerald, *Every Farm a Factory: The Industrial Ideal in American Agriculture* (New Haven: Yale University Press, 2003); Cunfer, *On the Great Plains.* An important exception is Joshua MacFadyen, "Hewers of Wood: A History of Wood Energy in Canada," in *Powering Up Canada: A History of Power, Fuel, and Energy from 1600,* ed. R.W. Sandwell (Montreal and Kingston: McGill-Queen's University Press, 2016), 129–61.

16 R.W. Sandwell, "An Introduction to Canada's Energy History," in Sandwell, *Powering Up Canada,* 3–36. Sandwell's work draws on the statistics compiled in Richard W. Unger and John Thistle, *Energy Consumption in Canada in the 19th and 20th Centuries: A Statistical Outline* (Napoli: Consiglio Nazionale delle Ricerche Istituto di Studi sulle Società del Mediterraneo, 2013).

17 For more on the ways that fairs reinforced community and best farming practices, see Wayne Caldwell Neely, *The Agricultural Fair* (New York: AMS Press, 1967); Thomas R. Irwin, "Government Funding of Agricultural Associations in Late Nineteenth Century Ontario" (PhD diss., University of Western Ontario, 1997); Ross D. Fair, "Gentlemen, Farmers, and Gentlemen Half-Farmers: The Development of Agricultural Societies in Upper Canada, 1792–1846" (PhD diss., Queen's University, 1998); and David Mizener, "Furrows and Fairgrounds: Agriculture, Identity, and Authority in Twentieth-Century Rural Ontario" (PhD diss., York University, 2009).

18 "Medora and Wood Agricultural Society Fall Fair Entry Book, 1907–1912," no accession number, MLM.

19 "Homer Ledger," Gravenhurst Public Library Archives.

20 Boyer, *Muskoka's Grand Hotels,* 74.

21 Tourism aside, the diverse ways that households provided for their own needs and generated income shared parallels with rural communities throughout Ontario in the late nineteenth and early twentieth centuries. Adam Crerar, "Ties That Bind: Farming, Agrarian Ideals, and Life in Ontario, 1890–1930" (PhD diss., University of Toronto, 1999).

22 "Diary of Julia 'Leena' Riley, Diary of Pioneers at Milford Bay," October 19, 1909–May 31, 1910, April–May 1910, 1912, 1913, October–November 1909–12, Archives of the Muskoka Steamship and Historical Society.

23 Ibid., June 1910, 1912.

24 Rogers, *Muskoka Lakes Bluebook, 1915.*

Notes to pages 141–55

25 John Rogers, *Muskoka Lakes Bluebook, Directory and Chart, 1918* (Port Sandfield, ON: Self-published, 1918).
26 "Homer Ledger," 609, 738 Gravenhurst Public Library Archives.
27 Hathaway, *Muskoka Memories*, 218.
28 Belisle, *Retail Nation*, chapter 1; "Canadian Mail Order Catalogues – History," 2019, LAC, https://www.bac-lac.gc.ca/eng/discover/postal-heritage-philately/canadian-mail-order -catalogues/Pages/catalogues-history.aspx.
29 Richard Tatley, *Windermere: The Jewel of Lake Rosseau* (Erin, ON: Boston Mills Press, 1999), 25.
30 *Summer Needs and Outing Goods*, 1899, T. Eaton Company fonds, F229–5-0–58, no. 2, AO.
31 *Campers' Supplies*, 1900, 26, T. Eaton Company fonds, F229–5-0–58, no. 2, AO.
32 The 1902 MLA Yearbook lists 182 member households, 159 of whom were cottagers. In 1918, the MLA membership had risen to 260 households, only 5 of whom were not cottagers. The 1918 *Muskoka Lakes Bluebook* lists 852 summer residents, so the MLA membership probably amounted to somewhere between a third to half of all the cottagers in Muskoka. J.D. McMurrich, ed., *Muskoka Lakes Association 1902 Yearbook* (Toronto: Oxford Press, 1902); Hugh Neilson, ed., *Muskoka Lakes Association 1918 Yearbook* (Toronto: Parker Bros., 1918); Rogers, *Muskoka Lakes Bluebook, 1918*.
33 *Summer Holiday Needs*, 1903, T. Eaton Company fonds, F229–5-0–60, no. 2, AO.
34 Belisle, *Retail Nation*, 49, 54.
35 *Outing Supply Catalogue*, 1906, 2, T. Eaton Company fonds, F229–5-0–60, no. 2, AO.
36 *Summer Catalogue*, 1901, 1–9, T. Eaton Company fonds, F229–5-0–58, no. 2, AO.
37 *Summer Holiday Needs*, 1903, 19–22, AO.
38 *Outing Supply Catalogue*, 1906, 2, AO.
39 McMurrich, *MLA 1902 Yearbook*, 64.
40 Tatley, *The Steamboat Era*, 1: 245.
41 "Summer Supply Season, 1905: Supply Boat 'Nymoca,'" LAC.
42 "Bracebridge Grocers and the Tourist Trade," *Bracebridge Gazette*, 29 June 1905, 1.
43 Katherine Hale, "Guests of Nature," *The Globe*, 5 July 1913, A3.
44 Belisle, *Retail Nation*, 27.
45 Rogers, *Muskoka Lakes Bluebook, 1915*, 3.
46 Scott, *Steam Tugs and Supply Boats*, 11.
47 Currie, *The Grand Trunk Railway*, 175, 207.
48 Ibid., 157.
49 Drummond, *Progress without Planning*, 253; M.J. Patton, "The Coal Resources of Canada," *Economic Geography* 1, 1 (March 1925): 73.
50 Canada, *Tables of the Trade and Navigation of the Province of Canada for the Year 1855* (Toronto: Stewart Derbishire and George Desbarats, 1856), 2.
51 David F. Walker, "Transportation of Coal into Southern Ontario, 1871–1921," *Ontario History* 63 (1971): 16.
52 Tatley, *The Steamboat Era*, 1: 273–74.
53 "Board Meeting Minutes of the Muskoka and Georgian Bay Navigation Company, 1896–1903," Minutes of Navig. Co. Bd. file, Steamships folder, AMSHS.
54 Tatley, *The Steamboat Era*, 1: 232; Smith, "A Room with a View," 137.
55 These numbers are estimates that would change rather significantly depending on the type of wood (hard versus soft) and coal (anthracite versus bituminous). The coal consumed

210 Notes to pages 155–59

by Muskoka steamers would most probably have been bituminous, whereas the cordwood sold through Homer to the Navigation Company in March 1897 was approximately one-quarter hardwood and three-quarters softwood. "Homer Ledger," 133, 280, 447, Gravenhurst Public Library Archives; "Unit 1: What Is Energy? Section C. Measuring and Quantifying Energy," K-12 Energy Education Program, University of Wisconsin, https://www.uwsp.edu/cnr-ap/KEEP/nres633/Pages/Unit1/Supplementary%20Pages/Energy-Conversion-and-Resource-Tables.aspx.

56 Tatley, *The Steamboat Era*, 1: 265.

57 McMurrich, *MLA 1902 Yearbook*.

58 Rogers, *Muskoka Lakes Bluebook, 1915*.

59 "Homer Ledger," 133, Gravenhurst Public Library Archives.

60 "Navigation Company Balance Sheets, 1897–1910," Royal Muskoka #4 file, Accounting Data.

61 Tatley, *The Steamboat Era*, 2: 15, 2: 51.

62 Drummond, *Progress without Planning*, 390–91.

63 Harold Williamson and Arnold R. Daum, *The American Petroleum Industry: The Age of Illumination, 1859–1899* (Evanston, IL: Northwestern University Press, 1959), 583.

64 Drummond, *Progress without Planning*, 96.

65 Samuel H. Schurr and Bruce C. Netschert, *Energy in the American Economy, 1850–1975: An Economic Study of Its History and Prospects* (Westport, CT: Greenwood Press, 1977), 116–17.

66 *Ontario Sessional Papers, 1929–30*.

67 Stephen James Davies, "Ontario and the Automobile, 1900–1930: Aspects of Technological Integration" (PhD diss., McMaster University, 1987), 390, appendix 4.

68 *Ontario Sessional Papers, 1920; Ontario Sessional Papers, 1929*.

69 *Ontario Sessional Papers, 1910*.

70 Lee Ann Eckhardt Smith, *Muskoka's Main Street: 150 Years of Courage and Adventure along the Muskoka Colonization Road* (Bracebridge: Muskoka Books, 2012), 143–44; Brendan O'Brien, *The Prettiest Spot in Muskoka* (Toronto: Bobolink Books, 1999), 142, 144.

71 McMurrich, *MLA 1902 Yearbook*, 62; Brendan O'Brien, "Memories: Cottage Life at the Turn of the Century," in Muskoka Lakes Association, *Summertimes*, 117.

72 Tatley, *The Steamboat Era*, 2: 27, 2: 33.

73 Ibid., 11, 70.

74 A.H. Duke and W.M. Gray, *The Boatbuilders of Muskoka* (Toronto: Self-published, 1985), 13–17.

75 They were A.H. Duke in 1908, both H.C. Minett and John Matheson in 1910, and W.J. Johnston in 1915. Ibid., 91–92; Paul Dodington, Paul W. Gockel, and Joe Fossey, *The Greatest Little Motor Boat Afloat: The Legendary Disappearing Propeller Boat* (Toronto: Stoddart, 1994), 29.

76 McMurrich, *MLA 1902 Yearbook*, 62; O'Brien, "Memories," 117.

77 Rogers, *Muskoka Lakes Bluebook, 1915*.

78 Dodington, Gockel, and Fossey, *The Greatest Little*, 29, 40.

79 Ibid., 43–45.

80 Rogers, *Muskoka Lakes Bluebook, 1918*, 82.

81 Ibid.

82 Michael Berger, *The Devil Wagon in God's Country: The Automobile and Social Change in Rural America, 1893–1929* (Hamden, CT: Archon Books, 1979); Davies, "Ontario and the

Notes to pages 159–68

Automobile"; Joseph Interrante, "You Can't Go to Town in a Bathtub: Automobile Movement and the Reorganization of Rural American Space, 1900–1930," *Radical History Review* 21 (Fall 1979): 151–68.

83 Petry, *Bala,* 95.

84 Duke and Gray, *The Boatbuilders,* 27.

85 Another tank depot, belonging to the British-American Oil Company, was located on Bala Park Island next to the siding. Petry, *Bala,* 95–96, 144–45; Duke and Gray, *The Boatbuilders,* 27, 29.

86 "Riley Diary," May 1910, June, November 1911, AMSHS.

87 O'Brien, *The Prettiest Spot,* 147.

88 Gray, *Lake Joseph,* 65.

89 "Correspondence with Muskoka Lakes Navigation and Hotel Company, March 16, 1918," Frederick W. Coate family fonds, F720, AO.

90 Ibid.

91 Boyer, *Muskoka's Grand Hotels,* 96.

92 Rogers, *Muskoka Lakes Bluebook, 1915,* 78, 85.

93 Rogers, *Muskoka Lakes Bluebook, 1918.*

94 McMurrich, *MLA 1902 Yearbook,* 56.

95 Rogers, *Muskoka Lakes Bluebook, 1915,* 4.

96 Liz Lundell, *Old Muskoka: Century Cottages and Summer Estates* (Erin, ON: Boston Mills Press, 2003), 108; Cameron Taylor, *Enchanted Summers: The Grand Hotels of Muskoka* (Toronto: Lynx Images, 1997), 47; Bessie Waters, *Country Tales: A Collection of Colourful Old-Time Reminiscences by a Muskoka Lady* (Bracebridge: MOS Graphics, 1992), 78–79.

97 "Correspondence with Muskoka Lakes Navigation and Hotel Company, June 19, 1915," Frederick W. Coate family fonds, F720, AO.

98 Ibid., October 5, 1917.

Conclusion

1 Lower, *Settlement and the Forest Frontier,* 75.

2 Muskoka Community Foundation, "Vital Signs 2018," 9, https://muskokacommunity foundation.ca/wp-content/uploads/2018/11/msk-vitalsigns-web.pdf.

3 Ibid., 3.

4 Ibid., 2.

5 Weaver, *The Great Land Rush.*

6 Sandwell, *Canada's Rural Majority.*

7 Tatley, *The Steamboat Era,* vol. 2.

8 Peter Stevens, "Cars and Cottages: The Automotive Transformation of Ontario's Summer Home Tradition," *Ontario History* 100, 1 (Spring 2008): 26–56.

9 Brownlie, *A Fatherly Eye.*

10 Calverley, *Who Controls the Hunt?*

11 Sharon Wall, "Totem Poles, Teepees, and Token Traditions: 'Playing Indian' at Ontario Summer Camps, 1920–1955," *Canadian Historical Review* 86, 3 (September 2005): 523–44.

12 Douglas McTaggart, *Bigwin Inn* (Erin, ON: Boston Mills Press, 1992).

13 Muskoka Steamships and Discovery Centre, "MSDC Revitalization Project," https:// realmuskoka.com/revitalization/.

212   Notes to pages 169–73

14 Stevens, "Getting Away from It," 27.
15 Ibid., 343; J.M.T. Engineering and Planning, "The Contribution of Recreation to the Muskoka Economy" (Planning Department, District Municipality of Muskoka, April 1973), 17, 23, 87; District Municipality of Muskoka, "2017 Second Home Study" (District Municipality of Muskoka, 2017), 11–12. Reports detailing the state of the tourism economy and demographics in the District of Muskoka refer variously to "cottages," "summer homes," and "seasonal dwellings," which I treat as interchangeable for the purposes of comparison. Also, it is important to remember that the District of Muskoka is a political unit that does not overlap completely with the Muskoka River watershed. These statistics therefore leave out a part of the geography included in this study, which is technically part of the District of Parry Sound.
16 District Municipality of Muskoka, "Muskoka Economic Strategy; Phase 1: Background Report" (District Municipality of Muskoka Planning and Economic Development Department, 2008), 60, 63–64.
17 Leacock, *Arcadian Adventures.*
18 Peter Stevens, "'Roughing It in Comfort': Family Cottaging and Consumer Culture in Postwar Ontario," *Canadian Historical Review* 94, 2 (June 2013): 234–62.
19 Ibid., 243.
20 Stevens, "Getting Away from It," 247–57, 263, 295.
21 Ibid., 124, 368; Roy I. Wolfe, "Summer Cottages in Ontario: Purpose-Built for an Inessential Purpose," in *Second Homes: Curse or Blessing?* ed. J.T. Coppock (Toronto: Pergamon Press, 1977), 17–33.
22 J.M.T. Engineering and Planning, "The Contribution of Recreation," 10; District Municipality of Muskoka, "Muskoka Economic Strategy," 17; District Municipality of Muskoka, "Muskoka: Let Us Show You Why" (Economic Development and Community Profile, 2019), 16.
23 John Michels, *The Permanent Weekend: Nature, Leisure, and Rural Gentrification* (Montreal and Kingston: McGill-Queen's University Press, 2017), 46.
24 Brett Grainger, "The Other Muskoka," *Toronto Life,* July 2005, 53.
25 Michels, *The Permanent Weekend.*
26 Ashley Gallant, "Understanding the Lived Experiences of Local Residents in Muskoka, Ontario: A Study on Cottaging" (master's thesis, University of Waterloo, 2017), 66.
27 Ibid., 67.
28 J.M.T. Engineering and Planning, "The Contribution of Recreation," 88; District Municipality of Muskoka, "Muskoka: Let Us Show You Why," 21.
29 Gallant, "Understanding the Lived Experiences," 69; Michels, *The Permanent Weekend,* 65, 113–16.
30 Muskoka Community Foundation, "Vital Signs 2018," 9.
31 Gallant, "Understanding the Lived Experiences," 69.
32 J.M.T. Engineering and Planning, "The Contribution of Recreation," 24; District Municipality of Muskoka, "Muskoka: Let Us Show You Why," 8.
33 Gallant, "Understanding the Lived Experiences"; Michels, *The Permanent Weekend;* Stevens, "Getting Away from It"; Harrison, *The View from Vermont;* Rothman, *Devil's Bargains;* Michael W. Childers, *Colorado Powder Keg: Ski Resorts and the Environmental Movement* (Lawrence, KS: University Press of Kansas, 2012).
34 J.M.T. Engineering and Planning, "The Contribution of Recreation," 125.

Notes to pages 173–76 213

35 Evan MacDonald et al., "Economic Valuation of Water Quality in the Muskoka Region" (Report prepared for the Muskoka Watershed Council, 2012), https://www.muskoka watershed.org/wp-content/uploads/2012/06/ValuingWaterQuality1.pdf; Julia Clapper and Steven B. Caudill, "Water Quality and Cottage Prices in Ontario," *Applied Economics* 46, 10 (2014): 1122–26.

36 Gregory Summers, *Consuming Nature: Environmentalism in the Fox River Valley, 1850–1950* (Lawrence, KS: University Press of Kansas, 2006); Harrison, *The View from Vermont,* 233.

37 Lower, *Settlement and the Forest Frontier,* 75.

38 Grainger, "The Other Muskoka," 57.

APPENDIX: A NOTE ON SOURCES

1 Fernand Braudel, *The Structures of Everyday Life: The Limits of the Possible,* translated by Slân Reynolds (Berkeley: University of California Press, 1981).

2 Virginia DeJohn Anderson, "Thomas Minor's World: Agrarian Life in Seventeenth-Century New England," *Agricultural History* 82, 4 (Fall 2008): 497.

3 Hamilton, *Guide Book and Atlas.*

4 G.W. Marshall, *Map and Chart of the Muskoka Lakes: Rosseau, Joseph, Muskoka* (Toronto: Self-published, 1899); Rogers, *Muskoka Lakes Bluebook, 1915;* Rogers, *Muskoka Lakes Bluebook, 1918.*

5 Donahue, *The Great Meadow;* Cunfer, *On the Great Plains.*

6 David Russo, *Keepers of Our Past: Local Historical Writing in the United States, 1820s–1930s* (Westport, CT: Greenwood Press, 1988); James Wilkinson, "A Choice of Fictions: Historians, Memory, and Evidence," *PMLA* 111, 1 (January 1996): 80–92; David Lowenthal, *Possessed by the Past: The Heritage Crusade and the Spoils of History* (New York: Free Press, 1996).

Bibliography

PRIMARY SOURCES

Archival Material

Archives of Ontario (AO)
Contract between Department of Public Works and J.T. Kirkpatrick for Improvement of
Washago and Gravenhurst Road. RG15–55–1.
Contract between Department of Public Works and John Ginty for a lock between Lakes
Muskoka and Rousseau. RG15–55–1.
Frederick W. Coate family fonds, F720.
T. Eaton Company fonds, F229.

Archives of the Muskoka Steamship and Historical Society (AMSHS)
"Accounts Ledger for Gravenhurst Sawmill of Snider Lumber Company, 1902–1907."
"Board Meeting Minutes of the Muskoka and Georgian Bay Navigation Company,
1896–1903." Minutes of Navig. Co. Bd. file, Steamships folder.
"Diary of Julia 'Leena' Riley, Diary of Pioneers at Milford Bay."
"Navigation Company Balance Sheets, 1897, 1902, 1905, 1906, 1908, 1910." Royal Muskoka
#4 file, Accounting Data.

Author's Private Collection
Diary of R.J. Maclennan. "A Few Weeks among the Northern Lakes and Islands, from My
Diary." August 1885.

Gravenhurst Public Library Archives
General Store Ledger of George Henry Homer, 1896–1901. Box 35.

Huntsville Public Library Archives
"Brief Synopsis of Leather Manufacture." April 26, 1967. Muskoka Local History Collection.
Huntsville Public Library, Huntsville, Ontario.

Bibliography

Conway, Abbott. "The Tanning Industry in Muskoka." In *Pioneer Muskoka: Notes on the History of Muskoka District, as Presented by Guest Speakers on Behalf of Georgian College* (Parry Sound: Algonquin Regional Library System, 1974), 19–22. Muskoka Local History Collection.

"The Tannery Journals, Part One." In *Vintage Muskoka,* 15–17. Muskoka Local History Collection, Leather Industry file.

Library and Archives Canada (LAC)

Amalgamation of Toronto, Simcoe and Muskoka Junction Railway Company and North Grey Railway Company as the Northern Extension Railways Company and Lease of Amalgamated Lines to the Northern Railways Company of Canada, June 29, 1871. RG12.

Department of Indian Affairs and Northern Development fonds. RG10.

James Bay Railway Company. General Claims, Claim of JJ Beaumont and Sons, 1905. RG30.

James Bay Railway Company and the Canadian Northern Ontario Railway Company. Regarding Agreement between the Muskoka Leather Company and James Bay Railways for construction of dam and sluice way at Stewart Lake outlet. RG30.

Muskoka Heritage Place Archives

"Anglo-Canadian Leather Company Tannery Grounds Maps, 1911 and 1921." Anglo-Canadian Leather Company: Tannery and Housing, Concert Band Binder of Collected documents, 785.06 ANG c. 1.

Smith, Gail. "Chapter Three: The Tanning Industry in Muskoka." Anglo-Canadian Leather Company: Tannery and Housing, Concert Band Binder of Collected documents, 785.06 ANG c. 1.

Muskoka Lakes Museum Archives (MLM)

"Farm Journal of John Oldham, 1868–1871." 978.20.1.

"Medora and Wood Agricultural Society Fall Fair Entry Book, 1907–1912." No accession number.

"Memoirs of Mabel Croucher Ames, 1884–1977." Oral memoirs originally shared with and transcribed by Vera Gross Ames, 1975, presented to Bill Gray by Lynda McClelland Stringer, 10 June 2006.

"Muskoka Leather Company Ledger, July 1905–August 1906."

University of Waterloo Archives and Special Collections

Muskoka Lakes Association fonds, GA 100.

Government Documents and Publications

Canada. *Tables of the Trade and Navigation of the Province of Canada for the Year 1855.* Toronto: Stewart Derbishire and George Desbarats, 1856.

Canada Land Inventory for Ontario. *Soil Capability for Agriculture.* Soil Research Institute, Research Branch, Agriculture Canada, based on maps prepared by the Canada-Ontario Soil Survey, with the support of the Lands Directorate, Environmental Management Service, Environment Canada. Ottawa, Surveys and Mapping Branch, Department of Energy, Mines, and Resources, 1975.

Canada Land Inventory for Quebec. *Soil Capability for Agriculture.* Soil Research Institute, Research Branch, Agriculture Canada, based on maps prepared by the Quebec Soil Survey, with the support of the Lands Directorate, Environmental Management Service, Environment Canada. Ottawa, Surveys and Mapping Branch, Department of Energy, Mines, and Resources, 1974. https://sis.agr.gc.ca/cansis/publications/maps/cli/1m/agr/index.html.

Census of Canada, 1871.

–. 1881.

–. 1891.

–. 1901.

–. 1911.

Davidson, Barry. "Forest Management Plan for the French/Severn Forest (360)." Ministry of Natural Resources, Parry Sound District, Southern Region and Westwind Forest Stewardship, 2008.

District Municipality of Muskoka. "Muskoka: Let Us Show You Why." Economic Development and Community Profile, 2019.

–. "Muskoka Economic Strategy; Phase 1: Background Report." District Municipality of Muskoka Planning and Economic Development Department, 2008.

–. "2017 Second Home Study." District Municipality of Muskoka, 2017.

Dominion of Canada. *Annual Reports of the Department of Indian Affairs.*

Jenness, Diamond. *The Ojibwa Indians of Parry Island, Their Social and Religious Life.* Department of Mines and National Museum of Canada Bulletin 78, Anthropological Series 17. Ottawa: J.O. Patenaude, I.S.O., 1935.

J.M.T. Engineering and Planning. "The Contribution of Recreation to the Muskoka Economy." Planning Department, District Municipality of Muskoka, April 1973.

Johnston, Darlene. "Connecting People to Place: Great Lakes Aboriginal History in Cultural Context." Prepared for the Ipperwash Commission of Inquiry, 2005. http://www.turtleisland.org/news/ipperwash2.pdf.

Muskoka and Lake Nipissing Districts: Information for Intending Settlers. Ottawa: Department of Agriculture, 1880.

Ontario Sessional Papers, 1870–1929.

Report of the Master Plan of Archaeological Resources of the District Municipality of Muskoka and the Wahta Mohawks. 3 vols. Toronto: Archaeological Services, 1994.

Report of the Royal Commission on Aboriginal Peoples. 7 vols. Ottawa: Royal Commission on Aboriginal Peoples, 1996.

Report of the Special Commissioners Appointed on the 8th of September, 1856, to Investigate Indian Affairs in Canada. Toronto: Stewart Derbishire and George Desbarats, 1858.

Teillet, Jean. "The Role of the Natural Resources Regulatory Regime in Aboriginal Disputes in Ontario." Prepared for the Ipperwash Commission of Inquiry, 2005.

Tough, Frank. "Ontario's Appropriation of Indian Hunting: Provincial Conservation Policies vs. Aboriginal and Treaty Rights, ca. 1892–1930." Paper prepared for the Ontario Native Affairs Secretariat. Toronto, January 1991.

Websites

"Canadian Mail Order Catalogues, History." 2019. Library and Archives Canada. https://www.bac-lac.gc.ca/eng/discover/postal-heritage-philately/canadian-mail-order-catalogues/Pages/catalogues-history.aspx.

Bibliography

Oester, Paul, and Steve Bowers. *Measuring Timber Products Harvested from Your Woodland.* The Woodland Workbook. Rev. ed. Oregon State University Extension Service, 2009. https://knowyourforest.org/sites/default/files/documents/Measuring_timber_products. pdfhttps://knowyourforest.org/sites/default/files/documents/Measuring_timber_ products.pdf.

Muskoka Community Foundation, "Vital Signs 2018," 9, https://muskokacommunity foundation.ca/wp-content/uploads/2018/11/msk-vitalsigns-web.pdf.

Muskoka Steamships and Discovery Centre, "MSDC Revitalization Project," https:// realmuskoka.com/revitalization/.

"Unit 1: What Is Energy? Section C. Measuring and Quantifying Energy." K-12 Energy Education Program, University of Wisconsin. https://www.uwsp.edu/cnr-ap/KEEP/ nres633/Pages/Unit1/Supplementary%20Pages/Energy-Conversion-and-Resource-Tables. aspx.

Newspapers
Bracebridge Gazette
The Globe
Huntsville Forester
The Mail
Northern Advocate
Toronto World

Interviews
Partridge, Carleen. 21 October 2011. Wasauksing First Nation.
Tabobondung, Joyce. 21 October 2011. Wasauksing First Nation.

Books and Articles

Adam, G. Mercer. "Georgian Bay and the Muskoka Lakes." In *Picturesque Spots of the North: Historical and Descriptive Sketches of the Scenery and Life in the Vicinity of Georgian Bay, the Muskoka Lakes, the Upper Lakes, in Central and Eastern Ontario, and in the Niagara District,* edited by George Munro Grant, 9–52. Chicago: Alexander Belford, 1899.

Ahlgren, Clifford E., and Isabel F. Ahlgren. "The Human Impact on Northern Forest Ecosystems." In *The Great Lakes Forest: An Environmental and Social History,* edited by Susan L. Flader, 33–51. Minneapolis: University of Minnesota Press, 1983.

Alexander, Rani. "Afterword: Toward an Archaeological Theory of Culture Conflict." In *Studies in Culture Contact: Interaction, Culture Change, and Archaeology,* edited by James Cusick, 476–95. Center for Archaeological Investigations Occasional Papers 25. Carbondale: Southern Illinois University Press, 1998.

Allen, William Arthur. "Wa-nant-git-che-ang: Canoe Route to Lake Huron through Southern Algonquia." *Ontario Archaeology* 73 (2002): 38–68.

Anderson, Virginia DeJohn. "Thomas Minor's World: Agrarian Life in Seventeenth-Century New England." *Agricultural History* 82, 4 (Fall 2008): 496–518.

Angus, James T. *A Deo Victoria: The Story of the Georgian Bay Lumber Company, 1871–1942.* Thunder Bay, ON: Severn, 1990.

Armstrong, John, and David M. Williams. "The Steamboat and Popular Tourism." *Journal of Transport History* 26, 1 (2005): 61–77.

Bibliography

Aron, Cindy. *Working at Play: A History of Vacations in the United States*. New York: Oxford University Press, 1999.

Barron, Hal S. *Mixed Harvest: The Second Great Transformation in the Rural North, 1870–1930*. Chapel Hill: University of North Carolina Press, 1997.

Bastedo, Jamie. *Shield Country: The Life and Times of the Oldest Piece of the Planet*. Red Deer, AB: Red Deer Press, 1994.

Belich, James. *Replenishing the Earth: The Settler Revolution and the Rise of the Angloworld*. Oxford: Oxford University Press, 2009.

Belisle, Donica. *Retail Nation: Department Stores and the Making of Modern Canada*. Vancouver: UBC Press, 2011.

–. "Toward a Canadian Consumer History." *Labour/Le travail* 52 (Fall 2003): 181–206.

Bello, David A. *Across Forest, Steppe, and Mountain: Environment, Identity, and Empire in Qing China's Borderlands*. New York: Cambridge University Press, 2015.

Berger, Michael. *The Devil Wagon in God's Country: The Automobile and Social Change in Rural America, 1893–1929*. Hamden, CT: Archon Books, 1979.

Blair, Peggy. *Lament for a First Nation: The Williams Treaties of Southern Ontario*. Vancouver: UBC Press, 2008.

Bohaker, Heidi. *Doodem and Council Fire: Anishinaabe Governance through Alliance*. Toronto: University of Toronto Press, 2020.

–. "'Nindoodemag': The Significance of Algonquin Kinship Networks in the Eastern Great Lakes Region, 1600–1701." *William and Mary Quarterly*, 3rd ser., 63, 1 (January 2006): 23–52.

Boone, Elaine A. "From Hot Streets to Lake Breezes: The Development of Tourism in Muskoka, 1860–1930." Master's thesis, Laurentian University, 1992.

Bouchard, Gérard. "Co-intégration et reproduction de la société rurale: Pour un modèle saguenayen de la marginalité." *Recherches sociographiques* 29, 2–8 (1988): 283–309.

–. "Marginality, Co-Integration and Change: Social History as a Critical Exercise." *Journal of the Canadian Historical Association* 8, 1 (1997): 19–38.

–. *Quelques arpents d'Amérique: Population, économie, famille au Saguenay, 1838–1971*. Montreal: Boréal, 1996.

Bourdo, Eric A. Jr. "The Forest the Settlers Saw." In *The Great Lakes Forest: An Environmental and Social History*, edited by Susan L. Flader, 3–16. Minneapolis: University of Minnesota Press, 1983.

Boyer, Barbaranne. *Muskoka's Grand Hotels*. Edited by Richard Tatley. Erin, ON: Boston Mills Press, 1987.

Bradley, Ben. *British Columbia by the Road: Car Culture and the Making of a Modern Landscape*. Vancouver: UBC Press, 2017.

Brandth, Berit, and Marit S. Haugen. "Farm Diversification into Tourism – Implications for Social Identity." *Journal of Rural Studies* 27 (2011): 35–44.

Braudel, Fernand. *The Structures of Everyday Life: The Limits of the Possible*. Translated by Sîân Reynolds. Berkeley: University of California Press, 1981.

Brody, Hugh. *The Other Side of Eden: Hunters, Farmers and the Shaping of the World*. Vancouver: Douglas and McIntyre, 2000.

Brown, Dona. *Inventing New England: Regional Tourism in the Nineteenth Century*. Washington, DC: Smithsonian Institution Press, 1995.

Brown, Robert Craig. "The Doctrine of Usefulness: Natural Resources and National Park Policy in Canada, 1887–1914." In *The Canadian National Parks: Today and Tomorrow*, edited by J.G. Nelson and R.C. Scace, 94–110. Calgary: National and Provincial Parks Association of Canada and the University of Calgary, 1969.

Brownlie, Robin. *A Fatherly Eye: Indian Agents, Government Power, and Aboriginal Resistance in Ontario, 1918–1939*. New York: Oxford University Press, 2003.

Brubaker, Rogers, and Frederick Cooper. "Beyond 'Identity.'" *Theory and Society* 29, 1 (February 2000): 1–47.

Buckley, Kenneth. "The Role of Staple Industries in Canada's Economic Development." *Journal of Economic History* 18 (1958): 439–60.

Burchardt, Jeremy. "Agricultural History, Rural History, or Countryside History?" *Historical Journal* 50, 2 (2007): 465–81.

Burd, Camden. "Imagining a Pure Michigan Landscape: Advertisers, Tourists, and the Making of Michigan's Northern Vacationlands." *Michigan Historical Review* 42, 2 (2016): 31–51.

Calverley, David. *Who Controls the Hunt? First Nations, Treaty Rights, and Wildlife Conservation in Ontario, 1783–1939*. Vancouver: UBC Press, 2018.

Campbell, Claire, ed. *A Century of Parks in Canada, 1911–2011*. Calgary: University of Calgary Press, 2011.

–. *Shaped by the West Wind: Nature and History in Georgian Bay*. Vancouver: UBC Press, 2005.

Caradonna, Jeremy L., ed. *Routledge Handbook of the History of Sustainability*. New York: Routledge, 2018.

–. *Sustainability: A History*. Oxford: Oxford University Press, 2014.

Careless, J.M.S. *Frontier and Metropolis: Regions, Cities, and Identities in Canada before 1914*. Toronto: University of Toronto Press, 1989.

Carter, Sarah. *Lost Harvests: Prairie Indian Reserve Farmers and Government Policy*. Montreal and Kingston: McGill-Queen's University Press, 1990.

Childers, Michael W. *Colorado Powder Keg: Ski Resorts and the Environmental Movement*. Lawrence, KS: University Press of Kansas, 2012.

Chute, Janet E. *The Legacy of Shingwaukonse: A Century of Leadership*. Toronto: University of Toronto Press, 1998.

Clapper, Julia, and Steven B. Caudill. "Water Quality and Cottage Prices in Ontario." *Applied Economics* 46, 10 (2014): 1122–26.

Clarke, John. *Land, Power, and Economics on the Frontier of Upper Canada*. Montreal and Kingston: McGill-Queen's University Press, 2001.

Clerk, Saloni, Roland Hall, Roberto Quinlan, and John P. Smol. "Quantitative Inferences of Past Hypolimnetic Anoxia and Nutrient Levels from a Canadian Precambrian Shield Lake." *Journal of Paleolimnology* 23 (2000): 319–36.

Cohen, Marjorie Griffin. *Women's Work, Markets, and Economic Development in Nineteenth-Century Ontario*. Toronto: University of Toronto Press, 1988.

Colombo, John. *Voices of Rama: Traditional Ojibwa Tales from the Rama Reserve, Lake Couchiching, Ontario*. Toronto: Self-published, 1994.

Conlin, Joseph. "Old Boy, Did You Get Enough Pie? A Social History of Food in Logging Camps." *Journal of Forest History* 23, 4 (October 1979): 164–85.

Conway, Abbott. *A History of Beardmore and Company Limited and Anglo Canadian Leather Company Limited*. Toronto: Canada Packers, 1990.

Costanza, Robert, and Bernard C. Patten. "Defining and Predicting Sustainability." *Ecological Economics* 15 (1995): 193–96.

Bibliography

Courville, Serge, and Normand Séguin. *Rural Life in Nineteenth Century Quebec*. CHA Booklet 47. Ottawa: Canadian Historical Association, 1989.

Cowan, Helen I. *British Emigration to British North America*. Toronto: University of Toronto Press, 1961.

Craig, Béatrice. *Backwoods Consumers and Homespun Capitalists: The Rise of a Market Culture in Eastern Canada*. Toronto: University of Toronto Press, 2009.

Creighton, Donald G. *The Commercial Empire of the St. Lawrence, 1760–1850*. Toronto: Ryerson Press, 1937.

Crerar, Adam. "Ties That Bind: Farming, Agrarian Ideals, and Life in Ontario, 1890–1930." PhD diss., University of Toronto, 1999.

Cronon, William. *Nature's Metropolis: Chicago and the Great West*. New York: W.W. Norton, 1991.

–. "The Trouble with Wilderness, or Getting Back to the Wrong Nature." In *Uncommon Ground: Rethinking the Human Place in Nature*, edited by William Cronon, 69–90. New York: W.W. Norton, 1995.

Cunfer, Geoff. *On the Great Plains: Agriculture and Environment*. College Station: Texas A&M University Press, 2005.

Currie, A.W. *The Grand Trunk Railway of Canada*. Toronto: University of Toronto Press, 1957.

Danbom, David B. *Born in the Country: A History of Rural America*. Baltimore: Johns Hopkins University Press, 1995.

Davies, Stephen James. "Ontario and the Automobile, 1900–1930: Aspects of Technological Integration." PhD diss., McMaster University, 1987.

Dawson, Michael. *Selling British Columbia: Tourism and Consumer Culture, 1890–1970*. Vancouver: UBC Press, 2004.

De la Fosse, Frederick Montague. *English Bloods: In the Backwoods of Muskoka, 1878*. Edited by Scott D. Shipman. Toronto: Natural Heritage Books, 2004.

de la Torre, Oscar. *The People of the River: Nature and Identity in Black Amazonia, 1835–1945*. Chapel Hill: University of North Carolina Press, 2018.

Denison, John. *Micklethwaite's Muskoka*. Toronto: Stoddart, 1993.

Deutsch, Tracey. *Building a Housewife's Paradise: Gender, Politics, and American Grocery Stores in the Twentieth Century*. Chapel Hill: University of North Carolina Press, 2010.

Dodington, Paul, Paul W. Gockel, and Joe Fossey. *The Greatest Little Motor Boat Afloat: The Legendary Disappearing Propeller Boat*. Toronto: Stoddart, 1994.

Doerfler, Jill. "A Philosophy for Living: Ignatia Broker and Constitutional Reform among the White Earth Anishinaabeg." In *Centering Anishinaabeg Studies: Understanding the World through Stories*, edited by Jill Doerfler, Niigaanwewidam James Sinclair, and Heidi Kiiwetinepinesiik Stark, 173–89. East Lansing, MI: Michigan State University Press, 2013.

Donahue, Brian. *The Great Meadow: Farmers and the Land in Colonial Concord*. New Haven: Yale University Press, 2004.

–. *Reclaiming the Commons: Community Farms and Forests in a New England Town*. New Haven: Yale University Press, 1999.

Donofrio, Gregory Alexander. "Feeding the City." *Gastronomica* 7, 4 (Fall 2007): 30–41.

Drache, Daniel. "Celebrating Innis: The Man, the Legacy, and Our Future." In *Staples, Markets, and Cultural Change: Selected Essays*, edited by Daniel Drache, xiii–lix. Montreal and Kingston: McGill-Queen's University Press, 1994.

Bibliography

Drummond, Ian. *Progress without Planning: The Economic History of Ontario.* Toronto: Ontario Historical Studies Series for the Government of Ontario by University of Toronto Press, 1987.

Duke, A.H., and W.M. Gray. *The Boatbuilders of Muskoka.* Toronto: Self-published, 1985.

Dunkin, Jessica. *Canoe and Canvas: Life at the Encampments of the American Canoe Association, 1880–1910.* Toronto: University of Toronto Press, 2019.

Durnin, J.V.G.A., and R. Passmore. *Energy, Work, and Leisure.* London: Heinemann, 1967.

Ehrenfeld, John R. "The Roots of Sustainability." *MIT Sloan Management Review* 46, 2 (2005): 23–25.

Fair, Ross D. "Gentlemen, Farmers, and Gentlemen Half-Farmers: The Development of Agricultural Societies in Upper Canada, 1792–1846." PhD diss., Queen's University, 1998.

Feldman, James. "The View from Sand Island: Reconsidering the Peripheral Economy, 1880–1940." *Western Historical Quarterly* 35, 3 (2004): 284–307.

Ferris, Neal. *The Archaeology of Native-Lived Colonialism: Challenging History in the Great Lakes.* Tucson: University of Arizona Press, 2009.

Fingard, Judith. "The Poor in Winter: Seasonality and Society in Pre-Industrial Canada." In *Pre-Industrial Canada: 1760–1849,* edited by Michael S. Cross and Gregory S. Kealey, 62–78. Toronto: University of Toronto Press, 1982.

Fitzgerald, Deborah. *Every Farm a Factory: The Industrial Ideal in American Agriculture.* New Haven: Yale University Press, 2003.

Flores, Dan. "An Argument for Bioregional History." *Environmental History Review* 18, 4 (Winter 1994): 1–18.

Forkey, Neil. *Shaping the Upper Canadian Frontier: Environment, Society, and Culture in the Trent Valley.* Calgary: University of Calgary Press, 2003.

Foster, David R., and John D. Aber. *Forests in Time: The Environmental Consequences of 1,000 Years of Change in New England.* New Haven: Yale University Press, 2004.

France, R.L. "Macroinvertebrate Colonization of Woody Debris in Canadian Shield Lakes following Riparian Clearcutting." *Conservation Biology* 11, 2 (April 1997): 513–21.

Fredericks, Sarah E. "Challenges to Measuring Sustainability." In *Berkshire Encyclopedia of Sustainability.* Vol. 6, *Measurements, Indicators, and Research Methods for Sustainability,* edited by Willis Jenkins and Whitney Bauman, 46–52. Great Barrington, MA: Berkshire, 2010.

Gabriel-Doxtater, Brenda Katlatont, and Arlette Kawanatatie Van den Hende. *At the Woods' Edge: An Anthology of the History of the People of Kanehsatà:ke.* Kanesatake, QC: Kanesatake Education Centre, 1995.

Gagan, David. *Hopeful Travellers: Families, Land and Social Change in Mid-Victorian Peel County, Canada West.* Toronto: University of Toronto Press, 1981.

Gallant, Ashley. "Understanding the Lived Experiences of Local Residents in Muskoka, Ontario: A Study on Cottaging." Master's thesis, University of Waterloo, 2017.

Gates, David M., C.H.D. Clarke, and James T. Harris. "Wildlife in a Changing Environment." In *The Great Lakes Forest: An Environmental and Social History,* edited by Susan L. Flader, 52–80. Minneapolis: University of Minnesota Press, 1983.

Grainger, Brett. "The Other Muskoka." *Toronto Life,* July 2005, 50–57.

Grand Trunk Railway Company of Canada. *Picturesque Muskoka: To the Highlands and Lakes of Northern Ontario.* Toronto: Grand Trunk Railway System and Muskoka Navigation Company, 1898.

Bibliography

Gray, William M. *Lake Joseph, 1860–1910: An Illustrated Notebook*. Toronto: Self-published, 1991.

Grober, Ulrich. *Sustainability: A Cultural History*. Translated by Ray Cunningham. Totnes, UK: Green Books, 2012.

Haberl, Helmut, Marina Fischer-Kowalski, Fridolin Krausmann, Helga Weisz, and Verena Winiwarter. "Progress towards Sustainability? What the Conceptual Framework of Material and Energy Flow Accounting (MEFA) Can Offer." *Land Use Policy* 21 (2004): 199–213.

Hak, Gordon. *Turning Trees into Dollars: The British Columbia Coastal Lumber Industry, 1858–1913*. Toronto: University of Toronto Press, 2000.

Hall, Roland I., and John P. Smol. "The Influence of Catchment Size on Lake Trophic Status during the Hemlock Decline and Recovery (4800 to 3500 BP) in Southern Ontario Lakes." *Hydrobiologia* 269–70 (1993): 371–90.

–. "Paleolimnological Assessment of Long-Term Water-Quality Changes in South-Central Ontario Lakes Affected by Cottage Development." *Canadian Journal of Fisheries and Aquatic Sciences* 53 (1996): 1–17.

Hamilton, W.E. *Guide Book and Atlas of Muskoka and Parry Sound Districts*. Maps by John Rogers, sketches by Seymour Penson. Toronto: H.R. Page, 1879.

Harris, Cole. *The Reluctant Land: Society, Space, and Environment in Canada before Confederation*. Vancouver: UBC Press, 2008.

Harris, Glenn. "The Hidden History of Agriculture in the Adirondack Park, 1825–1875." *New York State History* 83, 2 (Spring 2002): 165–202.

Harrison, Blake. *The View from Vermont: Tourism and the Making of an American Rural Landscape*. Burlington: University of Vermont Press, 2006.

Hathaway, Ann. *Muskoka Memories: Sketches from Real Life*. Toronto: William Briggs, 1904.

Havard, Gilles. *The Great Peace of Montreal of 1701: French-Native Diplomacy in the Seventeenth Century*. Translated by Phyllis Aronoff and Howard Scott. Montreal and Kingston: McGill-Queen's University Press, 2001.

Head, Grant. "An Introduction to Forest Exploitation in Nineteenth Century Ontario." In *Perspectives on Landscape and Settlement in Nineteenth Century Ontario*, edited by J. David Wood, 78–112. Toronto: McClelland and Stewart in association with the Institute of Canadian Studies, Carleton University, 1975.

Heinberg, Richard. "What Is Sustainability?" In *The Post Carbon Reader: Managing the 21st Century's Sustainability Crises*, edited by Richard Heinberg and Daniel Lerch, 13–24. Healdsburg, CA: Watershed Media, 2010.

Heinberg, Richard, and Daniel Lerch, eds. *The Post Carbon Reader: Managing the 21st Century's Sustainability Crises*. Healdsburg, CA: Watershed Media, 2010.

Henretta, James A. "Families and Farms: *Mentalité* in Pre-Industrial America." *William and Mary Quarterly* 35, 1 (January 1978): 3–32.

Hergert, Herbert H. "The Tannin Extraction Industry in the United States." *Journal of Forest History* 27, 2 (April 1983): 92–93.

Heron, Craig. *Booze: A Distilled History*. Toronto: Between the Lines, 2003.

Hind, Andrew, and Maria Da Silva. *Ghost Towns of Muskoka*. Toronto: Natural Heritage Books, 2008.

Hoganson, Kristin L. *Consumer's Imperium: The Global Production of American Domesticity, 1865–1920*. Chapel Hill: University of North Carolina Press, 2007.

Bibliography

Hoggart, Keith. "Let's Do Away with Rural." *Journal of Rural Studies* 6, 3 (1990): 245–57.

Holzkamm, Tim E., Victor T. Lytwyn, and Leo G. Weisberg. "Rainy River Sturgeon: An Ojibway Resource in the Fur Trade Economy." *Canadian Geographer* 32, 3 (September 1988): 194–205.

Horowitz, Daniel. *The Morality of Spending: Attitudes toward the Consumer Society in America, 1875–1940.* Baltimore, MD: Johns Hopkins University Press, 1985.

Innis, Harold A. "The Importance of Staple Products in Canadian Development." In *Staples, Markets, and Cultural Change: Selected Essays,* edited by Daniel Drache, 1–23. Montreal and Kingston: McGill-Queen's University Press, 1994.

Interrante, Joseph. "You Can't Go to Town in a Bathtub: Automobile Movement and the Reorganization of Rural American Space, 1900–1930." *Radical History Review* 21 (Fall 1979): 151–68.

Irwin, Thomas R. "Government Funding of Agricultural Associations in Late Nineteenth Century Ontario." PhD diss., University of Western Ontario, 1997.

Jacoby, Karl. *Crimes against Nature: Squatters, Poachers, Thieves, and the Hidden History of American Conservation.* Berkeley, CA: University of California Press, 2003.

Jasen, Patricia. *Wild Things: Nature, Culture, and Tourism in Ontario, 1790–1914.* Toronto: University of Toronto Press, 1995.

Jenkins, Willis. "Sustainability Theory." In *Berkshire Encyclopedia of Sustainability,* Vol. 1, *The Spirit of Sustainability,* edited by Willis Jenkins and Whitney Bauman, 380–84. Great Barrington, MA: Berkshire, 2010.

Johnston, Paul, Mark Everard, David Santillo, and Karl-Henrik Robèrt. "Reclaiming the Definition of Sustainability." *Environmental Science and Pollution Research* 14, 1 (2007): 60–66.

Judd, Richard W. "Reshaping Maine's Landscape: Rural Culture, Tourism, and Conservation, 1890–1929." *Journal of Forest History* 32, 4 (1988): 180–90.

Keller, Vagel Charles Jr. "Forgotten Brownfields: Rural Industrial Districts in Pennsylvania, 1870–1930." PhD diss., Carnegie Mellon University, 2005.

Kelly, Kenneth. "The Transfer of British Ideas on Improved Farming to Ontario during the First Half of the Nineteenth Century." *Ontario History* 63, 2 (1971): 103–11.

King, Harriet Barbara. *Letters from Muskoka, by an Emigrant Lady.* London: Richard Bentley and Son, 1878.

Kirkwood, Alexander, and J.J. Murphy. *The Undeveloped Land in Northern and Western Ontario: Collected and Compiled from Reports of Surveyors, Crown Land Agents, and Others, with the Sanction of the Honourable the Commissioner of Crown Lands.* Toronto: Hunter, Rose, 1878.

Koenig, Edwin C. *Culture and Ecologies: A Native Fishing Conflict on the Saugeen-Bruce Peninsula.* Toronto: University of Toronto Press, 2005.

Krech, Sheppard, III. *The Ecological Indian: Myth and History.* New York: W.W. Norton, 1999.

Kuhlberg, Mark. *In the Power of the Government: The Rise and Fall of Newsprint in Ontario, 1894–1932.* Toronto: University of Toronto Press, 2015.

Labelle, Kathryn Magee. *Dispersed but Not Destroyed: A History of the Seventeenth-Century Wendat People.* Vancouver: UBC Press, 2013.

Laforce, Philip. *History of Gibson Reserve.* Bracebridge: Bracebridge Gazette, n.d.

Lawson, Jamie, Marcelo Levy, and L. Anders Sandberg. "'Perpetual Revenues and the Delights of the Primitive': Change, Continuity, and Forest Policy Regimes in Ontario." In *Canadian Forest Policy: Adapting to Change*, edited by Michael Howlett, 279–315. Toronto: University of Toronto Press, 2001.

Leach, William. *Land of Desire: Merchants, Power, and the Rise of a New American Culture.* New York: Pantheon, 1993.

Leacock, Stephen. *Arcadian Adventures with the Idle Rich.* 1914. Reprint, Toronto: McClelland and Stewart, 1989.

Lears, T.J. Jackson. "From Salvation to Self-Realization: Advertising and the Therapeutic Roots of the Consumer Culture, 1880–1930." In *The Culture of Consumption: Critical Essays in American History, 1880–1980*, edited by Richard Wightman Fox and T.J. Jackson Lears, 1–38. New York: Pantheon Books, 1983.

LeCain, Timothy J. *The Matter of History: How Things Create the Past.* New York: Cambridge University Press, 2017.

Lerch, Daniel. "Preface." In *The Post Carbon Reader: Managing the 21st Century's Sustainability Crises*, edited by Richard Heinberg and Daniel Lerch, xix–xxiii. Healdsburg, CA: Watershed Media, 2010.

Little, J.I. *Nationalism, Capitalism and Colonization in Nineteenth Century Quebec: The Upper St. Francis District.* Montreal and Kingston: McGill-Queen's University Press, 1989.

–. "Scenic Tourism on the Northeastern Borderland: Lake Memphremagog's Steamboat Excursions and Resort Hotels, 1850–1900." *Journal of Historical Geography* 35, 4 (2009): 716–42.

Liverant, Bettina. *Buying Happiness: The Emergence of Consumer Consciousness in English Canada.* Vancouver: UBC Press, 2018.

Long, Gary. *This River the Muskoka.* Erin, ON: Boston Mills Press, 1989.

López-Ridaura, Santiago, Omar Masera, and Marta Astier. "Evaluating the Sustainability of Complex Socio-environmental Systems: The MESMIS Framework." *Ecological Indicators* 2, 1–2 (2002): 135–48.

Lovisek, Joan A.M. "Ethnohistory of the Algonkian Speaking Peoples of Georgian Bay – Precontact to 1850." PhD diss., McMaster University, 1991.

Lowenthal, David. *Possessed by the Past: The Heritage Crusade and the Spoils of History.* New York: Free Press, 1996.

Lower, A.R.M. *Great Britain's Woodyard: British America and the Timber Trade, 1763–1867.* Montreal and Kingston: McGill-Queen's University Press, 1973.

–. *The North American Assault on the Canadian Forest: A History of the Lumber Trade between Canada and the United States.* Toronto: Carnegie Endowment for International Peace, 1938.

–. *Settlement and the Forest Frontier in Eastern Canada.* Toronto: Macmillan, 1936.

Lundell, Liz. *Old Muskoka: Century Cottages and Summer Estates.* Erin, ON: Boston Mills Press, 2003.

Lutz, John S. *Makúk: A New History of Aboriginal-White Relations.* Vancouver: UBC Press, 2008.

Lyons, Scott Richard. *X-Marks: Native Signatures of Assent.* Minneapolis: University of Minnesota Press, 2010.

MacDonald, Edward. "A Landscape ... with Figures: Tourism and Environment on Prince Edward Island." *Acadiensis* 40, 1 (2011): 70–85.

Bibliography

MacDonald, Evan, Nicholas Lymer, Tim Bourne, and Alexis Godlington. "Economic Valuation of Water Quality in the Muskoka Region." Report prepared for the Muskoka Watershed Council, 2012.

MacEachern, Alan. *Natural Selections: National Parks in Atlantic Canada.* Montreal and Kingston: McGill-Queen's University Press, 2001.

MacFadyen, Joshua. "Hewers of Wood: A History of Wood Energy in Canada." In *Powering Up Canada: A History of Power, Fuel, and Energy from 1600,* edited by R.W. Sandwell, 129–61. Montreal and Kingston: McGill-Queen's University Press, 2016.

MacKay, Donald. *The Lumberjacks.* 3rd ed. Toronto: Dundurn, 2007.

MacKenzie, Norman Hall. "The Economic and Social Development of Muskoka, 1855–1888." PhD diss., University of Toronto, 1943.

Malin, James C. *History and Ecology: Studies of the Grassland.* Edited by Robert P. Swierenga. Lincoln, NB: University of Nebraska Press, 1984.

Mancke, Elizabeth. "At the Counter of the General Store: Women and the Economy in Eighteenth Century Nova Scotia." In *Intimate Relations: Family and Community in Planter Nova Scotia, 1759–1800,* edited by Margaret Conrad, 167–81. Fredericton: Acadiensis, 1995.

Marlatt, Michael. "The Calamity of the Initial Reserve Surveys under the Robinson Treaties." *Papers of the Thirty-Fifth Algonquian Conference,* edited by H.C. Wolfart, 281–335. Winnipeg: University of Manitoba Press, 2004.

Marshall, G.W. *Map and Chart of the Muskoka Lakes: Rosseau, Joseph, Muskoka.* Toronto: Self-published, 1899.

Marx, Leo. *The Machine in the Garden: Technology and the Pastoral Ideal in America.* New York: Oxford University Press, 1964.

Mason, D.H.C. *Muskoka: The First Islanders and After.* Bracebridge: Herald-Gazette Press, 1974.

Massie, Merle. *Forest Prairie Edge: Place History in Saskatchewan.* Winnipeg: University of Manitoba Press, 2014.

Maynard, Steven. "Rough Work and Rugged Men: The Social Construction of Masculinity in Working-Class History." *Labour/Le travail* 23 (Spring 1989): 159–69.

McCalla, Douglas. *Consumers in the Bush: Shopping in Rural Upper Canada.* Montreal and Kingston: McGill-Queen's University Press, 2015.

–. *Planting the Province: The Economic History of Upper Canada, 1784–1870.* Toronto: University of Toronto Press, 1993.

–. "Retailing in the Countryside: Upper Canadian General Stores in the Mid-Nineteenth Century." *Business and Economic History* 26, 2 (1997): 393–403.

McCallum, John. *Unequal Beginnings: Agriculture and Economic Development in Quebec and Ontario until 1870.* Toronto: University of Toronto Press, 1980.

McHugh, Joan E. *Beloved Muskoka: Diaries and Recollections of Elizabeth Penson.* Port Elgin, ON: Brucedale Press, 2009.

McInnis, Marvin. "The Changing Structure of Canadian Agriculture." *Journal of Economic History* 42, 1 (1982): 191–98.

McInnis, R.M. "Perspectives on Ontario Agriculture, 1815–1930." In *Canadian Papers in Rural History,* vol. 8, edited by Donald H. Akenson, 17–128. Gananoque, ON: Langdale Press, 1992.

McKay, Ian. *The Quest for the Folk: Antimodernism and Cultural Selection in Twentieth-Century Nova Scotia.* Montreal and Kingston: McGill-Queen's University Press, 1994.

Bibliography

McMichael, A.J., C.D. Butler, and Carl Foulke. "New Visions for Addressing Sustainability." *Science* 302 (12 December 2003): 1919–20.

McMurray, Thomas. *The Free Grant Lands of Canada from Practical Experience of Bush Farming in the Free Grant Districts of Muskoka and Parry Sound.* Bracebridge: Office of the Northern Advocate, 1871.

McMurrich, J.D., ed. *Muskoka Lakes Association 1902 Yearbook.* Toronto: Oxford Press, 1902.

McTaggart, Douglas. *Bigwin Inn.* Erin, ON: Boston Mills Press, 1992.

Michels, John. *The Permanent Weekend: Nature, Leisure, and Rural Gentrification.* Montreal and Kingston: McGill-Queen's University Press, 2017.

Miller, J.R. *Compact, Contract, Covenant: Aboriginal Treaty-Making in Canada.* Toronto: University of Toronto Press, 2009.

Mitman, Gregg. "Hay Fever Holiday: Health, Leisure, and Place in Gilded Age America." *Bulletin of the History of Medicine* 77, 3 (2003): 600–35.

Mizener, David. "Furrows and Fairgrounds: Agriculture, Identity, and Authority in Twentieth-Century Rural Ontario." PhD diss., York University, 2009.

Mochoruk, James David. *Formidable Heritage: Manitoba's North and the Cost of Development, 1870 to 1930.* Winnipeg: University of Manitoba Press, 2004.

Monod, David. *Store Wars: Shopkeepers and the Culture of Mass Marketing, 1890–1939.* Toronto: University of Toronto Press, 1996.

Murray, Florence B., ed. *Muskoka and Haliburton, 1615–1875: A Collection of Documents.* Toronto: Champlain Society for the Government of Ontario by University of Toronto Press, 1963.

Murton, James, Dean Bavington, and Carly Dokis, eds. *Subsistence under Capitalism: Historical and Contemporary Perspectives.* Montreal and Kingston: McGill-Queen's University Press, 2016.

Muskoka Community Foundation. "Vital Signs, 2018." Muskoka Community Foundation, 2018.

Muskoka Lakes Association, ed. *Summertimes: In Celebration of 100 Years of the Muskoka Lakes Association.* Erin, ON: Boston Mills Press, 1994.

Mwinyihija, Mwinyikione. *Ecotoxicological Diagnosis in the Tanning Industry.* New York: Springer, 2010.

Nash, Roderick. *Wilderness and American Mind.* New Haven: Yale University Press, 1967.

Neely, Wayne Caldwell. *The Agricultural Fair.* New York: AMS Press, 1967.

Neilson, Hugh, ed. *Muskoka Lakes Association 1918 Yearbook.* Toronto: Parker Bros., 1918.

Nelles, H.V. *The Politics of Development: Forests, Mines and Hydro-electric Power in Ontario, 1849–1941.* 2nd ed. Montreal and Kingston: McGill-Queen's University Press, 2005.

O'Brien, Brendan. "Memories: Cottage Life at the Turn of the Century." In *Summertimes: In Celebration of 100 Years of the Muskoka Lakes Association,* edited by Muskoka Lakes Association, 117–27. Erin, ON: Boston Mills Press, 1994.

–. *The Prettiest Spot in Muskoka.* Toronto: Bobolink Books, 1999.

Osborne, Thomas. *The Night the Mice Danced the Quadrille: Five Years in the Backwoods.* Erin, ON: Boston Mills Press, 1995.

Otis, Melissa. *Rural Indigenousness: A History of Iroquoian and Algonquian Peoples of the Adirondacks.* Syracuse, NY: Syracuse University Press, 2018.

Parenteau, Bill. "Angling, Hunting and the Development of Tourism in Late Nineteenth Century Canada: A Glimpse at the Documentary Record." *The Archivist* 117 (1998): 10–19.

Bibliography

Parkins, John R., and Maureen Reed, eds. *Social Transformation in Rural Canada: Community, Cultures, and Collective Action.* Vancouver: UBC Press, 2013.

Parr, Joy. "Hired Men: Ontario Agricultural Wage Labour in Historical Perspective." *Labour/Le travail* 15 (1985): 91–104.

Patton, M.J. "The Coal Resources of Canada." *Economic Geography* 1, 1 (March 1925): 73–88.

Penson, Seymour. "Seymour Penson and His Muskoka Neighbours, Part I." *East Georgian Bay Historical Society* 3 (1983): 166–226.

–. "Seymour Penson and His Muskoka Neighbours, Part II." *East Georgian Bay Historical Journal* 5 (1985).

Perry, Adele. *On the Edge of Empire: Gender, Race, and the Making of British Columbia, 1849–1871.* Toronto: University of Toronto Press, 2001.

Petry, Bob. *Bala, an Early Settlement in Muskoka: A Pictorial Story of Bala from the Late 1800s.* Bracebridge: Self-published, 1998.

Phillips, Ruth. *Trading Identities: The Souvenir in Native North American Art from the Northeast, 1700–1900.* Seattle: University of Washington Press, 1998.

Pierce, Jason. "The Winds of Change: The Decline of Extractive Industries and the Rise of Tourism in Hood River County, Oregon." *Oregon Historical Quarterly* 108, 3 (2007): 410–31.

Pike, Robert. *Tall Trees, Tough Men.* New York: W.W. Norton, 1967.

Piper, Liza. *The Industrial Transformation of Subarctic Canada.* Vancouver: UBC Press, 2009.

Pyne, Stephen J. *Awful Splendour: A Fire History of Canada.* Vancouver: UBC Press, 2007.

Radforth, Ian. *Bushworkers and Bosses: Logging in Northern Ontario, 1900–1980.* Toronto: University of Toronto Press, 1987.

–. "The Shantymen." In *Labouring Lives: Work and Workers in Nineteenth-Century Ontario,* edited by Paul Craven, 204–77. Toronto: University of Toronto Press, 1995.

Raibmon, Paige. *Authentic Indians: Episodes of Encounter from the Late-Nineteenth Century Northwest Coast.* Durham: Duke University Press, 2006.

Rees, William E. "Thinking 'Resilience.'" In *The Post Carbon Reader: Managing the 21st Century's Sustainability Crises,* edited by Richard Heinberg and Daniel Lerch, 25–40. Healdsburg, CA: Watershed Media, 2010.

Rogers, E.S., and Flora Tobobondung. "Parry Island Farmers: A Period of Change in the Way of Life of the Algonkains of Southern Ontario." In *Contributions of Canadian Ethnology, 1975,* edited by David Brez Carlisle, 247–366. National Museum of Man Mercury Series. Ottawa: National Museums of Canada, 1975.

Rogers, John. *Muskoka Lakes Bluebook, Directory and Chart, 1915.* Port Sandfield, ON: Self-published, 1915.

–. *Muskoka Lakes Bluebook, Directory and Chart, 1918.* Port Sandfield, ON: Self-published, 1918.

Rothman, Hal. *Devil's Bargains: Tourism in the Twentieth-Century American West.* Lawrence: University Press of Kansas, 1998.

Runte, Alfred. *National Parks: The American Experience.* Lincoln: University of Nebraska Press, 1979.

Russell, Peter A. "Upper Canada: A Poor Man's Country? Some Statistical Evidence." In *Canadian Papers in Rural History,* vol. 3, edited by Donald H. Akenson, 129–47. Gananoque, ON: Langdale Press, 1982.

Bibliography

Russo, David. *Keepers of Our Past: Local Historical Writing in the United States, 1820s–1930s.* Westport, CT: Greenwood Press, 1988.

Sandwell, R.W., ed. *Beyond the City Limits: Rural History in British Columbia.* Vancouver: UBC Press, 1999.

–. *Canada's Rural Majority: Households, Environments, and Economies, 1870–1940.* Toronto: University of Toronto Press, 2016.

–. *Contesting Rural Space: Land Policy and Practices of Resettlement on Saltspring Island, 1859–1891.* Montreal and Kingston: McGill-Queen's University Press, 2005.

Santink, Joy I. *Timothy Eaton and the Rise of His Department Store.* Toronto: University of Toronto Press, 1990.

Schivelbusch, Wolfgang. *The Railway Journey: The Industrialization of Time and Space in the Nineteenth Century.* Oakland: University of California Press, 1986.

Schmalz, Peter S. *The Ojibwa of Southern Ontario.* Toronto: University of Toronto Press, 1991.

Schultz, Jackson Smith. *The Leather Manufacture in the United States: A Dissertation on the Methods and Economies of Tanning.* New York: 'Shoe and Leather Reporter' Office, 1876.

Schurr, Samuel H., and Bruce C. Netschert. *Energy in the American Economy, 1850–1975: An Economic Study of Its History and Prospects.* Westport, CT: Greenwood Press, 1977.

Scott, Harley E. *Steam Tugs and Supply Boats of Muskoka.* Lancaster, NY: Cayuga Creek Historical Press, 1987.

Scott, James C. *The Art of Not Being Governed: An Anarchist History of Upland Southeast Asia.* New Haven, CT: Yale University Press, 2009.

Séguin, Normand. *La conquête du sol au 19e siècle.* Quebec City: Editions du Boreal Express, 1977.

Shapiro, Aaron. *The Lure of the North Woods: Cultivating Tourism in the Upper Midwest.* Minneapolis, MN: University of Minnesota Press, 2013.

–. "Promoting Cloverland: Regional Associations, State Agencies, and the Creation of Michigan's Upper Peninsula Tourist Industry." *Michigan Historical Review* 29, 1 (2003): 1–37.

–. "Up North on Vacation: Tourism and Resorts in Wisconsin's North Woods 1900–1945." *Wisconsin Magazine of History* 89, 4 (2006): 2–13.

Shifflett, Geoffrey. "The Evolving Muskoka Vacation Experience 1860–1945." PhD diss., University of Waterloo, 2012.

Smith, Graham. "A Room with a View: Cottage Architects and Builders." In *Summertimes: In Celebration of 100 Years of the Muskoka Lakes Association,* edited by Muskoka Lakes Association, 129–41. Erin, ON: Boston Mills Press, 1994.

Smith, Lee Ann Eckhardt. *Muskoka's Main Street: 150 Years of Courage and Adventure along the Muskoka Colonization Road.* Bracebridge, ON: Muskoka Books, 2012.

Stets, Jan E., and Peter J. Burke. "Identity Theory and Social Identity Theory." *Social Psychology Quarterly* 63, 3 (September 2000): 224–37.

Stevens, Peter. "Cars and Cottages: The Automotive Transformation of Ontario's Summer Home Tradition." *Ontario History* 100, 1 (Spring 2008): 26–56.

–. "Getting Away from It All: Family Cottaging in Postwar Ontario." PhD diss., York University, 2010.

Stilgoe, John. *Metropolitan Corridor: Railroads and the American Scene.* New Haven, CT: Yale University Press, 1983.

Stryker, Sheldon, and Peter J. Burke. "The Past, Present, and Future of an Identity Theory." *Social Psychology Quarterly* 63, 4 (December 2000): 284–97.

Bibliography

Summers, Gregory. *Consuming Nature: Environmentalism in the Fox River Valley, 1850–1950*. Lawrence, KS: University Press of Kansas, 2006.

Swift, Jamie. *Cut and Run: The Assault on Canada's Forests*. Toronto: Between the Lines, 1983.

Tatley, Richard. *Port Carling: The Hub of the Muskoka Lakes*. Erin, ON: Boston Mills Press, 1996.

–. *The Steamboat Era in the Muskokas*. Vol. 1, *To the Golden Years; A History of the Steam Navigation in the Districts of Muskoka and Parry Sound, 1866–1905*. Erin, ON: Boston Mills Press, 1983.

–. *The Steamboat Era in the Muskokas*. Vol. 2, *The Golden Years to Present; A History of the Steam Navigation in the Districts of Muskoka and Parry Sound, 1906–Present*. Erin, ON: Boston Mills Press, 1984.

–. "Timber! The Lumber Trade in Muskoka." In *Summertimes: In Celebration of 100 Years of the Muskoka Lakes Association*, edited by Muskoka Lakes Association, 75–87. Erin, ON: Boston Mills Press, 1994.

–. *Windermere: The Jewel of Lake Rosseau*. Erin, ON: Boston Mills Press, 1999.

Taylor, Cameron. *Enchanted Summers: The Grand Hotels of Muskoka*. Toronto: Lynx Images, 1997.

Taylor, Joseph E., III. *Persistent Callings: Seasons of Work and Identity on the Oregon Coast*. Corvallis, OR: Oregon State University Press, 2019.

Telford, Rhonda. "Anishinabe Interest in Islands, Fish and Water." In *Papers of the Thirty-First Algonquian Conference*, edited by John D. Nichols, 402–19. Winnipeg: University of Manitoba Press, 2000.

Thoms, J. Michael. "Ojibwa Fishing Grounds: A History of Ontario Fisheries Law, Science, and the Sportsmen's Challenge to Aboriginal Treaty Rights, 1650–1900." PhD diss., University of British Columbia, 2004.

Thorpe, Jocelyn. *Temagami's Tangled Wild: Race, Gender, and the Making of Canadian Nature*. Vancouver: UBC Press, 2012.

Trigger, Bruce G. *The Children of the Aataentsic: A History of the Huron People to 1660*. Montreal and Kingston: McGill-Queen's University Press, 1987.

–. *Natives and Newcomers: Canada's 'Heroic Age' Reconsidered*. Montreal and Kingston: McGill-Queen's University Press, 1986.

Unger, Richard W., and John Thistle. *Energy Consumption in Canada in the 19th and 20th Centuries: A Statistical Outline*. Napoli: Consiglio Nazionale delle Ricerche Istituto di Studi sulle Società del Mediterraneo, 2013.

Veblen, Thorstein. *The Theory of the Leisure Class*. Edited by Martha Banta. New York: Oxford University Press, 2007.

Walker, David F. "Transportation of Coal into Southern Ontario, 1871–1921." *Ontario History* 63 (1971): 15–30.

Wall, Geoffrey. "Pioneer Settlement in Muskoka." *Agricultural History* 44, 4 (October 1970): 393–400.

–. "Recreational Land Use in Muskoka." *Ontario Geography* 11 (1977): 11–28.

Wall, Sharon. "Totem Poles, Teepees, and Token Traditions: 'Playing Indian' at Ontario Summer Camps, 1920–1955." *Canadian Historical Review* 86, 3 (September 2005): 523–44.

Warde, Paul. *The Invention of Sustainability: Nature and Destiny, c. 1500–1870*. Cambridge, MA: Cambridge University Press, 2018.

Bibliography

Waters, Bessie. *Country Tales: A Collection of Colourful Old-Time Reminiscences by a Muskoka Lady.* Bracebridge: MOS Graphics, 1992.

Watson, Andrew. "Pioneering a Rural Identity on the Canadian Shield: Tourism, Household Economies, and Poor Soils in Muskoka, Ontario, 1870–1900." *Canadian Historical Review* 98, 2 (June 2017): 261–93.

–. "Supply Networks in the Age of Steamboat Navigation: Lakeside Mobility in Muskoka, Ontario, 1880–1930." In *Moving Natures: Mobility and Environment in Canadian History,* edited by Ben Bradley, Jay Young, and Colin Coates, 79–103. Calgary: University of Calgary Press, 2016.

Weaver, John C. *The Great Land Rush and the Making of the Modern World, 1650–1900.* Montreal and Kingston: McGill-Queen's University Press, 2003.

White, Mark A. "Sustainability: I Know It When I See It." *Ecological Economics* 86 (2013): 213–17.

White, Richard. *Land Use, Environment, and Social Change: The Shaping of Island County, Washington.* Seattle: University of Washington Press, 1980.

–. *The Middle Ground: Indians, Empires, and Republics in the Great Lakes Region, 1650–1815.* New York: Cambridge University Press, 1991.

–. *Railroaded: The Transcontinentals and the Making of Modern America.* New York: W.W. Norton, 2011.

Wilkinson, James. "A Choice of Fictions: Historians, Memory, and Evidence." *PMLA* III, 1 (January 1996): 80–92.

Williams, Raymond. *The Country and the City.* New York: Oxford University Press, 1973.

Wilson, Catherine Anne. "Reciprocal Work Bees and the Meaning of a Neighbourhood." *Canadian Historical Review* 82, 3 (September 2001): 431–64.

Wolfe, Roy I. "Summer Cottages in Ontario: Purpose-Built for an Inessential Purpose." In *Second Homes: Curse or Blessing?* edited by J.T. Coppock, 17–33. Toronto: Pergamon Press, 1977.

–. "The Summer Resorts of Ontario in the Nineteenth Century." *Ontario History* 54, 3 (1962): 149–61.

Wood, J. David. *Making Ontario: Agricultural Colonization and Landscape Re-Creation before the Railway.* Montreal and Kingston: McGill-Queen's University Press, 2000.

–. *Places of Last Resort: The Expansion of the Farm Frontier into the Boreal Forest in Canada, c. 1910–1940.* Montreal and Kingston: McGill-Queen's University Press, 2006.

Wrigley, E.A. *Continuity, Chance and Change: The Character of the Industrial Revolution in England.* Cambridge: Cambridge University Press, 1988.

Wynn, Graeme. "Notes on Society and Environment in Old Ontario." *Journal of Social History* 13, 1 (Fall 1979): 49–65.

–. *Timber Colony: An Historical Geography of Early Nineteenth Century New Brunswick.* Toronto: University of Toronto Press, 1981.

Index

Note: "(f)" following a page number indicates a figure.

abandonments: backwoods, 21, 31, 32, 35–37, 42–43; environmental conditions/limitations and, 20, 78; farming necessities vs., 38, 39; isolation and, 26; Osbornes and, 32; railways and, 45; rates of, 22, 23–24, 36–37; reasons for, 23–24; and rural identity, 43; soil quality and, 27, 43

Act to Amend and Consolidate the Laws Respecting Indians (1876). *See* Indian Act (1876)

Act to Amend the Law for the Sale and Settlement of the Public Lands (1853), 21–22

Act for the Protection of Game and Fur-bearing Animals (1892), 71

Act to Secure Free Grants and Homesteads to Actual Settlers on the Public Lands (1868) (Ontario). *See* Homestead Act (1868)

Adams, G. Mercer, 128

agriculture: and agricultural fairs, 138–39; Anishinaabeg and, 54, 56–59, 67, 75–76; automobiles and, 157; in backwoods, 29–31; in backwoods vs. lower lakes area, 20; Beausoleil Island band and, 60; capital/necessities for, 38; on Christian Island, 60; and colonial expansion, 20; de la Fosse and, 19–20; environmental limitations and, xiii–xv; gardens, 48, 86, 94, 139; Indigenous gardening rights, 48; King family, 29–31; Mohawk (Haudenosaunee) and, 69–70; and occupational pluralism, xviii, xix–xx; Oldham family, 28–29; orchards, 88, 94; Osborne family, 31–32; Parry Island band and, 61; potential of, xii–xiii, 27–28; Rama and, 58–59; resource extraction combined with, 11, 80, 105–6; rural history focus on, 9; and rural identity, 4, 46, 95, 137, 138–39; Sandy Island band and, 60; in seasonal cycle, 54; and sedentary society, 78–79; settler expectations of, 11; Snake Island band, 59; soils and, 5, 17; and tourism, 8, 77–78, 79–80, 88–89, 149, 165–66, 170. *See also* crops; fresh food(s); produce/produce sales; soils

agroforestry: in backwoods, 42–43, 166; decline in, 42, 79; and economic plurality, 202*n*32; logging camp employment and, 189*n*99, 202*n*34; and rural identity, 7, 40–41, 80; and subsistence, 20; and sustainability, 7. *See also* agriculture; logging; wood-resource harvesting

Aisance, John, 56, 60, 63, 68
Algonquian-speaking peoples, 52–53, 191–92n15, 196n87
Algonquin, Lake, 15–17
Algonquin Park, 67, 71, 167
Ames, Mabel Croucher, 91, 93, 100–1
Anglo-Canadian Leather Company, 122–23, 124, 126, 129(f), 130(f), 131
Anishinaabeg, xviii; agriculture, 54, 56–59, 67, 75–76; band formation, 54; and change and continuity, 50; crafts/craft selling, 70, 165; descent from Algonquian-speaking peoples, 191–92n15; dispersal of, 50–51, 58; *doodem*/clan organization, 54–55; fishing, 57–58, 63–65, 195n63; guiding/guides, 70-74, 165; and Haudenosaunee, 53, 71-72; home territory, 52; hunting, 57–58, 67–68; identity, 49; and Indigenous identity, 5–6, 12; model villages for, 56–58; moditional economy, 49, 70; population, 52; seasonal cycle, xix, 53–54, 67, 68, 75, 103; and seasonal cycle vs. sedentary life, 56; and sedentary life, 56–58, 63–64, 79–80; and Shield, 67–68; signing treaties, 56; and sustainability, xx, 14–15, 50, 54, 64, 166; and tourism, 4, 49, 67–68, 165, 166; tourism and rural identity, 12; trapping, 68; and treaties, xviii, 56; in US, 193n40; and waged labour, xviii, 70; and Wendat, 53. *See also* Beausoleil Island band; Christian Island First Nation; Georgina Island First Nation; Parry Island First Nation; Rama First Nation; Snake Island band
Arnprior and Ottawa Railway, 70
automobiles, xxi–xxii, 85, 157, 159, 167, 168, 169

backwoods: abandonments, 21, 31, 32, 35–37, 42–43; agroforestry in, 40–41, 42–43, 166; isolation in, 20–21, 31, 36, 43; King family in, 29–31; logging in, 43, 111, 166; occupational pluralism in, 169; railways and, 45; rural identity in, 30, 40–41; soils in, 43; steamboats in, 31; subsist-

ence, 37; tourism and, xx, 166, 169
Bailey, Alexander (Bee-to-beeg), 67–68
Bain, James Jr., 45–46, 80, 81
Baldwin, Aemilius, 33, 34, 35
Baxter Township: population, 52
Beardmore, George, 121–22, 123, 124–25, 128
Beaumaris cottage community, 87-88, 139
Beaumaris Hotel, 82, 86, 139
Beaumont, John James (J.J.), 97, 100, 133, 139–40, 148–49, 150
Beausoleil Island band (later Christian Island First Nation), 63; agriculture, 60; and fishing, 63. *See also* Christian Island First Nation (formerly Beausoleil Island band)
beaver meadows, 28–29, 31
Belisle, Donica, 136, 146
Bigcanoe, Charles, 68
Bigcanoe, George, 68
Bigwin, John, 68, 168
Bigwin Island, 167–68
boarding houses, 77, 82, 89, 139, 141, 141(f). *See also* hotels/resorts
boat locks, 24–25
Bouchard, Gérard, 12, 41, 105, 202n32
Bracebridge, 68; Anglo-Canadian Leather Company, 129(f); Anglo-Canadian tannery in, 124; Beardmore tannery in, 121, 123; British Lion Hotel, 19; leather tannery sheds, 128; Muskoka Colonization Road and, 21; Muskoka Leather Company tannery, 122(f); Northern Railway extension to, 43; railway reaching, 151; Shaw, Cassils and Company tannery, 122
Bridgland, J.W., 23, 113–14
British North America Act (1867), 51
Brooklands (Riley farm), 139
Brown, J.P., 89
Brownlie, Robin Jarvis, 56, 65, 72, 74, 167
Brunel Township, abandonments from, 35–37, 45; conditions in, 35–37; gardens/orchards in, 94; oats in, 41; patents, 36–37; potatoes in, 41; railway and settlement in, 45

Index

Buck Lake, cleared land at, 34(f); de la Fosse farm, 35; Harston home on, 33(f)

Campbell, Alexander, 23
Campbell, Claire, 79, 114
Campbell, John, 45–46, 80, 81, 91
Canada Land Inventory, 17, 33
Canadian Fairbanks–Morse Company, Residence Lighting and Water System, 162
Canadian Pacific Railway, 160
Cape Elizabeth, 88–89, 97, 162
Cardwell Township, Coate family in, 88
Carthew, John, 61
Chaffey Township, abandonments from, 43, 45; isolation, and road extension to, 26
Cherokee (passenger steamer), 151, 155, 156
Chippewa First Nations, 48, 51, 58, 63, 64, 71, 75, 167
Chitty, George L., 66
Christian Island, Beausoleil Island band move to, 60; farming on, 60; fishing on, 64, 65; trapping/fur sales, 68
Christian Island First Nation (formerly Beausoleil Island band): on ancestral rights, 48; and fishing, 63; formation of, 50; government identification as Chippewa, 63; and hunting, 67, 68; land rights, 167; population, 52; and tourism, 71; and treaties, 75; US Anishinaabeg joining, 193n40; work in sawmills, 70. *See also* Beausoleil Island band (later Christian Island band)
class. *See* social class
coal, 113, 151, 152(f), 154(f); cordwood vs., 134, 151, 153, 155–56; fuelwood vs., 156; imports, 151; and mineral energy, 157; and modernity, 155; power plants, 134; railways and, 151; steamboats and, 151, 156; tourism and, 137
Coate, Charlie, 161–62
Coate, Frederick, 88–89, 198n16
Coate, Hannah, 88
Coate, Harry, 88–89
Coate household, 198n16

Cockburn, A.P., 24, 25, 44, 81, 82, 85, 190n106
Colborne, John, 56
Coldwater reserve, xviii, 56–58, 193n36
Confederation (1867), xv, 27, 51, 75, 110
Conger Lumber Company, 124
Constance (supply boat), 98(f), 99(f), 150
consumer culture, xxi; in cities, 135; and conspicuous consumption, 135; defined, 136; and fossil fuels, 138; and local economy, 135; and local exchange networks, 143; and mass merchandising, 135–36; and national identity, 136; in rural areas, 136; and rural identity, 134, 163; and sustainability, 4, 163; and tourism, 4, 135, 143–44, 150; and tourist-settler relationship, 166
Cook Brothers, 108
cordwood, 154(f); abundance of, 152; coal vs., 93, 153, 155–56; Croucher cutting, 134; railways and, 151; sales, 155–56; steamboats and, 151–52, 153, 155; supply boats and, xx–xxi
cottager-local resident relationship, concern for resident welfare in, 174; cottage construction/repair in, 91, 170; cottager ignorance of impact of cottages, 170–71; cottager reliance in, 7; cottagers imagining selves as settlers, 170; environmentalism and, 173; fresh foods in, 89; goods/services in, 88, 89, 91, 93–94, 95; and governance, 173; and local farms, 170; produce sales in, 95; short-term rentals and, 173; and sustainability, 174; time-shares and, 173
cottagers: and environmentalism, 173; and local social conditions, 171–72; and motorboats, 159; population size, 82, 173; profitability from, vs. tourists staying at hotels, 89, 91; and steam yachts, 158; supply boats and, 142–43, 148–49; and wilderness experience, 170
cottages/cottaging, xvi; appearance of, 78; attainability of, 168–69; Beaumaris community, 139; at Cape Elizabeth, 89; on Cedar Island, 90(f); changing energy

234

Index

requirements, 161–62; and coal, 161–62; construction, 91–93; cordwood for, 93; costs of, 170; democratization of, 168–70, 171; electrification, 170; generators in, 162–63; isolation of, 94–95; on Lake Joseph, 90(f); and local economy, 170–71; locations, 89, 93–95; maps, 83(f); Muskoka Club and, 46, 81, 91; numbers of, 82, 89, 94, 152, 169; pattern books, 92–93; size of, xxiii, 78; Solid Comfort Camp and, 87–88; steam power plants, 161–62; and sustainability, 174; varieties among, 87–88; on Wegamind Island, 91, 92(f); and wilderness experience, 89; wood burning, 162–63

Cox, Enoch, 77, 82, 95, 142

Cox, Fanny. See Potts, Fanny (née Cox)

Cox, Sarah, 77, 82, 95

Cox family, 84–85

crafts/craft selling, xix, 71–72, 167; Anishinaabeg and, 70; Indigenous women and, 71–72

Craigie Lea, 91

crops, 20, 27–28, 30–31, 32, 36, 88

Croucher, George, 91, 93

Croucher, Mabel. See Ames, Mabel Croucher

Croucher, Ruth (nee Webb), 91

Crown Timber Act (1849), 110

Cunfer, Geoff, 14

de la Fosse, Frederick, 19–20, 32–33, 34–35, 36, 38, 40, 46–47, 185n1

Dennis, John S., 61–62

Department of Indian Affairs (DIA), 51, 65, 70, 74, 75, 167

Department of Labour, *Wage Rates and Salaries*, 113

department stores, 136–37. See also Eaton's department store

Disappearing Propellor Boat, 158–59, 159(f)

distant exchange networks, 7, 163, 166. See also department stores; mail order

Ditchburn, Henry, 158, 160

Dodge, A.G.P., 190n106, 201n16

Doerfler, Jill, 49

Donahue, Brian, 13–14

Drache, Daniel, 106

Draper Township, Hanna in, 96; Spring in, 44

Eaton, Timothy, 144

Eaton's department store, 134, 143–46, 148–50; catalogues, xxi, 144–45, 145(f), 147(f), 148

ecotones, xi

edges, x–xi

Edith May (steam yacht, later supply boat), 142–43, 150

Elgin House, 141, 161

employment insurance (EI), 172

environmental limitations: and abandonments, 78; and agriculture, xiii–xv; and construction of identity, 4; and rural identity, 20; and seasonal movement, 49; and settlement, 22; and sustainability, 174; and temporary occupation vs. sedentary life, 49; and tourism, 8, 46; and transportation, 22–23

environment/environmentalism, cottagers and, 173; household vs. camp/gang model of wood-resource harvesting and, 131–32; and identity, 10–11; and rural identity, 10–11; and tourist-settler relationship, 173

Ernescliffe, 140–41, 143(f)

farms/farming. See agriculture

Ferndale House, 84, 85, 85(f)

Ferris, Neal, 50, 52

First Nations. See Indigenous peoples

Fisheries Act (1857), 51, 63–64, 195n63

fishing/fisheries, Anishinaabeg and, 53, 54, 55, 57–58, 63–65, 195n63; Beausoleil Island band and, 60, 63; on Christian Island, 65; Christian Island band and, 64; commercial, 63–65; conservation laws and, 71, 74; First Nations and, 6; guiding, and rights to, 71; guiding and, xix, 72, 74, 167; Haudenosaunee, 69; Indigenous methods, vs. commercial, 64, 75; Indigenous peoples and, 52; Indigenous rights and, 63–65; law enforcement, 167; Osborne and, 32; Sandy

Index

Island band and, 61; in seasonal cycle, 53, 54; and settler subsistence, 20, 39–40; for sport, 39; treaties and, 56

Fitzgerald, F. Scott, *The Great Gatsby*, 170

foodstuffs: mail-order purchases, 136–37, 146–47; sales to logging camps, 41–42. *See also* fresh food(s); produce/produce sales

Forge, Francis (Frank), 95–96, 144

fossil fuels, changes resulting from, 138; and conspicuous consumption, 150; and consumer culture, 138; creation of new life patterns, 7; expanding consumption of, 162; organic energy vs., 137–38; and sustainability, 4; tourism and, 4, 137, 143; and tourist-settler relationship, 166. *See also* coal; gasoline

Fowlie, Albert, 61

Franklin Township, 32, 43; abandonment rates, 43; Osborne family in, 31–32

Fraser, Hamilton, 81

Freeman Township: population, 52; timber berths, 124

Freemason's Arms, 80

fresh food(s), 94; to cottagers, 89; to hotels, 89; motorboats and, 161; and permanent resident control over tourism, 134; sales to hotels, 140–41; sales to tourists, 84; supermarkets and, 170; supply boats and, 97, 148, 149, 161; and tourist-settler relationship, 138, 147. *See also* produce/produce sales

fuelwood, coal vs., 156; mineral energy vs., 134; and steamboat service, 150; and tourist-settler relationship, 138

furs, 50, 54, 62, 67–68, 74

Gallant, Ashley, 171–72

gardens. *See under* agriculture, gardens

Garrett, William, 33, 34, 35

gasoline: and consumer culture, 150; generators, 162–63; and mineral energy, 151, 157; motorboats and, 134, 156–57; power plants, 134; sales, 159–60; tourism and, 137

Gasoline Engine Company, 162

general stores, 94–95; Hanna and, 96–97; Homer and, 97, 99, 127, 142–43, 148, 155–56; hotels and, 142–43; log sales to, 118–19; Prowse and, 86, 87; and supply boats, 99, 148; transportation to, 95

Georgian Bay, Algonquian-speaking peoples along, 191–92n15, 196n87; Anishinaabeg on, 53; Beausoleil Island on, 53; fisheries, 52, 57, 60, 63; glaciation and, 16; Group of Seven and, xvi; Indigenous employment in lumber industry at, 70; Indigenous guides at, 74; and location of Muskoka, 15; logging along, 70, 107, 108; Northern Railway and, 44; and white pine as symbol, 114

Georgina Island First Nation, Bigwin and, 168; crafts selling, 167; formation of, 51; guiding, 167; and hunting, 67; land rights, 167; performances for tourists, 168; population, 52; on rights, 48; and tourism, 71; and treaties, 75. *See also* Snake Island band

Gibson, David, 22

Gibson reserve (later Wahta Mohawks), Mohawk (Haudenosaunee) at, 51, 69–70; population, 52. *See also* Wahta Mohawks (originally Gibson reserve)

Gibson Township, Mohawk reserve in, 51; population, 52

Goodman, A.K., 48

goods/services, 78; to hotels, 140–41; sales to cottagers, 88, 91, 93–94; and settler subsistence, 20; and tourism, xvii–xviii, 89, 139–40, 166, 169–70

Grand Trunk Railway, 85, 151

Gravenhurst, Muskoka Road/Colonization Road and, 21, 46; Muskoka Steamships and Discovery Centre, 168; Muskoka Wharf, 85; Northern Railway and, 43, 44, 46, 116, 151; Snider sawmilll in, 121

Great Peace of 1701, 53

Great Western Railway, 151

Grenkie, Julius, 118–19

Group of Seven, xvi–xvii

Guide Book and Atlas of Muskoka (Rogers), 118

236

Index

guiding/guides, 167; Anishinaabeg and, 70-74; city sportsmen hiring, 72; game laws and, 49; and hunting/fishing rights, xix, 71; income from, 72; Indigenous peoples and, xix; relationships with clients, 74

Hale, Katherine, 149
Hamilton Model Works, 158
Hanna, William, 96–97, 100, 101(f), 150
Harris, Lawren, xvi, xvii
Harrison, Blake, 8
Harston, Charles G., 19, 33(f), 33-35, 38, 40
Harston Agricultural School, 19, 33, 38, 40
Haudenosaunee, 53; agriculture, 69, 70; Anishinaabeg and, 53; and crafts, 165; fishing, 69; at Gibson reserve, 69–70; as guides, 165; and sustainability, 166; and tourism, 4, 165, 166. *See also* Mohawk (Haudenosaunee)
hay, 28–29, 31, 42, 70, 114
hemlock bark, 125(f); economic importance, 107; for leather tanning, 107, 121–31; tanneries and, 131. *See also* tanbark
hemlock trees: bark, 7; and commercial logging, 107; depletion, 105, 115, 123, 125, 128; household logging, 119; quantities, 121; removal, and ecology, 106; tannery move away from, 128–29, 131; tannins, 107
Homer, George Henry, 97, 99, 100, 102, 102(f), 128, 148, 150; general store, 118, 142–43, 155–56; supply boat *Constance*, 98(f), 99(f), 150
Homestead Act (1868), 27, 32, 35, 38, 40, 110–11, 188*n*76, 188*n*78
Hotchkiss, Hughson and Company, 108
hotels/resorts, xvi; automobiles and, xxii; Beaumaris Hotel, 82, 86, 139; Bigwin Inn, 167–68; changing energy requirements, 161–62; and coal, 161–62; delivery of goods to, 95; family costs of stay at, 91; fresh food sales to, 86, 89; general stores and, 142–43; generators in, 162–63; goods/services sales to, 89, 140–41; and goods/services sales to cottagers, 88; and local economy, 78; Maplehurst

Hotel, 88, 89; numbers of, 82, 152, 169; Paignton House, 141; produce sales to, 84, 88, 95; profitability of tourists staying at, vs. staying independently, 89, 91; Prospect House, 77, 82–83, 84–85, 91, 162; reliance on settlers, 6–7; Rosseau House, 81, 82, 84, 88; Scarcliff, 139, 141, 141(f), 160; settlers as proprietors of, xxii–xxiii; steam power plants, 161–62; and steam yachts, 158; Summit House, xxi, 81, 82, 84, 140, 142(f); supply boats and, 142–43; and varieties of tourists, 89; wood burning, 162–63. *See also* boarding houses
hunting, Algonquin Park and, 71; Anishinaabeg and, 53, 55, 57–58, 67–68; boundaries between territories, 68; Christian Island band, 68; conservation laws and, 71, 74; First Nations and, 6; game laws and, 49, 75; guides and, 167; guiding and, xix, 71, 72, 74; Indigenous peoples and, 52; Indigenous rights to, 48, 71; law enforcement, 167; Osborne and, 32; Parry Island band and, 61; and seasonal cycle, 53, 54; and settler subsistence, 20, 39–40; on Shield, 67–68; for sport, 39; treaties and, 56; Williams Treaties Commission and, 48–49
Huntsville: Anglo-Canadian Leather Company, 130(f), 131; leather tannery sheds, 128–29; Muskoka Colonization Road and, 21; Northern Railway extension to, 43; railway and, 45, 151; Shaw, Cassils and Company tannery, 122, 123
Hutton family, 140, 141(f)

ice houses, 93
identity, environment and, 9–11; malleability of, xix, 10; postmodernist/poststructuralist approaches, 10; social construction of, 4, 10–11. *See also* Indigenous identity; rural identity
Ilfracombe, 19, 34, 40, 46–47
Indian Act (1876), 6, 51, 65, 75, 165
Indian agents, 64–65, 70, 72, 74
Indigenous identity, Anishinaabeg and, 5–6, 12, 49; seasonal cycle and, 63, 76;

Index

settler colonialism and, 49; Shield environment and, 49; and sustainability, 50; tourism and, 71, 165

Indigenous peoples: camp, 73(f); crafts/craft selling, xix, 165; Department of Indian Affairs and, 51; dispossession of, 11; and gardening, 48; as guides, 165; in local histories, 194n54; and newcomers, xviii–xix; protected places and, 8; resilience, xix; seasonal cycle, 5–6; and seasonal occupation vs. sedentary existence, 79; settler colonialism and, xx, 6, 12, 49; subsistence strategies, 79; and tourism, xix, 49; wilderness experience and, xix, 71. *See also* Anishinaabeg; Haudenosaunee

Indigenous rights, colonization and, 50; conservation laws and, 71; and fisheries, 63–65; hunting, 48–49; Robinson-Huron Treaty and, 75; tourism and, 71; trapping, 48; treaties, and dispossession of, 51

Innis, Harold, 106

isolation: and abandonments, 26; of backwoods, 20–21, 26, 31, 36, 43; of cottages, 94–95; de la Fosse on, 32; and future of Muskoka, 23–24; goods/services sales to cottages, 91; King on, 29–30; Osborne on, 31; railways and, 43–46; steamboats and, 26, 27; transportation and, 20–21, 27, 78

Jackson, A.Y., xvi
Jenness, Diamond, 53
Johnston, William, 158–59
Joseph, Lake, 25(f); cottages on, 46, 90(f), 91; Elgin House, 141, 161; Summit House, 81, 82, 84, 140, 142(f)

Kadegegwon, Thomas, 68
Kaufman Furniture Company, 117; sawmill, 118(f)
Kaye, Norman, 92
Kayes family, 140
Kenozha (passenger steamer), 153
King, Harriet Barbara, 29–31, 32, 39, 40–41, 45, 111, 112, 113, 114; "Letters from

Muskoka," 104, 105; "Sonnet to the Muskoka Pines," 114
King, William (Mishoquetto), 194n59

Lady of the Lake (steamer), 97
Laforce, Philip, 69
Lake Muskoka, xxiii, 17, 61, 67, 68, 86(f), 108, 133, 139, 141(f), 148
land: as *doodem* territories vs. freehold private property, 66–67; free grant, xiii–xiv, 21–22, 27, 31, 186–87n29; importance of private property to settlers, 11; Indigenous dispossession of, 51; rush, 11, 21, 78, 165; sales by settlers, 78, 87, 89; sales to settlers, 21–22; speculation, 27, 111; surrender of Indigenous rights, 167; territorial treaties and, 50. *See also* reserves

Leacock, Stephen, 169; *Arcadian Adventures with the Idle Rich,* 135
leather tanneries/tanning: Beardmore tannery, 121, 123, 124–25; establishment of, 131; hair/flesh sales, 206n94; hemlock bark for, 7, 107, 121–31; liquid waste, 126; move away from hemlock, 128–29, 131; Muskoka Leather Company, 122(f), 123; origins of hides, 123, 205n84; and rural identity, 123; sawlog sales to, 105; Shaw, Cassils and Company, 122–23; sustainable alternative to tanbark, 126–28; tanbark disposal, 126; tanning process, 125–26, 129; tannins, 107, 129; volume of tanning, 123; waste, 125–26. *See also* tanbark
LeCain, Timothy J., 9–10
"Letters from Muskoka" (King), 104, 105
Lismer, Arthur, xvi
livestock, 36, 59, 88, 139–40
local exchange networks, consumer culture and, 143; mail order vs., 144; and rural identity, 138
Locke, John, 11
log selling/sales, 7; to general stores, 118–19; and household expenditures, 117–19; households forbidden from, 40–41, 121, 131; Parry Island band and, 66; rights to logging interests vs. homesteaders, 41;

238

Index

and rural identity, 131; to sawmills, 105; by settlers, 23–24, 27; Snider and, 117–18; soil quality and, 119–20; to tanneries, 105; waged labour in logging camps compared with, 106, 117

logging, agriculture vs., xv; in backwoods, 166; clear-cutting, 80; commercial vs. household, 117; decline of, 43; dues on amount cut, 110; and environment, 116–17; establishment in Ontario, 107; ground rents, 110; Homestead Act and, 27, 110–11; household, 117, 120–21; and imagining of landscape, 114; impacts of, 114, 115–17; licences, 110; log booms, 108, 108(f), 111, 112(f); Mohawk (Haudenosaunee) and, 70; and nutrition/diet of loggers, 113; Ontario government and, 110; Parry Island band and, 70; rapacity of, 106; and roads, 23; and rural identity, 42; and settler subsistence, 20; settler-logger tensions in, 201n20; square timber, 107; and sustainability, 14; sustainability of household vs. commercial, 117, 121; timber berths, 23, 41, 108, 110, 124, 131; timber speculation, 27, 111; tourism and, 165–66; Wahta and, 70; waterways and, 115–16; and white pine, 107, 131; as winter activity, 111; working conditions, 113. See also sawmilling/sawmills

logging camps, xx; in backwoods, 41, 43; conditions in, 113; decline of, 43; distance from home, 42, 112, 189n96; families of employees, 112; produce sales to, 41–42, 113–14; and rural identity, 42; waged labour in, 37, 41, 42, 106, 111–13, 131, 189n99, 202n34

Lovisek, Joan, 192n15, 195n81, 196n87

Lowe, Acton, 97

Lower, Arthur R.M., xiv, 106, 107, 164, 174

Lutz, John, 49, 192n16

MacDonald, D.F., 74

MacDonald, J.E.H., xvi–xvii

Maclennan, James, 91

mail order, 133, 144–48, 167; catalogues, 7, 134, 136, 145(f), 147(f), 148, 167; effects of, 7; food purchases, 136–37, 146–47; local exchange networks vs., 144; rural residents and, 136–37; supply boats vs., 133, 143, 147–50; and tourism, 143

Maplehurst Hotel, 88, 89

Martin, Louis, 89, 91

mass merchandising, xxi, 135–36, 167

McCabe, Mrs. (owner of Freemason's Arms), 80

McCulley, Joseph, 138

McGee, D'Arcy, 24

McGirr, John, 69

McLachlan Gasoline Engine Company, 158

McMurray, Thomas, 24, 38, 39, 45; The Free Grant Lands of Canada from Practical Experience of Bush Farming, 27–28

McMurrich Township, 188n74; abandonments from, 36–37; gardens/orchards in, 94; Garrett in, 34; oats in, 41–42; patents, 36–37

McPhee, D.J., 72

Medora Township, Coxes in, 77; Croucher family in, 91; gardens/orchards in, 94; Pensons in, 84; Prospect House, 77, 82–83, 84–85, 91, 162; selling logs from, 119–20; timber berths, 124

Medora and Wood Agricultural Society Fall Fair, 138–39

Megis, Peter, Chief (Muskato), 61, 63, 65, 66

mineral energy, coal-fuelled steamboats and, 156; effect of, 137; fuelwood vs., 134; motorboats and, 159–60; organic energy vs., 7, 137, 150, 151; and permanent resident control over tourism, 134; railways and, 151; and rural identity, 134, 163; transition to, 150–51

Mink (supply boat), 101(f), 102(f)

Misko-Aki, Chief. See Yellowhead, William, Chief (Misko-Aki)

Mississauga people, 58, 194n60

Mohawk (Haudenosaunee): reserve in Gibson Township, 51; and sedentary life, 70; timber cutting, 70. See also Gibson reserve (later Wahta Mohawks);

Wahta Mohawks (originally Gibson reserve)

Monague, Wesley, 68

Monck Township, 188*n*74; abandonments from, 35; Beaumaris Hotel, 82, 86, 139; gardens/orchards in, 94; oats in, 41; Oldham in, 29; potatoes in, 41; railway and settlement in, 45; Riley family in, 139–40

Monteith House, 88, 162

Moon River, logging along, 107

Moose Deer Point, 193*n*40

Morrison, John, 44

Moses, John, 72

Motor Queen (tanker), 160

motorboats, xxi, 157–61, 161(f), 166–67; builders, 158–59; and conspicuous consumption, 150; cottagers and, 159; and fresh food, 161; and gasoline, 134, 156–57; impact of, 157; and mail orders, 161; and organic energy, 150; popularity of, 158; steam yachts vs., 158; supply boats vs., 161; uses of, 160–61; and water transportation, 159–60

Muckata Mishoquet, Chief, 61, 63

Murray, Florence, 22, 111

Muskato, Chief (Peter Megis). *See* Megis, Peter, Chief (Muskato)

Muskoka: flora, xii; geography, 5, 5(f); geology, xii, 5, 5(f); glaciation, xii, 15–16; location, xii, 15; opening to resettlement, 66–67; origins of name, 15; tourist-settler relationship and development of, xvii. *See also* Lake Muskoka

Muskoka (steamboat), 154(f)

Muskoka Club, xxii, 46, 62, 72, 81, 81(f), 91

Muskoka Community Foundation, "Vital Signs," 164–65, 172

Muskoka Lakes Association (MLA), 126, 155, 161(f); Yearbook, 145–46, 148, 158

Muskoka Lakes Bluebook, 97, 140–41, 150, 155, 158, 159, 162

Muskoka Leather Company, 97, 122(f), 123, 124, 126, 127, 127(f), 128, 205–6*n*89

Muskoka Mill and Lumber Company, 70

Muskoka Navigation Company, 85, 97, 134, 151–53, 155, 156, 159, 160, 161, 162

Muskoka River: geography, 15–17; geology, 15–17; Indigenous peoples in watershed, 48–49, 52; logging along, 107; logs on, 112(f); tannery waste and, 126; watershed, 6(f), 15, 16(f)

Muskoka Road (Colonization Road), xiii, 21–23, 21(f), 26, 44, 46

Muskoka Steamships and Discovery Centre, 168

Muskoka Wood Product Company, 121

Muskokalite (tanker), 160

Musquash River, Indigenous use of, 67, 70; logging along, 69, 70, 107

Mutchenbacker family, 117

Nanigishkung, James, 67, 68

Napier, W.H.E., 65–66

Neutral people, 53

Newminko (supply boat), 150

Nipissing (steamboat), 26(f), 153

Nipissing people, 53

Northern Railway, 43, 44–46, 82, 85, 116

Nymoka (supply boat), 150

oats, 28, 41–42, 113–14

Obajawanung (later Port Carling), 61–62

O'Brien, Brendan, 160

occupational plurality, agriculture and, xviii, xix–xx; in backwoods, 169; co-integration strategy, 105–6; and construction of identity, 4; defined, 5; development of, xviii; Osborne and, 32; and rural identity, 11; and sedentary life, 5; tourism and, xix–xx, 165–66, 172

Odawa people, 53

oil. *See* gasoline

Ojibwe First Nations, 21, 51, 58, 61, 63, 75

Oldham family, 28-29

Oliver, J.D., 198*n*16

Oliver, R.J., 22

orchards. *See* agriculture, orchards

organic energy, fossil fuels vs., 137–38; mineral energy vs., 7, 137, 150, 151; railways and, 151; steamboats and, 151-56

Osborne, Thomas, 31–32, 36, 39, 43

Osborne household, 35, 38–39

Ottawa-Huron tract, xii–xiii, xv, 15, 27

240 Index

Paignton House, 141
Paisley, Joseph, 128
Pamosagay, Chief, 61
Parry Island First Nation (formerly Sandy Island band, later Wasauksing First Nation), 61–62, 194n52; crafts selling, 72; formation of, 51; governance, 65; government identification as Ojibwe, 63; and guiding, 72, 74; and logging employment, 70; population, 52; railway employment, 70; and Robinson-Huron Treaty, 75; and timber, 66; work in sawmills, 70. *See also* Sandy Island band (later Parry Island First Nation); Wasauksing First Nation (formerly Parry Island First Nation)
Parry Sound, 52, 54
Partridge, Carleen, 62
Peerless II (supply boat), xxi
Pegahmegahbow, James, Chief, 61–62, 65, 66, 194n59
Pennefather, R.T., 58, 60, 61, 65–66
Penson, Elizabeth (Eliza), 62, 84
Penson, Richard, 84
Penson, Seymour, 114
Peter, Alvin, 66
petroleum. *See* gasoline
Petun people, 53
Phillips, Alex, 118–19
Phillips, Louis, 128
pine trees, 42; exhaustion of, 105, 107–8, 109–10, 121; exports, 109–10; feet of logs cut, 109(f); as focus of commercial logging, 107; household sales, 40–41, 111, 131; logging industry and, 131; qualities of, 107; removal, and ecology, 106; on reserves, 66; as staple export, 131; as wilderness symbol, 114
Plummer, William, 64
Port Carling (formerly Obajawanung): agricultural fairs, 138–39; boatbuilders in, 158; crafts selling in, 72; Hanna in, 96–97; lock, 25; Parry Island First Nation and, 62
potatoes, 41–42, 60, 114
Potts, Edwin, 82–85

Potts, Fanny (née Cox), xxii, 3, 17–18, 82–85, 88, 93–94, 95, 99, 100, 102, 143
Pratt, William H., 81
produce/produce sales, Anishinaabeg and, 58; cost of living vs., 38; to cottages, 95; equitable access to, 102; fruits, 88; and hotels, 84, 86, 88, 95; and income in agroforestry economy, 41–42; to logging camps, 113–14; and settler subsistence, 20, 32; supply boats and, 100, 102; to tourists, 84. *See also* fresh food(s)
Prospect House, 77, 82–83, 84–85, 91, 162
Prowse, Edward, 85–88. *See also* Beaumaris Hotel
Prowse, Mary, 85–88

railways: and abandonments, 45; automobiles and, 167; and backwoods, 45; and coal, 151; continental expansion, 43–44; isolation and, 43–46; and mineral energy, 151; Parry Island band employment with, 70; and rural identity, 43, 45; and settlement, 45; and steamboats, 82, 85; and tourism, xxi, 43, 45–46; and wilderness experience, 87
Rama First Nation: about, 58–59; on ancestral rights, 48; crafts selling, 72, 167; and fishing, 63; formation of, 50; government identification as Chippewa, 63; guiding, 72, 167; and hunting, 67; land rights, 167; population, 52; and tourism, 71–72; and treaties, 75
regattas, 153(f), 160, 161(f)
reserves, Anishinaabeg dispersal into four bands as basis for, 50–51; Department of Indian Affairs and, 51, 65, 167; governance, 51, 65, 75, 165; income generation on, 65–66; Indian Act and, 51; Indian agents and, 65; map, 59(f); population numbers, 191n10; resource expropriation from, 65–66; timber on, 66; in US, 193n40
resorts. *See* hotels/resorts
resource extraction, agriculture and, 11, 80, 105–6; in waves of settler colonialism,

80. *See also* mining; wood-resource harvesting
Ricketts, Montague, 19, 20
Ridout Township, abandonment rates, 43
Riley, Leena (Julia), 139–40, 160
Riley family, 139–40
roads, automobiles and, 157, 167; bottle-necks, 23, 24, 31; and colonization, xii; construction, 24, 168; and cottage accessibility, 169; improvement to, 169; and logging, 23; and settlement, 21; Shield and, 157; stagecoaches and, 23. *See also* Muskoka Road (Colonization Road); transportation
Robinson, Thomas M., 62
Robinson, William Benjamin, 195n81–82
Robinson-Huron Treaty (1850), 21, 51, 61, 63, 71, 75, 195n81–82
Rogers, John, 198n8; *Guide Book and Atlas of Muskoka*, 118
Rosseau, 98(f), 125(f); Homer general store, 127, 155–56
Rosseau, Lake, 125(f); Paignton House, 141
Rosseau House, 81, 82, 84, 88
Royal Muskoka Hotel, 73(f)
rural history, farm focus in, 9; rural vs. urban experience in, 8–9
rural identity, abandonments and, 43; agriculture and, 4, 46, 95, 137, 138–39; agroforestry and, 7, 40–41, 80; in backwoods, 30; in backwoods vs. lower lakes area, 20, 46, 80; and concept of "rural," 9; consumer culture and, 134; environment and, 10–11; environmental limitations and, 4, 20; inter-household relationships and, 40; leather tanneries and, 123; local vs. city food purchases and, 137; local exchange networks and, 138; logging and, 42; materialism of analytical categories, 9–10; occupational pluralism and, 4, 11; railways and, 43, 45; seasonality and, 79, 88; strategies, 37; and subsistence, 80; sustainability and, 3–4, 12–13, 163, 165; timber sales and, 131; tourist-settler relationship and, 165–66, 173–74; waged labour and, 37;

waterways transportation and, 99; wood-resource harvesting and, 4, 104, 105, 132
rural identity and tourism, changes and, 166–67; community/economic evolution and, 8; consumer culture and, 163; environmental limitations and, 78; farming and, 149–50; Indigenous identity and, 12; in lower lakes area vs. backwoods, 37, 102–3; mail-order delivery vs., 134; mineral energy and, 134, 163; Potts on, 83; supply boats and, 100, 149–50; and sustainability, 3–4, 7

Sagamo (passenger steamer), 151, 152(f), 154(f), 155, 156
Saguenay region (Quebec), 11–12, 41
Sahanatien, Louis, Chief, 69
Sale and Settlement of the Public Lands Act (1853), 27
Sandwell, R.W., 5, 9, 137–38, 165
Sandy Island band (later Parry Island First Nation), 60–61; and fishing, 63; and rights to Shield, 63; and Robinson-Huron Treaty, 63; split, 61; US Anishinaabeg joining, 193n40. *See also* Parry Island First Nation (formerly Sandy Island band, later Wasauksing First Nation)
sawmilling/sawmills, 204n64; clear-cutting and, 80; and cottage construction, 91; decline of, 121; establishment of, 107; household sales to, 131–32; Kaufman, 118(f); mill closures, 121; sawlog sales to, 105; Snider and, 117; waged labour at, 70. *See also* logging
Scarcliff (boarding house), 139, 141, 141(f), 160
Scott, Harley, 100
Scott, William, 69–70
seasonal cycle/seasonality, Anishinaabeg and, xix, 53, 67, 68, 103; environmental limitations and, 49; and Indigenous identity, 63, 76; Indigenous peoples and, 5–6, 52, 79; model villages and, 57–58; and resilience, 75; and rural identity, 79, 88; settler colonialism and, 63; and

subsistence, 53–54; tourism and, xix, 6, 74, 79, 83, 103, 172; Wahta and, 70

sedentary life, agrarian society and, 78–79; Anishinaabeg and, 56–58, 63–64, 70; environmental limitations and, 49; Mohawk (Haudenosaunee) and, 70; occupational pluralism and, 5; Sandy Island band and, 61; tourism and, 79; unsuitability on Shield, 78–79; wood-resource harvesting and, 105

settler colonialism: and Anishinaabeg, 165; financial circumstances needed for settlement, 37–38; First Nations and, 6, 49; and Haudenosaunee, 165; and Indigenous identity, 49; and Indigenous people, xx, 12; and Indigenous rights, 50; and resiliency, 74; resource extraction in waves of, 80; and seasonal cycle, 63; and sustainability, 165; tourism and, 79–80, 166, 167; waves of, 55–56, 79–80

Shaw, Cassils and Company, 122–23

Shaw, Charles Orlando, 167

Shilling, Elisabeth, 67

Simon, Andrew, 48

Simon, Henry, 48

Sineah, Charles, Chief, 65

Six Mile Lake Provincial Park, xii

Skene, Charles, 64

Snake, Joseph, 56, 59, 63

Snake Island band, 59; and fishing, 63; government identification as Chippewa, 63; population, 52. *See also* Georgina Island First Nation

Snider, Elias, 117–20

Snider, William, 117–20

Snider Lumber Company, 117–21

Snike, George, 72

Snike, Richard, 72

social class, 168–69, 188*n*78

social conditions, local, 171–72

soils: and abandonment, 27, 43; and agriculture, 5, 17; in backwoods, 43; classes of, 17; erosion, 33–34, 38; glaciation and, 16–17; land clearing and, 33–34; and log selling, 119–20; quality of, 20; and tourism, xx. *See also* agriculture

Solid Comfort Camp, 86–87(f), 87

Spring, Albert, 44

Standard Chemical Company, 66, 70

staples economy, 105, 106–7

Star Island, 91

steam yachts, 142, 158

steamboats, xxi, 44, 161(f), 166–67; additions to fleets, 25; in backwoods, 31; and backwoods vs. lower lake area, 27; and coal, 151, 156; freight rates/shipping costs, 24; fuel costs, 152–53; introduction of, 24, 81; and isolation, 26, 27; and mineral energy, 156; navigation, 24–25; and Parry Island band, 62; and provisioning, 95; railways and, 82, 85; refuelling, 153; as supply boats, 96, 97; and tourism, 45–46; and wood, 150, 151–52, 153, 155

Stephenson Township, abandonments from, 35–37, 45; gardens/orchards in, 94; isolated farm in, 30(f); King family in, 29–31; oats in, 41; potatoes in, 41; railway and settlement in, 45; soil in, 31

Stevens, Peter, 168, 169–71

Stisted Township, 188*n*74; abandonments from, 36–37, 43, 45; Baldwin in, 34; gardens/orchards in, 94; Harston Agricultural School in, 19; oats in, 41–42; patents, 36–37; railway and, 45

subsistence, 20; backwoods, 37; employment insurance (EI) as form of, 172; relationships between households and, 40; rural identity and, 80; seasonal cycle and, 53–54; strategies, 39–43, 79

summer residences. *See* cottages/cottaging

Summit House, xxi, 81, 82, 84, 140, 142(f)

supply boats, xxi, 95, 96–102, 98(f), 99(f), 101(f), 102(f); amounts of transactions, 142–43; Beaumont and, 97, 133; cord-wood for, xx–xxi; and cottagers, 148–49; decline of, 150; and fresh food, 148, 149, 161; as gathering places, 100–1; general stores and, 99, 148; Hanna and, 97; Homer and, 98(f), 99(f); mail order and, 133, 143, 147–50; motorboats vs., 161; settler reliance on, 99–100; and tourism economy, 148–49

Index

243

sustainability, agroforestry and, 7; Anishinaabeg and, xx, 14–15, 50, 54, 55, 64, 166; of commercial vs. household logging, 117, 121; consumer culture and, 4, 163; cottaging and, 174; defined, 12-14; environmental historians and, 13–14; environmental limitations and, 174; fossil fuels and, 4; and Haudenosaunee, 166; in history of Muskoka, 14–15; Indigenous identity and, 50; in leather tanning, 126–28; log selling and, 7; logging and, 14; and rural identity, 3–4, 12–13, 163, 165; settler colonialism and, 165; tanbark collection and, 126–28; temporal/spatial variables, 13–14; tourism and, xx, 3–4, 7, 82, 165, 166, 171, 174; tourist-settler relationship and, 82; wood-resource harvesting and, 105

Tabobondung, Joyce, 72, 74, 196n87
tanbark, 205–6n89; bark gangs, 123, 124, 131, 206n92, 206n94; bark tickets, 124; decline in use, 128–29, 131; disposal, 126; harvesting, 123–25; household sales, 126–28; sales to tanneries, 105; sustainable alternatives to, 126–28. *See also* hemlock bark; leather tanneries/tanning tanneries. *See* leather tanneries/tanning tannins/tannic acid, 125, 129
Tatley, Richard, 158
Thompson, Alfred, 68
Thoms, J. Michael, 53, 55
Thomson, Tom, xvi
timber. *See* logging
timber berths, 23, 41, 108, 110, 124, 131. *See also* logging
Tondern Island, 86; Beaumaris Hotel, 82, 86, 139; cottages, 87–88; Solid Comfort Camp, 86–87(f), 87
Toronto, Simcoe and Muskoka Junction Railway Company (TSMJ), 44
Tothill, Richard, 33, 34
tourism: about, 3; agriculture and, 8, 77–78, 79–80, 88–89, 149, 165–66; Anishinaabeg and, 4, 49, 67–68, 165, 166; automobiles and, xxi–xxii; and backwoods, 166, 169; beginnings of, 80;

changes in, 166–67; as co-integration strategy, 12; consumer culture and, 4, 135, 143–44, 150; Eaton's and, 145–46; environmental limitations and, 8, 46; forests and, 80; fossil fuels and, 4, 137, 143; goods/services and, 166; growing transiency in, xxii; Haudenosaunee and, 4, 165, 166; health and, xv–xvi; and household economies, 88; importance to Muskoka, 165; Indigenous culture/history and, 168; and Indigenous identity, 71, 165; Indigenous peoples and, xix, 49; and Indigenous rights, 71; Indigenous seasonal cycle vs. seasonality of, 74; Indigenous women and, 71–72, 73(f); and local economy, 78–79, 164, 166, 172–74; and logging, 165–66; in lower lakes area vs. backwoods, xx; mail order and, 143; and modernity, 11; numbers of tourists, 77, 82, 94, 100, 103; and occupational pluralism, xix–xx, 165–66, 172; origins of tourists, 82, 87; railways and, xxi, 43, 45–46; and rural identity (*see* rural identity and tourism); scholarship on visitors vs. permanent residents, 7–8; and seasonal cycle/seasonality, xix, 6, 79, 83, 103, 172; and sedentary life, 79; settler colonialism and, 79–80, 166, 167; soils and, xx; steamboats and, 45–46; and summertime population, 82; supply boats and, 148–49; support of future generations, 174; as survival strategy, 5; and sustainability, xx, 3–4, 7, 82, 165, 166, 171, 174; tourists as renewable resources, 84; transportation and, 81–82; varieties of tourists, 89; waged labour in logging camps vs., 42; and wilderness experience, xix, 8, 11, 71, 79
tourist-settler relationship: attitudes toward each other, 83–84; butterflies/bees analogy, xxii, 3, 17–18, 83; coal vs. wood in, 155–56; concern for resident welfare, 174; consumer culture and, 163, 166; in cottage construction/repair, 91–93; development of, xvii–xviii; and development of Muskoka, xvii; distant exchange networks and, 163, 166;

environmentalism and, 173; erosion of settler control in, 147; within extended families, 88–89; fossil fuels and, 166; fresh food and, 138, 147; fuelwood and, 138; goods/services in, xvii–xviii, 93–94, 139–40, 169–70; household economy aligned within, 84; interdependence, and local economy, xviii, 163; mineral energy and, 163; motorboats and, 159; permanent resident control in, 134, 174; post-1900 changes and, xx–xxi; produce sales and, 84; and rural identity, 165–66, 173–74; supply boats and, 142; and sustainability, 82, 174; tourist reliance on settlers, 6–7, 78, 165

transportation, environmental limitations and, 22–23; to general stores, 95; and isolation, 20–21, 27, 78; and provisioning, 95; and settler success, 30; and standard of living, 24; and tourism, 81–82; waterway vs. land, 85. *See also* roads; steamboats

trapping, Anishinaabeg and, 68; Christian Island band, 68; game laws and, 75; Indigenous peoples and, 52; Indigenous rights to, 48; in seasonal cycle, 53; treaties and, 56. *See also* furs; hunting

treaties, and dispossession of rights, 51; Indian Act superseding, 65; and rights, 75; and rights to resources, 56; Robinson-Huron Treaty (1850), 21, 51, 61, 63, 71, 75; understandings of, 56, 66; Williams Treaties, 48–49, 50, 167, 168

Tully, Kivas, 23

Tyler, W.H., 151

United Farmers of Ontario, 157

United States, Anishinaabeg in, 193n40; competition over immigration, 22; Indian Removal Act (1830), 193n40; logging interests, 107; oil/petroleum in, 157; pace of settlement in, vs. Canada, xiv; reserves in, 193n40; tourists from, 45, 82, 87

Vankoughnet, P.M., 22

Veblen, Thorstein, *The Theory of the Leisure Class*, 135

Wadsworth, Vernon, 61

waged labour, Anishinaabeg and, 70; in backwoods, 111; and dependence on agroforestry, 202n34; household log selling vs., 106, 117; in logging camps, 37, 41, 42, 106, 111–13, 117, 131, 189n99; Mohawk (Haudenosaunee) and, 70; rural identity and, 37; and subsistence, 20

Wahta Mohawks (originally Gibson reserve): crafts selling, 72, 167; guiding, 72, 167; logging employment, 70; population, 52; sawmill employment, 70; and tourism, 72; and treaties, 75

Walton, Thomas, 65, 70

War of 1812, xviii, 50, 58

Wasauksing First Nation (formerly Parry Island First Nation), 62

waterways transportation, 25, 85, 96(f), 156; motorboats and, 159–60; and rural identity, 99. *See also* motorboats; steamboats; supply boats

Watt Township, 188n74; abandonments from, 35; Frank Forge in, 95–96; Oldham family in, 28–29; railway and settlement in, 45; selling logs from, 119–20

Weaver, John, 11, 21

Wegamind Island, 91, 92(f)

Welland Canal, 151

Wenonah (steamboat), 24

Wendat people, 53

wheat, 21, 22, 27–28, 31, 32, 41

white pine. *See* pine

wilderness experience, cottagers and, 89, 170; forests and, 103; and Indigenous peoples, xix, 71; Indigenous rituals and, 167; parks and, 79; railways and, 87; tourism and, xix, 8, 11, 71, 79; US tourists and, 87; white pine and, 114

Williams, Gilbert, 68

Williams, Raymond, 9

Williams Treaties/Commission, 48–49, 50, 67, 68, 75, 167, 168

Index

Wilmott, John, 86

Wood Township, gardens/orchards in, 94

wood-resource harvesting, xx; economic importance, 107; household vs. camp/gang model, and environment, 131–32; large-scale vs. household-based approach, 105; provincial rights to, 110; and rural identity, 4, 104, 105, 132; and sedentary life, 105; and sustainability, 105. *See also* cordwood; fuelwood; logging; tanbark

Wynn, Graeme, 42, 106, 112, 117, 189*n*95, 202*n*27, 202*n*33

year-round residence. *See* sedentary life

Yellowhead, Joseph, 48, 72

Yellowhead, William, Chief (Misko-Aki), 48, 56, 57, 58–59, 60

Yellowhead, William Jr., Chief, 56, 63

Yoho Island, 46, 91; Muskoka Club on, 46; Robinson's post on, 195*n*81–82

NATURE | HISTORY | SOCIETY

Claire Elizabeth Campbell, *Shaped by the West Wind: Nature and History in Georgian Bay*
Tina Loo, *States of Nature: Conserving Canada's Wildlife in the Twentieth Century*
Jamie Benidickson, *The Culture of Flushing: A Social and Legal History of Sewage*
John Sandlos, *Hunters at the Margin: Native People and Wildlife Conservation in the Northwest Territories*
William J. Turkel, *The Archive of Place: Unearthing the Pasts of the Chilcotin Plateau*
Greg Gillespie, *Hunting for Empire: Narratives of Sport in Rupert's Land, 1840–70*
James Murton, *Creating a Modern Countryside: Liberalism and Land Resettlement in British Columbia*
Stephen J. Pyne, *Awful Splendour: A Fire History of Canada*
Sharon Wall, *The Nurture of Nature: Childhood, Antimodernism, and Ontario Summer Camps, 1920–55*
Hans M. Carlson, *Home Is the Hunter: The James Bay Cree and Their Land*
Joy Parr, *Sensing Changes: Technologies, Environments, and the Everyday, 1953–2003*
Liza Piper, *The Industrial Transformation of Subarctic Canada*
Jamie Linton, *What Is Water? The History of a Modern Abstraction*
Dean Bavington, *Managed Annihilation: An Unnatural History of the Newfoundland Cod Collapse*
J. Keri Cronin, *Manufacturing National Park Nature: Photography, Ecology, and the Wilderness Industry of Jasper*
Shannon Stunden Bower, *Wet Prairie: People, Land, and Water in Agricultural Manitoba*
Jocelyn Thorpe, *Temagami's Tangled Wild: Race, Gender, and the Making of Canadian Nature*
Sean Kheraj, *Inventing Stanley Park: An Environmental History*
Darcy Ingram, *Wildlife, Conservation, and Conflict in Quebec, 1840–1914*
Caroline Desbiens, *Power from the North: Territory, Identity, and the Culture of Hydroelectricity in Quebec*

Daniel Macfarlane, *Negotiating a River: Canada, the US, and the Creation of the St. Lawrence Seaway*

Justin Page, *Tracking the Great Bear: How Environmentalists Recreated British Columbia's Coastal Rainforest*

Ryan O'Connor, *The First Green Wave: Pollution Probe and the Origins of Environmental Activism in Ontario*

John Thistle, *Resettling the Range: Animals, Ecologies, and Human Communities in British Columbia*

Jessica van Horssen, *A Town Called Asbestos: Environmental Contamination, Health, and Resilience in a Resource Community*

Nancy B. Bouchier and Ken Cruikshank, *The People and the Bay: A Social and Environmental History of Hamilton Harbour*

Carly A. Dokis, *Where the Rivers Meet: Pipelines, Participatory Resource Management, and Aboriginal-State Relations in the Northwest Territories*

Jonathan Peyton, *Unbuilt Environments: Tracing Postwar Development in Northwest British Columbia*

Mark R. Leeming, *In Defence of Home Places: Environmental Activism in Nova Scotia*

Jim Clifford, *West Ham and the River Lea: A Social and Environmental History of London's Industrialized Marshland, 1839–1914*

Michèle Dagenais, *Montreal, City of Water: An Environmental History*

David Calverley, *Who Controls the Hunt? First Nations, Treaty Rights, and Wildlife Conservation in Ontario, 1783–1939*

Jamie Benidickson, *Levelling the Lake: Transboundary Resource Management in the Lake of the Woods Watershed*

Daniel Macfarlane, *Fixing Niagara Falls: Environment, Energy, and Engineers at the World's Most Famous Waterfall*

Angela V. Carter, *Fossilized: Environmental Policy in Canada's Petro-Provinces*

Stéphane Castonguay, *The Government of Natural Resources: Science, Territory, and State Power in Quebec, 1867–1939*

Ronald Rudin, *Against the Tides: Reshaping Landscape and Community in Canada's Maritime Marshlands*

Printed and bound in Canada by Friesens
Set in Garamond by Artegraphica Design Co.
Copy editor: Deborah Kerr
Proofreader: Judith Earnshaw
Indexer: Noeline Bridge
Cartographer: Eric Leinberger
Cover designer: George Kirkpatrick